The Best
AMERICAN
ESSAYS
College Edition

D0111587

GUEST EDITORS OF
The Best American Essays

The Best
AMERICAN
ESSAYS
College Edition

Third Edition

Edited and with an Introduction
by ROBERT ATWAN

Houghton Mifflin Company   Boston   New York

Senior Sponsoring Editor: Dean Johnson
Editorial Associate: Bruce Cantley
Associate Project Editor: Mary Jane McTague
Production/Design Coordinator: Jodi O'Rourke
Senior Manufacturing Coordinator: Marie Barnes
Senior Marketing Manager: Nancy Lyman

Cover design: Sarah Melhado Bishins Design

Printed in the U.S.A.

Library of Congress Catalog Card Number: 01-30085

ISBN 0-618-04297-0

1 2 3 4 5 6 7 8 9 10-QFF-05 04 03 02 01

Credits

"The Telephone" by Anwar F. Accawi. From *The Boy from the Tower of the Moon* by Anwar Accawi. Copyright © 1999 by Anwar F. Accawi. Reprinted by permission of Beacon Press, Boston.

"Hair" by Marcia Aldrich. First published in *Northeast Review.* Copyright © 1992 by Marcia Aldrich. Reprinted by permission of the author.

"Yes, Oswald Alone Killed Kennedy" by Jacob Cohen. First published in *Commentary.* Copyright © 1992 by Jacob Cohen. Reprinted by permission of the author.

"Think About It" by Frank Conroy. First published in *Harper's Magazine.* Copyright © 1988 by Harper's Magazine. Reprinted by permission of Donadio & Ashworth, Inc.

"Shouting Fire" by Alan M. Dershowitz. First published in *The Atlantic Monthly.* Copyright © 1989 by Alan Dershowitz. Reprinted by permission of the author.

"Who Shot Johnny?" by Debra Dickerson. First published in *The New Republic.* Copyright © 1996 by Debra Dickerson. Reprinted by permission of the author.

"The Stunt Pilot" by Annie Dillard. First published in *Esquire.* Copyright © 1989 by Annie Dillard. Reprinted by permission of the author.

"Understanding Afrocentrism" by Gerald Early. First published in *Civilization.* Copyright © 1995 by Gerald Early. Reprinted by permission of the author.

In Memory of

Randy Shilts
(1951–1994)

Lewis Thomas
(1913–1993)

Contents

"As a woman and a writer, I have long wondered at the wellsprings of female masochism. Or what, in despair of a more subtle, less reductive phrase, we can call the congeries of predilections toward self-hurt, self-erasure, self-repudiation in women."

"The road to Fidel Castro's Palace of the Revolution leads through a memory lane of old American automobiles chugging along at about twenty-five miles an hour — springless, pre-embargo Ford coupes and Plymouth sedans, DeSotos and LaSalles, Nashes and Studebakers, and various vehicular collages created out of Cadillac grilles and Oldsmobile axles and Buick fenders patched with pieces of oil-drum metal and powered by engines interlinked with kitchen utensils and pre-Batista lawn mowers and other gadgets that have elevated the craft of tinkering in Cuba to the status of high art."

"I have not the slightest notion what goes on in the mind of my cat Jeoffry, beyond the conviction that it is a genuine mind, with genuine thoughts and a strong tendency to chaos, but in all other respects a mind totally unlike mine."

"Inhabiting a male body is much like having a bank account; as long as it's healthy, you don't think much about it. Compared to the female body, it is a low-maintenance proposition. . . ."

"For nearly thirty years, platoons of conspiracists have concertedly scavenged the record, floating their appalling and thrilling might-have-beens, unfazed by the contradictions and absurdities in their own wantonly selective accounts, often consciously, cunningly deceitful."

Preface

What Is *The Best American Essays* Series?

Back in the 1970s Edward Hoagland wondered why no one compiled an annual collection of the year's best essays, especially since comparable short story volumes had been around for decades. I agreed with Hoagland, and after a few false starts (I thought at first of calling the series "The E. B. White Awards" and later "The Emerson Awards"), I founded *The Best American Essays* as a companion volume to Houghton Mifflin's *The Best American Short Stories*. The first volume was published in 1986. Since then, the series has grown in popularity; each year more and more readers seem drawn to the vitality and versatility of the contemporary American essay.

For readers unfamiliar with the series, a brief introduction may be useful. As the series editor, I screen hundreds of essays from an enormous variety of general, specialized, and literary magazines. I then turn over a large number of candidates to a guest editor, a prominent American writer, who makes the final selection of approximately twenty essays. To qualify for selection, the essays must be works of high literary quality intended as fully developed, independent essays on subjects of general interest, originally written in English for first appearance in an American periodical during a calendar year. In general, selections for the book are included on the basis of literary achievement: they must be admirably written and demonstrate an awareness of craft as well as a forcefulness of thought. Since each guest editor, of course, possesses a different idea about what comprises a fine essay, each book also represents a unique literary sensibility. This variety of literary taste and opinion (which can be sampled in the prologue, "Essayists on the Essay") keeps the series healthy and diverse.

The College Edition

This version of *The Best American Essays* is designed for college students and classroom use. Essays have long been a staple of writing courses, so why not a collection of the "best" contemporary essays for today's students? I believe that many writing instructors wish to expose their students to high-quality, socially relevant, and intellectually challenging prose. With this end in mind, I selected particular essays from *The Best American Essays* series that I thought would work best for writing instructors and their students. Among the considerations for selection were length, topicality, diverse perspectives, and rhetorical and thematic variety.

Since the majority of essays we encounter today tend to fall into three general, though fairly distinct, categories — personal, informative, and argumentative — I arranged the selections accordingly. The book reflects the types of writing most often taught in introductory and even advanced composition courses. Instructors will find a generous number of selections to use if they want to teach excellent writing within the context of personal narratives, expository patterns, and persuasive strategies. In addition, I included within these three categories selections that also reflect many of the topics and issues that currently enliven discussion and debate: multiculturalism, race and gender, sexual and identity politics, popular culture, and media studies.

For instructors who prefer to teach essays along different lines, I've included three alternative arrangements: (a) a rhetorical table of contents that rearranges the essays into ten traditional modes or patterns; (b) a table of contents that focuses on salient literary and journalistic features; and (c) a thematic and topical organization that places the essays in a context of current issues. I've also drawn from the various "Forewords" I contribute to the annual volumes to develop an introduction to the literary and compositional features of the contemporary American essay. And, though space would not permit the inclusion of the fourteen guest-editor introductions, I orchestrated incisive excerpts into a prologue that should stimulate critical discussion of the genre and lead to writing assignments.

In addition, to help orient student readers, the volume contains an informative "lead-in" to each essay and a brief biographical note. "Reflections and Responses," a set of questions designed to assist class discussion or to instigate ideas for papers, follows each selection. The questions range from a consideration of compositional details to broader reflections on theme and issue. Instructors who wish to delve deeper into the literary and rhetorical features of the essays will appreciate the thorough and perceptive instructor's manual prepared by Elizabeth Huyck (Princeton University).

Given its arrangement, flexibility, and emphasis on recently published essays, the college edition of *The Best American Essays* is suitable for various writing courses. It can be used in mainstream freshman composition programs with a focus on personal, expository, and argumentative essays. Instructors who want to concentrate on the contemporary essay, creative nonfiction techniques, or the essay as a literary genre will also find the collection and its instructional apparatus extremely suitable.

For this new college edition, I revised a third of the book; of the thirty-six selections, twelve are new. Most of these selections are drawn from the 1998 and 1999 volumes, though I went back to earlier editions for a few additional essays. My choices were partially guided by several useful reviews from writing instructors who shared with me some of their classroom experiences with particular selections. For their thoughtful evaluations of the previous edition, I would like to thank Charlotte Alexander, City University of New York — College of Staten Island; Kathleen Byrd, South Puget Sound Community College (WA); Thom D. Chesney, Texas Wesleyan University; Bill Coyle, Salem State College (MA); Mark W. Cronin, Saint Anselm College (NH); Michel de Benedictis, Miami Dade Community College — Kendall (FL); Carol S. Franks, Portland State University (OR); Toni Graham, University of San Francisco (CA); Donna E. LaLonde, Washburn University (KS); and Daniel Patterson, California State University — San Bernardino. For this edition, I have also expanded my general introduction to the essay as well as added new material to the "Prologue: Essayists on the Essay."

No collection, of course, can entirely please everyone. I have listened carefully to reviewers and have relied on my own classroom experience in choosing contemporary essays that — in their variety of subject, style, and structure — would best serve as an introduction to the genre. I ought to add that I based my choices on the essays themselves, considering mainly their relevance to writing courses, not the reputations of their authors. You will certainly find many well-known essayists in the collection; but you will also discover several unfamiliar writers, some of whom have rarely been anthologized. A large part of my purpose in editing *The Best American Essays* series is to introduce to the reading public young and emerging writers.

I am always interested in comments and suggestions, especially regarding the book's classroom utility, and invite responses from teachers and students. Please address responses to: Robert Atwan/ Series Editor/The Best American Essays/P.O. Box 220/Readville, MA 02137.

Although anthologies such as this one may appear simple to construct, they actually involve the professional efforts of many people. I wish to extend my thanks, first of all, to the distinguished guest editors I've worked with and whose presence is felt throughout this edition: Elizabeth Hardwick, Gay Talese, Annie Dillard, Geoffrey Wolff, Justin Kaplan, Joyce Carol Oates, Susan Sontag, Joseph Epstein, Tracy Kidder, Jamaica Kincaid, Geoffrey C. Ward, Ian Frazier, Cynthia Ozick, and Edward Hoagland. Without them there would be no series. I appreciate the enthusiasm for the project and the help I've received from the Houghton Mifflin college staff: I especially appreciate the advice and support I received from my editors, Dean Johnson and Bruce Cantley. I would also like to thank Associate Project Editor Mary Jane McTague, who handled production; permissions editor Craig D. Mertens; and the copyeditor, Marianne L'Abbate. I'm especially grateful again to Elizabeth Huyck for producing a superb instructor's manual. As always, I'm indebted to my wife, Hélène, for her indispensable support and advice.

R. A.

Encountering the Essay

What Are Essays?

Like poems, plays, novels, and short stories, essays resist simple definition or classification. There are so many types of essays that any attempt to come up with a single, authoritative description of *the* essay is likely to be overly general or critically useless. A well-known handbook to literary terms, for example, doesn't even attempt to define the form: "A moderately brief prose discussion of a restricted topic," the entry begins. But it then goes on to say: "Because of the wide application of the term, no satisfactory definition can be arrived at; nor can a wholly acceptable 'classification' of essay types be made." So much writing today goes under the name of essay — celebrity profiles, interviews, political commentary, reviews, reportage, scientific papers, scholarly articles, snippets of humor, and newspaper columns — that it's virtually impossible for readers to obtain any clear and consistent impression of the form.

Though many illustrious examples of "brief prose discussion" can be found in classical Greek and Latin literature, the modern essay had its origins in the European Renaissance. At a time when writers and artists throughout Europe were exploring ways to express their personalities more freely in painting and literature, a French magistrate, Michel de Montaigne, retired to his Bordeaux estate in 1570 and began experimenting with a new kind of prose. Impatient with formal philosophy and academic disquisition, he soon found a way to create a more flexible and personal discourse. Realizing that his efforts fit no conventional category — they could not be termed letters, or memoirs, or treatises — he simply referred to them by the French word *essais*, meaning *attempts, trials*, or *experiments*. By adopting a casual, everyday word to describe his endeavors, Montaigne called attention to the informal character of this new literary genre. His essays were personal, tentative, highly digressive, and wholly unsystematic in their approach to a topic.

Montaigne's brand of essay became for many later writers *the* genuine essay. For William Hazlitt, Virginia Woolf, and E. B. White, this was the only type of essay that could be considered a literary form. It went under different names; sometimes it was called the periodical, informal, or familiar essay. This was to differentiate it from types of prose discourse composed in a more systematic and formal fashion, writing that conformed to objective rather than subjective standards. Some examples of the formal essay are philosophical and ethical arguments, historical and scientific papers, dissertations and critical articles. Today the informal essay is best represented by the personal essay, whereas the most popular type of formal essay is the magazine article. Although writers and editors may use the terms interchangeably, many periodicals routinely distinguish between essay and article in their tables of contents, a distinction that usually boils down to personal memoir or reflection as opposed to reportage, interviews, or feature stories.

Essays and Articles

If it's impossible to produce an airtight definition of an essay, it's equally impossible to define an article. Like "essay," this all-purpose literary label has a long, complex history. The word goes back to the Latin term for a joint *(artus)* connecting two parts of a body, and its literal use was eventually extended to include the components of writing and discourse. By the eighteenth century, "article" was used regularly for literary compositions that treated a specific topic. The first to use the term in its modern journalistic sense was one of English literature's foremost essayists, Joseph Addison.

Articles require not just a topic, but a timely topic. Unlike essays, articles are usually (a) about something specific and (b) about something of *current* interest. Essays, on the other hand, can take large liberties with subject, theme, organization, and point of view. Essayists tend to be personal, reflective, leisurely; article writers (they used to be called "articlers") usually stay close to the facts, rarely stray from "the point," and seldom interrupt the flow of information with personal opinion or reflection. The essayist will feel comfortable writing about various general topics — friendship, envy, manners, nature. The article writer is often looking for an angle, or "hook," that will directly relate the article to some current event or fashionable trend.

For example: assign the topic of "revenge" to two authors — one who prefers to write personal or familiar essays and one who specializes in journalistic articles or feature stories. Chances are the essayist will take a first-person, reflective look at the nature of revenge, blending together personal experience and literary references. The journalist will most likely conduct several interviews with psychologists and then skillfully choreograph these into an informative piece on how to deal constructively with vengeful emotions. These are, of course, extremes, but they suggest the divergent routes of the essay and article in today's literature. In general, the personal, reflective essay is often found in the literary quarterlies and periodicals; articles, like the example above, are the mainstay of popular magazines.

With a few exceptions, our major magazines print relatively few personal essays. Editors believe that their readers want news and information, not personal reminiscence or leisurely reflection. As a result, the weekly and monthly magazines depend on hard news stories, interviews, profiles, and "service articles" that offer readers practical advice on everything from child rearing to the latest diet. Few of these pieces could be called "literary"; most of them fall rapidly out of date and are not likely to be read even a few months after their appearance. If the personal essayist faces the challenge of making his or her experiences and reflections interesting and relevant, the article writer faces a different challenge: how to handle current issues and topics in such a way that people will still read the work with pleasure long after those issues and topics have vanished from public discussion.

Yet, as the selections in this volume show, most good prose is not easy to pigeonhole. At either end of the spectrum, it's fairly easy to distinguish a literary essay from a journalistic article. But as we move toward the center of the spectrum, the distinctions become less clear. We begin to find a compositional mix: personal essays that depend on research and reporting, topical articles that feature a personal voice and individual viewpoint. Such literary mixtures have become increasingly prevalent in today's magazines and literary periodicals. Note, for example, the selection by Gay Talese, the writer who was one of the founders of a literary movement known as "The New Journalism." This movement attracted many prominent authors (Joan Didion, Truman Capote, Norman Mailer, among others) who wanted to incorporate a variety of literary techniques — many borrowed from novels and essays — into the conventionally "objective" magazine article. In Talese's talented hands, the ordinary celebrity profile becomes infused with mood, atmosphere, and conflict as personalities develop within a narrative that bristles with dramatic tension. Many readers coming across "Ali in Havana" (see page 236) in *Esquire* magazine would naturally consider Talese's profile of the world's most famous athlete an article; yet a close reading will demonstrate not only Talese's meticulous skills as a journalist but his mastery of dramatic irony and literary form. Readers will want to note, too, how Annie Dillard (see page 134) elevates a "profile" of a famous stunt pilot into an essay of astonishing lyric power. In a number of the essays collected here, the writers move between the topical requirements of an article and the literary demands of an essay, adroitly balancing fact and observation with the nuances of voice and style, irony and wit.

Essays and Fiction

What ultimately makes a piece of prose an essay is usually found in the personal quality of its writing. Many of the essays in this book are not only written in the first-person singular but they are also *about* the first-person singular. As Montaigne proved long ago, the essay is the perfect literary vehicle for both self-disclosure and self-discovery: "The wisdom of my lesson," he wrote, "is wholly in truth, in freedom, in reality." Writers today use the essay to explore their personal relationships, their individual identities, and their ethnic or racial heritages. Personal essays like Judith Ortiz Cofer's "Silent Dancing" and Scott Russell Sanders's "The Inheritance of Tools" are intimate, candid, revealing, close to the pulse of everyday human experience.

Yet *personal* can be a tricky term. Its roots reach back to the Latin *persona,* the literal term for "mask." The word was traditionally used for a theatrical character, a *dramatis persona.* Thus, oddly enough, the word we use to convey intimacy and sincerity — we often approvingly speak of someone's *personal* touch — has hidden overtones of disguise and performance. Readers may overlook this double sense of the term, but personal essayists rarely do. They know that the first-person singular is not a simple equivalent of the self, a mere matter of slapping down the word "I" in front of every sentence. They know that the single letter "I" is one of the English language's most complex words.

Who is the "I" of the essay — a real person or a *dramatis persona?* Did Scott Russell Sanders really bang his thumb with a hammer just before learning of his father's death? Did Ann Hodgman actually sample Gaines-burgers to see if they tasted like human food? Or have these essayists contrived incidents and fabricated moods in the interests of creating a story or endorsing a position? Unless we personally know the writers, how can we verify their accounts?

When the essay is philosophical or argumentative, we can decide whether we accept an essayist's opinions or not on the basis of logic, evidence, proof, or internal consistency. For example, we would base our agreement or disagreement with Jacob Cohen's "Yes, Oswald Alone Killed Kennedy" entirely on information that has nothing to do with the author's personal life. But once essayists begin to tell stories — about sampling dog food or playing with their children — they move dangerously close to fiction, especially when they add characters, dialogue, episodes, and climaxes. When constructing personal narratives, the essayist confronts the toughest challenge of the craft: telling stories that are at once artful, true, and *believable.* One of the essayist's most frustrating moments is when he or she relates a true story with the utmost candor and discovers that nobody believes it.

The personal essayist, then, must balance craft and credibility, aesthetics and accuracy. The first-person singular is both person and *persona,* a real person and a literary construct. The "I" is both reporting a story and simultaneously *shaping* one. If essayists hope to be wholly believable, however, they need to worry about too much shaping. A true story doesn't usually come prepackaged in a compellingly dramatic shape — many elements just don't fit in. To be believable, the essayist may narrate a story that doesn't — like much of life itself — possess a satisfying narrative closure. Sometimes what one expects to happen doesn't happen. "The writer in me," writes Frank Conroy in "Think About It," "is tempted to create a scene here — to invent one for dramatic purposes — but of course I can't do that." His literary impulse as a novelist is to create a scene; his honesty as an essayist won't let him. An essay like "Think About It" places the reader directly inside the conflict between essay and story. In fact, the tension between personal essays and stories recurs throughout this collection and is especially apparent in such selections as Anwar F. Accawi's "The Telephone" and Garrett Hongo's "Kubota."

Essays and the Writing Process

Many students who enter their first-year writing courses already know how to manufacture the "perfect paper." For some reason, they know it should begin with an introductory paragraph that contains a thesis statement and often cites an expert named Webster. It then pursues its expository path through three paragraphs that develop the main idea until it finally reaches a concluding paragraph that industriously summarizes all three previous paragraphs. The conclusion often begins, "Thus we see that . . . ." If the paper tells a personal story, it might conclude, "Suddenly I realized . . . ." Epiphanies abound.

What is especially maddening about the typical five-paragraph paper has less to do with its tedious, predictable structure than with its implicit message that writing should be the end product of thought and not the enactment of its process. Many students seem unaware that writing can be an act of discovery, an opportunity to say something they had never before thought of saying. The worst papers instructors receive are largely the products of premature conclusions, of unearned assurances, of minds irrevocably made up. As Robert Frost once put it, for many people thinking merely means voting. Why go through the trouble of writing papers on an issue when all that's required is an opinion poll? Do you agree?

Disagree? It makes sense to call such productions "papers" (or "themes" or "assignments") since what is written has almost no connection with the true sense of "essaying"— trying out ideas and positions, writing while in a state of uncertainty, of not knowing.

The five-paragraph theme is also a charade. It not only parades in lock-step toward its conclusion; it begins with its conclusion. It is all about its conclusion. Its structure permits no change of direction, no reconsideration, no wrestling with ideas. It is — and has long been — the perfect vehicle for the sort of reader who solemnly likes to ask: "And your point is . . . ?"

The most talented essayists have aims other than merely getting a point across or a position announced or an identity established. It may help to imagine an essay as a sort of Cubist rendition of an idea: the essayist would rather you consider all sides and aspects of a thought or concept, much in the same multi-perspectival fashion that Picasso or Braque portrayed an ordinary table on canvas. Some essayists — Montaigne again was the first — seem literally to be turning ideas over in their minds. The intellectual essay is nothing if not ruminative; the autobiographical essay may continually lose its sense of direction. Both kinds of essays, like Samuel Johnson's eighteenth-century fable, *Rasselas,* will often reach a "conclusion in which nothing is concluded."

Can a Computer Evaluate an Essay?

This question has been on people's minds since Educational Testing Service recently unveiled "e-rater," their new computer program that will grade essay questions on the Graduate Management Admissions Test. As news of e-rater spread, newspaper reports appeared across the nation nervously wondering how essays can be machine-scored. Objective tests, with their multiple choices, are one thing; but aren't sentences, paragraphs, and organization quite another?

The answer is that a computer can very easily score the results of essay questions, assuming that all anyone wanted to know was whether the writing conformed to standard English usage and reflected a few other elements of style, like syntactic variety, that can be measured conveniently and objectively. Computers have been able to do this for quite some time, and most word-processing applications currently provide a few (though still rudimentary) tools to check grammar and style. But can a computer detect humor and irony (which sometimes skilled readers themselves fail to catch)? Can it evaluate the use of imagery and metaphor, or discern the nuances of a writer's tone of voice? E-rater's developer honestly admitted to the *New York Times* that it cannot: "It's not designed to score Montaigne," she said. "It's designed for a specific purpose: to score the kinds of essays we see on standardized tests." Admittedly, these would be "standard" essays.

Are these what we talk about when we talk about essays? Montaigne's term for his eccentric and digressive meditations is now employed so broadly and indiscriminately that its traditional literary meaning is all but forgotten. An essay, it seems, is anything we want it to be. Our dailies, weeklies, and monthlies are chock full of nonfiction prose, but very little of it is either creative or literary. Most of it is informative, functional, or advisory, and that's as it should be. Produced with built-in obsolescence, such writing is made for the month (at best) and not for the years. E-rater may do fine evaluating standardized expression, but it is educationally unfortunate that its name and use will continue to confuse people about the true literary nature of essays.

The Essay and Risk

"Where there's a will there's a way," an excited William Hazlitt says to himself as he hurries down Chancery Lane "about half-past six o'clock, on Monday the 10th of December, to enquire at Jack Randall's where the fight the next day was to be." The year is 1821, the city is London, and Hazlitt is pursuing his way to an out-of-town boxing match, his first fight ever. He's eager to see big Bill Neate, the raging Bristol "Bull," take on the "Gas-Man," Tom Hickman, the bravest and cruelest fighter in all of England. "I was determined to see this fight, come what would, and see it I did, in great style."

You can consult all the handbooks on literary fiction for all the elements of style, structure, and composition, but you'll rarely find mention of what Hazlitt just noted — *determination*. Yet its literary value is inestimable.

This collection is filled with determination. You can see the fight in great style. You can narrate it with equally great style. But as Hazlitt reminds us, you first have to get there. No sitting in your study with a boxing encyclopedia, no telephone interviews with experts, no electronic highway; and the travel involved takes you beyond your local library.

Such narratives can be a risky business. For one thing, the destinations are often uncertain. When Jamaica Kincaid decides to see England for the first time, or when Barry Lopez strays far from the beaten track in search of an ancient stone horse, or even when Ian Frazier journeys around his Ohio and Montana neighborhoods, they have no idea what surprising emotions or events they will encounter. But there's an additional risk. After writing "The Fight," Hazlitt was surprised to find that people considered his eyewitness report a "vulgar thing." This wasn't simply because his story took readers into an unfamiliar subculture, but because it took them into unfamiliar prose territory as well. In other words, Hazlitt risked the unliterary; he was determined to find a way to develop an essay out of "unsuitable" material. We can find a similar determination throughout this volume: look at how such writers as Marcia Aldrich, Natalie Kusz, Frank Conroy, or Debra Dickerson creatively confront ordinary, unpromising, uncomfortable, or even intractable subjects. Where there's a will there's a way.

Risk and determination — at both a personal and creative level — will often transform a piece of nonfiction prose into a memorable literary work. Our finest essayists seek out challenges, go for the toughest questions on the board. The challenges may spring from the demands of the assignment or of the composition — or both. These essayists resist the plodding memoir, the facile discovery of identity, the predictable opinion, or the unearned assertion. What many of the essays collected here have in common is their determination to take on the tough assignment, to raise the difficulty level of the game.

The Contemporary American Essay: A Diversity of Forms and Voices

The personal essay has long existed in a literary twilight zone. Because it presumes to tell a true story yet often employs fictional or poetic techniques, it stands awkwardly with one foot in and one foot out of "imaginative" literature. It was partially for this reason that one of America's foremost essayists, E. B. White, complained in 1977 that the essayist "unlike the novelist, the poet, and the playwright, must be content in his self-imposed role of second-class citizen." Writers who have their eyes on a Nobel Prize or "other earthly triumphs," White continued, "had best write a novel, a poem, or a play." White was responding not only to the critical reception of his own work but to a general decline in the literary quality of the American essay. Essays struck a lot of readers as "old-fashioned." When readers thought of essays, they thought of writing that was stiff, stuffy, textbookish — things teachers forced them to read and write in school.

A century ago, however, the essay occupied a prominent position in American literature. It fell into the class of writing that critics called "polite letters." The essayists, mostly men, addressed the literate world in an urbane, congenial, comfortable manner. These gentlemen, it seemed, always possessed three names — James Russell Lowell, Oliver Wendell Holmes, Thomas Wentworth Higginson — and more often than not lived in New England. In this era, when "coming out" referred only to a young woman's debut, the typical essay was proper, genteel, and Anglophilic. Although it atrophied during the 1930s, the polite essay retained for many years an insidious power over American students, who were often forced to imitate its polished civility in that shadow genre known as the "freshman theme." The goal of English teachers, Kurt Vonnegut recalls, was to get you "to write like cultivated Englishmen of a century or more ago."

Essays began to seem old-fashioned to the American reader mainly because they were too slow in coming to terms with twentieth-century modernism. While William Faulkner, T. S. Eliot, and Eugene O'Neill were radically transforming fiction, poetry, and drama, the essay retained much of its relaxed, genteel manner. Adventurous writers considered the essay a holdover from Victorian times. With few exceptions, the essay broke no new ground, violated no literary conventions. Instead of standing as modern works of literature in themselves, essays simply tried to explain those works. For the academic community as well as for many general readers, the essay gradually grew synonymous with literary criticism. Essays were written *about* literature, not *as* literature.

Since E. B. White issued his complaint, the literary status of the essay has been steadily improving. As Annie Dillard says, the essay "has joined the modern world." Essays are now written in the same imaginative spirit as fiction and poetry. Contemporary essays can rival the best fiction and poetry in artistic accomplishment. Far from being hesitant about literary aims and methods, today's essayists delight in the use of imagery, symbol, and metaphor, often interweaving them into such complex mosaic patterns as those we find in Gretel Ehrlich's "Spring" and Joyce Carol Oates's "They All Just Went Away." Boundary lines — between life and art, prose and poetry, truth and fiction, the world and self — are often blurred, as essayists take greater liberties with language and form. This is true even of essays grounded in information and explanation. In Diana Kappel-Smith's lovely meditation on the natural world, ordinary salt becomes a metaphor for the mysterious ways the world and the human body are tied together, all things "inextricably mixed."

Nor can the essay be characterized any longer by its homogeneity. In fact, its diversity may now be its most noticeable feature. In light of the essay's transformation, today's poetry and fiction appear stagnant: the essay may be our most exciting literary form. We see narrative essays that are indistinguishable from short stories, mosaic essays that read like prose poems. We find literary criticism with an autobiographical spin, journalism sensitively attuned to drama and metaphor, reflection with a heavy dose of information. Some essayists write polemic that sounds like poetry. Physicists, mathematicians, and philosophers are finding that complex ideas and a memorable prose style are not irreconcilable. Even law review articles have taken a literary turn. Today's essays are incredibly difficult to categorize and pin down.

This volume collects and celebrates the contemporary American essay. Never before — except perhaps in the days of Ralph Waldo Emerson and Henry David Thoreau — have so many fine young American writers begun to explore the essay's literary possibilities. They come to the form with a renewed enthusiasm for its astonishing flexibility and versatility — the essay can incorporate an enormously wide range of subjects and styles. The personal essay has grown increasingly candid, more intimate, less polite. Essayists seem willing to take greater emotional risks. Essayists today seem less relaxed and more eager to confront urgent social questions. Journalism has contributed to this sense of risk and urgency, encouraging essayists to fuse within a single style both personal experience and public issues, dual themes that Barry Lopez brilliantly combines in "The Stone Horse."

The Essay and Cyberspace

The year 1995 marked the 400th anniversary of the first complete edition of Montaigne's essays. Over the next few years, it will be natural to speculate on how the essay will change in the next millennium. Will essays be shaped in new, surprising ways by the digital revolution? Will cyberspace breed new essayists and new kinds of essays? Will original, literary prose works begin appearing in underground sites without benefit of agents, editors, publishers, and prestige periodicals? Will young, struggling writers find a quicker and less stressful way to break into print? As voice and video become increasingly common, will we be entering a new age of graphic/audio texts that will dramatically alter the reading habits of a future generation? In 2020, as one commentator wondered, will book publishers as a trade be as obsolete as blacksmiths?

Predictions of a bookless future have, of course, been commonplace for decades, and there's good reason to be skeptical about the announced "end" of anything, whether it be books, literature, or history itself. When Bill Gates wanted to evangelize on America's electronic future, he didn't go on-line but produced an old-fashioned thirty-dollar hardcover book with a first printing of 800,000 copies. The first thing most young people probably did when they got the book, however, was run the inserted "companion interactive CD-ROM" that contained the complete text, multimedia hyperlinks, video demonstrations, and an audio interview with Gates. Unbelievers continually say that nobody wants to read a book on a screen, and for that reason alone they consider books to be irreplaceable. But for the next generation, books may routinely be read on screen, a cozy lightweight "papery" screen you can pop a CD into, carry anywhere, and comfortably curl up with and read in the dark. Why not? The practical advantages will be tremendous, and parents will finally be able to lift their kids' backpacks.

The issue really isn't about the future of books but of reading, and since people were reading long before the paginated book was developed some 500 years ago, chances are that they'll be reading long after it has been radically transformed. It is hardly a coincidence that the essay was invented not long after the book, for we owe to the physical feature of books the personal essay's idiosyncratic and circuitous manner. Montaigne equipped his home office with one of the earliest book-lined studies, where he loved to spend his time *browsing.* His mind too mercurial to concentrate wholeheartedly on any one volume, he would "leaf through now one book, now another, without order and without plan, by disconnected fragments." An idea took hold; he began to write just the way he read. His medium became his message, and the personal essay was born.

It will be exciting to see what new shapes the American essay will assume ten years from now, when we're well past the millennium mark and "twentieth century" will no longer be synonymous with "modern." Expect some surprises.

Robert Atwan

Essayists on the Essay

Each edition of The Best American Essays *features a guest editor who makes the final selections and writes an introduction to the volume. The guest editors themselves are distinguished American writers, many of whom have excelled in various literary forms. In their introductions, they almost always address the question of the essay: its history, definition, style, audience, composition. Their essays on the essay would in themselves make an interesting collection. What follows are some of their most incisive remarks.*

What Is an Essay?

What *is* an essay, and what, if anything, is it about? "Formal" and "informal," "personal," "familiar," "review-essay," "article-essay," "critical essay," essays literary, biographical, polemic, and historical — the standard lit-crit lexicon and similar attempts at genre definition and subclassification in the end simply tell you how like an eel this essay creature is. It wriggles between narcissism and detachment, opinion and fact, the private party and the public meeting, omphalos and brain, analysis and polemics, confession and reportage, persuasion and provocation. All you can safely say is that it's not poetry and it's not fiction.

— Justin Kaplan

Resisting Definitions

AN ESSAY! The fixed form or the fixed category of any kind, any definition at all, fills me with such despair that I feel compelled to do or be its opposite. And if I cannot do its opposite, if I can in fact complete the task that is the fixed form, or fill the fixed category, I then deny it, I then decline to participate at all. Is this a complex view? But I believe I have stated it simply: anything that I might do, anything that I might be, I cannot bear to be enclosed by, I cannot bear to have its meaning applied to me.

The Essay: and this is not a form of literary expression unfamiliar to me. I can remember being introduced to it. It was the opinions and observations of people I did not know, and their opinions and observations bore no relationship to my life as I lived it then. But even now, especially now, I do not find anything peculiar or wrong about this; after all, the opinions and observations of people you do not know are the most interesting, and even the most important, for your own opinions and observations can only, ultimately, fix you, categorize you — the very thing that leads me to dissent or denial.

    — Jamaica Kincaid

The Essay As Object

If kids still write essays in school the way people my age used to, they meet the essay first as pure object. In school, it is (or was) a written paper of a certain length, on an assigned subject, with specified margins and neatness, due on the teacher's desk at a certain date. From about fourth grade on, I wrote many essays. "An essay a week" was a philosophy lots of grammar school teachers subscribed to back then. Recently I came across an essay of mine I'd saved from the fifth grade. It's called "If I Had Three Wishes." My first wish, as I described it, was for lots of fishing equipment, my second was for a canoe in which to go fishing, and my third was for a cabin in the woods somewhere near good fishing. I have more or less gotten those wishes, writing occasional essays about fishing all the while. Even in its present state as childhood artifact, "If I Had Three Wishes" retains its purposeful object-ness: the three-ring-binder paper with regular lines and space at the top for student's name, teacher's name, and date; the slow, newly-learned script, in blue ballpoint, almost without mistakes; and the circled good grade in the teacher's hand.

    — Ian Frazier

The Essay As Action

Beneath the object, the physical piece of writing with its unpredictable content, is the action that produced it. The action, it seems to me, is easier to predict. The difference is like that between a golf ball in the air and the swing of the golfer that propelled it; the flight of a struck ball varies, but the swing tends always to be the same. An essay is a golf swing, an angler's cast, a tennis serve. For example, say, an experience happens to you, one that seems to have literary potential. You wait for it to grow in your mind into a short story or even just an episode of "Friends," but somehow it doesn't. Then a further experience, or an odd chance, or something a friend says, or something in the newspaper chimes with the first experience, and suddenly you understand you can write about it, and you do. You quit longing for form and write what's there, with whatever serviceable prose comes to hand, for no better reason than the fun and release of saying. That sequence — that combination of patience with sudden impatience, that eventual yielding to the simple desire to tell — identifies the essay.

— Ian Frazier

Essays and the Real World

The essay can do everything a poem can do, and everything a short story can do — everything but fake it. The elements in any nonfiction should be true not only artistically — the connections must hold at base and must be veracious, for that is the convention and the covenant between the nonfiction writer and his reader. Veracity isn't much of a drawback to the writer; there's a lot of truth out there to work with. And veracity isn't much of a drawback to the reader. The real world arguably exerts a greater fascination on people than any fictional one; many people, at least, spend their whole lives there, apparently by choice. The essayist does what we do with our lives; the essayist thinks about actual things. He can make sense of them analytically or artistically. In either case he renders the real world coherent and meaningful, even if only bits of it, and even if that coherence and meaning reside only inside small texts.

— Annie Dillard

No Standard Essay

As there is no standard human type who writes essays, so is there no standard essay: no set style, length, or subject. But what does unite almost all successful essays, no matter how divergent the subject, is that a strong personal presence is felt behind them. This is so even if the essayist never comes out to tell you his view of the matter being discussed, never attempts directly to assert his personality, never even slips into the first-person singular. Without that strong personal presence, the essay doesn't quite exist; it becomes an article, a piece, or some other indefinable verbal construction. Even when the subject seems a distant and impersonal one, the self of the writer is in good part what the essay is about.

— Joseph Epstein

The Essay's Diversity

It is not only that the essay *could* be about anything. It usually was. The good health of essay writing depends on writers continuing to address eccentric subjects. In contrast to poetry and fiction, the nature of the essay is diversity — diversity of level, subject, tone, diction. Essays on being old and falling in love and the nature of poetry are still being written. And there are also essays on Rita Hayworth's zipper and Mickey Mouse's ears.

— Susan Sontag

The Memorable Essay

I am predisposed to the essay with knowledge to impart — but, unlike journalism, which exists primarily to present facts, the essays transcend their data, or transmute it into personal meaning. The memorable essay, unlike the article, is not place- or time-bound; it survives the occasion of its original composition. Indeed, in the most brilliant essays, language is not merely the medium of communication; it *is* communication.

— Joyce Carol Oates

The Author's Gumption

Given the confusion of genre minglings and overlaps, what finally distinguishes an essay from an article may just be the author's gumption, the extent to which personal voice, vision, and style are the prime movers and shapers, even though the authorial "I" may be only a remote energy, nowhere visible but everywhere present. ("We commonly do not remember," Thoreau wrote in the opening paragraphs of *Walden,* "that it is, after all, always the first person that is speaking.")

— Justin Kaplan

Essays and the Imagination

An essay is a thing of the imagination. If there is information in an essay, it is by-the-by, and if there is an opinion in it, you need not trust it for the long run. A genuine essay has no educational, polemical, or sociopolitical use; it is the movement of a free mind at play. Though it is written in prose, it is closer in kind to poetry than to any other form. Like a poem, a genuine essay is made out of language and character and mood and temperament and pluck and chance.

— Cynthia Ozick

Essays Versus Articles

And if I speak of a genuine essay, it is because fakes abound. Here the old-fashioned term poetaster may apply, if only obliquely. As the poetaster is to the poet — a lesser aspirant — so the article is to the essay: a look-alike knockoff guaranteed not to wear well. An article is gossip. An essay is reflection and insight. An article has the temporary advantage of social heat — what's hot out there right now. An essay's heat is interior. An article is timely, topical, engaged in the issues and personalities of the moment; it is likely to be stale within the month. In five years it will have acquired the quaint aura of a rotary phone. An article is Siamesetwinned to its date of birth. An essay defies its date of birth, and ours too.

— Cynthia Ozick

Essays Versus Stories

In some ways the essay can deal in both events and ideas better than the short story can, because the essayist — unlike the poet — may introduce the plain, unadorned thought without the contrived entrances of long-winded characters who mouth discourses. This sort of awful device killed "the novel of idea." (But eschewing it served to limit fiction's materials a little further, and likely contributed to our being left with the short story of scant idea.) The essayist may reason; he may treat of historical, cultural, or natural events, as well as personal events, for their interest and meaning alone, without resort to fabricated dramatic occasions. So the essay's materials are larger than the story's.

— Annie Dillard

Essays Versus Poems

The essay may deal in metaphor better than the poem can, in some ways, because prose may expand what the lyric poem must compress. Instead of confining a metaphor to half a line, the essayist can devote to it a narrative, descriptive, or reflective couple of pages, and bring forth vividly its meanings. Prose welcomes all sorts of figurative language, of course, as well as alliteration, and even rhyme. The range of rhythms in prose is larger and grander than that of poetry. And it can handle discursive idea, and plain fact, as well as character and story.

— Annie Dillard

Essays Are Not Scientific Documents

An essay is not a scientific document. It can be serendipitous or domestic, satire or testimony, tongue-in-cheek or a wail of grief.

Mulched perhaps in its own contradictions, it promises no sure objectivity, just the condiment of opinion on a base of observation, and sometimes such leaps of illogic or superlogic that they may work a bit like magic realism in a novel: namely, to simulate the mind's own processes in a murky and incongruous world. More than being instructive, as a magazine article is, an essay has a slant, a seasoned personality behind it that ought to weather well. Even if we think the author is telling us the earth is flat, we might want to listen to him elaborate upon the fringes of his premise because the bristle of his narrative and what he's seen intrigues us. He has a cutting edge, yet balance too. A given body of information is going to be eclipsed, but what lives in art is spirit, not factuality, and we respond to Montaigne's human touch despite four centuries of technological and social change.

— Edward Hoagland

The Essayist's Defensiveness

No poet has a problem saying, I am a poet. No fiction writer hesitates to say, I am writing a story. "Poem" and "story" are still relatively stable, easily identified literary forms or genres. The essay is not, in that sense, a genre. Rather, "essay" is just one name, the most sonorous name, bestowed on a wide range of writings. Writers and editors usually call them "pieces." This is not just modesty or American casualness. A certain defensiveness now surrounds the notion of the essay. And many of the best essayists today are quick to declare that their best work lies elsewhere: in writing that is more "creative" (fiction, poetry) or more exacting (scholarship, theory, philosophy).

— Susan Sontag

On Being an Essayist

As someone who takes some pride in being known as "Joseph Epstein, an essayist" — or, even better, "the essayist Joseph Epstein" — who takes the term "essayist" as an honorific, I have both an interest and a stake in the form. I hate to see it put down, defamed, spat upon, even mildly slighted. The best luck that any writer can have is to find his or her form, and I feel fortunate in having found mine some twenty years ago in the familiar essay. It happened quite by luck: I was not then a frequent reader of Montaigne and Hazlitt; in those days I was even put off by Charles Lamb, who sometimes seemed to me a bit precious. For me the novel was the form of forms, and easily the one I most admired and should most have liked to master. Although I have published a dozen or so short stories, I have not yet written a novel — nor have I one in mind to write — and so I have to conclude that despite my enormous regard for that form, it just isn't mine. Perhaps it is quite useless for a writer to search for his perfect form; that form, it may well be, has to find him.

— Joseph Epstein

Essayists Must Tell the Truth

I work by Hemingway's precept that a writer's root charge is to distinguish what you really felt in the moment from the false sentiment of what you now believe you should have felt. The personal essay, autobiography, has been a red flag to professional classifiers and epistemologists; a critical industry has flourished for the refinement of generic protocols (many in French, with as much fine print as an installment purchase agreement), subcontracted principally to skeptics. In the judgment of Northrop Frye, for instance, a piece of work is shelved with autobiography or with fiction according to whether the librarian chooses to believe it.

Well. I've written one, and I've written the other, and I'm here to testify that the issue is at once weightier and simpler: a personal essayist means to tell the truth. The contract between a personal essayist and a reader is absolute, an agreement about intention. Because memory is fallible, and point of view by its nature biased, the personal essayist will tell a slant tale, willy-nilly. But not by design.

— Geoffrey Wolff

The Essayist's Voice

The influential essayist is someone with an acute sense of what has not been (properly) talked about, what should be talked about

(but differently). But what makes essays last is less their argument
than the display of a complex mind and a distinctive prose voice.

— Susan Sontag

The Demands of the First Person Singular

The thoroughgoing first person is a demanding mode. It asks
for the literary equivalent of perfect pitch. Even good writers occasionally lose control of their tone and let a self-congratulatory
quality slip in. Eager to explain that their heart is in the right
place, they baldly state that they care deeply about matters with
which they appear to be only marginally acquainted. Pretending to
confess to their bad behavior, they revel in their colorfulness. In-
sistently describing their own biases, they make it all too obvious
that they wish to appear uncommonly reliable. Obviously, the first
person doesn't guarantee honesty. Just because they are committing words to paper does not mean that writers stop telling themselves the lies that they've invented for getting through the night.
Not everyone has Montaigne's gift for candor. Certainly some people are less likely to write honestly about themselves than about
anyone else on earth.

— Tracy Kidder

The "Who Cares?" Factor

Not every voice a great soliloquy makes, a truth at odds with
the education of many an American writer, with the education of
this American writer. I remember (see how difficult, even now,
to break the habit of that pronoun, that solipsistic verb), at board-
ing school in England, writing about Cordelia in the moment
when she recognizes how mistaken is her father's measurement of
affection. I spent the greater part of my allotted space telling
about a tangled misunderstanding between my dad and myself:
"So I understand just how Cordelia felt." Of course my teacher
wrote "who cares?" Of course he was right to write that: to filter all
data through the mesh of personal relevance is the voice's tyranni-
cal sway over listener and speaker alike. Sometimes it should be

okay to take facts in, quietly manipulate them behind an opaque scrim, and display them as though the arranger never arranged. It should be all right to mediate, let another voice speak through your spirit medium, pretend as a writer not to be front and center on stage.

— Geoffrey Wolff

How the Essayist Acquires Authority

Essays are how we speak to one another in print — caroming thoughts not merely in order to convey a certain packet of information, but with a special edge or bounce of personal character in a kind of public letter. As a writer you multiply yourself, gaining height as though jumping on a trampoline, if you can catch the gist of what other people have also been feeling and clarify it for them. Classic essay subjects, like the flux of friendship, "On Greed," "On Religion," "On Vanity," or solitude, lying, self-sacrifice, can be major-league yet not require Bertrand Russell to handle them. A layman who has diligently looked into something, walking in the mosses of regret after the death of a parent, for instance, may acquire an intangible authority, even without being memorably angry or funny or possessing a beguiling equanimity. *He* cares; therefore, if he has tinkered enough with his words, we do too.

— Edward Hoagland

The Conversational Style

While there is no firmly set, single style for the essayist, styles varying with each particular essayist, the best general description of essayistic style was written in 1827 by William Hazlitt in his essay "Familiar Style." "To write a genuine familiar or truly English style," Hazlitt wrote, "is to write as any one would speak in common conversation who had a thorough command and choice of words, who could discourse with ease, force, and perspicuity, setting aside all pedantic and oratorical flourishes." The style of the essayist is that of an extremely intelligent, highly commonsensical person talking, without stammer and with impressive coherence, to him- or herself and to anyone else who cares to eavesdrop. This self-reflexivity, this notion of talking to oneself, has always seemed to me to mark the essay off from the lecture. The lecturer is always teaching; so, too, frequently is the critic. If the essayist does so, it is usually only indirectly.

— Joseph Epstein

The Attractions of Autobiography

Contemporary critical theory lends authority to the autobiographical impulse. As every graduate student knows, only a fool would try to think or bear witness to events objectively anymore, and only an intellectual crook would claim to have done so. There's a line of reasoning that goes like this: writers ought to acknowledge that they are subjective filtering agents and let themselves appear on the page; or, in greater honesty, describe themselves in detail; or, most honest of all, make themselves their main subject matter, since one's own self is the only subject one can really know. Maybe widespread psychotherapy has made literary self-revelation popular. Certainly there are economic reasons. Editors and agents seem to think that the public's hunger for intimate true-life stories has grown large enough to include the private lives of literary figures as well as those of movie stars, mass murderers, and athletes. And the invitation to write about oneself has intrinsic attractions. The subject interests most writers. The research doesn't usually require travel or phone calls or hours in a library. The enterprise *looks* easy.

— Tracy Kidder

The Essayist's Audience

Essays are addressed to a public in which some degree or equity exists between the writer and the reader. Shared knowledge is a necessity, although the information need not be concrete. Perhaps it is more to be thought of as a sharing of the experience of reading certain kinds of texts, texts with omissions and elisions, leaps. The essayist does not stop to identify the common ground; he will not write, "Picasso, the great Spanish painter who lived long in

France." On the other hand, essays are about something, something we may not have had reason to study and master, often matters about which we are quite ignorant. Elegance of presentation,
reflection made interesting and significant, easily lead us to engage our reading minds with Zulus, herbaceous borders in the
English garden, marriage records in eighteenth-century France,
Japanese scrolls.

— Elizabeth Hardwick

Essays Start Out in Magazines

Essays end up in books, but they start their lives in magazines.
(It's hard to imagine a book of recent but previously unpublished
essays.) The perennial comes now mainly in the guise of the topical and, in the short run, no literary form has as great and
immediate an impact on contemporary readers. Many essays are
discussed, debated, reacted to in a way that poets and writers of
fiction can only envy.

— Susan Sontag

On Certain Magazine Interviews

I myself have been interviewed by writers carrying recorders,
and as I sit answering their questions, I see them half-listening,
nodding pleasantly, and relaxing in the knowledge that the little
wheels are rolling. But what they are getting from me (and I assume from other people they talk to) is not the insight that comes
from deep probing and perceptive analysis and old-fashioned
legwork; it is rather the first-draft drift of my mind, a once-over-
lightly dialogue that — while perhaps symptomatic of a society permeated by fast-food computerized bottom-line impersonalized
workmanship — too frequently reduces the once-artful craft of
magazine writing to the level of talk radio on paper.

— Gay Talese

Listening to People Think

Quoting people verbatim, to be sure, has rarely blended well
with my narrative style of writing or with my wish to observe and
describe people actively engaged in ordinary but revealing situations rather than to confine them to a room and present them
in the passive posture of a monologist. Since my earliest days in
journalism, I was far less interested in the exact words that came
out of people's mouths than in the essence of their meaning. More
important than what people say is what they think, even though
the latter may initially be difficult for them to articulate and
may require much pondering and reworking within the inter-
viewee's mind — which is what I gently try to prod and stimulate
as I query, interrelate, and identify with my subjects as I personally accompany them whenever possible, be it on their errands,
their appointments, their aimless peregrinations before dinner or
after work. Wherever it is, I try physically to be there in my role as
a curious confidant, a trustworthy fellow traveler searching into
their interior, seeking to discover, clarify, and finally to describe in
words (my words) what they personify and how they think.

— Gay Talese

On the Subjects of Essays

Those with the least gift are most anxious to receive a commission. It seems to them that there lies waiting a topic, a new
book, a performance, and that this is known as material. The true
prose writer knows there is nothing given, no idea, no text or
play seen last evening until an assault has taken place, the forced
domination that we call "putting it in your own words." Talking
about, thinking about a project bears little relation to the composition; enthusiasm boils down with distressing speed to a paragraph, often one of mischievous banality. To proceed from musing
to writing is to feel a robbery has taken place. And certainly there
has been a loss; the loss of the smiles and ramblings and discussions so much friendlier to ambition than the cold hardship of
writing.

— Elizabeth Hardwick

The Essay's Unlimited Possibilities

The essay is, and has been, all over the map. There's nothing you cannot do with it; no subject matter is forbidden, no structure is proscribed. You get to make up your own structure every time, a structure that arises from the materials and best contains them. The material is the world itself, which, so far, keeps on keeping on. The thinking mind will analyze, and the creative imagination will link instances, and time itself will churn out scenes — scenes unnoticed and lost, or scenes remembered, written, and saved.

In his essay "Home," William Kittredge remembers Jack Ray, his boyhood hero, whom he later hired as a hand on his Oregon ranch. After a bout in jail, Jack Ray would show up in the bunkhouse grinning. "Well, hell, Jack," Kittredge would say. "It's a new day."

"Kid," he would say, "she's a new world every morning."

— Annie Dillard

1

The Personal Voice: Identity, Diversity, Self-Discovery

ANWAR F. ACCAWI

The Telephone

Newspapers and popular magazines indirectly encourage readers to think essays are synonymous with opinion pieces—columns and articles in which writers speak their minds and air their views on topics in the news. But essays can be effective means of storytelling, as Anwar Accawi proves in the following account of his childhood in a very small village in southern Lebanon. In "The Telephone," Accawi offers an unpretentious description of how the modern world began its intrusion into a timeless and insulated culture, where "there was no real need for a calendar or a watch to keep track of the hours, days, months, and years." As Accawi says of village life: "We lived and loved and toiled and died without ever needing to know what year it was, or even the time of day."

Accawi, who was born in Lebanon in 1943 and came to the United States in 1965, began writing essays as a way to preserve a disappearing culture for his young children who knew nothing of the old country. A teacher at the English Language Institute at the University of Tennessee, Knoxville, he is the author of a memoir, The Boy *from the Tower of the* Moon *(1999). "The Telephone," which originally appeared in* The Sun *(1997), was one of Accawi's first publications and was selected by Cynthia Ozick for* The Best American Essays, *1998.*

When I was growing up in Magdaluna, a small Lebanese village in the terraced, rocky mountains east of Sidon, time didn't mean much to anybody, except maybe to those who were dying, or those waiting to appear in court because they had tampered with the boundary markers on their land. In those days, there was no real need for a calendar or a watch to keep track of the hours, days, months, and years. We knew what to do and when to do it, just as the Iraqi geese knew when to fly north, driven by the hot wind that blew in from the desert, and the ewes knew when to give birth to wet lambs that stood on long, shaky legs in the chilly March wind and baaed hesitantly, because they were small and cold and did not know where they were or what to do now that they were here. The only timepiece we had need of then was the sun. It rose and set, and the seasons rolled by, and we sowed seed and harvested and ate and played and married our cousins and had babies who got whooping cough and chickenpox — and those children who survived grew up and married *their* cousins and had babies who got whooping cough and chickenpox. We lived and loved and toiled and died without ever needing to know what year it was, or even the time of day.

It wasn't that we had no system for keeping track of time and of the important events in our lives. But ours was a natural — or, rather, a divine — calendar, because it was framed by acts of God. Allah himself set down the milestones with earthquakes and droughts and floods and locusts and pestilences. Simple as our calendar was, it worked just fine for us.

Take, for example, the birth date of Teta Im Khalil, the oldest woman in Magdaluna and all the surrounding villages. When I first met her, we had just returned home from Syria at the end of the Big War and were living with Grandma Mariam. Im Khalil came by to welcome my father home and to take a long, myopic look at his foreign-born wife, my mother. Im Khalil was so old that the skin of her cheeks looked like my father's grimy tobacco pouch, and when I kissed her (because Grandma insisted that I show her old friend affection), it was like kissing a soft suede glove that had been soaked with sweat and then left in a dark closet for a season. Im Khalil's face got me to wondering how old one had to be to look and taste the way she did. So, as soon as she had hobbled off on her cane, I asked Grandma, "How old is Teta Im Khalil?"

Grandma had to think for a moment; then she said, "I've been told that Teta was born shortly after the big snow that caused the roof on the mayor's house to cave in."

"And when was that?" I asked.

"Oh, about the time we had the big earthquake that cracked the wall in the east room."

Well, that was enough for me. You couldn't be more accurate

than that, now, could you? Satisfied with her answer, I went back to playing with a ball made from an old sock stuffed with other, much older socks.

And that's the way it was in our little village for as far back as anybody could remember: people were born so many years before or after an earthquake or a flood; they got married or died so many years before or after a long drought or a big snow or some other disaster. One of the most unusual of these dates was when Antoinette the seamstress and Saeed the barber (and tooth puller) got married. That was the year of the whirlwind during which fish and oranges fell from the sky. Incredible as it may sound, the story of the fish and oranges was true, because men — respectable men, like Abu George the blacksmith and Abu Asaad the mule skinner, men who would not lie even to save their own souls — told and retold that story until it was incorporated into Magdaluna's calendar, just like the year of the black moon and the year of the locusts before it. My father, too, confirmed the story for me. He told me that he had been a small boy himself when it had rained fish and oranges from heaven. He'd gotten up one morning after a stormy night and walked out into the yard to find fish as long as his forearm still flopping here and there among the wet navel oranges.

The year of the fish-bearing twister, however, was not the last remarkable year. Many others followed in which strange and wonderful things happened: milestones added by the hand of Allah to Magdaluna's calendar. There was, for instance, the year of the drought, when the heavens were shut for months and the spring from which the entire village got its drinking water slowed to a trickle. The spring was about a mile from the village, in a ravine that opened at one end into a small, flat clearing covered with fine gray dust and hard, marble-sized goat droppings, because every afternoon the goatherds brought their flocks there to water them. In the year of the drought, that little clearing was always packed full of noisy kids with big brown eyes and sticky hands, and their mothers — sinewy, overworked young women with protruding collarbones and cracked, callused brown heels. The children ran around playing tag or hide-and-seek while the women talked, shooed flies, and awaited their turns to fill up their jars with drinking water to bring home to their napping men and wet babies. There were days when we had to wait from sunup until late afternoon just to fill a small clay jar with precious, cool water.

Sometimes, amid the long wait and the heat and the flies and the smell of goat dung, tempers flared, and the younger women, anxious about their babies, argued over whose turn it was to fill up her jar. And sometimes the arguments escalated into full-blown, knockdown-dragout fights; the women would grab each other by the hair and curse and scream and spit and call each other names that made my ears tingle. We little brown boys who went with our mothers to fetch water loved these fights, because we got to see the women's legs and their colored panties as they grappled and rolled around in the dust. Once in a while, we got lucky and saw much more, because some of the women wore nothing at all under their long dresses. God, how I used to look forward to those fights. I remember the rush, the excitement, the sun dancing on the dust clouds as a dress ripped and a young white breast was revealed, then quickly hidden. In my calendar, that year of drought will always be one of the best years of my childhood, because it was then, in a dusty clearing by a trickling mountain spring, I got my first glimpses of the wonders, the mysteries, and the promises hidden beneath the folds of a woman's dress. Fish and oranges from heaven . . . you can get over that.

But, in another way, the year of the drought was also one of the worst of my life, because that was the year that Abu Raja, the retired cook who used to entertain us kids by cracking walnuts on his forehead, decided it was time Magdaluna got its own telephone. Every civilized village needed a telephone, he said, and Magdaluna was not going to get anywhere until it had one. A telephone would link us with the outside world. At the time, I was too young to understand the debate, but a few men — like Shukri, the retired Turkish-army drill sergeant, and Abu Hanna the vineyard keeper — did all they could to talk Abu Raja out of having a telephone brought to the village. But they were outshouted and ignored and finally shunned by the other villagers for resisting progress and trying to keep a good thing from coming to Magdaluna.

One warm day in early fall, many of the villagers were out in their fields repairing walls or gathering wood for the winter when the shout went out that the telephone-company truck had arrived at Abu Raja's *dikkan*, or country store. There were no roads in those days, only footpaths and dry streambeds, so it took the telephone-company truck almost a day to work its way up the rocky terrain from Sidon — about the same time it took to walk. When the truck came into view, Abu George, who had a huge voice and, before the telephone, was Magdaluna's only long-distance communication system, bellowed the news from his front porch. Everybody dropped what they were doing and ran to Abu Raja's house to see what was happening. Some of the more dignified villagers, however, like Abu Habeeb and Abu Nazim, who had been to big cities like Beirut and Damascus and had seen things like telephones and telegraphs, did not run the way the rest did; they walked with their canes hanging from the crooks of their arms, as if on a Sunday afternoon stroll.

It did not take long for the whole village to assemble at Abu Raja's *dikkan.* Some of the rich villagers, like the widow Farha and the gendarme Abu Nadeem, walked right into the store and stood at the elbows of the two important-looking men from the telephone company, who proceeded with utmost gravity, like priests at Communion, to wire up the telephone. The poorer villagers stood outside and listened carefully to the details relayed to them by the not-so-poor people who stood in the doorway and could see inside.

"The bald man is cutting the blue wire," someone said.

"He is sticking the wire into the hole in the bottom of the black box," someone else added.

"The telephone man with the mustache is connecting two pieces of wire. Now he is twisting the ends together," a third voice chimed in.

Because I was small and unaware that I should have stood outside with the other poor folk to give the rich people inside more room (they seemed to need more of it than poor people did), I wriggled my way through the dense forest of legs to get a firsthand look at the action. I felt like the barefoot Moses, sandals in hand, staring at the burning bush on Mount Sinai. Breathless, I watched as the men in blue, their shirt pockets adorned with fancy lettering in a foreign language, put together a black machine that supposedly would make it possible to talk with uncles, aunts, and cousins who lived more than two days' ride away.

It was shortly after sunset when the man with the mustache announced that the telephone was ready to use. He explained that all Abu Raja had to do was lift the receiver, turn the crank on the black box a few times, and wait for an operator to take his call. Abu Raja, who had once lived and worked in Sidon, was impatient with

the telephone man for assuming that he was ignorant. He grabbed
the receiver and turned the crank forcefully, as if trying to start a
Model T Ford. Everybody was impressed that he knew what to do.
He even called the operator by her first name: "Centralist." Within
moments, Abu Raja was talking with his brother, a concierge in
Beirut. He didn't even have to raise his voice or shout to be heard.

If I hadn't seen it with my own two eyes and heard it with my
own two ears, I would not have believed it — and my friend Kameel
didn't. He was away that day watching his father's goats, and when
he came back to the village that evening, his cousin Habeeb and I
told him about the telephone and how Abu Raja had used it to
speak with his brother in Beirut. After he heard our report, Kameel
made the sign of the cross, kissed his thumbnail, and warned us
that lying was a bad sin and would surely land us in purgatory.
Kameel believed in Jesus and Mary, and wanted to be a priest
when he grew up. He always crossed himself when Habeeb, who
was irreverent, and I, who was Presbyterian, were around, even
when we were not bearing bad news.

And the telephone, as it turned out, was bad news. With its coming, the face of the village began to change. One of the first effects
was the shifting of the village's center. Before the telephone's arrival, the men of the village used to gather regularly at the house
of Im Kaleem, a short, middle-aged widow with jet-black hair and a
raspy voice that could be heard all over the village, even when she
was only whispering. She was a devout Catholic and also the village
shlikki — whore. The men met at her house to argue about politics
and drink coffee and play cards or backgammon. Im Kaleem was
not a true prostitute, however, because she did not charge for her
services — not even for the coffee and tea (and, occasionally, the
strong liquor called arrack) that she served the men. She did not
need the money; her son, who was overseas in Africa, sent her
money regularly. (I knew this because my father used to read her
son's letters to her and take down her replies, as Im Kaleem could
not read and write.) Im Kaleem was no slut either — unlike some
women in the village — because she loved all the men she enter-
tained, and they loved her, every one of them. In a way, she was
married to all the men in the village. Everybody knew it — the
wives knew it; the itinerant Catholic priest knew it; the Presbyterian minister knew it — but nobody objected. Actually, I suspect

the women (my mother included) did not mind their husbands' visits to Im Kaleem. Oh, they wrung their hands and complained to one another about their men's unfaithfulness, but secretly they were relieved, because Im Kaleem took some of the pressure off them and kept the men out of their hair while they attended to their endless chores. Im Kaleem was also a kind of confessor and troubleshooter, talking sense to those men who were having family problems, especially the younger ones.

Before the telephone came to Magdaluna, Im Kaleem's house was bustling at just about any time of day, especially at night, when its windows were brightly lit with three large oil lamps, and the loud voices of the men talking, laughing, and arguing could be heard in the street below — a reassuring, homey sound. Her house was an island of comfort, an oasis for the weary village men, exhausted from having so little to do.

But it wasn't long before many of those men — the younger ones especially — started spending more of their days and evenings at Abu Raja's *dikkan*. There, they would eat and drink and talk and play checkers and backgammon, and then lean their chairs back against the wall — the signal that they were ready to toss back and forth, like a ball, the latest rumors going around the village. And they were always looking up from their games and drinks and talk to glance at the phone in the corner, as if expecting it to ring any minute and bring news that would change their lives and deliver them from their aimless existence. In the meantime, they smoked cheap, hand-rolled cigarettes, dug dirt out from under their fingernails with big pocketknives, and drank lukewarm sodas they called Kacula, Seffen-Ub, and Bebsi. Sometimes, especially when it was hot, the days dragged on so slowly that the men turned on Abu Saeed, a confirmed bachelor who practically lived in Abu Raja's *dikkan,* and teased him for going around barefoot and unshaven since the Virgin had appeared to him behind the olive press.

The telephone was also bad news for me personally. It took away my lucrative business — a source of much-needed income. Before the telephone came to Magdaluna, I used to hang around Im Kaleem's courtyard and play marbles with the other kids, waiting for some man to call down from a window and ask me to run to the store for cigarettes or arrack, or to deliver a message to his wife, such as what he wanted for supper. There was always something in it for me: a ten- or even a twenty-five-piaster piece. On a good day, I ran nine or ten of those errands, which assured a steady supply of marbles that I usually lost to Sami or his cousin Hani, the basket weaver's boy. But as the days went by, fewer and fewer men came to Im Kaleem's, and more and more congregated at Abu Raja's to wait by the telephone. In the evenings, no light fell from her window onto the street below, and the laughter and noise of the men trailed off and finally stopped. Only Shukri, the retired Turkish-army drill sergeant, remained faithful to Im Kaleem after all the other men had deserted her; he was still seen going into or leaving her house from time to time. Early that winter, Im Kaleem's hair suddenly turned gray, and she got sick and old. Her legs started giving her trouble, making it hard for her to walk. By spring she hardly left her house anymore.

At Abu Raja's *dikkan,* the calls did eventually come, as expected, and men and women started leaving the village the way a hailstorm begins: first one, then two, then bunches. The army took them. Jobs in the cities lured them. And ships and airplanes carried them to such faraway places as Australia and Brazil and New Zealand. My friend Kameel, his cousin Habeeb, and their cousins and my cousins all went away to become ditch diggers and mechanics and butcher-shop boys and deli owners who wore dirty aprons sixteen hours a day, all looking for a better life than the one they had left behind. Within a year, only the sick, the old, and the maimed were left in the village. Magdaluna became a skeleton of its former self, desolate and forsaken, like the tombs, a place to get away from.

Finally, the telephone took my family away, too. My father got a call from an old army buddy who told him that an oil company in southern Lebanon was hiring interpreters and instructors. My father applied for a job and got it, and we moved to Sidon, where I went to a Presbyterian missionary school and graduated in 1962. Three years later, having won a scholarship, I left Lebanon for the United States. Like the others who left Magdaluna before me, I am still looking for that better life.

Reflections and Responses

1. Why do you think Accawi begins his recollections of childhood by focusing on the way the passage of time was measured by the villagers? Does Accawi see the village's attitude toward time in positive or negative ways? How do his word choices and images reflect his position?

2. Consider the way Accawi introduces the telephone into the village. How does he prepare for its appearance? From whose perspective do we view the installation? How are the class lines of the village drawn when the telephone is installed? Finally, why did the telephone turn out to be "bad news" for the village as a whole?

3. How would you assess Accawi's attitude in the final paragraph? How did the telephone personally change his life? Do you think the change was for the worse? Do you think Accawi himself believes it was for the worse? How do you interpret his final sentence?

MARCIA ALDRICH

Hair

Montaigne, the first essayist, would have enjoyed Marcia Aldrich's wonderful meditation on hairstyles and the way they reflect our personal identity. When Montaigne began writing personal essays in the 1570s, he initiated a new style of self-portrayal. He brought his whole body into his writing, inviting his readers to see his essays not simply as thoughts on a page but as an extension of his physical being. Not having (as he put it) an "imposing presence" in actual life, he tried to create one in and through his remarkable essays. A very "physical" writer, he would discuss his looks, height, voice, and complexion, the way he walked, and his habit of scratching the inside of his ears. A persistent self-reviser, Montaigne would also appreciate Aldrich's resistance to a settled style ("a new hairstyle," she says, "will write over the last") and to a coherent philosophy.

Marcia Aldrich is a professor of English who specializes in twentieth-century poetry at Michigan State University. She is the author of a memoir about growing up in the '50s, Girl Rearing *(1998). She is also working on a study of the poet Louise Bogan. "Hair" originally appeared in* The Northwest Review *(1992) and was selected by Joseph Epstein for* The Best American Essays *1993.*

I've been around and seen the Taj Mahal and the Grand Canyon and Marilyn Monroe's footprints outside Grauman's Chinese Theater, but I've never seen my mother wash her own hair. After my mother married, she never washed her own hair again. As a girl and an unmarried woman — yes — but, in my lifetime, she never washed her hair with her own two hands. Upon matrimony, she began weekly treks to the beauty salon where Julie washed and styled her hair. Her appointment on Fridays at two o'clock was never cancelled or rescheduled; it was the bedrock of her week, around which she pivoted and planned. These two hours were indispensable to my mother's routine, to her sense of herself and what, as a woman, she should concern herself with — not to mention their being her primary source of information about all sorts of things she wouldn't otherwise come to know. With Julie my mother discussed momentous decisions concerning hair color and the advancement of age and what could be done about it, hair length and its effect upon maturity, when to perm and when not to perm, the need to proceed with caution when a woman desperately wanted a major change in her life like dumping her husband or sending back her newborn baby and the only change she could effect was a change in her hair. That was what Julie called a "dangerous time" in a woman's life. When my mother spoke to Julie, she spoke in conspiratorial, almost confessional, tones I had never heard before. Her voice was usually tense, on guard, the laughter forced, but with Julie it dropped much lower, the timbre darker than the upper-register shrills sounded at home. And most remarkably, she listened to everything Julie said.

As a child I was puzzled by the way my mother's sense of self-worth and mood seemed dependent upon how she thought her hair looked, how the search for the perfect hairstyle never ended. Just as Mother seemed to like her latest color and cut, she began to agitate for a new look. The cut seemed to have become a melancholy testimony, in my mother's eyes, to time's inexorable passage. Her hair never stood in and of itself; it was always moored to a complex set of needs and desires her hair couldn't in itself satisfy. She wanted her hair to illuminate the relationship between herself and the idea of motion while appearing still, for example. My mother wanted her hair to be fashioned into an event with a complicated narrative past. However, the more my mother attempted to impose a hairstyle pulled from an idealized image of herself, the more the hairstyle seemed to be at odds with my mother. The more the hairstyle became substantial, the more the woman underneath was obscured. She'd riffle through women's magazines and stare for long dreamy hours at a particular woman's coiffure. Then she'd ask my father in an artificially casual voice: "How do you think I'd look with really short hair?" or "Would blonde become me?" My father never committed himself to an opinion. He had learned from long experience that no response he made could turn out well; anything he said would be used against him, if not in the immediate circumstances, down the line, for my mother never forgot anything anyone ever said about her hair. My father's refusal to engage the "hair question" irritated her.

So too, I was puzzled to see that unmarried women washed their own hair, and married women, in my mother's circle at least, by some unwritten dictum never touched their own hair. I began studying before and after photographs of my mother's friends. These photographs were all the same. In the pre-married mode, their hair was soft and unformed. After the wedding, the women's hairstyles bore the stamp of property, looked constructed from grooming talents not their own, hairstyles I'd call produced, requiring constant upkeep and technique to sustain the considerable loft and rigidity — in short, the antithesis of anything I might naively call natural. This was hair no one touched, crushed, or ran fingers through. One poked and prodded various hair masses back into formation. This hair presented obstacles to embrace, the scent of the hair spray alone warded off man, child, and pests. I never saw my father stroke my mother's head. Children whimpered when my mother came home fresh from the salon with a potent do. Just when a woman's life was supposed to be opening out into daily affection, *the* sanctioned affection of husband and children, the women of my mother's circle encased themselves in a helmet of hair not unlike Medusa's.

In so-called middle age, my mother's hair never moved, never blew, never fell in her face: her hair became a museum piece. When she went to bed, she wore a blue net, and when she took short showers, short because, after all, she wasn't washing her hair and she was seldom dirty, she wore a blue plastic cap for the sake of preservation. From one appointment to the next, the only change her hair could be said to undergo was to become crestfallen. Taking extended vacations presented problems sufficiently troublesome to rule out countries where she feared no beauty parlors existed. In the beginning, my parents took overnighters, then week jaunts, and thereby avoided the whole hair dilemma. Extending their vacations to two weeks was eventually managed by my mother applying more hair spray and sleeping sitting up. But after the two week mark had been reached, she was forced to either return home or venture into an unfamiliar salon and subject herself to scrutiny, the kind of scrutiny that leaves no woman unscathed. Then she faced Julie's disapproval, for no matter how expensive and expert the salon, my mother's hair was to be lamented. Speaking just for myself, I had difficulty distinguishing Julie's cunning from the stranger's. In these years my mother's hair looked curled, teased, and sprayed into a waved tossed monument with holes poked through for glasses. She believed the damage done to her hair was tangible proof she had been somewhere, like stickers on her suitcases.

My older sisters have worked out their hair positions differently. My oldest sister's solution has been to fix upon one hairstyle and never change it. She wants to be thought of in a singular fashion. She may vary the length from long to longer, but that is the extent of her alteration. Once, after having her first baby, the "dangerous time" for women, she recklessly cut her hair to just below the ear. She immediately regretted the decision and began growing it back as she walked home from the salon, vowing not to repeat the mistake. Her signature is dark, straight hair pulled heavily off her face in a large silver clip, found at any Woolworth's. When one clip breaks, she buys another just like it. My mother hates the timelessness of my sister's hair. She equates it with a refusal to face growing old. My mother says, "It's immature to wear your hair the same way all your life." My sister replies,

"It's immature to never stop thinking about your hair. If this hairstyle was good enough when I was twenty, it's good enough when I'm forty, if not better."

"But what about change?" my mother asks.

"Change is overrated," my sister says flipping her long hair over her shoulder definitively. "I feel my hair."

My other sister was born with thin, lifeless, nondescript hair: a cross she has had to bear. Even in the baby pictures, the limp strands plastered on her forehead in question marks wear her down. Shame and self-effacement are especially plain in the pictures where she posed with our eldest sister, whose dark hair dominates the frame. She's spent her life attempting to disguise the real state of her hair. Some years she'd focus on style, pulling it back in ponytails so that from the front no one could see there wasn't much hair in the back. She tried artless, even messy styles — as if she had just tied it up any old way before taking a bath or bunched it to look deliberately snarled. There were the weird years punctuated by styles that looked as if she had taken sugar water and lemon juice and squeezed them onto her wet hair and then let them crystallize. The worst style was when she took her hair and piled it on the top of her head in a cone shape and then crimped the ponytail into a zigzag. Personally, I thought she had gone too far. No single approach solved the hair problem, and so now, in maturity, she combines the various phases of attack in hope something will work. She frosts both the grey strands and the pale brown, and then perms for added body and thickness. She's forced to keep her hair short because chemicals do tend to destroy. My mother admires my sister's determination to transform herself, and never more than in my sister's latest assault upon middle age. No one has known for many years nor does anyone remember what the untreated color or texture of either my mother's or my sister's hair might be.

As the youngest by twelve years, there was little to distract Mother's considerable attention from the problem of my hair. I had cowlicks, a remarkable number of them, which like little arrows shot across my scalp. They refused to be trained, to lie down quietly in the same direction as the rest of my hair. One at the front insisted on sticking straight up while two on either side of my ears jutted out seeking sun. The lack of uniformity, the fact that my hair had a mind of its own, infuriated my mother and she saw to it that Julie cut my hair as short as possible in order to curtail its wanton expression. Sitting in the swivel chair before the mirror while Julie snipped, I felt invisible, as if I was unattached to my hair.

Just when I started to menstruate, my mother decided the battle plan needed a change, and presto, the page boy replaced the pixie. Having not outgrown the thicket of cowlicks, Mother bought a spectrum of brightly colored stretch bands to hold my hair back off my face. Then she attached thin pink plastic curlers with snap on lids to the ends of my hair to make them flip up or under, depending on her mood. The stretch bands pressed my hair flat until the very bottom, at which point the ends formed a tunnel with ridges from the roller caps — a point of emphasis, she called it. Coupled with the aquamarine eyeglasses, newly acquired, I looked like an overgrown insect that had none of its kind to bond with.

However, I was not alone. Unless you were the last in a long line of sisters, chances were good that your hair would not go unnoticed by your mother. Each of my best friends was subjected to her mother's hair dictatorship, although with entirely different results. Perry Jensen's mother insisted that all five of her daughters peroxide their hair blonde and pull it back into high ponytails. All the girls' hair turned green in the summer from chlorine. Melissa Matson underwent a look-alike "home perm" with her mother, an experience she never did recover from. She developed a phobic reaction to anything synthetic, which made life very expensive. Not only did mother and daughter have identical tight curls and wear mother-daughter outfits, later they had look-alike nose jobs.

In my generation, many women who survived hair bondage to their mothers now experiment with hairstyles as one would test a new design: to see how it works, what it will withstand, and how it can be improved. Testing requires boldness, for often the style fails dramatically, as when I had my hair cut about a half inch long at the top, and it stood straight up like a tacky shag carpet. I had to live with the results, bear daily witness to the kinks in its design for nine months until strategies of damage control could be deployed. But sometimes women I know create a look that startles in its originality and suggests a future not yet realized.

The women in my family divide into two general groups: those who fasten upon one style, become identified with a look, and are impervious to change, weathering the years steadfastly, and those who, for a variety of reasons, are in the business of transforming themselves. In my sister's case, the quest for perfect hair originates in a need to mask her own appearance; in my mother's case, she wants to achieve a beauty of person unavailable in her own life story. Some women seek transformation, not out of dissatisfaction with themselves, but because hair change is a means of moving along in their lives. These women create portraits of themselves that won't last forever, a new hairstyle will write over the last.

Since my mother dictated my hair, I never took a stand on the hair issue. In maturity, I'm incapable of assuming a coherent or consistent philosophy. I have wayward hair: it's always becoming something else. The moment it arrives at a recognizable style, it begins to undo itself, it grows, the sun colors it, it waves. When one hair pin goes in, another seems to come out. Sometimes I think I should follow my oldest sister — she claims to never give more than a passing thought to her hair and can't see what all the angst is about. She asks, "Don't women have better things to think about than their hair?"

I bite back: "But don't you think hair should reflect who you are?"

"To be honest, I've never thought about it. I don't think so. Cut your hair the same way, and lose your self in something else. You're distracted from the real action."

I want to do what my sister says, but when I walk out into shop-lined streets, I automatically study women's hair and always with the same question: How did they arrive at their hair? Lately, I've been feeling more and more like my mother. I hadn't known how to resolve the dilemma until I found Rhonda. I don't know if I found Rhonda or made her up. She is not a normally trained hair-dresser: she has a different set of eyes, unaffected. One day while out driving around to no place in particular, at the bottom of a hill, I found: "Rhonda's Hair Salon — Don't Look Back" written on a life-size cardboard image of Rhonda. Her shop was on the top of this steep orchard planted hill, on a plateau with a great view that opened out and went on forever. I parked my car at the bottom and walked up. Zigzagging all the way up the hill, leaning against or sticking out from behind the apple trees were more life-sized cardboard likenesses of Rhonda. Except for the explosive sun-bursts in her hair, no two signs were the same. At the bottom, she wore long red hair falling below her knees and covering her entire body like a shawl. As I climbed the hill, Rhonda's hair gradually be-came shorter and shorter, and each length was cut differently, until when I reached the top, her head was shaved and glistening in the sun. I found Rhonda herself out under one of the apple trees wearing running shoes. Her hair was long and red and looked as if it had never been cut. She told me she had no aspira-tions to be a hairdresser, "she just fell into it." "I see hair," she con-tinued, "as an extension of the head and therefore I try to do hair with a lot of thought." Inside there were no mirrors, no swivel chairs, no machines of torture with their accompanying stink. She said, "Nothing is permanent, nothing is forever. Don't feel ham-pered or hemmed in by the shape of your face or the shape of your past. Hair is vital, sustains mistakes, can be born again. You don't have to marry it. Now tip back and put your head into my hands."

Reflections and Responses

---

1. Consider how Aldrich invites you to see hairstyles in terms of personal identity. Compare the different female members of her family. How does each reflect a different philosophical attitude through her hairstyle? What are they? Why do you think Aldrich left her father out of these reflections?

2. How does Aldrich establish a relationship between hairstyle and writing style? For Aldrich, what do the two have in common? In going through her essay, identify some features of her writing style that also reflect her attitude toward her hair.

3. Reread Aldrich's final paragraph carefully. It's tricky. What do you think is happening? Is "Rhonda" real or fictitious? What makes you think she is real? Alternatively, what makes you think Aldrich made her up? Why do you think Aldrich concluded her essay with this visit to Rhonda's Hair Salon?

JUDITH ORTIZ COFER

Silent Dancing

Nothing rekindles childhood memories better than old photographs or home movies. In this vivid essay, a grainy and poorly focused five-minute home movie of a New Year's Eve party helps a writer capture the spirit of a Puerto Rican community in Paterson, New Jersey. That the movie is fragmented and silent adds to its documentary value and, for a lyrical essayist, it evokes much more than it can possibly reveal. "Even the home movie," Cofer writes, "cannot fill in the sensory details such a gathering left imprinted in a child's brain." Those sensory details — "the flavor of Puerto Rico" — must be supplied through the art of writing.

A professor of English and creative writing at the University of Georgia, Judith Ortiz Cofer has published prize-winning books in a number of genres: a novel, The Line of the Sun *(1989);* two poetry collections, Terms of Survival *(1987)* and Reaching for the Mainland *(1986); two autobiographical books combining prose and poetry,* Silent Dancing *(1990) and* The Latin Deli *(1993); and* An Island Like You: Stories of the Barrio *(1995). She has recently published* The Year of Our Revolution: New and Selected Stories and Poems *(1998). Cofer has received many prestigious awards, including fellowships from the National Endowment for the Arts, the Witter Bynner Foundation for Poetry, and the Bread Loaf Writers' Conference. "Silent Dancing" originally appeared in* The Georgia Review *(1990) and was selected by Joyce Carol Oates for* The Best American Essays *1991. Ms. Cofer courteously supplied the notes to this selection.*

We have a home movie of this party. Several times my mother and I have watched it together, and I have asked questions about the silent revelers coming in and out of focus. It is grainy and of short duration, but it's a

great visual aid to my memory of life at that time. And it is in color — the
only complete scene in color I can recall from those years.

We lived in Puerto Rico until my brother was born in 1954. Soon
after, because of economic pressures on our growing family, my father joined the United States Navy. He was assigned to duty on a
ship in Brooklyn Yard — a place of cement and steel that was to be
his home base in the States until his retirement more than twenty
years later. He left the Island first, alone, going to New York City
and tracking down his uncle who lived with his family across the
Hudson River in Paterson, New Jersey. There my father found a
tiny apartment in a huge tenement that had once housed Jewish
families but was just being taken over and transformed by Puerto
Ricans, overflowing from New York City. In 1955 he sent for us.
My mother was only twenty years old, I was not quite three, and my
brother was a toddler when we arrived at *El Building,* as the place
had been christened by its newest residents.

My memories of life in Paterson during those first few years are
all in shades of gray. Maybe I was too young to absorb vivid colors
and details, or to discriminate between the slate blue of the winter
sky and the darker hues of the snow-bearing clouds, but that single
color washes over the whole period. The building we lived in was
gray, as were the streets, filled with slush the first few months of my
life there. The coat my father had bought for me was similar in
color and too big; it sat heavily on my thin frame.

I do remember the way the heater pipes banged and rattled,
startling all of us out of sleep until we got so used to the sound that
we automatically shut it out or raised our voices above the racket.
The hiss from the valve punctuated my sleep (which has always
been fitful) like a nonhuman presence in the room — a dragon
sleeping at the entrance of my childhood. But the pipes were also
a connection to all the other lives being lived around us. Having
come from a house designed for a single family back in Puerto
Rico — my mother's extended-family home — it was curious to
know that strangers lived under our floor and above our heads,
and that the heater pipe went through everyone's apartments. (My
first spanking in Paterson came as a result of playing tunes on the
pipes in my room to see if there would be an answer.) My mother
was as new to this concept of beehive life as I was, but she had been

given strict orders by my father to keep the doors locked, the noise down, ourselves to ourselves.

It seems that Father had learned some painful lessons about prejudice while searching for an apartment in Paterson. Not until years later did I hear how much resistance he had encountered with landlords who were panicking at the influx of Latinos into a neighborhood that had been Jewish for a couple of generations. It made no difference that it was the American phenomenon of ethnic turnover which was changing the urban core of Paterson, and that the human flood could not be held back with an accusing finger.

"You Cuban?" one man had asked my father, pointing at his name tag on the Navy uniform — even though my father had the fair skin and light-brown hair of his northern Spanish background, and the name Ortiz is as common in Puerto Rico as Johnson is in the U.S.

"No," my father had answered, looking past the finger into his adversary's angry eyes. "I'm Puerto Rican."

"Same shit." And the door closed.

My father could have passed as European, but we couldn't. My brother and I both have our mother's black hair and olive skin, and so we lived in El Building and visited our great-uncle and his fair children on the next block. It was their private joke that they were the German branch of the family. Not many years later that area too would be mainly Puerto Rican. It was as if the heart of the city map were being gradually colored brown — *café con leche* brown. Our color.

The movie opens with a sweep of the living room. It is "typical" immigrant Puerto Rican decor for the time: the sofa and chairs are square and hard-looking, upholstered in bright colors (blue and yellow in this instance), and covered with the transparent plastic that furniture salesmen then were so adept at convincing women to buy. The linoleum on the floor is light blue; if it had been subjected to spike heels (as it was in most places), there were dime-sized indentations all over it that cannot be seen in this movie. The room is full of people dressed up: dark suits for the men, red dresses for the women. When I have asked my mother why most of the women are in red that night, she has shrugged, "I don't remember. Just a coincidence." She doesn't have my obsession for assigning symbolism to everything.

The three women in red sitting on the couch are my mother, my eighteen-year-old cousin, and her brother's girlfriend. The novia *is just up from the Island, which is apparent in her body language. She sits up formally, her dress pulled over her knees. She is a pretty girl, but her posture makes her look insecure, lost in her full-skirted dress, which she has carefully tucked around her to make room for my gorgeous cousin, her future sister-in-law. My cousin has grown up in Paterson and is in her last year of high school. She doesn't have a trace of what Puerto Ricans call* la mancha *(literally, the stain: the mark of the new immigrant — something about the posture, the voice, or the humble demeanor that makes it obvious to everyone the person has just arrived on the mainland). My cousin is wearing a tight, se-quined, cocktail dress. Her brown hair has been lightened with peroxide around the bangs, and she is holding a cigarette expertly between her fin-gers, bringing it up to her mouth in a sensuous arc of her arm as she talks animatedly. My mother, who has come up to sit between the two women, both only a few years younger than herself, is somewhere between the poles they represent in our culture.*

It became my father's obsession to get out of the barrio, and thus we were never permitted to form bonds with the place or with the people who lived there. Yet El Building was a comfort to my mother, who never got over yearning for *la isla.* She felt sur-rounded by her language: the walls were thin, and voices speaking and arguing in Spanish could be heard all day. *Salsas* blasted out of radios, turned on early in the morning and left on for company. Women seemed to cook rice and beans perpetually — the strong aroma of boiling red kidney beans permeated the hallways.

Though Father preferred that we do our grocery shopping at the supermarket when he came home on weekend leaves, my mother insisted that she could cook only with products whose la-bels she could read. Consequently, during the week I accompa-nied her and my little brother to *La Bodega* — a hole-in-the-wall grocery store across the street from El Building. There we squeezed down three narrow aisles jammed with various products. Goya's and Libby's — those were the trademarks that were trusted by *her mamá,* so my mother bought many cans of Goya beans, soups, and condiments, as well as little cans of Libby's fruit juices for us. And she also bought Colgate toothpaste and Palmolive soap. (The final *e* is pronounced in both these products in Spanish, so for many years I believed that they were manufactured on the Island. I remember my surprise at first hearing a commercial on television in which Colgate rhymed with "ate.") We always lingered at La Bodega, for it was there that Mother breathed best, taking in the familiar aromas of the foods she knew from Mamá's kitchen. It was also there that she got to speak to the other women of El Building without violating outright Father's dictates against fraternizing with our neighbors.

Yet Father did his best to make our "assimilation" painless. I can still see him carrying a real Christmas tree up several flights of stairs to our apartment, leaving a trail of aromatic pine. He carried it formally, as if it were a flag in a parade. We were the only ones in El Building that I knew of who got presents on both Christmas day AND *día de Reyes,* the day when the Three Kings brought gifts to Christ and to Hispanic children.

Our supreme luxury in El Building was having our own television set. It must have been a result of Father's guilt feelings over the isolation he had imposed on us, but we were among the first in the barrio to have one. My brother quickly became an avid watcher of Captain Kangaroo and Jungle Jim, while I loved all the series showing families. By the time I started first grade, I could have drawn a map of Middle America as exemplified by the lives of characters in *Father Knows Best, The Donna Reed Show, Leave It to Beaver, My Three Sons,* and (my favorite) *Bachelor Father,* where John Forsythe treated his adopted teenage daughter like a princess because he was rich and had a Chinese houseboy to do everything for him. In truth, compared to our neighbors in El Building, *we* were rich. My father's Navy check provided us with financial security and a standard of life that the factory workers envied. The only thing his money could not buy us was a place to live away from the barrio — his greatest wish, Mother's greatest fear.

In the home movie the men are shown next, sitting around a card table set up in one corner of the living room, playing dominoes. The clack of the ivory pieces was a familiar sound. I heard it in many houses on the Island and in many apartments in Paterson. In Leave It to Beaver, *the Cleavers played bridge in every other episode; in my childhood, the men started every social occasion with a hotly debated round of dominoes. The women would sit around and watch, but they never participated in the games.*

Here and there you can see a small child. Children were always brought to parties and, whenever they got sleepy, were put to bed in the host's bedroom. Babysitting was a concept unrecognized by the Puerto Rican women I knew: a responsible mother did not leave her children with any stranger. And in a culture where children are not considered intrusive, there was no need to leave the children at home. We went where our mother went.

Of my preschool years I have only impressions: the sharp bite of the wind in December as we walked with our parents towards the brightly lit stores downtown; how I felt like a stuffed doll in my heavy coat, boots, and mittens; how good it was to walk into the five-and-dime and sit at the counter drinking hot chocolate. On Saturdays our whole family would walk downtown to shop at the big department stores on Broadway. Mother bought all our clothes at Penney's and Sears, and she liked to buy her dresses at the women's specialty shops like Lerner's and Diana's. At some point we'd go into Woolworth's and sit at the soda fountain to eat.

We never ran into other Latinos at these stores or when eating out, and it became clear to me only years later that the women from El Building shopped mainly in other places — stores owned by other Puerto Ricans or by Jewish merchants who had philosophically accepted our presence in the city and decided to make us their good customers, if not real neighbors and friends. These establishments were located not downtown but in the blocks around our street, and they were referred to generically as *La Tienda, El Bazar, La Bodega, La Botánica.* Everyone knew what was meant. These were the stores where your face did not turn a clerk to stone, where your money was as green as anyone else's.

One New Year's Eve we were dressed up like child models in the Sears catalogue: my brother in a miniature man's suit and bow tie, and I in black patent-leather shoes and a frilly dress with several layers of crinoline underneath. My mother wore a bright-red dress that night, I remember, and spike heels; her long black hair hung to her waist. Father, who usually wore his Navy uniform during his short visits home, had put on a dark civilian suit for the occasion: we had been invited to his uncle's house for a big celebration. Everyone was excited because my mother's brother Hernan — a bachelor who could indulge himself with luxuries — had bought a home movie camera, which he would be trying out that night.

Even the home movie cannot fill in the sensory details such a gathering left imprinted in a child's brain. The thick sweetness of women's perfumes mixing with the ever-present smells of food cooking in the kitchen: meat and plantain *pasteles,* as well as the ubiquitous rice dish made special with pigeon peas — *gandules* — and seasoned with precious *sofrito** sent up from the Island by somebody's mother or smuggled in by a recent traveler. *Sofrito* was one of the items that women hoarded, since it was hardly ever in stock at La Bodega. It was the flavor of Puerto Rico.

The men drank Palo Viejo rum, and some of the younger ones got weepy. The first time I saw a grown man cry was at a New Year's Eve party: he had been reminded of his mother by the smells in the kitchen. But what I remember most were the boiled *pasteles* — plantain or yucca rectangles stuffed with corned beef or other meats, olives, and many other savory ingredients, all wrapped in banana leaves. Everybody had to fish one out with a fork. There was always a "trick" pastel — one without stuffing — and whoever got that one was the "New Year's Fool."

There was also the music. Long-playing albums were treated like precious china in these homes. Mexican recordings were popular, but the songs that brought tears to my mother's eyes were sung by the melancholy Daniel Santos, whose life as a drug addict was the stuff of legend. Felipe Rodríguez was a particular favorite of couples, since he sang about faithless women and brokenhearted men. There is a snatch of one lyric that has stuck in my mind like a needle on a worn groove: *De piedra ha de ser mi cama, de piedra la cabezera . . . la mujer que a mi me quiera . . . ha de quererme de veras. Ay, Ay, Ay, corazón, porque no amas[†]. . . .* I must have heard it a thousand times since the idea of a bed made of stone, and its connection to love, first troubled me with its disturbing images.

The five-minute home movie ends with people dancing in a circle — the creative filmmaker must have set it up, so that all of

Author's note — ***sofrito:** A cooked condiment. A sauce composed of a mixture of fatback, ham, tomatoes, and many island spices and herbs. It is added to many typical Puerto Rican dishes for a distinctive flavor.

Author's note — [†]**"De piedra ha de ser . . ."** Lyrics from a popular romantic ballad (called a *bolero* in Puerto Rico). Freely translated: "My bed will be made of stone, of stone also my headrest (or pillow), the woman who (dares to) loves me, will have to love me for real. *Ay, Ay, Ay,* my heart, why can't you (let me) love. . . ."

them could file past him. It is both comical and sad to watch silent dancing. Since there is no justification for the absurd movements that music provides for some of us, people appear frantic, their faces embarrassingly intense. It's as if you were watching sex. Yet for years, I've had dreams in the form of this home movie. In a recurring scene, familiar faces push themselves forward into my mind's eye, plastering their features into distorted close-ups. And I'm asking them: "Who is she? Who is the old woman I don't recognize? Is she an aunt? Somebody's wife? Tell me who she is."

"See the beauty mark on her cheek as big as a hill on the lunar landscape of her face — well, that runs in the family. The women on your father's side of the family wrinkle early; it's the price they pay for that fair skin. The young girl with the green stain on her wedding dress is *La Novia* — just up from the Island. See, she lowers her eyes when she approaches the camera, as she's supposed to. Decent girls never look at you directly in the face. *Humilde,* humble, a girl should express humility in all her actions. She will make a good wife for your cousin. He should consider himself lucky to have met her only weeks after she arrived here. If he marries her quickly, she will make him a good Puerto Rican–style wife; but if he waits too long, she will be corrupted by the city — just like your cousin there."

"She means me. I do what I want. This is not some primitive island I live on. Do they expect me to wear a black mantilla on my head and go to mass every day? Not me. I'm an American woman, and I will do as I please. I can type faster than anyone in my senior class at Central High, and I'm going to be a secretary to a lawyer when I graduate. I can pass for an American girl anywhere — I've tried it. At least for Italian, anyway — I never speak Spanish in public. I hate these parties, but I wanted the dress. I look better than any of these *humildes* here. *My* life is going to be different. I have an American boyfriend. He is older and has a car. My parents don't know it, but I sneak out of the house late at night sometimes to be with him. If I marry him, even my name will be American. I hate rice and beans — that's what makes these women fat."

"Your *prima** is pregnant by that man she's been sneaking around with. Would I lie to you? I'm your *Tiá Política,*† your great-uncle's

Author's note — **prima:** Female cousin.

Author's note — †**tía política:** Aunt by marriage.

common-law wife — the one he abandoned on the Island to go marry your cousin's mother. *I* was not invited to this party, of course, but I came anyway. I came to tell you that story about your cousin that you've always wanted to hear. Do you remember the comment your mother made to a neighbor that has always haunted you? The only thing you heard was your cousin's name, and then you saw your mother pick up your doll from the couch and say: 'It was as big as this doll when they flushed it down the toilet.' This image has bothered you for years, hasn't it? You had nightmares about babies being flushed down the toilet, and you wondered why anyone would do such a horrible thing. You didn't dare ask your mother about it. She would only tell you that you had not heard her right, and yell at you for listening to adult conversations. But later, when you were old enough to know about abortions, you suspected.

I am here to tell you that you were right. Your cousin was growing an *Americanito* in her belly when this movie was made. Soon after she put something long and pointy into her pretty self, thinking maybe she could get rid of the problem before breakfast and still make it to her first class at the high school. Well, *Niña,** her screams could be heard downtown. Your aunt, her mamá, who had been a midwife on the Island, managed to pull the little thing out. Yes, they probably flushed it down the toilet. What else could they do with it — give it a Christian burial in a little white casket with blue bows and ribbons? Nobody wanted that baby — least of all the father, a teacher at her school with a house in West Paterson that he was filling with real children, and a wife who was a natural blond.

Girl, the scandal sent your uncle back to the bottle. And guess where your cousin ended up? Irony of ironies. She was sent to a village in Puerto Rico to live with a relative on her mother's side: a place so far away from civilization that you have to ride a mule to reach it. A real change in scenery. She found a man there — women like that cannot live without male company — but believe me, the men in Puerto Rico know how to put a saddle on a woman like her. *La Gringa,*[†] they call her. Ha, ha, ha. *La Gringa* is what she always wanted to be. . . ."

The old woman's mouth becomes a cavernous black hole I fall into. And as I fall, I can feel the reverberations of her laughter. I hear the echoes of her last mocking words: *La Gringa, La Gringa!*

Author's note — *niña: Girl.

Author's note — †La gringa: Derogatory epithet used here to ridicule a Puerto Rican girl who wants to look like a blonde North American.

And the conga line keeps moving silently past me. There is no music in my dream for the dancers.

When Odysseus visits Hades to see the spirit of his mother, he makes an offering of sacrificial blood, but since all the souls crave an audience with the living, he has to listen to many of them before he can ask questions. I, too, have to hear the dead and the forgotten speak in my dream. Those who are still part of my life remain silent, going around and around in their dance. The others keep pressing their faces forward to say things about the past.

My father's uncle is last in line. He is dying of alcoholism, shrunken and shriveled like a monkey, his face a mass of wrinkles and broken arteries. As he comes closer I realize that in his features I can see my whole family. If you were to stretch that rubbery flesh, you could find my father's face, and deep within *that* face — my own. I don't want to look into those eyes ringed in purple. In a few years he will retreat into silence, and take a long, long time to die. *Move back, Tío,* I tell him. *I don't want to hear what you have to say. Give the dancers room to move. Soon it will be midnight. Who is the New Year's Fool this time?*

Reflections and Responses

1. Consider the idea of "silence" in the essay. Why is it significant that the home movie has no soundtrack? What does Cofer do with that missing element? How does silence contribute to the theme of the essay?

2. What connections does Cofer make between the home movie and her dreams? In what ways is the movie dreamlike? In what ways does the essay become more nightmarish as it proceeds?

3. Consider Cofer's final paragraph. How does it pull together the various strands of the essay?

HENRY LOUIS GATES, JR.

In the Kitchen

In recent years, the memoir has become an attractive genre for many Ameri-can writers. Once written only toward the close of a career, as a kind of summary of a successful life (Benjamin Franklin's Autobiography *is the leading American prototype), the memoir is today often composed by indi-viduals in early or midcareer. As a result, such memoirs tend to be fash-ioned around the family, childhood, and the formative years. This is especially true with memoirs that introduce us to cultural worlds we may be unfamiliar with, or, as in the case of Henry Louis Gates, Jr., to acquaint us with a world that has vanished. He begins his celebrated memoir* Colored People *(1994) with an address to his children: "Dear Maggie and Liza: I have written to you because a world into which I was born, a world that nurtured and sustained me, has mysteriously disappeared."*

Henry Louis Gates, Jr., is W. E. B. Du Bois Professor of the Humanities and chair of the Afro-American Studies Department at Harvard Univer-sity, as well as director of the W. E. B. Du Bois Institute for Afro-American Research at Harvard. He received his Ph.D. in English literature from the University of Cambridge. Well-known for his work in recovering black writ-ers from obscurity, Dr. Gates, a "literary archaeologist," has brought to light thousands of previously lost or neglected works of nineteenth-century black literature. Among his books are: Figures in Black: Words, Signs, and the Racial Self *(1987);* The Signifying Monkey: A Theory of Afro-American Literary Criticism *(1988);* Loose Canons: Notes on the Culture Wars *(1992); and* Thirteen Ways of Looking at a Black Man *(1997). An essay-chapter of* Colored People, *"In the Kitchen" orig-inally appeared in* The New Yorker *(1994) and was selected by Jamaica Kincaid for* The Best American Essays *1995.*

We always had a gas stove in the kitchen, in our house in Piedmont, West Virginia, where I grew up. Never electric, though using
electric became fashionable in Piedmont in the sixties, like using
Crest toothpaste rather than Colgate, or watching Huntley and
Brinkley rather than Walter Cronkite. But not us: gas, Colgate, and
good ole Walter Cronkite, come what may. We used gas partly out
of loyalty to Big Mom, Mama's mama, because she was mostly blind
and still loved to cook, and could feel her way more easily with gas
than with electric. But the most important thing about our gas-
equipped kitchen was that Mama used to do hair there. The "hot
comb" was a fine-toothed iron instrument with a long wooden handle and a pair of iron curlers that opened and closed like scissors.
Mama would put it in the gas fire until it glowed. You could smell
those prongs heating up.

I liked that smell. Not the smell so much, I guess, as what the
smell meant for the shape of my day. There was an intimate
warmth in the women's tones as they talked with my mama, doing
their hair. I knew what the women had been through to get their
hair ready to be "done," because I would watch Mama do it to herself. How that kink could be transformed through grease and fire
into that magnificent head of wavy hair was a miracle to me, and
still is.

Mama would wash her hair over the sink, a towel wrapped
around her shoulders, wearing just her slip and her white bra. (We
had no shower — just a galvanized tub that we stored in the
kitchen — until we moved down Rat Tail Road into Doc Wolver-
ton's house, in 1954). After she dried it, she would grease her scalp
thoroughly with blue Bergamot hair grease, which came in a short,
fat jar with a picture of a beautiful colored lady on it. It's important
to grease your scalp real good, my mama would explain, to keep
from burning yourself. Of course, her hair would return to its natural kink almost as soon as the hot water and shampoo hit it. To
me, it was another miracle how hair so "straight" would so quickly
become kinky again the second it even approached some water.

My mama had only a few "clients" whose heads she "did" — did,
I think, because she enjoyed it, rather than for the few pennies it
brought in. They would sit on one of our red plastic kitchen
chairs, the kind with the shiny metal legs, and brace themselves for
the process. Mama would stroke that red-hot iron — which by this
time had been in the gas fire for half an hour or more — slowly but

firmly through their hair, from scalp to strand's end. It made a scorching, crinkly sound, the hot iron did, as it burned its way through kink, leaving in its wake straight strands of hair, standing long and tall but drooping over at the ends, their shape like the top of a heavy willow tree. Slowly, steadily, Mama's hands would transform a round mound of Odetta kink* into a darkened swamp of everglades. The Bergamot made the hair shiny; the heat of the hot iron gave it a brownish-red cast. Once all the hair was as straight as God allows kink to get, Mama would take the well-heated curling iron and twirl the straightened strands into more or less loosely wrapped curls. She claimed that she owed her skill as a hairdresser to the strength in her wrists, and as she worked her little finger would poke out, the way it did when she sipped tea. Mama was a southpaw, and wrote upside down and backward to produce the cleanest, roundest letters you've ever seen.

The "kitchen" she would all but remove from sight with a hand-held pair of shears, bought just for this purpose. Now, the kitchen was the room in which we were sitting — the room where Mama did hair and washed clothes, and where we all took a bath in that galvanized tub. But the word has another meaning, and the kitchen that I'm speaking of is the very kinky bit of hair at the back of your head, where your neck meets your shirt collar. If there was ever a part of our African past that resisted assimilation, it was the kitchen. No matter how hot the iron, no matter how powerful the chemical, no matter how stringent the mashed-potatoes-and-lye formula of a man's "process," neither God nor woman nor Sammy Davis, Jr., could straighten the kitchen. The kitchen was permanent, irredeemable, irresistible kink. Unassimilably African. No matter what you did, no matter how hard you tried, you couldn't de-kink a person's kitchen. So you trimmed it off as best you could.

When hair had begun to "turn," as they'd say — to return to its natural kinky glory — it was the kitchen that turned first (the kitchen around the back, and nappy edges at the temples). When the kitchen started creeping up the back of the neck, it was time to get your hair done again.

* * *

Odetta kink: Odetta Holmes Felious Gorden, the African-American folk singer of the 1960s, helped popularize the "afro" hair style. — Ed.

Sometimes, after dark, a man would come to have his hair done. It was Mr. Charlie Carroll. He was very light-complected and had a ruddy nose — it made me think of Edmund Gwenn, who played Kris Kringle in *Miracle on 34th Street*. At first, Mama did him after my brother, Rocky, and I had gone to sleep. It was only later that we found out that he had come to our house so Mama could iron his hair — not with a hot comb or a curling iron but with our very own Proctor-Silex steam iron. For some reason I never understood, Mr. Charlie would conceal his Frederick Douglass–like mane* under a big white Stetson hat. I never saw him take it off except when he came to our house, at night, to have his hair pressed. (Later, Daddy would tell us about Mr. Charlie's most prized piece of knowledge, something that the man would only confide after his hair had been pressed, as a token of intimacy. "Not many people know this," he'd say, in a tone of circumspection, "but George Washington was Abraham Lincoln's daddy." Nodding solemnly, he'd add the clincher: "A white man told me." Though he was in dead earnest, this became a humorous refrain around our house — "a white man told me" — which we used to punctuate especially preposterous assertions.)

My mother examined my daughters' kitchens whenever we went home to visit, in the early eighties. It became a game between us. I had told her not to do it, because I didn't like the politics it suggested — the notion of "good" and "bad" hair. "Good" hair was "straight," "bad" hair kinky. Even in the late sixties, at the height of Black Power, almost nobody could bring themselves to say "bad" for good and "good" for bad. People still said that hair like white people's hair was "good," even if they encapsulated it in a disclaimer, like "what we used to call 'good.'"

Maggie would be seated in her highchair, throwing food this way and that, and Mama would be cooing about how cute it all was, how I used to do just like Maggie was doing, and wondering whether her flinging her food with her left hand meant that she was going to be left-handed like Mama. When my daughter was just about covered with Chef Boyardee Spaghetti-O's, Mama would

---

*Frederick Douglass–like mane: Photographs of Frederick Douglass (1817?–1895), the escaped slave who became a prominent African-American writer and abolitionist, show that he had an impressive head of hair. — Ed.

seize the opportunity: wiping her clean, she would tilt Maggie's head to one side and reach down the back of her neck. Sometimes Mama would even rub a curl between her fingers, just to make sure that her bifocals had not deceived her. Then she'd sigh with satisfaction and relief: no kink . . . yet. Mama! I'd shout, pretending to be angry. Every once in a while, if no one was looking, I'd peek, too.

I say "yet" because most black babies are born with soft, silken hair. But after a few months it begins to turn, as inevitably as do the seasons or the leaves on a tree. People once thought baby oil would stop it. They were wrong.

Everybody I knew as a child wanted to have good hair. You could be as ugly as homemade sin dipped in misery and still be thought attractive if you had good hair. "Jesus moss," the girls at Camp Lee, Virginia, had called Daddy's naturally "good" hair during the war. I know that he played that thick head of hair for all it was worth, too.

My own hair was "not a bad grade," as barbers would tell me when they cut it for the first time. It was like a doctor reporting the results of the first full physical he has given you. Like "You're in good shape" or "Blood pressure's kind of high — better cut down on salt."

I spent most of my childhood and adolescence messing with my hair. I definitely wanted straight hair. Like Pop's. When I was about three, I tried to stick a wad of Bazooka bubble gum to that straight hair of his. I suppose what fixed that memory for me is the spanking I got for doing so: he turned me upside down, holding me by my feet, the better to paddle my behind. Little *nigger*, he had shouted, walloping away. I started to laugh about it two days later, when my behind stopped hurting.

When black people say "straight," of course, they don't usually mean literally straight — they're not describing hair like, say, Peggy Lipton's (she was the white girl on *The Mod Squad*), or like Mary's of Peter, Paul & Mary fame; black people call that "stringy" hair. No, "straight" just means not kinky, no matter what contours the curl may take. I would have done *anything* to have straight hair — and I used to try everything, short of getting a process.

Of the wide variety of techniques and methods I came to master in the challenging prestidigitation of the follicle, almost all had two things in common: a heavy grease and the application of pressure. It's not an accident that some of the biggest black-owned companies in the fifties and sixties made hair products. And I tried them all, in search of that certain silken touch, the one that would leave neither the hand nor the pillow sullied by grease.

I always wondered what Frederick Douglass put on *his* hair, or what Phillis Wheatley* put on hers. Or why Wheatley has that rag on her head in the little engraving in the frontispiece of her book. One thing is for sure: you can bet that when Phillis Wheatley went to England and saw the Countess of Huntingdon, she did not stop by the Queen's coiffeur on her way there. So many black people still get their hair straightened that it's a wonder we don't have a national holiday for Madame C. J. Walker, the woman who invented the process of straightening kinky hair. Call it Jheri-Kurled or call it "relaxed," it's still fried hair.

I used all the greases, from sea-blue Bergamot and creamy vanilla Duke (in its clear jar with the orange, white, and green label) to the godfather of grease, the formidable Murray's. Now, Murray's was some *serious* grease. Whereas Bergamot was like oily jello and Duke was viscous and sickly sweet, Murray's was light brown and *hard*. Hard as lard and twice as greasy, Daddy used to say. Murray's came in an orange can with a press-on top. It was so hard that some people would put a match to the can, just to soften the stuff and make it more manageable. Then, in the late sixties, when Afros came into style, I used Afro Sheen. From Murray's to Duke to Afro Sheen: that was my progression in black consciousness.

We used to put hot towels or washrags over our Murray-coated heads, in order to melt the wax into the scalp and the follicles. Unfortunately, the wax also had the habit of running down your neck, ears, and forehead. Not to mention your pillowcase. Another problem was that if you put two palmfuls of Murray's on your head your hair turned white. (Duke did the same thing.) The challenge was to get rid of that white color. Because if you got rid of the white stuff you had a magnificent head of wavy hair. That was the beauty of it: Murray's was so hard that it froze your hair into the wavy style

---

***Phillis Wheatley:** An African born slave in a prosperous Boston family, Phillis Wheatley (1753?–1784) became America's first major black poet.

you brushed it into. It looked really good if you wore a part. A lot of guys had parts *cut* into their hair by a barber, either with the clippers or with a straightedge razor. Especially if you had kinky hair — then you'd generally wear a short razor cut, or what we called a Quo Vadis.

We tried to be as innovative as possible. Everyone knew about using a stocking cap, because your father or your uncle wore one whenever something really big was about to happen, whether sacred or secular: a funeral or a dance, a wedding or a trip in which you confronted official white people. Any time you were trying to look really sharp, you wore a stocking cap in preparation. And if the event was really a big one, you made a new cap. You asked your mother for a pair of her hose, and cut it with scissors about six inches or so from the open end — the end with the elastic that goes up to the top of the thigh. Then you knotted the cut end, and it became a beehive-shaped hat, with an elastic band that you pulled down low on your forehead and down around your neck in the back. To work well, the cap had to fit tightly and snugly, like a press. And it had to fit that tightly because it *was* a press: it pressed your hair with the force of the hose's elastic. If you greased your hair down real good, and left the stocking cap on long enough, voilà: you got a head of pressed-against-the-scalp waves. (You also got a ring around your forehead when you woke up, but it went away.) And then you could enjoy your concrete do. Swore we were bad, too, with all that grease and those flat heads. My brother and I would brush it out a bit in the mornings, so that it looked — well, "natural." Grown men still wear stocking caps — especially older men, who generally keep their stocking caps in their top drawers, along with their cufflinks and their see-through silk socks, their *Maverick* ties, their silk handkerchiefs, and whatever else they prize the most.

A Murrayed-down stocking cap was the respectable version of the process, which, by contrast, was most definitely not a cool thing to have unless you were an entertainer by trade. Zeke and Keith and Poochie and a few other stars of the high school basketball team all used to get a process once or twice a year. It was expensive, and you had to go somewhere like Pittsburgh or D.C. or Uniontown — somewhere where there were enough colored people to support a trade. The guys would disappear, then reappear

a day or two later, strutting like peacocks, their hair burned slightly red from the lye base. They'd also wear "rags"— cloths or handkerchiefs — around their heads when they slept or played basketball. Do-rags, they were called. But the result was straight hair, with just a hint of wave. No curl. Do-it-yourselfers took their chances at home with a concoction of mashed potatoes and lye.

The most famous process of all, however, outside of the process Malcolm X describes in his *Autobiography*, and maybe the process of Sammy Davis, Jr., was Nat King Cole's process. Nat King Cole had patent-leather hair. That man's got the finest process money can buy, or so Daddy said the night we saw Cole's TV show on NBC. It was November 5, 1956. I remember the date because everyone came to our house to watch it and to celebrate one of Daddy's buddies' birthdays. Yeah, Uncle Joe chimed in, they can do shit to his hair that the average Negro can't even *think* about — secret shit.

Nat King Cole was *clean*. I've had an ongoing argument with a Nigerian friend about Nat King Cole for twenty years now. Not about whether he could sing — any fool knows that he could — but about whether or not he was a handkerchief head for wearing that patent-leather process.

Sammy Davis, Jr.'s process was the one I detested. It didn't look good on him. Worse still, he liked to have a fried strand dangling down the middle of his forehead, so he could shake it out from the crown when he sang. But Nat King Cole's hair was a thing unto itself, a beautifully sculpted work of art that he and he alone had the right to wear. The only difference between a process and a stocking cap, really, was taste; but Nat King Cole, unlike, say, Michael Jackson, looked *good* in his. His head looked like Valentino's head in the twenties, and some say it was Valentino the process was imitating. But Nat King Cole wore a process because it suited his face, his demeanor, his name, his style. He was as clean as he wanted to be.

I had forgotten all about that patent-leather look until one day in 1971, when I was sitting in an Arab restaurant on the island of Zanzibar surrounded by men in fezzes and white caftans, trying to learn how to eat curried goat and rice with the fingers of my right hand and feeling two million miles from home. All of a sudden, an

old transistor radio sitting on top of a china cupboard stopped blaring out its Swahili music and started playing "Fly Me to the Moon," by Nat King Cole. The restaurant's din was not affected at all, but in my mind's eye I saw it: the King's magnificent sleek black tiara. I managed, barely, to blink back the tears.

Reflections and Responses

1. Of what importance is the kitchen to the family's identity? Of what importance is it to African American identity? What does "kitchen" have to do with assimilation?

2. Evaluate Gates's position on processed hair. What are the politics of "good" and "bad" hair? Which kind does Gates most identify himself with? What makes his response difficult to pin down?

3. Read Gates's last paragraph again carefully. What does its setting suggest? What is the concluding paragraph's relation to the essay as a whole? What is Gates's emotional state — and why do you think he feels the way he does about Nat King Cole?

DAGOBERTO GILB

Victoria

Essays often hang on slight anecdotes, casual incidents that, at first glance, do not seem dramatic enough to be memorable. Such incidents play a large part in most people's lives, and essayists often enjoy taking a trivial event and bringing it center stage. In "Victoria," Dagoberto Gilb demonstrates how a momentary encounter with a glamorous television actress transformed one of the most miserable days he had ever known: "My brain was swollen with the vision of her, of her and me sitting there, saying hi, saying bye. I couldn't get it out of my mind."

Dagoberto Gilb is the author of a collection of short stories, The Magic of Blood *(1993), and a novel,* The Last Known Residence of Mickey Acuna *(1994). In addition to a Whiting Writers' Award, he has received Guggenheim and NEA fellowships. His work has recently appeared in* The New Yorker, The Nation, *and* DoubleTake, *and another of his essays was selected for* The Best American Essays 1997. *He lives in Austin, Texas. "Victoria" originally appeared in* The Washington Post Magazine *and was selected by Edward Hoagland for* The Best American Essays 1999.

I'll even blame the heat for my inability to remember which year it was —1986, give or take. It was hot like never before, my skin so porous it was hard to distinguish which side of it I was on. Like I could sweat and become a puddle. A dirty puddle, because I'd absorbed that construction site. And because this was Los Angeles, and it was smoggy too. But you know what, it wasn't the smog or the dirt or the cement dust, it was the heat that seemed to drain all the color into an overexposed gauze. It was so hot. I'm talking about three digits, so don't think I'm exaggerating. It was so hot. It was so hot everybody had to say it again and again. So hot I don't remember if the heat lasted three weeks, a month, two, three. It was day and night hot, as forever and endless as boredom.

I remember the fan. That's what I had going in the apartment when I got back from the job. I can still hear its shuddering fizz as it rotated, the clacks as it teetered at far left and far right until it shifted direction. I'd rigged together electrician's tape and no. 9 tie wire to keep the plastic base joined to the plastic stem, too cheap to buy a new one. I carried it with me wherever I sat because I wanted it close. Right after work, that was on the couch, near the tube. I'd have already downed one beer, and I'd have already put three cans of an already refrigerated six-pack in the freezer, and I'd be almost done with the third when I would turn on my show to drink two more almost frozen: *Dallas* was on every weekday evening. It was going around probably a second time, and so some of the episodes I'd seen, but who knows why you hook onto a particular TV program. For me it had always been cop shows, so I can't explain my deal with *Dallas*. I didn't like the city of Dallas, did not want to live there and never had. There was nobody I identified with and nothing these Ewings owned that I dreamed of having. Besides Pam. Besides Victoria Principal. You see, I didn't watch television much, and when I did it was reruns, not prime time. I didn't flip through the *Star* or *People,* and I knew nothing about Hollywood even if my apartment was a few blocks from it. Obviously a woman as stunning as Victoria Principal had a past that brought her to the show, obviously everybody knew how beautiful she was. But since I'd never seen or heard of her outside either *Dallas* or my own television set, my brain didn't register obvious. And of course it didn't matter. I alone saw and discovered her, how sweet and gorgeous she was. I wouldn't even joke to my wife about my infatuation with her. Pale as she was, I wanted her to have Mexican blood — you know, like Rita Hayworth, Raquel Welch, even, I thought I heard, Vanna White. And if she didn't, well, I didn't care that much.

The job was called a Class-A high-rise, and it was a steel building going several stories up and a few down. We were pouring decks and nonstructural beams and wrapping columns. It was in Beverly Hills, and it was on Rodeo Drive. Which sounds good but isn't. It meant that, because of Beverly Hills noise ordinances, starting time was an hour later than a job anywhere else. Because of morning L.A. traffic, it meant getting there at the same time as any job and leaving an hour later than usual, right in the worst evening traffic. I needed the money bad. My first days — or was it weeks? — were at the bottom level, in dirt, sharing air with a Bobcat — a miniature backhoe, like a Go Kart compared with the real thing — whose purpose, as I recall, was to fuse abused earth and unfiltered exhaust fumes into, first, a paste that lathered my sweaty arms and face black, and, second, a dyeing agent for snot and phlegm whose blow and hack you don't want to read about.

It was down there where I first met the guy I remember only as Pretty Boy. He was sent to assist me a couple of times. I'm fairly sure we were doing the same work, together, those hours, but you wouldn't know it by looking at him. I think he maybe perspired some, but he did it in such a way that it could have been a spray-on. You know how they use those little misting bottles on wealthy beaches to keep cool, or on a movie set, where they dapple a V on the gray T-shirt between the pecs and shoulder blades? Pretty Boy had puffy blond hair like an Aryan, like a surfer, like a New York model. If he didn't have to wear a hard hat, I'm sure a head twitch would have sent a cute curlicue off his forehead. He loved Reagan. He had an apartment in Santa Monica. He was single. That is to say, he did not live with a wife, he did not have two children. He smiled much more than was acceptable and, unlike me and everybody else panting in the L.A. basin, said he didn't mind the heat. He'd admit it was hot, it was hotter than anything he'd lived through, but . . . But *what?* He just shrugged his shoulders, a smile more than a wink — he treated himself to colder air conditioning when he got home, turned it *way* down. That is to say, he had air conditioning. Do I remember that remark, its surrounding image lingering dreamy. He was such a short, thin pretty boy. What good would it do for me to reply? What good to beat him with my steel Estwing hammer?

My hammer brings up Modesto Rodriguez, he of somewhere a hundred kilometers or so from Acapulco, where he was a *mero mero,* a big cheese, in a village, not as in Los Angeles, where he was mostly unemployed and struggling. And a lot of that struggle was with the English language. He had been working on the job with a young laborer, Matthew, who was related to someone and so was allowed to do all kinds of jobs laborers aren't supposed to, like this union carpenter's work with Modesto Rodriguez. I'd been brought up from the darkness below to set beams on the first level because, though Matthew spoke Spanish, Modesto's wasn't the same — the suggestion being that Modesto's was "Mexican," not "Castilian"— and therefore they were having trouble communicating. The other laborers on this job were a Polish guy from Poland and a black guy from Compton. Modesto was very happy to be with me, because these other two were about as fluent in this "Castilian" Spanish as Matthew. That is to say, they went around saying *no problema* a lot. What nobody ever understood, thinking that Spanish alone is a lot to have in common, is how little Modesto and I had to talk about — unlike, for instance, me and that laborer from Compton. Modesto had great enthusiasm, though, and he wanted to know everything. If someone did come up to us to say something, he wanted it translated. He wanted everything anyone said translated, everything I said back translated. Once I started not doing that, it was often the topic of discussion while we were working. I told him it was too hot for talking, period.

I do remember clearly the beginning of the end of this job for me. It was before lunch, and the super was standing there. Modesto barked words of greeting in an overly voweled English, wagging energetically. The super was shaped like a heavily mustached and bearded and eyebrowed cantaloupe. You wouldn't be able to tell by staring whether he smiled or not. Take that back. He didn't smile. He never smiled around me, anyway. It could've been the heat. But then sometimes, for reasons unknown, or instinctual, or born of karmic resentments from previous lives, people don't like you. It could be the nose. Could be a hard hat worn backward, the bandanna under it. Could be the laugh. Could be the teeth, though not the silver ones in Modesto's mouth — I thought they were too glary in the sun, wondered if they got too hot when he grinned — because the super wasn't bothered, looking right at them when he wanted to know what we were doing. And he continued looking at them as I translated and then stepped forward, skipping the Spanish. He did not want to look at me while I explained why we were going about our project the way we were, which was not how it was being done before I got there. It's true, I made decisions, and I made one about installing these beam sides. I was a journeyman, and sometimes I knew what I was doing, and this saved time and made it easier on us. The super heard me explain. He knew it wasn't wrong, because we were putting them in and stripping them out much faster. He didn't like it anyway, because, probably, of my nose type.

It was just hot, I knew it. It was so hot. Nobody was in a good mood. Well, Modesto was okay. At lunch, we went up on the roof, where some Pacific breezes might pass by. Modesto would have another T-shirt and change into it and let the sweat-soaked one dry, then eat. A great idea I copied. Pretty Boy was up there, too. Miserable as it was, he'd be in a good mood. Why shouldn't he be, all those breezes going to him alone? Even his depressing stories didn't make him feel bad: He went to a nightclub on the Sunset Strip called Coconut Teasers. I'd been there once. It was one of those bright, pink-decorated places peopled by men and women who had their hair styled, who wore clothes with names and worked out in gyms with names on machines with names and drank colored drinks with names. Men as beautiful as Pretty Boy, buttons done and undone just so. Women with lots of cleavage and revealed thigh. A place, in other words, I went to once for a short visit. Pretty Boy liked to go there because he liked to sleep with lots of pretty girls and that was the place for him. He said he took pictures. What kind of pictures? You know. No, what kind? Of the women. Everyone you slept with? Yeah. He brought a photo another day to show me. A Polaroid. She was lying on a bed, and she didn't have anything on. She let you? They all do. Whaddaya mean, they *all* do? I take pictures of them all. I have a collection. You just ask them? He nodded. And they do this? He smiled. You just *ask* them? He nodded, smiling. And you have a collection? In a binder. He smiled.

Sometimes I didn't want to be there and watch the cool breezes billowing into him. And I was with Modesto all day. Sometimes I'm grouchy. I wanted to eat lunch alone sometimes. So I found a bench at the edge of the site, at a driveway at the back entrance of the I. Magnin department store — maybe we were building an addition to it. I liked sitting there, watching the rich ladies step out of their Jaguars and Mercedes and BMWs, all dressed like it was an opera night, then high-heel clicking those twenty-five feet into the autumn climate of the luxury store. The red-coated attendants sprinted up and down the parking structure, whistling like birds, those radial tires squealing like peacocks into the parking struc-

ture. I sat there one lunch break with my feet up on the bumper of
a Bentley. I was sitting there this other lunch break when Victoria
Principal came and sat next to me.

Victoria Principal, of *Dallas*. She sat down a yard from me.
Maybe less when I think of it. Yes, less. Expert with a carpenter's
tape, I assure you, reconsidering it now, it was less. Her precious
hips were between sixteen and twenty inches from mine once she
sat down. I saw her coming before she sat. It seemed like a mirage
at first, bad eyesight. And I didn't want to stare while she sat there.
I was eating. I can't remember what I was eating. Tacos? Yogurt? I
think of both when I strain to remember. I said hi. She turned and
said hi back. Victoria. She was very pleasant about saying hi, not
self-conscious or worried in the unnatural heat about sitting next
to me, a sweaty, dirty construction worker. Of course I wanted to
talk. We both watched the boys in red coats sprinting, whistling.
Did I want to offer her my food? I don't remember that. I didn't
want to tell her I was a fan. I didn't want to tell her I watched the
reruns. I almost did say something. All I could think of: I'm a carpenter here. That would've been the opening. Once we got to talking I would tell her more about me, that I wasn't just a carpenter,
but a writer. Really. I never told anybody that, but I wanted her to
know, to know that my working poverty wasn't without its other
value — artistic, or spiritual, some higher implication like that. I
would have to talk both casually and with sophistication. Instead I
sat there. I did peek over at her a few times. I didn't want her to
think I was a weirdo, but I couldn't resist. She was beautiful. And
then her Jaguar Mercedes BMW appeared and she was getting up
and I said bye. She turned to me and she said bye back. She was
nice. Nice like a kiss is nice. Like a kiss that, even when you can
only imagine it, makes you remember, right then, that you are
happy to be alive.

Modesto didn't know who Victoria Principal was. Pretty Boy said
he said hi to Kareem Abdul-Jabbar when he walked by a couple of
weeks before and Kareem waved to him. What did Pretty Boy know
about love? My brain was swollen with the vision of her, of her and
me sitting there, saying hi, saying bye. I couldn't get it out of my
mind.

Modesto and I had to haul some long sticks of two-by-fours up
several levels of stairs. This was a laborer's job, but Matthew didn't

have to do this sort of thing. Somewhere along the way, my hammer fell out of its sling, and when we were done, I went up and down trying to find it. That's when the super decided to look me right in the eyes. What are you doing? he asked. I'm looking for my hammer, I told him. Why? Because I lost it somewhere. Where did you lose it? I couldn't believe he was actually staring at me, either. And I didn't know what else to say, except, if I knew where I lost it, it wouldn't be lost.

And that was the end, though I don't remember what happened after. Nothing specifically dramatic, I don't mean to imply that. I simply cannot remember whether I got my check, whether I quit, whether it was a day later or a week or two. I've had so many jobs, and I've been laid off and fired and quit so many times that no details stick. Just that it was the hottest, most miserable summer ever, and I hated this job. That on a bench near Rodeo Drive, at lunch, I sat so close to Victoria Principal we could have been holding hands, we could have been sharing tacos, or yogurt, talking, getting to know each other.

Reflections and Responses

1. Why do you think Dagoberto Gilb decided to open his essay with a description of the heat? In what ways does the heat set an appropriate mood for the entire essay? How does Gilb establish a relationship between heat and memory? Many people would write only about something they remember clearly. Why do you think Gilb calls attention repeatedly to his inability to remember?

2. Why are Gilb's job and coworkers so important to his essay? If he had minimized his description of work and expanded his description of his meeting with Victoria Principal, would that have changed your impression of the essay's significance?

3. Do you find any connection between Gilb's encounter with Victoria Principal and the loss of his job? Why does one event follow the other? Is it only coincidence? Why do you think Gilb decides not to state any connection?

LUCY GREALY

Mirrorings

Survival has become one of the dominant themes of our times. Today's essayists seem to be especially candid about personal pain and more willing to disclose the details of illnesses and injuries than were essayists in the past. This literary phenomenon may be stimulated by the public's vast interest in authentic medical case histories, an interest more popularly manifested in the growing number of on-line support groups and numerous television and film portrayals based on actual cases. One of the finest recent books in this memoir genre is Lucy Grealy's Autobiography of a Face, *which is remarkable not only for its intense level of self-examination but for its elegant and engaging prose.*

An award-winning poet who lives in New York City, Lucy Grealy attended the Iowa Writer's Workshop and has received fellowships at the Bunting Institute of Radcliffe and the Fine Arts Work Center in Provincetown. Published in 1994, Autobiography of a Face *was based on the essay "Mirrorings," which originally appeared in* Harper's Magazine *and which also won the National Magazine Award. The essay was selected by Tracy Kidder for* The Best American Essays 1994.

There was a long period of time, almost a year, during which I never looked in a mirror. It wasn't easy, for I'd never suspected just how omnipresent are our own images. I began by merely avoiding mirrors, but by the end of the year I found myself with an acute knowledge of the reflected image, its numerous tricks and wiles, how it can spring up at any moment: a glass tabletop, a well-polished door handle, a darkened window, a pair of sunglasses, a restaurant's otherwise magnificent brass-plated coffee machine sitting innocently by the cash register.

At the time, I had just moved, alone, to Scotland and was surviving on the dole, as Britain's social security benefits are called. I didn't know anyone and had no idea how I was going to live, yet I went anyway because by happenstance I'd met a plastic surgeon there who said he could help me. I had been living in London, working temp jobs. While in London, I'd received more nasty comments about my face than I had in the previous three years, living in Iowa, New York, and Germany. These comments, all from men and all odiously sexual, hurt and disoriented me. I also had journeyed to Scotland because after more than a dozen operations in the States my insurance had run out, along with my hope that further operations could make any *real* difference. Here, however, was a surgeon who had some new techniques, and here, amazingly enough, was a government willing to foot the bill: I didn't feel I could pass up yet another chance to "fix" my face, which I confusedly thought concurrent with "fixing" my self, my soul, my life.

Twenty years ago, when I was nine and living in America, I came home from school one day with a toothache. Several weeks and misdiagnoses later, surgeons removed most of the right side of my jaw in an attempt to prevent the cancer they found there from spreading. No one properly explained the operation to me, and I awoke in a cocoon of pain that prevented me from moving or speaking. Tubes ran in and out of my body, and because I was temporarily unable to speak after the surgery and could not ask questions, I made up my own explanations for the tubes' existence. I remember the mysterious manner the adults displayed toward me. They asked me to do things: lie still for x-rays, not cry for needles, and so on, tasks that, although not easy, never seemed equal to the praise I received in return. Reinforced to me again and again was how I was "a brave girl" for not crying, "a good girl" for not complaining, and soon I began defining myself this way, equating strength with silence.

Then the chemotherapy began. In the seventies chemo was even cruder than it is now, the basic premise being to poison patients right up to the very brink of their own death. Until this point I almost never cried and almost always received praise in return. Thus I got what I considered the better part of the deal. But now it was like a practical joke that had gotten out of hand. Chemotherapy was a nightmare and I wanted it to stop; I didn't want to be brave anymore. Yet I had grown so used to defining myself as "brave" — i.e., *silent* — that the thought of losing this sense of myself was even more terrifying. I was certain that if I broke down I would be despicable in the eyes of both my parents and the doctors.

The task of taking me into the city for the chemo injections fell mostly on my mother, though sometimes my father made the trip. Overwhelmed by the sight of the vomiting and weeping, my father developed the routine of "going to get the car," meaning that he left the doctor's office before the injection was administered, on the premise that then he could have the car ready and waiting when it was all over. Ashamed of my suffering, I felt relief when he was finally out of the room. When my mother took me, she stayed in the room, yet this only made the distance between us even more tangible. She explained that it was wrong to cry *before* the needle went in; afterward was one thing, but before, that was mere fear, and hadn't I demonstrated my bravery earlier? Every Friday for two and a half years I climbed up onto that big doctor's table and told myself not to cry, and every week I failed. The two large syringes were filled with chemicals so caustic to the vein that each had to be administered very slowly. The whole process took about four minutes; I had to remain utterly still. Dry retching began in the first fifteen seconds, then the throb behind my eyes gave everything a yellow-green aura, and the bone-deep pain of alternating extreme hot and cold flashes made me tremble, yet still I had to sit motionless and not move my arm. No one spoke to me — not the doctor, who was a paradigm of the cold-fish physician; not the nurse, who told my mother I reacted much more violently than many of "the other children"; and not my mother, who, surely overwhelmed by the sight of her child's suffering, thought the best thing to do was remind me to be brave, to try not to cry. All the while I hated myself for having wept before the needle went in, convinced that the nurse and my mother were right, that I was "overdoing it," that the throwing up was psychosomatic, that my mother was angry with me for not being good or brave enough.

Yet each week, two or three days after the injection, there came the first flicker of feeling better, the always forgotten and gratefully rediscovered understanding that to simply be well in my body was the greatest thing I could ask for. I thought other people felt this appreciation and physical joy all the time, and I felt cheated because I was able to feel it only once a week.

Because I'd lost my hair, I wore a hat constantly, but this fooled no one, least of all myself. During this time, my mother worked in a nursing home in a Hasidic community. Hasidic law dictates that married women cover their hair, and most commonly this is done with a wig. My mother's friends were now all willing to donate their discarded wigs, and soon the house seemed filled with them. I never wore one, for they frightened me even when my mother insisted I looked better in one of the few that actually fit. Yet we didn't know how to say no to the women who kept graciously offering their wigs. The cats enjoyed sleeping on them and the dogs playing with them, and we grew used to having to pick a wig up off a chair we wanted to sit in. It never struck us as odd until one day a visitor commented wryly as he cleared a chair for himself, and suddenly a great wave of shame overcame me. I had nightmares about wigs and flushed if I even heard the word, and one night I put myself out of my misery by getting up after everyone was asleep and gathering all the wigs except for one the dogs were fond of and that they had chewed up anyway. I hid all the rest in an old chest.

When you are only ten, which is when the chemotherapy began, two and a half years seem like your whole life, yet it finally did end, for the cancer was gone. I remember the last day of treatment clearly because it was the only day on which I succeeded in not crying, and because later, in private, I cried harder than I had in years; I thought now I would no longer be "special," that without the arena of chemotherapy in which to prove myself no one would ever love me, that I would fade unnoticed into the background. But this idea about *not being different* didn't last very long. Before, I foolishly believed that people stared at me because I was bald. After my hair eventually grew in, it didn't take long before I understood that I looked different for another reason. My face. People stared at me in stores, and other children made fun of me to the point that I came to expect such reactions constantly, wherever I went. School became a battleground.

Halloween, that night of frights, became my favorite holiday because I could put on a mask and walk among the blessed for a few brief, sweet hours. Such freedom I felt, walking down the street, my face hidden! Through the imperfect oval holes I could peer out at other faces, masked or painted or not, and see on those faces nothing but the normal faces of childhood looking back at me, faces I mistakenly thought were the faces everyone else but me saw all the time, faces that were simply curious and ready for fun, not the faces I usually braced myself for, the cruel, lonely, vicious ones I spent every day other than Halloween waiting to see around each corner. As I breathed in the condensed, plastic-scented air under the mask, I somehow thought that I was breathing in normality, that this joy and weightlessness were what the world was composed of, and that it was only my face that kept me from it, my face that was my own mask that kept me from knowing the joy I was sure everyone but me lived with intimately. How could the other children not know it? Not know that to be free of the fear of taunts and the burden of knowing no one would ever love you was all that anyone could ever ask for? I was a pauper walking for a short while in the clothes of the prince, and when the day ended I gave up my disguise with dismay.

I was living in an extreme situation, and because I did not particularly care for the world I was in, I lived in others, and because the world I did live in was dangerous now, I incorporated this danger into my secret life. I imagined myself to be an Indian. Walking down the streets, I stepped through the forest, my body ready for any opportunity to fight or flee one of the big cats that I knew stalked me. Vietnam and Cambodia, in the news then as scenes of catastrophic horror, were other places I walked through daily. I made my way down the school hall, knowing a land mine or a sniper might give themselves away at any moment with the subtle metal click I'd read about. Compared with a land mine, a mere insult about my face seemed a frivolous thing.

In those years, not yet a teenager, I secretly read — knowing it was somehow inappropriate — works by Primo Levi and Elie Wiesel, and every book by a survivor I could find by myself without asking the librarian. Auschwitz, Birkenau: I felt the blows of the capos and somehow knew that because any moment we might be called upon to live for a week on one loaf of bread and some water called soup, the peanut-butter sandwich I found on my plate was nothing less than a miracle, an utter and sheer miracle capable of making me literally weep with joy.

I decided to become a "deep" person. I wasn't exactly sure what this would entail, but I believed that if I could just find the right philosophy, think the right thoughts, my suffering would end. To try to understand the world I was in, I undertook to find out what was "real," and I quickly began seeing reality as existing in the lowest common denominator, that suffering was the one and only dependable thing. But rather than spend all of my time despairing, though certainly I did plenty of that, I developed a form of defensive egomania: I felt I was the only one walking about in the world who understood what was really important. I looked upon people complaining about the most mundane things — nothing on TV, traffic jams, the price of new clothes — and felt joy because I knew how unimportant those things really were and felt unenlightened superiority because other people didn't. Because in my fantasy life I had learned to be thankful for each cold, blanketless night that I survived on the cramped wooden bunks, my pain and despair were a stroll through the country in comparison. I was often miserable, but I knew that to feel warm instead of cold was its own kind of joy, that to eat was a reenactment of the grace of some god whom I could only dimly define, and that to simply be alive was a rare, ephemeral gift.

As I became a teenager, my isolation began. My nonidentical twin sister started going out with boys, and I started — my most tragic mistake of all — to listen to and believe the taunts thrown at me daily by the very boys she and the other girls were interested in. I was a dog, a monster, the ugliest girl they had ever seen. Of all the remarks, the most damaging wasn't even directed at me but was really an insult to "Jerry," a boy I never saw because every day between fourth and fifth periods, when I was cornered by a particular group of kids, I was too ashamed to lift my eyes off the floor. "Hey, look, it's Jerry's girlfriend!" they shrieked when they saw me, and I felt such shame, knowing that this was the deepest insult to Jerry that they could imagine.

When pressed to it, one makes compensations. I came to love winter, when I could wrap up the disfigured lower half of my face in a scarf: I could speak to people and they would have no idea to whom and to what they were really speaking. I developed the bad habit of letting my long hair hang in my face and of always covering my chin and mouth with my hand, hoping it might be mistaken as a thoughtful, accidental gesture. I also became interested in horses and got a job at a rundown local stable. Having those horses to go to each day after school saved my life; I spent all of my time either with them or thinking about them. Completely and utterly repressed by the time I was sixteen, I was convinced that I would never want a boyfriend, not ever, and wasn't it convenient for me, even a blessing, that none would ever want me. I told myself I was free to concentrate on the "true reality" of life, whatever that was. My sister and her friends put on blue eye shadow, blow-dried their hair, and spent interminable hours in the local mall, and I looked down on them for this, knew they were misleading themselves and being overly occupied with the "mere surface" of living. I'd had thoughts like this when I was younger, ten or twelve, but now my philosophy was haunted by desires so frightening I was unable even to admit they existed.

Throughout all of this, I was undergoing reconstructive surgery in an attempt to rebuild my jaw. It started when I was fifteen, two years after chemo ended. I had known for years I would have operations to fix my face, and at night I fantasized about how good my life would finally be then. One day I got a clue that maybe it wouldn't be so easy. An older plastic surgeon explained the process of "pedestals" to me, and told me it would take *ten years* to fix my face. Ten years? Why even bother, I thought; I'll be ancient by then. I went to a medical library and looked up the "pedestals" he talked about. There were gruesome pictures of people with grotesque tubes of their own skin growing out of their bodies, tubes of skin that were harvested like some kind of crop and then rearranged, with results that did not look at all normal or acceptable to my eye. But then I met a younger surgeon, who was working on a new way of grafting that did not involve pedestals, and I became more hopeful and once again began to await the fixing of my face, the day when I would be whole, content, loved.

Long-term plastic surgery is not like in the movies. There is no one single operation that will change everything, and there is certainly no slow unwrapping of the gauze in order to view the final, remarkable result. There is always swelling, sometimes to a grotesque degree, there are often bruises, and always there are scars. After each operation, too frightened to simply go look in the mirror, I developed an oblique method, with several stages. First, I tried to catch my reflection in an overhead lamp: the roundness of the metal distorted my image just enough to obscure details and give no true sense of size or proportion. Then I slowly worked my way up to looking at the reflection in someone's eyeglasses, and from there I went to walking as briskly as possible by a mirror, glancing only quickly. I repeated this as many times as it would take me, passing the mirror slightly more slowly each time until finally I was able to stand still and confront myself.

The theory behind most reconstructive surgery is to take large chunks of muscle, skin, and bone and slap them into the roughly appropriate place, then slowly begin to carve this mess into some sort of shape. It involves long, major operations, countless lesser ones, a lot of pain, and many, many years. And also, it does not always work. With my young surgeon in New York, who with each passing year was becoming not so young, I had two or three soft-tissue grafts, two skin grafts, a bone graft, and some dozen other operations to "revise" my face, yet when I left graduate school at the age of twenty-five I was still more or less in the same position I had started in: a deep hole in the right side of my face and a rapidly shrinking left side and chin, a result of the radiation I'd had as a child and the stress placed upon the bone by the other operations. I was caught in a cycle of having a big operation, one that would force me to look monstrous from the swelling for many months, then having the subsequent revision operations that improved my looks tremendously, and then slowly, over the period of a few months or a year, watching the graft reabsorb back into my body, slowly shrinking down and leaving me with nothing but the scarred donor site the graft had originally come from.

It wasn't until I was in college that I finally allowed that maybe, just maybe, it might be nice to have a boyfriend. I went to a small, liberal, predominantly female school and suddenly, after years of alienation in high school, discovered that there were other people I could enjoy talking to who thought me intelligent and talented. I was, however, still operating on the assumption that no one, not ever, would be physically attracted to me, and in a curious way this shaped my personality. I became forthright and honest in the way that only the truly self-confident are, who do not expect to be rejected, and in the way of those like me, who do not even dare to ask acceptance from others and therefore expect no rejection. I

had come to know myself as a person, but I would be in graduate
school before I was literally, physically able to use my name and
the word "woman" in the same sentence.

Now my friends repeated for me endlessly that most of it was in
my mind, that, granted, I did not look like everyone else, but that
didn't mean I looked bad. I am sure now that they were right some
of the time. But with the constant surgery I was in a perpetual state
of transfiguration. I rarely looked the same for more than six
months at a time. So ashamed of my face, I was unable even to
admit that this constant change affected me; I let everyone who
wanted to know that it was only what was inside that mattered, that
I had "grown used to" the surgery, that none of it bothered me at
all. Just as I had done in childhood, I pretended nothing was
wrong, and this was constantly mistaken by others for bravery. I
spent a great deal of time looking in the mirror in private, posi-
tioning my head to show off my eyes and nose, which were not
only normal but quite pretty, as my friends told me often. But I
could not bring myself to see them for more than a moment: I
looked in the mirror and saw not the normal upper half of my face
but only the disfigured lower half.

People still teased me. Not daily, as when I was younger, but in
ways that caused me more pain than ever before. Children stared
at me, and I learned to cross the street to avoid them; this bothered me, but not as much as the insults I got from men. Their
taunts came at me not because I was disfigured but because I was a
disfigured *woman*. They came from boys, sometimes men, and almost always from a group of them. I had long, blond hair, and I
also had a thin figure. Sometimes, from a distance, men would see
a thin blonde and whistle, something I dreaded more than anything else because I knew that as they got closer, their tune, so to
speak, would inevitably change; they would stare openly or, worse,
turn away quickly in shame or repulsion. I decided to cut my hair
to avoid any misconception that anyone, however briefly, might
have about my being attractive. Only two or three times have I ever
been teased by a single person, and I can think of only one time
when I was ever teased by a woman. Had I been a man, would I
have had to walk down the street while a group of young women
followed and denigrated my sexual worth?

Not surprisingly, then, I viewed sex as my salvation. I was sure
that if only I could get someone to sleep with me, it would mean I

wasn't ugly, that I was attractive, even lovable. This line of reasoning led me into the beds of several manipulative men who liked themselves even less than they liked me, and I in turn left each short-term affair hating myself, obscenely sure that if only I had been prettier it would have worked — he would have loved me and it would have been like those other love affairs that I was certain "normal" women had all the time. Gradually, I became unable to say "I'm depressed" but could say only "I'm ugly," because the two had become inextricably linked in my mind. Into that universal lie, that sad equation of "if only . . ." that we are all prey to, I was sure that if only I had a normal face, then I would be happy.

The new surgeon in Scotland, Oliver Fenton, recommended that I undergo a procedure involving something called a tissue expander, followed by a bone graft. A tissue expander is a small balloon placed under the skin and then slowly blown up over the course of several months, the object being to stretch out the skin and create room and cover for the new bone. It's a bizarre, nightmarish thing to do to your face, yet I was hopeful about the end results and I was also able to spend the three months that the expansion took in the hospital. I've always felt safe in hospitals: they're the one place I feel free from the need to explain the way I look. For this reason the first tissue expander was bearable — just — and the bone graft that followed it was a success; it did not melt away like the previous ones.

The surgical stress this put upon what remained of my original jaw instigated the deterioration of that bone, however, and it became unhappily apparent that I was going to need the same operation I'd just had on the right side done to the left. I remember my surgeon telling me this at an outpatient clinic. I planned to be traveling down to London that same night on an overnight train, and I barely made it to the station on time, such a fumbling state of despair I was in.

I could not imagine going through it *again,* and just as I had done all my life, I searched and searched through my intellect for a way to make it okay, make it bearable, for a way to *do* it. I lay awake all night on that train, feeling the tracks slip beneath me with an odd eroticism, when I remembered an afternoon from my three months in the hospital. Boredom was a big problem those long afternoons, the days marked by meals and television programs. Waiting for the afternoon tea to come, wondering desperately how I could make time pass, it had suddenly occurred to me that I didn't have to make time pass, that it would do it of its own accord, that I simply had to relax and take no action. Lying on the train, remembering that, I realized I had no obligation to improve my situation, that I didn't have to explain or understand it, that I could just simply let it happen. By the time the train pulled into King's Cross station, I felt able to bear it yet again, not entirely sure what other choice I had.

But there was an element I didn't yet know about. When I returned to Scotland to set up a date to have the tissue expander inserted, I was told quite casually that I'd be in the hospital only three or four days. Wasn't I going to spend the whole expansion time in the hospital? I asked in a whisper. What's the point of that? came the answer. You can just come in every day to the outpatient ward to have it expanded. Horrified by this, I was speechless. I would have to live and move about in the outside world with a giant balloon inside the tissue of my face? I can't remember what I did for the next few days before I went into the hospital, but I vaguely recall that these days involved a great deal of drinking alone in bars and at home.

I had the operation and went home at the end of the week. The only things that gave me any comfort during the months I lived with my tissue expander were my writing and Franz Kafka. I started a novel and completely absorbed myself in it, writing for hours each day. The only way I could walk down the street, could stand the stares I received, was to think to myself, "I'll bet none of them are writing a novel." It was that strange, old, familiar form of egomania, directly related to my dismissive, conceited thoughts of adolescence. As for Kafka, who had always been one of my favorite writers, he helped me in that I felt permission to feel alienated, and to have that alienation be okay, bearable, noble even. In the same way that imagining I lived in Cambodia helped me as a child, I walked the streets of my dark little Scottish city by the sea and knew without doubt that I was living in a story Kafka would have been proud to write.

The one good thing about a tissue expander is that you look so bad with it in that no matter what you look like once it's finally removed, your face has to look better. I had my bone graft and my

fifth soft-tissue graft and, yes, even I had to admit I looked better.
But I didn't look like me. Something was wrong: was *this* the face I
had waited through eighteen years and almost thirty operations
for? I somehow just couldn't make what I saw in the mirror corre-
spond to the person I thought I was. It wasn't only that I continued
to feel ugly; I simply could not conceive of the image as belonging
to me. My own image was the image of a stranger, and rather than
try to understand this, I simply stopped looking in the mirror. I
perfected the technique of brushing my teeth without a mirror,
grew my hair in such a way that it would require only a quick, simple brush, and wore clothes that were simply and easily put on, no
complex layers or lines that might require even the most minor of
visual adjustments.

On one level I understood that the image of my face was merely
that, an image, a surface that was not directly related to any true,
deep definition of the self. But I also knew that it is only through
appearances that we experience and make decisions about the
everyday world, and I was not always able to gather the strength to
prefer the deeper world to the shallower one. I looked for ways to
find a bridge that would allow me access to both, rather than riding out the constant swings between peace and anguish. The only
direction I had to go in to achieve this was to strive for a state of
awareness and self-honesty that sometimes, to this day, occasionally rewards me. I have found, I believe, that our whole lives are
dominated, though it is not always so clearly translatable, by the
question "How do I look?" Take all the many nouns in our
lives — car, house, job, family, love, friends — and substitute the
personal pronoun "I." It is not that we are all so self-obsessed; it is
that all things eventually relate back to ourselves, and it is our own
sense of how we appear to the world by which we chart our lives,
how we navigate our personalities, which would otherwise be
adrift in the ocean of *other* people's obsessions.

One evening toward the end of my year-long separation from the
mirror, I was sitting in a café talking to someone — an attractive
man, as it happened — and we were having a lovely, engaging conversation. For some reason I suddenly wondered what I looked like
to him. What was he *actually* seeing when he saw me? So many times
I've asked this of myself, and always the answer is this: a warm,
smart woman, yes, but an unattractive one. I sat there in the café

and asked myself this old question, and startlingly, for the first time in my life, I had no answer readily prepared. I had not looked in a mirror for so long that I quite simply had no clue as to what I looked like. I studied the man as he spoke; my entire life I had seen my ugliness reflected back to me. But now, as reluctant as I was to admit it, the only indication in my companion's behavior was positive.

And then, that evening in that café, I experienced a moment of the freedom I'd been practicing for behind my Halloween mask all those years ago. But whereas as a child I expected my liberation to come as a result of gaining something, a new face, it came to me now as the result of shedding something, of shedding my image. I once thought that truth was eternal, that when you understood something it was with you forever. I know now that this isn't so, that most truths are inherently unretainable, that we have to work hard all our lives to remember the most basic things. Society is no help; it tells us again and again that we can most be ourselves by looking like someone else, leaving our own faces behind to turn into ghosts that will inevitably resent and haunt us. It is no mistake that in movies and literature the dead sometimes know they are dead only after they can no longer see themselves in the mirror; and as I sat there feeling the warmth of the cup against my palm, this small observation seemed like a great revelation to me. I wanted to tell the man I was with about it, but he was involved in his own topic and I did not want to interrupt him, so instead I looked with curiosity toward the window behind him, its night-darkened glass reflecting the whole café, to see if I could, now, recognize myself.

Reflections and Responses

1. Note how Grealy opens her essay with a description of mirroring objects. Why do you think she begins in this fashion? Why doesn't she start by telling the reader first about her physical condition?

2. How does Grealy introduce images of disguise into her essay? What sort of disguises does she invent? In what ways do Grealy's

discoveries about self-deception and self-honesty apply to all readers, not just those with similar afflictions? How does Grealy extend
those discoveries to others?

3. Consider carefully Grealy's final paragraph. What "small observation" does she make? Why does it seem like a "great revelation"?
Try putting her observation into your own words.

GARRETT HONGO

Kubota

"I was not made yet, and he was determined that his stories be part of my making," Garrett Hongo says of his Hawaiian-born Japanese grandfather, Kubota, whose nightly "talk story" bore testimony to the trials endured by Japanese Americans soon after the attack on Pearl Harbor. Hongo's essay is more than a personal recollection; it is a fulfillment of his grandfather's injunction to retain these stories as part of his heritage. Having encouraged Hongo to "learn speak dah good Ing-rish," Kubota then leaves him with the command: "You tell story." Such injunctions, Hongo reminds us, are the inspiration behind many enduring works of literature — a character frequently encountered in the classics is the "witness who gives personal testimony about an event the rest of his community cannot even imagine."

Garrett Hongo is a poet born in Volcano, Hawaii, a place which figures in his recent book Volcano: A Memoir of Hawaii *(1995). He was educated at Pomona College, the University of Michigan, and the University of California, Irvine, where he received an M.F.A. in English. The author of two highly praised volumes of poetry,* Yellow Light *(1982) and* The River of Heaven *(1988), and the editor of* The Open Boat: Poems from Asian America *(1993), Hongo is Professor of Creative Writing at the University of Oregon. He has received many literary awards, including fellowships from the National Endowment for the Arts and the John Simon Guggenheim Foundation. "Kubota" originally appeared in* Ploughshares *(1990) and was selected by Joyce Carol Oates for* The Best American Essays *1991.*

On December 8, 1941, the day after the Japanese attack on Pearl Harbor in Hawaii, my grandfather barricaded himself with his family — my grandmother, my teenage mother, her two sisters and two brothers — inside of his home in La'ie, a sugar plantation village on Oahu's North Shore. This was my maternal grandfather, a man most villagers called by his last name, Kubota. It could mean either "Wayside Field" or else "Broken Dreams," depending on which ideograms he used. Kubota ran La'ie's general store, and the previous night, after a long day of bad news on the radio, some locals had come by, pounded on the front door, and made threats. One was said to have brandished a machete. They were angry and shocked, as the whole nation was in the aftermath of the surprise attack. Kubota was one of the few Japanese Americans in the village and president of the local Japanese language school. He had become a target for their rage and suspicion. A wise man, he locked all his doors and windows and did not open his store the next day, but stayed closed and waited for news from some official.

He was a *kibei*, a Japanese American born in Hawaii (a U.S. territory then, so he was thus a citizen) but who was subsequently sent back by his father for formal education in Hiroshima, Japan, their home province. *Kibei* is written with two ideograms in Japanese: one is the word for "return" and the other is the word for "rice." Poetically, it means one who returns from America, known as the Land of Rice in Japanese (by contrast, Chinese immigrants called their new home Mountain of Gold).

Kubota was graduated from a Japanese high school and then came back to Hawaii as a teenager. He spoke English — and a Hawaiian creole version of it at that — with a Japanese accent. But he was well liked and good at numbers, scrupulous and hard working like so many immigrants and children of immigrants. Castle & Cook, a grower's company that ran the sugarcane business along the North Shore, hired him on first as a stock boy and then appointed him to run one of its company stores. He did well, had the trust of management and labor — not an easy accomplishment in any day — married, had children, and had begun to exert himself in community affairs and excel in his own recreations. He put together a Japanese community organization that backed a Japanese language school for children and sponsored teachers from Japan. Kubota boarded many of them, in succession, in his own home. This made dinners a silent affair for his talkative, Hawaiian-bred children, as their stern *sensei*, or teacher, was nearly always at the table and their own abilities in the Japanese language were as delinquent as their attendance. While Kubota and the *sensei* rattled on about things Japanese, speaking Japanese, his children hurried through their suppers and tried to run off early to listen to the radio shows.

After dinner, while the *sensei* graded exams seated in a wicker chair in the spare room and his wife and children gathered around the radio in the front parlor, Kubota sat on the screened porch outside, reading the local Japanese newspapers. He finished reading about the same time as he finished the tea he drank for his digestion — a habit he'd learned in Japan — and then he'd get out his fishing gear and spread it out on the plank floors. The wraps on his rods needed to be redone, gears in his reels needed oil, and, once through with those tasks, he'd painstakingly wind on hundreds of yards of new line. Fishing was his hobby and his passion. He spent weekends camping along the North Shore beaches with his children, setting up umbrella tents, packing a rice pot and hibachi along for meals. And he caught fish. *Ulu'a* mostly, the huge surf-feeding fish known on the mainland as the jack crevalle, but he'd go after almost anything in its season. In Kawela, a plantation-owned bay nearby, he fished for mullet Hawaiian-style with a throw net, stalking the bottom-hugging, gray-backed schools as they gathered at the stream mouths and in the freshwater springs. In an outrigger out beyond the reef, he'd try for *aku*— the skipjack tuna prized for steaks and, sliced raw and mixed with fresh seaweed and cut onions, for *sashimi* salad. In Kahaluu and Ka'awa and on an offshore rock locals called Goat Island, he loved to go torching, stringing lanterns on bamboo poles stuck in the sand to attract *kumu'u*, the red goatfish, as they schooled at night just inside the reef. But in Lai'e on Laniloa Point near Kahuku, the northernmost tip of Oahu, he cast twelve- and fourteen-foot surf rods for the huge, varicolored, and fast-running *ulu'a* as they ran for schools of squid and baitfish just beyond the biggest breakers and past the low sand flats wadable from the shore to nearly a half mile out. At sunset, against the western light, he looked as if he walked on water as he came back, fish and rods slung over his shoulders, stepping along the rock and coral path just inches under the surface of a running tide.

When it was torching season, in December or January, he'd drive out the afternoon before and stay with old friends, the Tanakas or

Yoshikawas, shopkeepers like him who ran stores near the fishing grounds. They'd have been preparing for weeks, selecting and cutting their bamboo poles, cleaning the hurricane lanterns, tearing up burlap sacks for the cloths they'd soak with kerosene and tie onto sticks they'd poke into the soft sand of the shallows. Once lit, touched off with a Zippo lighter, these would be the torches they'd use as beacons to attract the schooling fish. In another time, they might have made up a dozen paper lanterns of the kind mostly used for decorating the summer folk dances outdoors on the grounds of the Buddhist church during O-Bon, the Festival for the Dead. But now, wealthy and modern and efficient killers of fish, Tanaka and Kubota used rag torches and Colemans and cast rods with tips made of Tonkin bamboo and butts of American-spun fiberglass. After just one good night, they might bring back a prize bounty of a dozen burlap bags filled with scores of bloody, rigid fish delicious to eat and even better to give away as gifts to friends, family, and special customers.

It was a Monday night, the day after Pearl Harbor, and there was a rattling knock at the front door. Two FBI agents presented themselves, showed identification, and took my grandfather in for questioning in Honolulu. He didn't return home for days. No one knew what had happened or what was wrong. But there was a roundup going on of all those in the Japanese-American community suspected of sympathizing with the enemy and worse. My grandfather was suspected of espionage, of communicating with offshore Japanese submarines launched from the attack fleet days before war began. Torpedo planes and escort fighters, decorated with the insignia of the Rising Sun, had taken an approach route from northwest of Oahu directly across Kahuku Point and on toward Pearl. They had strafed an auxiliary air station near the fishing grounds my grandfather loved and destroyed a small gun battery there, killing three men. Kubota was known to have sponsored and harbored Japanese nationals in his own home. He had a radio. He had wholesale access to firearms. Circumstances and an undertone of racial resentment had combined with wartime hysteria in the aftermath of the tragic naval battle to cast suspicion on the loyalties of my grandfather and all other Japanese Americans. The FBI reached out and pulled hundreds of them in for questioning in dragnets cast throughout the West Coast and Hawaii.

My grandfather was lucky; he'd somehow been let go after only a few days. Others were not as fortunate. Hundreds, from small communities in Washington, California, Oregon, and Hawaii, were rounded up and, after what appeared to be routine questioning, shipped off under Justice Department orders to holding centers in Leuppe on the Navaho reservation in Arizona, in Fort Missoula in Montana, and on Sand Island in Honolulu Harbor. There were other special camps on Maui in Ha'iku and on Hawaii — the Big Island — in my own home village of Volcano.

Many of these men — it was exclusively the Japanese-American men suspected of ties to Japan who were initially rounded up — did not see their families again for more than four years. Under a suspension of due process that was only after the fact ruled as warranted by military necessity, they were, if only temporarily, "disappeared" in Justice Department prison camps scattered in particularly desolate areas of the United States designated as militarily "safe." These were grim forerunners of the assembly centers and concentration camps for the 120,000 Japanese-American evacuees that were to come later.

I am Kubota's eldest grandchild, and I remember him as a lonely, habitually silent old man who lived with us in our home near Los Angeles for most of my childhood and adolescence. It was the fifties, and my parents had emigrated from Hawaii to the mainland in the hope of a better life away from the old sugar plantation. After some success, they had sent back for my grandparents and taken them in. And it was my grandparents who did the work of the household while my mother and father worked their salaried city jobs. My grandmother cooked and sewed, washed our clothes, and knitted in the front room under the light of a huge lamp with a bright three-way bulb. Kubota raised a flower garden, read up on soils and grasses in gardening books, and planted a zoysia lawn in front and a dichondra one in back. He planted a small patch near the rear block wall with green onions, eggplant, white Japanese radishes, and cucumber. While he hoed and spaded the loamless, clayey earth of Los Angeles, he sang particularly plangent songs in Japanese about plum blossoms and bamboo groves.

Once, in the mid-sixties, after a dinner during which, as always, he had been silent while he worked away at a meal of fish and rice spiced with dabs of Chinese mustard and catsup thinned with soy sauce, Kubota took his own dishes to the kitchen sink and washed them up. He took a clean jelly jar out of the cupboard — the glass was thick and its shape squatty like an old-fashioned. He reached around to the hutch below where he kept his bourbon. He made himself a drink and retired to the living room where I was expected to join him for "talk story," the Hawaiian idiom for chewing the fat.

I was a teenager and, though I was bored listening to stories I'd heard often enough before at holiday dinners, I was dutiful. I took my spot on the couch next to Kubota and heard him out. Usually, he'd tell me about his schooling in Japan where he learned judo along with mathematics and literature. He'd learned the *soroban* there — the abacus, which was the original pocket calculator of the Far East — and that, along with his strong, judo-trained back, got him his first job in Hawaii. This was the moral. "Study *ha-ahd*," he'd say with pidgin emphasis. "Learn read good. Learn speak da kine *good* English." The message is the familiar one taught to any children of immigrants: succeed through education. And imitation. But this time, Kubota reached down into his past and told me a different story. I was thirteen by then, and I suppose he thought me ready for it. He told me about Pearl Harbor, how the planes flew in wing after wing of formations over his old house in La'ie in Hawaii, and how, the next day, after Roosevelt had made his famous "Day of Infamy" speech about the treachery of the Japanese, the FBI agents had come to his door and taken him in, hauled him off to Honolulu for questioning, and held him without charge for several days. I thought he was lying. I thought he was making up a kind of horror story to shock me and give his moral that much more starch. But it was true. I asked around. I brought it up during history class in junior high school, and my teacher, after silencing me and stepping me off to the back of the room, told me that it was indeed so. I asked my mother and she said it was true. I asked my schoolmates, who laughed and ridiculed me for being so ignorant. We lived in a Japanese-American community, and the parents of most of my classmates were the *nisei* who had been interned as teenagers all through the war. But there was a strange silence around all of this. There was a hush, as if one were invoking the ill powers of the dead when one brought it up. No one cared to speak about the evacuation and relocation for very long. It wasn't in our history books, though we were studying World War II at the time. It wasn't in the family albums of the people I knew and whom I'd visit staying over weekends with friends. And it wasn't anything that the family talked about or allowed me to keep bringing up either. I was given the facts, told sternly and pointedly that "it was war" and that "nothing could be done." *"Shikatta ga nai"* is the phrase in Japanese, a kind of resolute and determinist pronouncement on how to deal with inexplicable tragedy. I was to know it but not to dwell on it. Japanese Americans were busy trying to forget it ever happened and were having a hard enough time building their new lives after "camp." It was as if we had no history for four years and the relocation was something unspeakable.

But Kubota would not let it go. In session after session, for months it seemed, he pounded away at his story. He wanted to tell me the names of the FBI agents. He went over their questions and his responses again and again. He'd tell me how one would try to act friendly toward him, offering him cigarettes while the other, who hounded him with accusations and threats, left the interrogation room. Good cop, bad cop, I thought to myself, already superficially streetwise from stories black classmates told of the Watts riots and from my having watched too many episodes of *Dragnet* and *The Mod Squad*. But Kubota was not interested in my experiences. I was not made yet, and he was determined that his stories be part of my making. He spoke quietly at first, mildly, but once into his narrative and after his drink was down, his voice would rise and quaver with resentment and he'd make his accusations. He gave his testimony to me and I held it at first cautiously in my conscience like it was an heirloom too delicate to expose to strangers and anyone outside of the world Kubota made with his words. "I give you story now," he once said, "and you learn speak good, eh?" It was my job, as the disciple of his preaching I had then become, Ananda to his Buddha, to reassure him with a promise. "You learn speak good like the Dillingham," he'd say another time, referring to the wealthy scion of the grower family who had once run, unsuccessfully, for one of Hawaii's first senatorial seats. Or he'd then invoke a magical name, the name of one of his heroes, a man he thought particularly exemplary and righteous. "Learn speak dah good Ing-rish like *Mistah Inouye*," Kubota shouted. "He *lick* dah Dillingham even in debate. I saw on *terre-bision* myself." He was remembering the debates before the first senatorial election just before Hawaii was admitted to the Union as its fiftieth state. "You *tell* story," Kubota would end. And I had my injunction.

The town we settled in after the move from Hawaii is called Gardena, the independently incorporated city south of Los Angeles and north of San Pedro harbor. At its northern limit, it borders on Watts and Compton, black towns. To the southwest are Torrance and Redondo Beach, white towns. To the rest of L.A., Gardena is primarily famous for having legalized five-card draw poker after the war. On Vermont Boulevard, its eastern border, there is a dingy little Vegas-like strip of card clubs with huge parking lots and flickering neon signs that spell out "The Rainbow" and "The Horseshoe" in timed sequences of varicolored lights. The town is only secondarily famous as the largest community of Japanese Americans in the United States outside of Honolulu, Hawaii. When I was in high school there, it seemed to me that every *sansei* kid I knew wanted to be a doctor, an engineer, or a pharmacist. Our fathers were gardeners or electricians or nurserymen or ran small businesses catering to other Japanese Americans. Our mothers worked in civil service for the city or as cashiers for Thrifty Drug. What the kids wanted was a good job, good pay, a fine home, and no troubles. No one wanted to mess with the law — from either side — and no one wanted to mess with language or art. They all talked about getting into the right clubs so that they could go to the right schools. There was a certain kind of sameness, an intensely enforced system of conformity. Style was all. Boys wore moccasin-sewn shoes from Flagg Brothers, black A-1 slacks, and Kensington shirts with high collars. Girls wore their hair up in stiff bouffants solidified in hairspray and knew all the latest dances from the slauson to the funky chicken. We did well in chemistry and in math, no one who was Japanese but me spoke in English class or in history unless called upon, and no one talked about World War II. The day after Robert Kennedy was assassinated, after winning the California Democratic primary, we worked on calculus and elected class coordinators for the prom, featuring the 5th Dimension. We avoided grief. We avoided government. We avoided strong feelings and dangers of any kind. Once punished, we tried to maintain a concerted emotional and social discipline and would not willingly seek to fall out of the narrow margin of protective favor again.

But when I was thirteen, in junior high, I'd not understood why it was so difficult for my classmates, those who were themselves Japanese American, to talk about the relocation. They had cringed, too, when I tried to bring it up during our discussions of World War II. I was Hawaiian-born. They were mainland-born. Their parents had been in camp, had been the ones to suffer the complicated experience of having to distance themselves from their own history and all things Japanese in order to make their way back and into the American social and economic mainstream. It was out of this sense of shame and a fear of stigma I was only beginning to understand that the *nisei* had silenced themselves. And, for their children, among whom I grew up, they wanted no heritage, no culture, no contact with a defiled history. I recall the silence very well. The Japanese-American children around me were burdened in a way I was not. Their injunction was silence. Mine was to speak.

Away at college, in another protected world in its own way as magical to me as the Hawaii of my childhood, I dreamed about my grandfather. Tired from studying languages, practicing German conjugations or scripting an army's worth of Chinese ideograms on a single sheet of paper, Kubota would come to me as I drifted off into sleep. Or I would walk across the newly mown ball field in back of my dormitory, cutting through a street-side phalanx of ancient eucalyptus trees on my way to visit friends off campus, and I would think of him, his anger, and his sadness.

I don't know myself what makes someone feel that kind of need to have a story they've lived through be deposited somewhere, but I can guess. I think about *The Iliad, The Odyssey, The Peloponnesian Wars* of Thucydides, and a myriad of the works of literature I've studied. A character, almost a *topoi* he occurs so often, is frequently the witness who gives personal testimony about an event the rest of his community cannot even imagine. The sibyl is such a character. And Procne, the maid whose tongue is cut out so that she will not tell that she has been raped by her own brother-in-law, the king of Thebes. There are the dime novels, the epic blockbusters Hollywood makes into miniseries, and then there are the plain, relentless stories of witnesses who have suffered through horrors major and minor that have marked and changed their lives. I myself haven't talked to Holocaust victims. But I've read their survival stories and their stories of witness and been revolted and moved by them. My father-in-law, Al Thiessen, tells me his war stories again and again and I listen. A Mennonite who set aside the strictures of his own church in order to serve, he was a Marine codeman in the Pacific during World War II, in the Signal Corps on Guadalcanal, Morotai, and Bougainville. He was part of the island-hopping maneuver MacArthur had devised to win the war in the Pacific. He saw friends die from bombs which exploded not ten yards away. When he was with the 298th Signal Corps attached to the Thirteenth Air Force, he saw plane after plane come in and crash, just short of the runway, killing their crews, setting the jungle ablaze with oil and gas fires. Emergency wagons would scramble, bouncing over newly bulldozed land men used just the afternoon before for a football game. Every time we go fishing together, whether it's in a McKenzie boat drifting for salmon in Tillamook Bay or taking a lunch break from wading the riffles of a stream in the Cascades, he tells me about what happened to him and the young men in his unit. One was a Jewish boy from Brooklyn. One was a foul-mouthed kid from Kansas. They died. And he *has* to tell me. And I *have* to listen. It's a ritual payment the young owe their elders who have survived. The evacuation and relocation is something like that.

Kubota, my grandfather, had been ill with Alzheimer's disease for some time before he died. At the house he'd built on Kamehameha Highway in Hau'ula, a seacoast village just down the road from La'ie where he had his store, he'd wander out from the garage or greenhouse where he'd set up a workbench, and trudge down to the beach or up toward the line of pines he'd planted while employed by the Work Projects Administration during the thirties. Kubota thought he was going fishing. Or he thought he was back at work for Roosevelt, planting pines as a windbreak or soilbreak on the windward flank of the Ko'olau Mountains, emerald monoliths rising out of sea and cane fields from Waialua to Kaneohe. When I visited, my grandmother would send me down to the beach to fetch him. Or I'd run down Kam Highway a quarter mile or so and find him hiding in the cane field by the roadside, counting stalks, measuring circumferences in the claw of his thumb and forefinger. The look on his face was confused or concentrated, I didn't know which. But I guessed he was going fishing again. I'd grab him and walk him back to his house on the highway. My grandmother would shut him in a room.

Within a few years, Kubota had a stroke and survived it, then he had another one and was completely debilitated. The family decided to put him in a nursing home in Kahuku, just set back from the highway, within a mile or so of Kahuku Point and the Tanaka Store where he had his first job as a stock boy. He lived there three years, and I visited him once with my aunt. He was like a potato that had been worn down by cooking. Everything on him — his eyes, his teeth, his legs and torso — seemed like it had been sloughed away. What he had been was mostly gone now and I was looking at the nub of a man. In a wheelchair, he grasped my hands and tugged on them — violently. His hands were still thick and, I believed, strong enough to lift me out of my own seat into his lap. He murmured something in Japanese — he'd long ago ceased to speak any English. My aunt and I cried a little, and we left him.

I remember walking out on the black asphalt of the parking lot of the nursing home. It was heat-cracked and eroded already, and grass had veined itself into the interstices. There were coconut trees around, a cane field I could see across the street, and the ocean I knew was pitching a surf just beyond it. The green Ko'olaus came up behind us. Somewhere nearby, alongside the beach, there was an abandoned airfield in the middle of the canes. As a child, I'd come upon it playing one day, and my friends and I kept returning to it, day after day, playing war or sprinting games or coming to fly kites. I recognize it even now when I see it on TV — it's used as a site for action scenes in the detective shows Hollywood always sets in the islands: a helicopter chasing the hero racing away in a Ferrari, or gun dealers making a clandestine rendezvous on the abandoned runway. It was the old airfield strafed by Japanese planes the day the major flight attacked Pearl Harbor. It was the airfield the FBI thought my grandfather had targeted in his night fishing and signaling with the long surf poles he'd stuck in the sandy bays near Kahuku Point.

Kubota died a short while after I visited him, but not, I thought, without giving me a final message. I was on the mainland, in

California studying for Ph.D. exams, when my grandmother called me with the news. It was a relief. He'd suffered from his debilitation a long time and I was grateful he'd gone. I went home for the funeral and gave the eulogy. My grandmother and I took his ashes home in a small, heavy metal box wrapped in a black *furoshiki*, a large silk scarf. She showed me the name the priest had given to him on his death, scripted with a calligraphy brush on a long, narrow talent of plain wood. Buddhist commoners, at death, are given priestly names, received symbolically into the clergy. The idea is that, in their next life, one of scholarship and leisure, they might meditate and attain the enlightenment the religion is aimed at. *"Shaku Shūchi,"* the ideograms read. It was Kubota's Buddhist name, incorporating characters from his family and given names. It meant "Shining Wisdom of the Law." He died on Pearl Harbor Day, December 7, 1983.

After years, after I'd finally come back to live in Hawaii again, only once did I dream of Kubota, my grandfather. It was the same night I'd heard HR 442, the redress bill for Japanese Americans, had been signed into law. In my dream that night Kubota was "torching," and he sang a Japanese song, a querulous and wavery folk ballad, as he hung paper lanterns on bamboo poles stuck into the sand in the shallow water of the lagoon behind the reef near Kahuku Point. Then he was at a work table, smoking a hand-rolled cigarette, letting it dangle from his lips Bogart-style as he drew, daintily and skillfully, with a narrow trim brush, ideogram after ideogram on a score of paper lanterns he had hung in a dark shed to dry. He had painted a talismanic mantra onto each lantern, the ideogram for the word "red" in Japanese, a bit of art blended with some superstition, a piece of sympathetic magic appealing to the magenta coloring on the rough skins of the schooling, night-feeding fish he wanted to attract to his baited hooks. He strung them from pole to pole in the dream then, hiking up his khaki worker's pants so his white ankles showed and wading through the shimmering black waters of the sand flats and then the reef. "The moon is leaving, leaving," he sang in Japanese. "Take me deeper in the savage sea." He turned and crouched like an ice racer then, leaning forward so that his unshaven face almost touched the light film of water. I could see the light stubble of beard like a fine, gray ash covering the lower half of his face. I could see his gold-rimmed spectacles. He held a small wooden boat in his cupped hands and placed it lightly on the sea and pushed it away. One of his lanterns was on it and, written in small neat rows like a sutra scroll, it had been decorated with the silvery names of all our dead.

Reflections and Responses

1. What do you think Hongo means when he states that his grandfather "was determined that his stories be part of my making"? What is being "made" and how do family stories contribute?

2. Why do you think Hongo places his grandfather's stories in the context of "a myriad of the works of literature" he studied? What effect does this have on the way we consider both the stories and works of literature?

3. Why do you think Hongo decided to conclude his essay with a dream? What does the imagery suggest? How does it refer to other images in the essay?

NATALIE KUSZ

Ring Leader

As should be readily apparent from the selections in this chapter, candor and honesty are essential ingredients of the personal essay. That sounds perhaps like easy writing advice: just be candid and honest. The problem is, of course, that candor and honesty usually require us to say some unflattering things about ourselves. Mark Twain realized this when he tried to write his autobiography: "I have been dictating this autobiography of mine daily for three months; I have thought of fifteen hundred or two thousand incidents in my life which I am ashamed of but I have not gotten one of them to consent to go on paper yet." In "Ring Leader," Natalie Kusz, a writer noted for her ability to cut through pretense and self-deception, offers a self-portrait that resists the natural lure of self-flattery: "The fact is, I grew up ugly — no, worse than that, I grew up unusual, that unforgivable sin among youth."

Kusz (whose last name rhymes with push*) teaches creative nonfiction at Harvard University. In 1989, she received the prestigious Whiting Writers' Award and in 1990 both the Christopher Award and the General Electric Award for Younger Writers.* Road Song, *a memoir of her childhood published in 1990, remains one of the finest memoirs of the decade. "Ring Leader" originally appeared in* Allure *magazine and was selected by Ian Frazier for* The Best American Essays 1997.

I was thirty years old when I had my right nostril pierced, and back-home friends fell speechless at the news, lapsing into long telephone pauses of the sort that June Cleaver would employ if the Beave had ever called to report, "Mom, I'm married. His name's Eddie." Not that I resemble a Cleaver or have friends who wear pearls in the shower, but people who have known me the longest would say that for me to *draw* attention to my body rather than to work all out to *repel* it is at least as out of character as the Beave's abrupt urge for his-and-his golf ensembles. A nose ring, they might tell you, would be my last choice for a fashion accessory, way down on the list with a sag-enhancing specialty bra or a sign on my butt reading "Wide Load."

The fact is, I grew up ugly — no, worse than that, I grew up *unusual,* that unforgivable sin among youth. We lived in Alaska, where, despite what you might have heard about the Rugged Individualist, teenagers still adhere to the universal rules of conformity: if Popular Patty wears contact lenses, then you will by gum get contacts too, or else pocket those glasses and pray you can distinguish the girls' bathroom door from the boys'. The bad news was that I had only one eye, having lost the other in a dog attack at age seven; so although contacts, at half the two-eyed price, were easy to talk my parents into, I was still left with an eye patch and many facial scars, signs as gaudy as neon, telling everyone, "Here is a girl who is Not Like You." And Not Like Them, remember, was equivalent to Not from This Dimension, only half (maybe one third) as interesting.

The rest of my anatomy did nothing to help matters. I come from a long line of famine-surviving ancestors — on my father's side, Polish and Russian, on my mother's, everything from Irish to French Canadian — and thus I have an excellent, thrifty, Ebenezer Scrooge of a metabolism. I can ingest but a single calorie, and before quitting time at the Scrooge office, my system will have spent that calorie to replace an old blood cell, to secrete a vital hormone, to send a few chemicals around the old nervous system, and still have enough left over to deposit ten fat cells in my inner thigh — a nifty little investment for the future, in case the Irish potato famine ever recurs. These metabolic wonders are delightful if you are planning a move to central Africa, but for an American kid wiggling to Jane Fonda as if her life depended on it (which, in high school, it did), the luckiest people on earth seemed to be anorexics, those wispy and hollow-cheeked beings whose primary part in the locker room drama was to stand at the mirror and announce, "My God, I disgust myself, I am *so fat.*" While the other girls recited their lines ("No, Samantha, don't talk like that, you're beautiful, you really *are!*"), I tried to pull on a gym shirt without removing any other shirt first, writhing inside the cloth like a cat trapped among the bedsheets.

Thus, if you add the oversized body to the disfigured face, and add again my family's low income and my secondhand wardrobe, you have a formula for pure, excruciating teenage angst. Hiding from public scrutiny became for me, as for many people like me, a way of life. I developed a bouncy sense of humor, the kind that makes people say, "That Natalie, she is always so *up*," and keeps them from probing for deep emotion. After teaching myself to sew, I made myself cheap versions of those Popular Patty clothes or at least the items (*never* halter tops, although this was the seventies) that a large girl could wear with any aplomb. And above all, I studied the other kids, their physical posture, their music, their methods of blow-dryer artistry, hoping one day to emerge from my body, invisible. I suppose I came as close to invisibility as my appearance would allow, for if you look at the yearbook photos from that time, you will find on my face the same "too cool to say 'cheese' " expression as on Popular Patty's eleven-man entourage.

But at age thirty, I found myself living in the (to me) incomprehensible politeness of America's Midwest, teaching at a small private college that I found suffocating, and anticipating the arrival of that all-affirming desire of college professors everywhere, that professional certification indicating you are now "one of the family"; academic tenure. A first-time visitor to any college campus can easily differentiate between tenured and nontenured faculty by keeping in mind a learning institution's two main expectations: (1) that a young professor will spend her first several years on the job proving herself indispensable (sucking up), working to advance the interests of the college (sucking up), and making a name for herself in her field of study (sucking up); and (2) that a senior, tenured professor, having achieved indispensability, institutional usefulness, and fame will thereafter lend her widely recognized name to the school's public relations office, which will use that name to attract prospective new students and faculty, who will in turn be encouraged to call on senior professors for the purpose of asking deep, scholarly questions (sucking up). Thus, a visitor touring any random campus can quickly distinguish tenured faculty persons from nontenured ones simply by noting the habitual shape and amount of chapping of their lips.

I anticipated a future of senior-faculty meetings with academia's own version of Popular Patty — not a nubile, cheerleading fashion plate, but a somber and scholarly denture wearer who, under the legal terms of tenure, cannot be fired except for the most grievous unprofessional behavior, such as igniting plastique under the dean's new Lexus. When that official notice landed in my In box, my sucking-up days would be over. I would have arrived. I would be family.

I couldn't bear it. In addition to the fact that I possessed all my own teeth, I was unsuited to Become As One with the other tenured beings because I was by nature boisterous, a collector of Elvis memorabilia, and given to not washing my car — in short, I was and always would be from Alaska.

Even in my leisure hours, my roots made my life of that period disorienting. Having moved to the immaculate Midwest from the far-from-immaculate wilderness, I found myself incapable of understanding, say, the nature of cul-de-sacs, those little circles of pristine homes where all the children were named Chris, and where all the parents got to vote on whether the Johnsons (they were all Johnsons) could paint their house beige. I would go to potluck suppers where the dishes were foreign to me, and twelve people at my table would take a bite, savor it with closed eyes, and say, "Ah, Tater Tot casserole. Now *that* takes me back." It got to the point where I felt defensive all the time, professing my out-of-townness whenever I was mistaken for a local, someone who understood the conversational subtexts and genteel body language of a Minnesotan. Moreover, I could never be sure what I myself said to these people with my subtextual language or my body. For all I knew, my posture during one of those impossible kaffeeklatsches proclaimed to everyone, "I am about to steal the silverware," or "I subscribe to the beliefs of Reverend Sun Myung Moon."

I grew depressed. Before long, I was feeling nostalgic for Alaskan eccentricities I had avoided even when I had lived there — unshaven legs and armpits, for example, and automobiles held together entirely by duct tape. I began decorating my office with absurd and nonprofessional items: velvet paintings, Mr. Potato Head, and a growing collection of snow globes from each of the fifty states. Students took to coming by to play with Legos, or to blow bubbles from those little circular wands, and a wish started to grow in my brain, a yearning for some way to transport the paraphernalia around with me, to carry it along as an indication that I was truly unconventional at heart.

So the week that I received tenure, when they could no longer fire me and when a sore nose would not get bumped during the course of any future sucking-up maneuver, I entered a little shop in the black-leather part of town and emerged within minutes with my right nostril duly pierced. The gesture was, for me, a celebration, a visible statement that said, "Assume nothing. I might be a punk from Hennepin Avenue, or a belly dancer with brass knuckles in my purse." Polite as was the society of that region, my colleagues never referred to my nose, but I could see them looking and wondering a bit, which was exactly the thing I had wanted — a lingering question in the minds of the natives, the possibility of forces they had never fathomed.

After this, my comfort level changed some, and almost entirely for the better. I had warned my father, who lived with me those years, that I was thinking of piercing my nose. When I arrived home that day and the hole was through the side instead of in the center — he had expected, I found out, a Maori-style bone beneath the nostrils — he looked at me, his color improved, and he asked if I wanted chicken for dinner. So that was all fine. At school, students got over their initial shock relatively quickly, having already seen the trailer-park ambience of my office, and they became less apt to question my judgment on their papers; I could hear them thinking, She looks like she must understand *something* about where I'm coming from. And my daughter — this is the best part of all — declared I was the hippest parent she knew, and decided it was O.K. to introduce me to her junior high friends; even Cool Chris — the Midwestern variety of Popular Patty — couldn't boast a body-pierced mom.

I have since moved away from Minnesota, and old friends (those of the aforementioned June Cleaver–type stunned silence) have begun to ask if I have decided to stop wearing a nose stud now that my initial reason for acquiring it has passed. And here, to me, is the interesting part: the answer, categorically, is no. Nonconformity, or something like it, may have been the initial reason behind shooting a new hole through my proboscis, but a whole set of side effects, a broad and unexpected brand of liberation, has provided me a reason for keeping it. Because the one-eyed fat girl who couldn't wear Popular Patty's clothes, much less aspire to steal her boyfriends, who was long accustomed to the grocery-store stares of adults and small children ("Mommy, what happened to that fat lady's face?"), who had learned over the years to hide whenever possible, slathering her facial scars with cover stick, is now — am I dreaming? — in charge. I have now, after all, deliberately chosen a "facial flaw," a remarkable aspect of appearance. Somehow now, the glances of strangers seem less invasive, nothing to incite me to nunhood; a long look is just that — a look — and what of it? I've invited it, I've made room for it, it is no longer inflicted upon me against my will.

Reflections and Responses

1. Natalie Kusz wrote "Ring Leader" for *Allure,* a magazine specializing in advice for young women who want to look their best. In what ways is her subject appropriate for the magazine's content? In what ways could her approach appear ironic?

2. Kusz writes with a clear sense of humor. Find a few examples of her humor. Do they have anything in common?

3. Consider Kusz's final paragraph. What has she come to realize about her looks? How does the nose stud help her come to this realization? The final paragraph is more subtle than it may first appear. Explain in your own words her final sentence.

JOHN MCPHEE

Silk Parachute

As originally appeared in *The New Yorker*

Personal memoirs can be hundreds of pages long or — like this one — very short. Whether long or short, they are fueled by the writer's recollection of evocative details. In "Silk Parachute," John McPhee constructs a complex miniature memoir around a number of details concerning his relationship with his mother; some of the details he claims he cannot vouch for and others he alleges he can. The reader is invited to wonder why he vividly recalls certain moments and denies any recollection of others: "The assertion is absolutely false that when I came home from high school with an A-minus she demanded an explanation for the minus."

One of America's most celebrated nonfiction writers, John McPhee was born in Princeton, New Jersey, in 1931 and is the author of numerous award-winning books. His first book, A Sense of Where You Are, *is a profile of basketball star Bill Bradley and appeared in 1965. He has published nearly a book every year since then, all of them with the same publisher, Farrar, Straus & Giroux. Although his subjects range from sports to science, McPhee has written extensively in the fields of nature and geology. He has been a staff writer for* The New Yorker *magazine since 1965 and a professor of journalism at Princeton University since 1975. "Silk Parachute" originally appeared in* The New Yorker *and was selected by Cynthia Ozick for* The Best American Essays 1998.

When your mother is ninety-nine years old, you have so many memories of her that they tend to overlap, intermingle, and blur. It is extremely difficult to single out one or two, impossible to remember any that exemplify the whole.

It has been alleged that when I was in college she heard that I had stayed up all night playing poker and wrote me a letter that used the word "shame" forty-two times. I do not recall this.

I do not recall being pulled out of my college room and into the church next door.

It has been alleged that on December 24, 1936, when I was five years old, she sent me to my room at or close to 7 P.M. for using four-letter words while trimming the Christmas tree. I do not recall that,

The assertion is absolutely false that when I came home from high school with an A-minus she demanded an explanation for the minus.

It has been alleged that she spoiled me with protectionism, because I was the youngest child and therefore the most vulnerable to attack from overhead — an assertion that I cannot confirm or confute, except to say that facts don't lie.

We lived only a few blocks from the elementary school and routinely ate lunch at home. It is reported that the following dialogue and ensuing action occurred on January 22, 1941:

"Eat your sandwich."

"I don't want to eat my sandwich."

"I made that sandwich, and you are going to eat it, Mister Man. You filled yourself up on penny candy on the way home, and now you're not hungry."

"I'm late. I have to go. I'll eat the sandwich on the way back to school."

"Promise?"

"Promise."

Allegedly, I went up the street with sandwich in my hand and buried it in a snowbank in front of Dr. Wright's house. My mother, holding back the curtain in the window of the side door, was watching. She came out in the bitter cold, wearing only a light dress, ran to the snowbank, dug out the sandwich, chased me up Nassau Street,* and rammed the sandwich down my throat, snow and all. I do not recall any detail of that story. I believe it to be a total fabrication.

There was the case of the missing Cracker Jack at Lindel's corner store. Flimsy evidence pointed to Mrs. McPhee's smallest child.

*Nassau Street: Princeton's main street.

It has been averred that she laid the guilt on with the following words: "'Like mother, like son' is a saying so true, the world will judge largely of mother by you." It has been asserted that she immediately repeated that proverb three times, and also recited it on other occasions too numerous to count. I have absolutely no recollection of her saying that about the Cracker Jack or any other controlled substance.

We have now covered everything even faintly unsavory that has been reported about this person in ninety-nine years, and even those items are a collection of rumors, half-truths, prevarications, false allegations, inaccuracies, innuendos, and canards.

This is the mother who — when Alfred Knopf* wrote her twenty-two-year-old son a letter saying, "The readers' report in the case of your manuscript would not be very helpful, and I think might discourage you completely" — said, "Don't listen to Alfred Knopf. Who does Alfred Knopf think he is, anyway? Someone should go in there and k-nock his block off." To the best of my recollection, that is what she said.

I also recall her taking me, on or about March 8, my birthday, to the theater in New York every year, beginning in childhood. I remember those journeys as if they were today. I remember *A Connecticut Yankee*. Wednesday, March 8, 1944. Evidently, my father had written for the tickets, because she and I sat in the last row of the second balcony. Mother knew what to do about that. She gave me for my birthday an elegant spyglass, sufficient in power to bring the Connecticut Yankee back from Vermont. I sat there watching the play through my telescope, drawing as many guffaws from the surrounding audience as the comedy on the stage.

On one of those theater days — when I was eleven or twelve — I asked her if we could start for the city early and go out to La Guardia Field to see the comings and goings of airplanes. The temperature was well below the freeze point and the March winds were so blustery that the wind-chill factor was forty below zero. Or seemed to be. My mother figured out how to take the subway to a stop in Jackson Heights and a bus from there — a feat I am unable to duplicate to this day. At La Guardia, she accompanied me to the

*__Alfred Knopf:__ founder of the prominent New York publishing house that bears his name; the "K" is sounded.

observation deck and stood there in the icy wind for at least an hour, maybe two, while I, spellbound, watched the DC-3s coming in on final, their wings flapping in the gusts. When we at last left the observation deck, we went downstairs into the terminal, where she bought me what appeared to be a black rubber ball but on closer inspection was a pair of hollow hemispheres hinged on one side and folded together. They contained a silk parachute. Opposite the hinge, each hemisphere had a small nib. A piece of string wrapped round and round the two nibs kept the ball closed. If you threw it high into the air, the string unwound and the parachute blossomed. If you sent it up with a tennis racket, you could put it into the clouds. Not until the development of the ten-megabyte hard disk would the world ever know such a fabulous toy. Folded just so, the parachute never failed. Always, it floated back to you — silkily, beautifully — to start over and float back again. Even if you abused it, whacked it really hard — gracefully, lightly, it floated back to you.

Reflections and Responses

1. Note the style of McPhee's opening paragraphs. Why do you think he repeats the phrase "It has been alleged . . ."? What does the tone of the phrase suggest, along with such words as *reported, assertion,* and *averred*? Who do you imagine has made the assertions and allegations?

2. Why is McPhee careful to say that he can't recall some details and events yet specifically remembers others? Can you detect any differences between what he recalls and what he doesn't?

3. Given its title role and its final emphasis, the silk parachute McPhee's mother bought for him at La Guardia Airport is clearly the essay's dominant image. How does McPhee enlarge its significance? What do you think the parachute represents?

CYNTHIA OZICK

The Break

Throughout history, essayists have continually returned to a favorite topic: the self. This is not surprising, since the essay, like the lyric poem, is among the most subjective of literary forms. An entire anthology could be assembled containing essays titled (with slight variations) "On Myself." In "The Break," Cynthia Ozick takes this traditional topic and gives it a remarkable spin, allowing a new self to break away from the old. Her description of this psychic split crosses a few conventional boundaries and pushes the personal essay into new imaginative territory.

*Cynthia Ozick is the author of three collections of essays —*Art & Ardor *(1983),* Metaphor & Memory *(1989), and* Fame & Folly *(1996) — as well as three collections of short stories and five novels, the most recent of which is* The Puttermesser Papers *(1997). She has also published a volume of critical writing,* What Henry James Knew and Other Essays on Writers *(1994). A member of the American Academy of Arts and Letters, she has received numerous literary awards, including a Guggenheim fellowhip and the Rea Award for the Short Story. Her essays have been selected several times for* The Best American Essays *series and she served as guest editor of the 1998 volume. "The Break," which originally appeared in* Antaeus, *was chosen by Jamaica Kincaid for the 1995 collection.*

I write these words at least a decade after the terrifying operation that separated us. Unfortunately, no then-current anesthesia, and no then-accessible surgical technique, was potent enough to suppress consciousness of the knife as it made its critical blood-slice through the area of our two warring psyches. It is the usual case in medicine that twins joined at birth are severed within the first months of life. Given the intransigence of my partner (who until this moment remains recalcitrant and continues to wish to convert me to her loathsome outlook), I had to wait many years until I could obtain her graceless and notoriously rancorous consent to our divergence.

The truth is I have not spoken to her since the day we were wheeled, side by side as usual, on the same stretcher, into the operating room. Afterward it was at once observed (especially by me) that the surgery had not altered her character in any respect, and I felt triumphantly justified in having dragged her into it. I had done her no injury — she was as intractable as ever. As for myself, I was freed from her proximity and her influence. The physical break was of course the end, not the beginning, of our rupture; psychologically, I had broken with her a long time ago. I disliked her then, and though shut of her daily presence and unavoidable attachment, I dislike her even now. Any hint or symptom of her discourages me; I have always avoided reading her. Her style is clotted, parenthetical, self-indulgent, long-winded, periphrastic, in every way excessive — hard going altogether. One day it came to me: why bother to keep up this fruitless connection? We have nothing in common, she and I. Not even a name. Since our earliest school years she has masqueraded as Cynthia, a Latin fancifulness entirely foreign to me. To my intimates I am Shoshana, the name given me at birth: Hebrew for Lily (anciently mistransliterated as Susanna).

To begin with, I am honest; she is not. Or, to spare her a moral lecture (but why should I? What has she ever spared *me*?), let me put it that she is a fantasist and I am not. Never mind that her own term for her condition, is not surprisingly, realism. It is precisely her "realism" that I hate. It is precisely her "facts" that I despise.

Her facts are not my facts. For instance, you will never catch me lying about my age, which is somewhere between seventeen and twenty-two. She, on the other hand, claims to be over sixty. A preposterous declaration, to be sure — but see how she gets herself up to look the part! She is all dye, putty, greasepaint. She resembles nothing so much as Gravel Gertie in the old Dick Tracy strip. There she is, done up as a white-haired, dewlapped, thick-waisted, thick-lensed hag, seriously myopic. A phenomenal fake. (Except for the nearsightedness, which, to be charitable, I don't hold against her, being seriously myopic myself.)

Aging is certainly not her only pretense. She imagines herself to be predictable; fixed; irrecoverable. She reflects frequently — tediously — on the trajectory of her life, and supposes that its arc and direction are immutable. What she has done she has done. She believes she no longer has decades to squander. I know better than to subscribe to such fatalism. Here the radical difference in our ages (which began to prove itself out at the moment of surgery) is probably crucial. It is her understanding that she is right to accept her status. She is little known or not known at all, relegated to marginality, absent from the authoritative anthologies that dictate which writers matter.

She knows she does not matter. She argues that she has been in rooms with the famous and felt the humiliation of her lesserness, her invisibility, her lack of writerly weight or topical cachet. In gilded chambers she has seen journalists and cultural consuls cluster around and trail after the stars; at conferences she has been shunted away by the bureaucratic valets of the stars. She is aware that she has not written enough. She is certainly not read. She sees with a perilous clarity that she will not survive even as "minor."

I will have none of this. There was a time — a tenuous membrane still hung between us, a remnant of sentiment or nostalgia on my part — when she was fanatically driven to coerce me into a similar view of myself. The blessed surgery, thank God, put an end to all that. My own ambition is fresh and intact. I can gaze at her fearfulness, her bloodless perfectionism and the secret crisis of confidence that dogs it, without a drop of concern. You may ask, Why am I so pitiless? Don't I know (I know to the lees) her indiscipline, her long periods of catatonic paralysis, her idleness, her sleepiness? Again you ask, Do you never pity her? Never. Hasn't she enough self-pity for the two of us? It is not that I am any more confident or less fearful; here I am, standing at the threshold still, untried, a thousand times more diffident, tremulous, shy. My heart is vulnerable to the world's distaste and dismissiveness. But oh, the difference between us! I have the power to scheme and to construct — a power that time has eroded in her, a power that she regards as superseded, useless. Null and void. Whatever shreds remain of her own ambitiousness embarrass her now. She is resigned to her failures. She is shamed by them. To be old and unachieved: ah.

Yes, ah! Ah! This diminution of hunger in her disgusts me; I detest it. She is a scandal of sorts, a superannuated mourner: her Promethean wounds (but perhaps they are only Procrustean?) leak on her bed when she wakes, on the pavement when she walks. She considers herself no more than an ant in an anthill. I have heard her say of the round earth, viewed on films sent back from this or that space shuttle, that Isaiah and Shakespeare are droplets molten into that tiny ball, and as given to evaporation as the pointlessly rotating ball itself. Good God, what have I do to with any of that? I would not trade places with her for all the china in Teaneck.

Look, there is so much ahead! Forms of undiminished luminescence; specifically, novels. A whole row of novels. All right, let her protest if it pleases her — when *she* set out, the written word was revered; reputations were rooted in the literariness of poets, novelists. Stories are electronic nowadays, and turn up in pictures: the victory, technologically upgraded, of the comic book. The writer is at last delectably alone, dependent on no acclaim. It is all for the sake of the making, the finding, the doing: the *Ding-an-Sich.** The wild *interestingness* of it! I will be a novelist yet! I feel myself becoming a voluptuary of human nature, a devourer, a spewer, a seer, an ironist. A hermit-toiler. I dream of nights without sleep.

She, like so many of her generation, once sought work and recognition. Perhaps she labored for the sake of fame, who knows? Five or six of her contemporaries, no more, accomplished that ubiquitous desire. But here in the gyre of my eighteenth year, my goatish and unbridled twentieth, my muscular and intemperate and gluttonous prime, it is fruitfulness I am after: despite the unwantedness of it — and especially despite *her* — I mean to begin a life of novel-writing. A jagged heap of interferences beclouds the year ahead, but what do I care? I have decades to squander.

As for her: I deny her, I denounce her, I let her go. Whining, wizened, hoary fake, with her cowardice, her fake name!

---

*Ding-an-Sich: German phrase meaning "thing in itself." The philosopher Immanuel Kant (1724–1804) used this expression to refer to the nonsensory reality we can never know.

Reflections and Responses

---

1. Reread the essay's opening paragraphs. Where in the essay do you first become aware that Ozick is describing two sides of the same person? What indicates this to you?

2. Why do you think Ozick decided to write the essay from the perspective of one side of the psychic split (Shoshana's) and not the other (Cynthia's)? How do we learn what the other side is like? What do you think Cynthia's voice would sound like?

3. What role does age play in the essay? How does it determine important aspects of both identities? What do you believe is the biggest difference between Ozick's two identities? Why do you think Shoshana considers Cynthia a "fake"?

SCOTT RUSSELL SANDERS

The Inheritance of Tools

A heritage is not only ethnic or cultural; it can also be a code of behavior, a system of manners, or even the practical skills that grandparents and parents often pass along to their children. In this widely reprinted personal essay, a writer, upon hearing of his father's sudden death, is reminded of the tools and techniques he inherited from his grandfather and father, which he in turn is now passing along to his own children. Though these tools and techniques have literally to do with carpentry, they take on extra duty in this finely crafted essay in which the hand tools themselves become equivalent to works of art: "I look at my claw hammer, the distillation of a hundred generations of carpenters, and consider that it holds up well be-side those other classics—Greek vases, Gregorian chants, Don Quixote, *barbed fish hooks, candles, spoons."*

Scott Russell Sanders is the author of more than a dozen books of fiction, science fiction, essays, and nonfiction; these include Stone Country *(1985),* The Paradise of Bombs *(1987),* Secrets of the Universe *(1991),* Staying Put *(1993), and* Hunting for Hope: A Father's Jour-neys *(1998). A recent book,* Writing from the Center *(1994) is a vol-ume of essays about living and working in the Midwest. The recipient of many prestigious writing awards and fellowships, Sanders is a professor of English at Indiana University. "The Inheritance of Tools" originally ap-peared in* The North American Review *(1986) and was selected by Gay Talese for* The Best American Essays 1987.

At just about the hour when my father died, soon after dawn one February morning when ice coated the windows like cataracts, I banged my thumb with a hammer. Naturally I swore at the ham-mer, the reckless thing, and in the moment of swearing I thought of what my father would say: "If you'd try hitting the nail it would go in a whole lot faster. Don't you know your thumb's not as hard as that hammer?" We both were doing carpentry that day, but far apart. He was building cupboards at my brother's place in Oklahoma; I was at home in Indiana, putting up a wall in the basement to make a bedroom for my daughter. By the time my mother called with news of his death — the long distance wires whittling her voice until it seemed too thin to bear the weight of what she had to say — my thumb was swollen. A week or so later a white scar in the shape of a crescent moon began to show above the cuticle, and month by month it rose across the pink sky of my thumbnail. It took the better part of a year for the scar to disappear, and every time I noticed it I thought of my father.

The hammer had belonged to him, and to his father before him. The three of us have used it to build houses and barns and chicken coops, to upholster chairs and crack walnuts, to make doll furniture and bookshelves and jewelry boxes. The head is scratched and pockmarked, like an old plowshare that has been working rocky fields, and it gives off the sort of dull sheen you see on fast creek water in the shade. It is a finishing hammer, about the weight of a bread loaf, too light, really, for framing walls, too heavy for cabinet work, with a curved claw for pulling nails, a rounded head for pounding, a fluted neck for looks, and a hickory handle for strength.

The present handle is my third one, bought from a lumberyard in Tennessee, down the road from where my brother and I were helping my father build his retirement house. I broke the previous one by trying to pull sixteen-penny nails out of floor joists — a foolish thing to do with a finishing hammer, as my father pointed out. "You ever hear of a crowbar?" he said. No telling how many handles he and my grandfather had gone through before me. My grandfather used to cut down hickory trees on his farm, saw them into slabs, cure the planks in his hayloft, and carve handles with a drawknife. The grain in hickory is crooked and knotty, and therefore tough, hard to split, like the grain in the two men who owned this hammer before me.

After proposing marriage to a neighbor girl, my grandfather used this hammer to build a house for his bride on a stretch of river bottom in northern Mississippi. The lumber for the place, like the hickory for the handle, was cut on his own land. By the day of the wedding he had not quite finished the house, and so right after the ceremony he took his wife home and put her to work. My grandmother had worn her Sunday dress for the wedding, with a fringe of lace tacked on around the hem in honor of the occasion. She removed this lace and folded it away before going out to help my grandfather nail siding on the house. "There she was in her good dress," he told me some fifty-odd years after that wedding day, "holding up them long pieces of clapboard while I hammered, and together we got the place covered up before dark." As the family grew to four, six, eight, and eventually thirteen, my grandfather used this hammer to enlarge his house room by room, like a chambered nautilus expanding its shell.

By and by the hammer was passed along to my father. One day he was up on the roof of our pony barn nailing shingles with it, when I stepped out the kitchen door to call him for supper. Before I could yell, something about the sight of him straddling the spine of that roof and swinging the hammer caught my eye and made me hold my tongue. I was five or six years old, and the world's commonplaces were still news to me. He would pull a nail from the pouch at his waist, bring the hammer down, and a moment later the *thunk* of the blow would reach my ears. And that is what had stopped me in my tracks and stilled my tongue, that momentary gap between seeing and hearing the blow. Instead of yelling from the kitchen door, I ran to the barn and climbed two rungs up the ladder — as far as I was allowed to go — and spoke quietly to my father. On our walk to the house he explained that sound takes time to make its way through air. Suddenly the world seemed larger, the air more dense, if sound could be held back like any ordinary traveler.

By the time I started using this hammer, at about the age when I discovered the speed of sound, it already contained houses and mysteries for me. The smooth handle was one my grandfather had made. In those days I needed both hands to swing it. My father would start a nail in a scrap of wood, and I would pound away until I bent it over.

"Looks like you got ahold of some of those rubber nails," he would tell me. "Here, let me see if I can find you some stiff ones." And he would rummage in a drawer until he came up with a fistful

of more cooperative nails. "Look at the head," he would tell me.
"Don't look at your hands, don't look at the hammer. Just look at
the head of that nail and pretty soon you'll learn to hit it square."

Pretty soon I did learn. While he worked in the garage cutting
dovetail joints for a drawer or skinning a deer or tuning an engine,
I would hammer nails. I made innocent blocks of wood look like
porcupines. He did not talk much in the midst of his tools, but
he kept up a nearly ceaseless humming, slipping in and out of a
dozen tunes in an afternoon, often running back over the same
stretch of melody again and again, as if searching for a way out.
When the humming did cease, I knew he was faced with a task requiring great delicacy or concentration, and I took care not to distract him.

He kept scraps of wood in a cardboard box — the ends of two-by-
fours, slabs of shelving and plywood, odd pieces of molding — and
everything in it was fair game. I nailed scraps together to fashion
what I called boats or houses, but the results usually bore only faint
resemblance to the visions I carried in my head. I would hold up
these constructions to show my father, and he would turn them
over in his hands admiringly, speculating about what they might be.
My cobbled-together guitars might have been alien spaceships, my
barns might have been models of Aztec temples, each wooden con-
traption might have been anything but what I had set out to make.

Now and again I would feel the need to have a chunk of wood
shaped or shortened before I riddled it with nails, and I would
clamp it in a vise and scrape at it with a handsaw. My father would
let me lacerate the board until my arm gave out, and then he
would wrap his hand around mine and help me finish the cut,
showing me how to use my thumb to guide the blade, how to pull
back on the saw to keep it from binding, how to let my shoulder do
the work.

"Don't force it," he would say, "just drag it easy and give the
teeth a chance to bite."

As the saw teeth bit down, the wood released its smell, each kind
with its own fragrance, oak or walnut or cherry or pine — usually
pine because it was the softest, easiest for a child to work. No matter how weathered or gray the board, no matter how warped and
cracked, inside there was this smell waiting, as of something
freshly baked. I gathered every smidgen of sawdust and stored it

away in coffee cans, which I kept in a drawer of the workbench. When I did not feel like hammering nails, I would dump my sawdust on the concrete floor of the garage and landscape it into highways and farms and towns, running miniature cars and trucks along miniature roads. Looming as huge as a colossus, my father worked over and around me, now and again bending down to inspect my work, careful not to trample my creations. It was a landscape that smelled dizzyingly of wood. Even after a bath my skin would carry the smell, and so would my father's hair, when he lifted me for a bedtime hug.

I tell these things not only from memory but also from recent observation, because my own son now turns blocks of wood into nailed porcupines, dumps cans full of sawdust at my feet and sculpts highways on the floor. He learns how to swing a hammer from the elbow instead of the wrist, how to lay his thumb beside the blade to guide a saw, how to tap a chisel with a wooden mallet, how to mark a hole with an awl before starting a drill bit. My daughter did the same before him, and even now, on the brink of teenage aloofness, she will occasionally drag out my box of wood scraps and carpenter something. So I have seen my apprenticeship to wood and tools re-enacted in each of my children, as my father saw his own apprenticeship renewed in me.

The saw I use belonged to him, as did my level and both of my squares, and all four tools had belonged to his father. The blade of the saw is the bluish color of gun barrels, and the maple handle, dark from the sweat of hands, is inscribed with curving leaf designs. The level is a shaft of walnut two feet long, edged with brass and pierced by three round windows in which air bubbles float in oil-filled tubes of glass. The middle window serves for testing if a surface is horizontal, the others for testing if a surface is plumb or vertical. My grandfather used to carry this level on the gun rack behind the seat in his pickup, and when I rode with him I would turn around to watch the bubbles dance. The larger of the two squares is called a framing square, a flat steel elbow, so beat up and tarnished you can barely make out the rows of numbers that show how to figure the cuts on rafters. The smaller one is called a try square, for marking right angles, with a blued steel blade for the shank and a brass-faced block of cherry for the head.

I was taught early on that a saw is not to be used apart from a square: "If you're going to cut a piece of wood," my father insisted, "you owe it to the tree to cut it straight."

Long before studying geometry, I learned there is a mystical virtue in right angles. There is an unspoken morality in seeking the level and the plumb. A house will stand, a table will bear weight, the sides of a box will hold together, only if the joints are square and the members upright. When the bubble is lined up between two marks etched in the glass tube of a level, you have aligned yourself with the forces that hold the universe together. When you miter the corners of a picture frame, each angle must be exactly forty-five degrees, as they are in the perfect triangles of Pythagoras, not a degree more or less. Otherwise the frame will hang crookedly, as if ashamed of itself and of its maker. No matter if the joints you are cutting do not show. Even if you are butting two pieces of wood together inside a cabinet, where no one except a wrecking crew will ever see them, you must take pains to ensure that the ends are square and the studs are plumb.

I took pains over the wall I was building on the day my father died. Not long after that wall was finished — paneled with tongue-and-groove boards of yellow pine, the nail holes filled with putty and the wood all stained and sealed — I came close to wrecking it one afternoon when my daughter ran howling up the stairs to announce that her gerbils had escaped from their cage and were hiding in my brand new wall. She could hear them scratching and squeaking behind her bed. Impossible! I said. How on earth could they get inside my drum-tight wall? Through the heating vent, she answered. I went downstairs, pressed my ear to the honey-colored wood, and heard the *scritch scritch* of tiny feet.

"What can we do?" my daughter wailed. "They'll starve to death, they'll die of thirst, they'll suffocate."

"Hold on," I soothed. "I'll think of something."

While I thought and she fretted, the radio on her bedside table delivered us the headlines: Several thousand people had died in a city in India from a poisonous cloud that had leaked overnight from a chemical plant. A nuclear-powered submarine had been launched. Rioting continued in South Africa. An airplane had been hijacked in the Mediterranean. Authorities calculated that several thousand homeless people slept on the streets within sight of the Washington Monument. I felt my usual helplessness in the face of all these calamities. But here was my daughter, weeping because her gerbils were holed up in a wall. This calamity I could handle.

"Don't worry," I told her. "We'll set food and water by the heating vent and lure them out. And if that doesn't do the trick, I'll tear the wall apart until we find them."

She stopped crying and gazed at me. "You'd really tear it apart? Just for my gerbils? The wall?" Astonishment slowed her down only for a second, however, before she ran to the workbench and began tugging at drawers, saying, "Let's see, what'll we need? Crowbar. Hammer. Chisels. I hope we don't have to use them — but just in case."

We didn't need the wrecking tools. I never had to assault my handsome wall, because the gerbils eventually came out to nibble at a dish of popcorn. But for several hours I studied the tongue-and-groove skin I had nailed up on the day of my father's death, considering where to begin prying. There were no gaps in that wall, no crooked joints.

I had botched a great many pieces of wood before I mastered the right angle with a saw, botched even more before I learned to miter a joint. The knowledge of these things resides in my hands and eyes and the webwork of muscles, not in the tools. There are machines for sale — powered miter boxes and radial arm saws, for instance — that will enable any casual soul to cut proper angles in boards. The skill is invested in the gadget instead of the person who uses it, and this is what distinguishes a machine from a tool. If I had to earn my keep by making furniture or building houses, I suppose I would buy powered saws and pneumatic nailers; the need for speed would drive me to it. But since I carpenter only for my own pleasure or to help neighbors or to remake the house around the ears of my family, I stick with hand tools. Most of the ones I own were given to me by my father, who also taught me how to wield them. The tools in my workbench are a double inheritance, for each hammer and level and saw is wrapped in a cloud of knowing.

All of these tools are a pleasure to look at and to hold. Merchants would never paste NEW NEW NEW! signs of them in stores. Their designs are old because they work, because they serve their purpose well. Like folk songs and aphorisms and the grainy bits of language, these tools have been pared down to essentials. I look at my claw hammer, the distillation of a hundred generations of carpenters, and consider that it holds up well beside those other classics — Greek vases, Gregorian chants, *Don Quixote,* barbed fish hooks, candles, spoons. Knowledge of hammering stretches back to the earliest humans who squatted beside fires, chipping flints. Anthropologists have a lovely name for those unworked rocks that served as the earliest hammers. "Dawn stones," they are called. Their only qualification for the work, aside from hardness, is that they fit the hand. Our ancestors used them for grinding corn, tapping awls, smashing bones. From dawn stones to this claw hammer is a great leap in time, but no great distance in design or imagination.

On that iced-over February morning when I smashed my thumb with the hammer, I was down in the basement framing the wall that my daughter's gerbils would later hide in. I was thinking of my father, as I always did whenever I built anything, thinking how he would have gone about the work, hearing in memory what he would have said about the wisdom of hitting the nail instead of my thumb. I had the studs and plates nailed together all square and trim, and was lifting the wall into place when the phone rang upstairs. My wife answered, and in a moment she came to the basement door and called down softly to me. The stillness in her voice made me drop the framed wall and hurry upstairs. She told me my father was dead. Then I heard the details over the phone from my mother. Building a set of cupboards for my brother in Oklahoma, he had knocked off work early the previous afternoon because of cramps in his stomach. Early this morning, on his way into the kitchen of my brother's trailer, maybe going for a glass of water, so early that no one else was awake, he slumped down on the linoleum and his heart quit.

For several hours I paced around inside my house, upstairs and down, in and out of every room, looking for the right door to open and knowing there was no such door. My wife and children followed me and wrapped me in arms and backed away again, circling and staring as if I were on fire. Where was the door, the door, the door? I kept wondering. My smashed thumb turned purple and throbbed, making me furious. I wanted to cut it off and rush outside and scrape away the snow and hack a hole in the frozen earth and bury the shameful thing.

I went down into the basement, opened a drawer in my workbench, and stared at the ranks of chisels and knives. Oiled and sharp, as my father would have kept them, they gleamed at me like teeth. I took up a clasp knife, pried out the longest blade, and tested the edge on the hair of my forearm. A tuft came away cleanly, and I saw my father testing the sharpness of tools on his own skin, the blades of axes and knives and gouges and hoes, saw the red hair shaved off in patches from his arms and the backs of his hands. "That will cut bear," he would say. He never cut a bear with his blades, now my blades, but he cut deer, dirt, wood. I closed the knife and put it away. Then I took up the hammer and went back to work on my daughter's wall, snugging the bottom plate against a chalk line on the floor, shimming the top plate against the joists overhead, plumbing the studs with my level, making sure before I drove the first nail that every line was square and true.

Reflections and Responses

1. Consider the way Sanders opens the essay. Given the significance of his father's death, why does he mention his injured thumb in the same sentence? Why is this a relevant detail? How does it figure later in the essay?

2. Note the many concrete references to carpentry in the essay. In what ways is the language of tools and carpentry related to other aspects of life? Why is there "a mystical virtue in right angles"?

3. In rereading the essay, try to reconstruct the chronology of the February day that Sanders's father died. First, consider how Sanders constructs his narrative. Why does he deviate from a straightforward, hour-by-hour account? Why, for example, does he introduce the story about his daughter's gerbils? In what ways does that anecdote deepen the essay's theme?

AMY TAN

Mother Tongue

*For many American students, the language spoken at home is far different
from the one spoken in school. For that reason, many students learn to
switch back and forth between two languages, the one they use with their
family and the one required for their education. Such switching, however,
need not be confining or demoralizing. Rather, it can enhance one's sensitivity to language and can even be creatively enabling, as the Chinese
American novelist Amy Tan suggests in this charming personal essay.
"Language is the tool of my trade," Tan writes. "And I use them all — all
the Englishes I grew up with."*

*Born into a Chinese family that had recently arrived in California,
Amy Tan began writing as a child and after graduation from college
worked for several years as a freelance business writer. In the mid-eighties,
she began writing fiction, basing much of her work on family stories. She is
the author of two best-selling novels:* The Joy Luck Club *(1989), which
was a finalist for both the National Book Award and National Book Critics
Circle Award and was made into a motion picture directed by Wayne
Wang,* The Kitchen God's Wife *(1991), and* The Hundred Secret
Senses *(1995). In 1992 she published a popular children's book,* The
Moon Lady. *She lives in San Francisco, where she is at work on a new
novel. "Mother Tongue" originally appeared in* The Threepenny Review *(1990) and was selected by Joyce Carol Oates for* The Best American Essays 1991.

I am not a scholar of English or literature. I cannot give you much
more than personal opinions on the English language and its variations in this country or others.

I am a writer. And by that definition, I am someone who has always loved language. I am fascinated by language in daily life. I

spend a great deal of my time thinking about the power of language — the way it can evoke an emotion, a visual image, a complex idea, or a simple truth. Language is the tool of my trade. And I use them all — all the Englishes I grew up with.

Recently, I was made keenly aware of the different Englishes I do use. I was giving a talk to a large group of people, the same talk I had already given to half a dozen other groups. The nature of the talk was about my writing, my life, and my book, *The Joy Luck Club*. The talk was going along well enough, until I remembered one major difference that made the whole talk sound wrong. My mother was in the room. And it was perhaps the first time she had heard me give a lengthy speech, using the kind of English I have never used with her. I was saying things like, "The intersection of memory upon imagination" and "There is an aspect of my fiction that relates to thus-and-thus"— a speech filled with carefully wrought grammatical phrases, burdened, it suddenly seemed to me, with nominalized forms, past perfect tenses, conditional phrases, all the forms of standard English that I had learned in school and through books, the forms of English I did not use at home with my mother.

Just last week, I was walking down the street with my mother, and I again found myself conscious of the English I was using, the English I do use with her. We were talking about the price of new and used furniture and I heard myself saying this: "Not waste money that way." My husband was with us as well, and he didn't notice any switch in my English. And then I realized why. It's because over the twenty years we've been together I've often used that same kind of English with him, and sometimes he even uses it with me. It has become our language of intimacy, a different sort of English that relates to family talk, the language I grew up with.

So you'll have some idea of what this family talk I heard sounds like, I'll quote what my mother said during a recent conversation which I videotaped and then transcribed. During this conversation, my mother was talking about a political gangster in Shanghai who had the same last name as her family's, Du, and how the gangster in his early years wanted to be adopted by her family, which was rich by comparison. Later, the gangster became more powerful, far richer than my mother's family, and one day showed up at my mother's wedding to pay his respects. Here's what she said in part:

"Du Yusong having business like fruit stand. Like off the street kind. He is Du like Du Zong — but not Tsung-ming Island people. The local people call putong, the river east side, he belong to that side local people. That man want to ask Du Zong father take him in like become own family. Du Zong father wasn't look down on him, but didn't take seriously, until that man big like become a mafia. Now important person, very hard to inviting him. Chinese way, came only to show respect, don't stay for dinner. Respect for making big celebration, he shows up. Mean gives lots of respect. Chinese custom. Chinese social life that way. If too important won't have to stay too long. He come to my wedding. I didn't see, I heard it. I gone to boy's side, they have YMCA dinner. Chinese age I was nineteen."

You should know that my mother's expressive command of English belies how much she actually understands. She reads the *Forbes* report, listens to *Wall Street Week,* converses daily with her stockbroker, reads all of Shirley MacLaine's books with ease — all kinds of things I can't begin to understand. Yet some of my friends tell me they understand 50 percent of what my mother says. Some say they understand 80 to 90 percent. Some say they understand none of it, as if she were speaking pure Chinese. But to me, my mother's English is perfectly clear, perfectly natural. It's my mother tongue. Her language, as I hear it, is vivid, direct, full of observation and imagery. That was the language that helped shape the way I saw things, expressed things, made sense of the world.

Lately, I've been giving more thought to the kind of English my mother speaks. Like others, I have described it to people as "broken" or "fractured" English. But I wince when I say that. It has always bothered me that I can think of no way to describe it other than "broken," as if it were damaged and needed to be fixed, as if it lacked a certain wholeness and soundness. I've heard other terms used, "limited English," for example. But they seem just as bad, as if everything is limited, including people's perceptions of the limited English speaker.

I know this for a fact, because when I was growing up, my mother's "limited" English limited *my* perception of her. I was ashamed of her English. I believed that her English reflected the quality of

what she had to say. That is, because she expressed them imper-
fectly her thoughts were imperfect. And I had plenty of empirical
evidence to support me: the fact that people in department stores,
at banks, and at restaurants did not take her seriously, did not give
her good service, pretended not to understand her, or even acted
as if they did not hear her.

My mother has long realized the limitations of her English as
well. When I was fifteen, she used to have me call people on the
phone to pretend I was she. In this guise, I was forced to ask for
information or even to complain and yell at people who had
been rude to her. One time it was a call to her stockbroker in New
York. She had cashed out her small portfolio and it just so happened we were going to go to New York the next week, our very
first trip outside California. I had to get on the phone and say in
an adolescent voice that was not very convincing, "This is Mrs.
Tan."

And my mother was standing in the back whispering loudly,
"Why he don't send me check, already two weeks late. So mad he
lie to me, losing me money."

And then I said in perfect English, "Yes, I'm getting rather concerned. You had agreed to send the check two weeks ago, but it
hasn't arrived."

Then she began to talk more loudly. "What he want, I come to
New York tell him front of his boss, you cheating me?" And I was
trying to calm her down, make her be quiet, while telling the
stockbroker, "I can't tolerate any more excuses. If I don't receive
the check immediately, I am going to have to speak to your manager when I'm in New York next week." And sure enough, the following week there we were in front of this astonished stockbroker,
and I was sitting there red-faced and quiet, and my mother, the
real Mrs. Tan, was shouting at his boss in her impeccable broken
English.

We used a similar routine just five days ago, for a situation that
was far less humorous. My mother had gone to the hospital for an
appointment, to find out about a benign brain tumor a CAT scan
had revealed a month ago. She said she had spoken very good
English, her best English, no mistakes. Still, she said, the hospital
did not apologize when they said they had lost the CAT scan and
she had come for nothing. She said they did not seem to have any

sympathy when she told them she was anxious to know the exact diagnosis, since her husband and son had both died of brain tumors. She said they would not give her any more information until the next time and she would have to make another appointment for that. So she said she would not leave until the doctor called her daughter. She wouldn't budge. And when the doctor finally called her daughter, me, who spoke in perfect English — lo and behold — we had assurances the CAT scan would be found, promises that a conference call on Monday would be held, and apologies for any suffering my mother had gone through for a most regrettable mistake.

I think my mother's English almost had an effect on limiting my possibilities in life as well. Sociologists and linguists probably will tell you that a person's developing language skills are more influenced by peers. But I do think that the language spoken in the family, especially in immigrant families which are more insular, plays a large role in shaping the language of the child. And I believe that it affected my results on achievement tests, IQ tests, and the SAT. While my English skills were never judged as poor, compared to math, English could not be considered my strong suit. In grade school I did moderately well, getting perhaps B's, sometimes B-pluses, in English and scoring perhaps in the sixtieth or seventieth percentile on achievement tests. But those scores were not good enough to override the opinion that my true abilities lay in math and science, because in those areas I achieved A's and scored in the ninetieth percentile or higher.

This was understandable. Math is precise; there is only one correct answer. Whereas, for me at least, the answers on English tests were always a judgment call, a matter of opinion and personal experience. Those tests were constructed around items like fill-in-the-blank sentence completion, such as, "Even though Tom was ____, Mary thought he was ____." And the correct answer always seemed to be the most bland combinations of thoughts, for example, "Even though Tom was shy, Mary thought he was charming," with the grammatical structure "even though" limiting the correct answer to some sort of semantic opposites, so you wouldn't get answers like, "Even though Tom was foolish, Mary thought he was ridiculous." Well, according to my mother, there were very few limitations as to what Tom could have been and what Mary might have thought of him. So I never did well on tests like that.

The same was true with word analogies, pairs of words in which you were supposed to find some sort of logical, semantic relationship — for example, "*Sunset* is to *nightfall* as ___ is to ___." And here you would be presented with a list of four possible pairs, one of which showed the same kind of relationship: *red* is to *stoplight*, *bus* is to *arrival*, *chills* is to *fever, yawn* is to *boring*. Well, I could never think that way. I knew what the tests were asking, but I could not block out of my mind the images already created by the first pair, "*sunset* is to *nightfall*" — and I would see a burst of colors against a darkening sky, the moon rising, the lowering of a curtain of stars. And all the other pairs of words — red, bus, stoplight, boring — just threw up a mass of confusing images, making it impossible for me to sort out something as logical as saying: "A sunset precedes nightfall" is the same as "a chill precedes a fever." The only way I would have gotten that answer right would have been to imagine an associative situation, for example, my being disobedient and staying out past sunset, catching a chill at night, which turns into feverish pneumonia as punishment, which indeed did happen to me.

I have been thinking about all this lately, about my mother's English, about achievement tests. Because lately I've been asked, as a writer, why there are not more Asian Americans represented in American literature. Why are there few Asian Americans enrolled in creative writing programs? Why do so many Chinese students go into engineering? Well, these are broad sociological questions I can't begin to answer. But I have noticed in surveys — in fact, just last week — that Asian students, as a whole, always do significantly better on math achievement tests than in English. And this makes me think that there are other Asian-American students whose English spoken in the home might also be described as "broken" or "limited." And perhaps they also have teachers who are steering them away from writing and into math and science, which is what happened to me.

Fortunately, I happen to be rebellious in nature and enjoy the challenge of disproving assumptions made about me. I became an English major my first year in college, after being enrolled as pre-med. I started writing nonfiction as a freelancer the week after I was told by my former boss that writing was my worst skill and I should hone my talents toward account management.

But it wasn't until 1985 that I finally began to write fiction. And at first I wrote using what I thought to be wittily crafted sentences, sentences that would finally prove I had mastery over the English language. Here's an example from the first draft of a story that later made its way into *The Joy Luck Club,* but without this line: "That was my mental quandary in its nascent state." A terrible line, which I can barely pronounce.

Fortunately, for reasons I won't get into today, I later decided I should envision a reader for the stories I would write. And the reader I decided upon was my mother, because these were stories about mothers. So with this reader in mind — and in fact she did read my early drafts — I began to write stories using all the Englishes I grew up with: the English I spoke to my mother, which for lack of a better term might be described as "simple"; the English she used with me, which for lack of a better term might be described as "broken"; my translation of her Chinese, which could certainly be described as "watered down"; and what I imagined to be her translation of her Chinese if she could speak in perfect English, her internal language, and for that I sought to preserve the essence, but neither an English nor a Chinese structure. I wanted to capture what language ability tests can never reveal: her intent, her passion, her imagery, the rhythms of her speech and the nature of her thoughts.

Apart from what any critic had to say about my writing, I knew I had succeeded where it counted when my mother finished reading my book and gave me her verdict: "So easy to read."

Reflections and Responses

1. What are the "Englishes" that Amy Tan grew up with? Why does she feel uncomfortable with the term "broken English"? Why do you think she still uses that term toward the end of her essay?

2. What point is Tan making about language tests? Why did she not perform as well on them as she did on math and science? In her opinion, what aspects of language do the tests fail to take into account?

3. Tan cites a sentence — "That was my mental quandary in its nascent state" — that she deleted from *The Joy Luck Club*. What do you think she dislikes about that sentence? What kind of English does it represent? Does it or doesn't it demonstrate a "mastery" of the English language?

2

The Attentive Mind: Observation, Reflection, Insight

ANNIE DILLARD

The Stunt Pilot

Creative expression can take many forms; it need not refer only to literature, painting, or music. We can find creativity in craft and design, in the movements of dancers and athletes, and even — as the following essay reveals — in the aerobatics of a stunt pilot. Observing the breathtaking dives and spins, the "loops and arabesques" of a celebrated pilot, Annie Dillard is struck by their resemblance to artistic expression. She finds in the pilot's use of space a new kind of beauty, one that seems to encompass all the arts — poetry, painting, music, sculpture: "The black plane dropped spinning, and flattened out spinning the other way; it began to carve the air into forms that built wildly and musically on each other and never ended."

Annie Dillard is one of America's preeminent essayists, someone for whom, as she puts it, the essay is not an occasional piece but her "real work." Her many award-winning books of essays and nonfiction include Pilgrim at Tinker Creek, *which won the Pulitzer Prize for General Nonfiction in 1975,* Holy the Firm *(1977),* Living by Fiction *(1982),* Teaching a Stone to Talk *(1982),* An American Childhood *(1987),* The Writing Life *(1989), and* For the Time Being *(1999). Dillard has taught creative writing at Wesleyan University in Middletown, Connecticut, since 1979. In 1992, she published her first novel,* The Living. *"The Stunt Pilot" originally appeared in* Esquire *(1989) and was selected by Justin Kaplan for* The Best American Essays 1990.

Dave Rahm lived in Bellingham, Washington, north of Seattle. Bellingham, a harbor town, lies between the alpine North Cascade Mountains and the San Juan Islands in Haro Strait above Puget Sound. The latitude is that of Newfoundland. Dave Rahm was a stunt pilot, the air's own genius.

In 1975, with a newcomer's willingness to try anything once, I attended the Bellingham Air Show. The Bellingham airport was a wide clearing in a forest of tall Douglas firs; its runways suited small planes. It was June. People wearing blue or tan zipped jackets stood loosely on the concrete walkways and runways outside the coffee shop. At that latitude in June, you stayed outside because you could, even most of the night, if you could think up something to do. The sky did not darken until ten o'clock or so, and it never got very dark. Your life parted and opened in the sunlight. You tossed your dark winter routines, thought up mad projects, and improvised everything from hour to hour. Being a stunt pilot seemed the most reasonable thing in the world; you could wave your arms in the air all day and night, and sleep next winter.

I saw from the ground a dozen stunt pilots; the air show scheduled them one after the other, for an hour of aerobatics. Each pilot took up his or her plane and performed a batch of tricks. They were precise and impressive. They flew upside down, and straightened out; they did barrel rolls, and straightened out; they drilled through dives and spins, and landed gently on a far runway.

For the end of the day, separated from all other performances of every sort, the air show director had scheduled a program titled "Dave Rahm." The leaflet said that Rahm was a geologist who taught at Western Washington University. He had flown for King Hussein in Jordan. A tall man in the crowd told me Hussein had seen Rahm fly on a visit the king made to the United States; he had invited him to Jordan to perform at ceremonies. Hussein was a pilot, too. "Hussein thought he was the greatest thing in the world."

Idly, paying scant attention, I saw a medium-sized, rugged man dressed in brown leather, all begoggled, climb in a black biplane's open cockpit. The plane was a Bücker Jungman, built in the thirties. I saw a tall, dark-haired woman seize a propeller tip at the plane's nose and yank it down till the engine caught. He was off; he climbed high over the airport in his biplane, very high until he was barely visible as a mote, and then seemed to fall down the air, diving headlong, and streaming beauty in spirals behind him.

The black plane dropped spinning, and flattened out spinning the other way; it began to carve the air into forms that built wildly and musically on each other and never ended. Reluctantly, I started paying attention. Rahm drew high above the world an inexhaustibly glorious line; it piled over our heads in loops and arabesques. It was like a Saul Steinberg* fantasy; the plane was the pen. Like Steinberg's contracting and billowing pen line, the line Rahm spun moved to form new, punning shapes from the edges of the old. Like a Klee[†] line, it smattered the sky with landscapes and systems.

The air show announcer hushed. He had been squawking all day, and now he quit. The crowd stilled. Even the children watched dumbstruck as the slow, black biplane buzzed its way around the air. Rahm made beauty with his whole body; it was pure pattern, and you could watch it happen. The plane moved every way a line can move, and it controlled three dimensions, so the line carved massive and subtle slits in the air like sculptures. The plane looped the loop, seeming to arch its back like a gymnast; it stalled, dropped, and spun out of it climbing; it spiraled and knifed west on one side's wings and back east on another; it turned cartwheels, which must be physically impossible; it played with its own line like a cat with yarn. How did the pilot know where in the air he was? If he got lost, the ground would swat him.

Rahm did everything his plane could do: tailspins, four-point rolls, flat spins, figure eights, snap rolls, and hammerheads. He did pirouettes on the plane's tail. The other pilots could do these stunts too, skillfully, one at a time. But Rahm used the plane inexhaustibly, like a brush marking thin air.

His was pure energy and naked spirit. I have thought about it for years. Rahm's line unrolled in time. Like music, it split the bulging rim of the future along its seam. It pried out the present. We watchers waited for the split-second curve of beauty in the present to reveal itself. The human pilot, Dave Rahm, worked in the cockpit right at the plane's nose; his very body tore into the future for us and reeled it down upon us like a curling peel.

---

*Saul Steinberg: Contemporary artist (b. 1914) who also created numerous covers for *The New Yorker* magazine.

[†]Klee: Paul Klee (1879–1940), a Swiss artist known for his highly distinctive abstract paintings.

Like any fine artist, he controlled the tension of the audience's longing. You desired, unwittingly, a certain kind of roll or climb, or a return to a certain portion of the air, and he fulfilled your hope slantingly, like a poet, or evaded it until you thought you would burst, and then fulfilled it surprisingly, so you gasped and cried out.

The oddest, most exhilarating and exhausting thing was this: he never quit. The music had no periods, no rests or endings; the poetry's beautiful sentence never ended; the line had no finish; the sculptured forms piled overhead, one into another without surcease. Who could breathe, in a world where rhythm itself had no periods?

It had taken me several minutes to understand what an extraordinary thing I was seeing. Rahm kept all that embellished space in mind at once. For another twenty minutes I watched the beauty unroll and grow more fantastic and unlikely before my eyes. Now Rahm brought the plane down slidingly, and just in time, for I thought I would snap from the effort to compass and remember the line's long intelligence; I could not add another curve. He brought the plane down on a far runway. After a pause, I saw him step out, an ordinary man, and make his way back to the terminal.

The show was over. It was late. Just as I turned from the runway, something caught my eye and made me laugh. It was a swallow, a blue-green swallow, having its own air show, apparently inspired by Rahm. The swallow climbed high over the runway, held its wings oddly, tipped them, and rolled down the air in loops. The inspired swallow. I always want to paint, too, after I see the Rembrandts. The blue-green swallow tumbled precisely, and caught itself and flew up again as if excited, and looped down again, the way swallows do, but tensely, holding its body carefully still. It was a stunt swallow.

I went home and thought about Rahm's performance that night, and the next day, and the next.

I had thought I knew my way around beauty a little bit. I knew I had devoted a good part of my life to it, memorizing poetry and focusing my attention on complexity of rhythm in particular, on force, movement, repetition, and surprise, in both poetry and prose. Now I had stood among dandelions between two asphalt runways in Bellingham, Washington, and begun learning about beauty. Even the Boston Museum of Fine Arts was never more inspiriting than this small northwestern airport on this time-killing Sunday afternoon in June. Nothing on earth is more gladdening than knowing we must roll up our sleeves and move back the boundaries of the humanly possible once more.

Later I flew with Dave Rahm; he took me up. A generous geographer, Dick Smith, at Western Washington University, arranged it, and came along. Rahm and Dick Smith were colleagues at the university. In geology, Rahm had published two books and many articles. Rahm was handsome in a dull sort of way, blunt-featured, wide-jawed, wind-burned, keen-eyed, and taciturn. As anyone would expect. He was forty. He wanted to show me the Cascade Mountains; these enormous peaks, only fifty miles from the coast, rise over nine thousand feet; they are heavily glaciated. Whatcom County has more glaciers than the lower forty-eight states combined; the Cascades make the Rocky Mountains look like hills. Mount Baker is volcanic, like most Cascade peaks. That year, Mount Baker was acting up. Even from my house at the shore I could see, early in the morning on clear days, volcanic vapor rise near its peak. Often the vapor made a cloud that swelled all morning and hid the snows. Every day the newspapers reported on Baker's activity: Would it blow? (A few years later, Mount St. Helens did blow.)

Rahm was not flying his trick biplane that day, but a faster enclosed plane, a single-engine Cessna. We flew from a bumpy grass airstrip near my house, out over the coast and inland. There was coastal plain down there, but we could not see it for clouds. We were over the clouds at five hundred feet and inside them too, heading for an abrupt line of peaks we could not see. I gave up on everything, the way you do in airplanes; it was out of my hands. Every once in a while Rahm saw a peephole in the clouds and buzzed over for a look. "That's Larsen's pea farm," he said, or "That's Nooksack Road," and he changed our course with a heave.

When we got to the mountains, he slid us along Mount Baker's flanks sideways.

Our plane swiped at the mountain with a roar. I glimpsed a

windshield view of dirty snow traveling fast. Our shaking, swooping belly seemed to graze the snow. The wings shuddered; we peeled away and the mountain fell back and the engines whined. We felt flung, because we were in fact flung; parts of our faces and internal organs trailed pressingly behind on the curves. We came back for another pass at the mountain, and another. We dove at the snow headlong like suicides; we jerked up, down, or away at the last second, so late we left our hearts, stomachs, and lungs behind. If I forced myself to hold my heavy head up against the G's,* and to raise my eyelids, heavy as barbells, and to notice what I saw, I could see the wrinkled green crevasses cracking the glaciers' snow.

Pitching snow filled all the windows, and shapes of dark rock. I had no notion which way was up. Everything was black or gray or white except the fatal crevasses; everything made noise and shook. I felt my face smashed sideways and saw rushing abstractions of snow in the windshield. Patches of cloud obscured the snow fleetingly. We straightened out, turned, and dashed at the mountainside for another pass, which we made, apparently, on our ear, an inch or two away from the slope. Icefalls and cornices jumbled and fell away. If a commercial plane's black box, such as the FAA painstakingly recovers from crash sites, could store videotapes as well as pilots' last words, some videotapes would look like this: a mountainside coming up at the windows from all directions, ice and snow and rock filling the screen up close and screaming by.

Rahm was just being polite. His geographer colleague wanted to see the fissure on Mount Baker from which steam escaped. Everybody in Bellingham wanted to see that sooty fissure, as did every geologist in the country; no one on earth could fly so close to it as Rahm. He knew the mountain by familiar love and feel, like a face; he knew what the plane could do and what he dared to do.

When Mount Baker inexplicably let us go, he jammed us into cloud again and soon tilted. "The Sisters!" someone shouted, and I saw the windshield fill with red rock. This mountain looked infernal, a drear and sheer plane of lifeless rock. It was red and sharp; its gritty blades cut through the clouds at random. The mountain was quiet. It was in shade. Careening, we made sideways passes at these brittle peaks too steep for snow. Their rock was full of iron,

---

*G's: A measure of gravitational force.

somebody shouted at me then or later; the iron had rusted, so they were red. Later, when I was back on the ground, I recalled that, from a distance, the two jagged peaks called the Twin Sisters looked translucent against the sky; they were sharp, tapered, and fragile as arrowheads.

I talked to Rahm. He was flying us out to the islands now. The islands were fifty or sixty miles away. Like many other people, I had picked Bellingham, Washington, by looking at an atlas. It was clear from the atlas that you could row in the salt water and see snow-covered mountains; you could scale a glaciated mountainside with an ice ax in August, skirting green crevasses two hundred feet deep, and look out on the islands in the sea. Now, in the air, the clouds had risen over us; dark forms lay on the glinting water. There was almost no color to the day, just blackened green and some yellow. I knew the islands were forested in dark Douglas firs the size of skyscrapers. Bald eagles scavenged on the beaches; robins the size of herring gulls sang in the clearings. We made our way out to the islands through the layer of air between the curving planet and its held, thick clouds.

"When I started trying to figure out what I was going to do with my life, I decided to become an expert on mountains. It wasn't much to be, it wasn't everything, but it was something. I was going to know everything about mountains from every point of view. So I started out in geography." Geography proved too pedestrian for Rahm, too concerned with "how many bushels of wheat an acre." So he ended up in geology. Smith had told me that geology departments throughout the country used Rahm's photographic slides — close-ups of geologic features from the air.

"I used to climb mountains. But you know, you can get a better feel for a mountain's power flying around it, flying all around it, than you can from climbing it tied to its side like a flea."

He talked about his flying performances. He thought of the air as a line, he said. "This end of the line, that end of the line — like a rope." He improvised. "I get a rhythm going and stick with it." While he was performing in a show, he paid attention, he said, to the lighting. He didn't play against the sun. That was all he said about what he did.

In aerobatic maneuvers, pilots pull about seven positive G's on some stunts and six negative G's on others. Some gyrations push;

others pull. Pilots alternate the pressures carefully, so they do not gray out or black out.

Later I learned that some stunt pilots tune up by wearing gravity boots. These are boots made to hook over a doorway; wearing them, you hang in the doorway upside down. It must startle a pilot's children to run into their father or mother in the course of their home wanderings — the parents hanging wide-eyed, upside down in the doorway like a bat.

We were landing; here was the airstrip on Stuart Island — that island to which Ferrar Burn was dragged by the tide. We put down, climbed out of the plane, and walked. We wandered a dirt track through fields to a lee shore where yellow sandstone ledges slid into the sea. The salt chuck, people there called salt water. The sun came out. I caught a snake in the salt chuck; the snake, eighteen inches long, was swimming in the green shallows.

I had a survivor's elation. Rahm had found Mount Baker in the clouds before Mount Baker found the plane. He had wiped it with the fast plane like a cloth and we had lived. When we took off from Stuart Island and gained altitude, I asked if we could turn over — could we do a barrel roll? The plane was making a lot of noise, and Dick Smith did not hear any of this, I learned later. "Why not?" Rahm said, and added surprisingly, "It won't hurt the plane." Without ado he leaned on the wheel and the wing went down and we went somersaulting over it. We upended with a roar. We stuck to the plane's sides like flung paint. All the blood in my body bulged on my face; it piled between my skull and skin. Vaguely I could see the chrome sea twirling over Rahm's head like a baton, and the dark islands sliding down the skies like rain.

The G's slammed me into my seat like thugs and pinned me while my heart pounded and the plane turned over slowly and compacted each organ in turn. My eyeballs were newly spherical and full of heartbeats. I seemed to hear a crescendo; the wing rolled shuddering down the last 90 degrees and settled on the flat. There were the islands, admirably below us, and the clouds, admirably above. When I could breathe, I asked if we could do it again, and we did. He rolled the other way. The brilliant line of the sea slid up the side window bearing its heavy islands. Through the shriek of my blood and the plane's shakes I glimpsed the line of the sea over the windshield, thin as a spear. How in performance did Rahm keep track while his brain blurred and blood roared in his ears without ceasing? Every performance was a tour de force and a show of will, a *Machtspruch.* * I had seen the other stunt pilots straighten out after a trick or two; their blood could drop back and the planet simmer down. An Olympic gymnast, at peak form, strings out a line of spins ten stunts long across a mat, and is hard put to keep his footing at the end. Rahm endured much greater pressure on his faster spins using the plane's power, and he could spin in three dimensions and keep twirling till he ran out of sky room or luck.

When we straightened out, and had flown straightforwardly for ten minutes toward home, Dick Smith, clearing his throat, brought himself to speak. "What was that we did out there?"

"The barrel rolls?" Rahm said. "They were barrel rolls." He said nothing else. I looked at the back of his head; I could see the serious line of his cheek and jaw. He was in shirtsleeves, tanned, strong-wristed. I could not imagine loving him under any circumstance; he was alien to me, unfazed. He looked like GI Joe. He flew with that matter-of-fact, bored gesture pilots use. They click overhead switches and turn dials as if only their magnificent strength makes such dullness endurable. The half circle of wheel in their big hands looks like a toy they plan to crush in a minute; the wiggly stick the wheel mounts seems barely attached.

A crop-duster pilot in Wyoming told me the life expectancy of a crop-duster pilot is five years. They fly too low. They hit buildings and power lines. They have no space to fly out of trouble, and no space to recover from a stall. We were in Cody, Wyoming, out on the north fork of the Shoshone River. The crop duster had wakened me that morning flying over the ranch house and clearing my bedroom roof by half an inch. I saw the bolts on the wheel assembly a few feet from my face. He was spraying with pesticide the plain old grass. Over breakfast I asked him how long he had been dusting crops. "Four years," he said, and the figure stalled in the air between us for a moment. "You know you're going to die at it someday," he added. "We all know it. We accept that; it's part of it." I think now that, since the crop duster was in his twenties, he ac-

*__Machtspruch:__ German, meaning "power speech."

cepted only that he had to say such stuff; privately he counted on skewing the curve.

I suppose Rahm knew the fact too. I do not know how he felt about it. "It's worth it," said the early French aviator Mermoz. He was Antoine de Saint-Exupéry's friend. "It's worth the final smashup."

Rahm smashed up in front of King Hussein, in Jordan, during a performance. The plane spun down and never came out of it; it nosedived into the ground and exploded. He bought the farm. I was living then with my husband out on that remote island in the San Juans, cut off from everything. Battery radios picked up the Canadian Broadcasting Company out of Toronto, half a continent away; island people would, in theory, learn if the United States blew up, but not much else. There were no newspapers. One friend got the Sunday *New York Times* by mail boat on the following Friday. He saved it until Sunday and had a party, every week; we all read the Sunday *Times* and no one mentioned that it was last week's.

One day, Paul Glenn's brother flew out from Bellingham to visit; he had a seaplane. He landed in the water in front of the cabin and tied up to our mooring. He came in for coffee, and he gave out news of this and that, and — Say, did we know that stunt pilot Dave Rahm had cracked up? In Jordan, during a performance: he never came out of a dive. He just dove right down into the ground, and his wife was there watching. "I saw it on CBS News last night." And then — with a sudden sharp look at my filling eyes — "What, did you know him?" But no, I did not know him. He took me up once. Several years ago. I admired his flying. I had thought that danger was the safest thing in the world, if you went about it right.

Later, I found a newspaper. Rahm was living in Jordan that year; King Hussein invited him to train the aerobatics team, the Royal Jordanian Falcons. He was also visiting professor of geology at the University of Jordan. In Amman that day he had been flying a Pitt Special, a plane he knew well. Katy Rahm, his wife of six months, was sitting beside Hussein in the viewing stands, with her daughter. Rahm died performing a Lomcevak combined with a tail slide and hammerhead. In a Lomcevak, the pilot brings the plane up on a slant and pirouettes. I had seen Rahm do this: the falling plane twirled slowly like a leaf. Like a ballerina, the plane seemed to hold its head back stiff in concentration at the music's slow, painful beauty. It was one of Rahm's favorite routines. Next the pilot flies straight up, stalls the plane, and slides down the air on his tail. He brings the nose down — the hammerhead — kicks the engine, and finishes with a low loop.

It is a dangerous maneuver at any altitude, and Rahm was doing it low. He hit the ground on the loop; the tail slide had left him no height. When Rahm went down, King Hussein dashed to the burning plane to pull him out, but he was already dead.

A few months after the air show, and a month after I had flown with Rahm, I was working at my desk near Bellingham, where I lived, when I heard a sound so odd it finally penetrated my concentration. It was the buzz of an airplane, but it rose and fell musically, and it never quit; the plane never flew out of earshot. I walked out on the porch and looked up: it was Rahm in the black and gold biplane, looping all over the air. I had been wondering about his performance flight: could it really have been so beautiful? It was, for here it was again. The little plane twisted all over the air like a vine. It trailed a line like a very long mathematical proof you could follow only so far, and then it lost you in its complexity. I saw Rahm flying high over the Douglas firs, and out over the water, and back over farms. The air was a fluid, and Rahm was an eel.

It was as if Mozart could move his body through his notes, and you could walk out on the porch, look up, and see him in periwig and breeches, flying around in the sky. You could hear the music as he dove through it; it streamed after him like a contrail.

I lost myself; standing on the firm porch, I lost my direction and reeled. My neck and spine rose and turned, so I followed the plane's line kinesthetically. In his open-cockpit black plane, Rahm demonstrated curved space. He slid down ramps of air, he vaulted and wheeled. He piled loops in heaps and praised height. He unrolled the scroll of air, extended it, and bent it into Möbius strips; he furled line in a thousand new ways, as if he were inventing a script and writing it in one infinitely recurring utterance until I thought the bounds of beauty must break.

From inside, the looping plane had sounded tinny, like a kazoo. Outside, the buzz rose and fell to the Doppler effect as the plane looped near or away. Rahm cleaved the sky like a prow and tossed out time left and right in his wake. He performed for forty minutes; then he headed the plane, as small as a wasp, back to the airport inland. Later I learned Rahm often practiced acrobatic flights over this shore. His idea was that if he lost control and was going to go down, he could ditch in the salt chuck, where no one else would get hurt.

If I had not turned two barrel rolls in an airplane, I might have fancied Rahm felt good up there, and playful. Maybe Jackson Pollock felt a sort of playfulness, in addition to the artist's usual deliberate and intelligent care. In my limited experience, painting, unlike writing, pleases the senses while you do it, and more while you do it than after it is done. Drawing lines with an airplane, unfortunately, tortures the senses. Jet bomber pilots black out. I knew Rahm felt as if his brain were bursting his eardrums, felt that if he let his jaws close as tight as centrifugal force pressed them, he would bite through his lungs.

"All virtue is a form of acting," Yeats said. Rahm deliberately turned himself into a figure. Sitting invisible at the controls of a distant airplane, he became the agent and the instrument of art and invention. He did not tell me how he felt when we spoke of his performance flying; he told me instead that he paid attention to how his plane and its line looked to the audience against the lighted sky. If he had noticed how he felt, he could not have done the work. Robed in his airplane, he was as featureless as a priest. He was lost in his figural aspect like an actor or a king. Of his flying, he had said only, "I get a rhythm and stick with it." In its reticence, this statement reminded me of Veronese's* "Given a large canvas, I enhanced it as I saw fit." But Veronese was ironic, and Rahm was not; he was as literal as an astronaut; the machine gave him tongue.

When Rahm flew, he sat down in the middle of art and strapped himself in. He spun it all around him. He could not see it himself. If he never saw it on film, he never saw it at all — as if Beethoven could not hear his final symphonies not because he was deaf but because he was inside the paper on which he wrote. Rahm must have felt it happen, that fusion of vision and metal, motion and idea. I think of this man as a figure, a college professor with a Ph.D. upside down in the loud band of beauty. What are we here for? *Propter chorum,* the monks say: for the sake of the choir.

"Purity does not lie in separation from but in deeper pene-

---

*Veronese: Paolo Veronese (1528–1588), famous Venetian painter.

tration into the universe," Teilhard de Chardin* wrote. It is hard to imagine a deeper penetration into the universe than Rahm's last dive in his plane, or than his inexpressible wordless selfless line's inscribing the air and dissolving. Any other art may be permanent. I cannot recall one Rahm sequence. He improvised. If Christo† wraps a building or dyes a harbor, we join his poignant and fierce awareness that the work will be gone in days. Rahm's plane shed a ribbon in space, a ribbon whose end unraveled in memory while its beginning unfurled as surprise. He may have acknowledged that what he did could be called art, but it would have been, I think, only in the common misusage, which holds art to be the last extreme of skill. Rahm rode the point of the line to the possible; he discovered it and wound it down to show. He made his dazzling probe on the run. "The world is filled, and filled with the Absolute," Teilhard de Chardin wrote. "To see this is to be made free."

Reflections and Responses

1. How does Dillard establish a connection between stunt piloting and artistic performance? Identify the various moments in her essay when she makes such a connection. What do these moments have in common? What images do they share?

2. Note that Dillard doesn't wait until the very end of her essay to introduce Rahm's death. Why do you think she avoids this kind of climax? What advantage does this give her?

3. "The Stunt Pilot" also appears as an untitled chapter in Dillard's book *The Writing Life*. Why is this an appropriate context for the essay? What does the essay tell us about expression and composition?

---

*Teilhard de Chardin:** Pierre Teilhard de Chardin (1881–1953), a noted paleontologist and Catholic priest whose most famous book, *The Phenomenon of Man*, attempts to bridge the gap between science and religion.

†**Christo:** A contemporary Bulgarian artist known for staging spectacular environmental effects.

GRETEL EHRLICH

Spring

"Recuperation is like spring," writes Gretel Ehrlich in a lyrical essay that sensitively charts the changes both within a Wyoming season and a woman's psyche. A model of the modern reflective essay, her meditation on her slow recovery from pneumonia and the death of a young rancher branches out into thoughts about time and space, sex and death, dream and reality, cosmology and Jurassic landscapes. As she considers the way life and thought move between the linear and the circular, particle and wave, she shapes her essay accordingly, at some moments pursuing a narrative, at others following the trail of an image: "In March I'm ramshackle, weak in the knees, giddy, dazzled by broken-backed clouds, the passing of Halley's comet, the on-and-off strobe of sun."

Ehrlich is the author of The Solace of Open Spaces *(1985),* Wyoming Stories *(1986),* Heart Mountain *(1988),* Islands, the Universe, Home *(1991),* Arctic Heart: A Poem Cycle *(1992),* A Match to the Heart *(1994), and* Questions of Heaven: The Chinese Journeys of an American Buddhist *(1997). Her essays have appeared in* Harper's, The Atlantic, Time, *the* New York Times, *and many other national periodicals. She divides her time between the central coast of California and Wyoming. "Spring" originally appeared in* Antaeus *(1986) and was selected by Gay Talese for* The Best American Essays 1987.

We have a nine-acre lake on our ranch and a warm spring that feeds it all winter. By mid-March the lake ice begins to melt where the spring feeds in, and every year the same pair of mallards come ahead of the others and wait. Though there is very little open water they seem content. They glide back and forth through a thin estuary, brushing watercress with their elegant folded wings, then tip end-up to eat and, after, clamber onto the lip of ice that retreats, hardens forward, and retreats again.

Mornings, a transparent pane of ice lies over the meltwater. I peer through and see some kind of waterbug — perhaps a leech — paddling like a sea turtle between green ladders of lakeweed. Cattails and sweetgrass from the previous summer are bone dry, marked with black mold spots, and bend like elbows into the ice. They are swords that cut away the hard tenancy of winter. At the wide end a mat of dead waterplants has rolled back into a thick, impregnable breakwater. Near it, bubbles trapped under the ice are lenses focused straight up to catch the coming season.

It's spring again and I wasn't finished with winter. That's what I said at the end of summer too. I stood on the twenty-foot-high haystack and yelled "No!" as the first snow fell. We had been up since four in the morning picking the last bales of hay from the oatfield by hand, slipping under the weight of them in the mud, and by the time we finished the stack, six inches of snow had fallen.

It's spring but I was still cataloguing the different kinds of snow: snow that falls dry but is rained on; snow that melts down into hard crusts; wind-driven snow that looks blue; powder snow on hardpack on powder — a Linzertorte of snow. I look up. The troposphere is the seven-to-ten-mile-wide sleeve of air out of which all our weather shakes. A bank of clouds drives in from the south. Where in it, I wonder, does a snowflake take on its thumbprint uniqueness? Inside the cloud where schools of flakes are flung this way and that like schools of fish? What gives the snowflake its needle, plate, column, branching shapes — the battering wind or the dust particles around which water vapor clings?

Near town the river ice breaks up and lies stacked in industrial-sized hunks — big as railway cars — on the banks, and is flecked black by wheeling hurricanes of newly plowed topsoil. That's how I feel when winter breaks up inside me: heavy, onerous, upended, inert against the flow of water. I had thought about ice during the cold months too. How it is movement betrayed, water seized in the moment of falling. In November, ice thickened over the lake like a cataract, and from the air looked like a Cyclops, one bad eye. Under its milky spans over irrigation ditches, the sound of water running south was muffled. One solitary spire of ice hung noise-lessly against dark rock at the Falls as if mocking or mirroring the broom-tail comet on the horizon. Then, in February, I tried for words not about ice, but words hacked from it — the ice at the end of the mind, so to speak — and failed.

Those were winter things and now it is spring, though one name can't describe what, in Wyoming, is a three-part affair: false spring, the vernal equinox, and the spring when flowers come and the grass grows.

Spring means restlessness. The physicist I've been talking to all winter says if I look more widely, deeply, and microscopically all at once I might see how springlike the whole cosmos is. What I see as order and stillness — the robust, time-bound determinacy of my life — is really a mirage suspended above chaos. "There's a lot of random jiggling going on all the time, everywhere," he tells me. Winter's tight sky hovers. Under it, the hayfields are green, then white, then green growing under white. The confinement I've felt since November resembles the confinement of subatomic parti-cles, I'm told. A natural velocity finally shows itself. The particle moves; it becomes a wave.

The sap rises in trees and in me and the hard knot of persever-ance I cultivated to meet winter dissipates; I walk away from the obsidian of bitter nights. Now, when snow comes, it is wet and heavy, but the air it traverses feels light. I sleep less and dream not of human entanglements, but of animals I've never seen: a cater-pillar fat as a man's thumb, made of linked silver tubes, has two heads — one human, one a butterfly's.

Last spring at this time I was coming out of a bout with pneumo-nia. I went to bed on January first and didn't get up until the end of February. Winter was a cocoon in which my gagging, basso cough shook the dark figures at the end of my bed. Had I read too much Hemingway? Or was I dying? I'd lie on my stomach and look out. Nothing close up interested me. All engagements of mind — the circumlocutions of love interests and internal gossip — ap-peared false. Only my body was true. And my body was trying to close down, go out the window without me.

I saw things out there. Our ranch faces south down a long tree-less valley whose vanishing point is two gray hills, folded one in front of the other like two hands, and after that — space, cerulean air, clouds like pleated skirts, and red mesas standing up like breaching whales in a valley three thousand feet below. After-noons, our young horses played, rearing up on back legs and paw-ing oh so carefully at each other, reaching around, ears flat back, nipping manes and withers. One of those times their falsetto squeals looped across the pasture and hung on frozen currents of air. But when I tried to ingest their sounds of delight, I found my lungs had no air.

It was thirty-five below zero that night. Our plumbing froze, and because I was very weak my husband had to bundle me up and help me to the outhouse. Nothing close at hand seemed to register with me: neither the cold nor the semicoziness of an uninsulated house. But the stars were lurid. For a while I thought I saw the horses, dead now, and eating each other, and spinning round and round in the ice of the air.

My scientist friends talk with relish about how insignificant we humans are when placed against the time-scale of geology and the cosmos. I had heard it a hundred times, but never felt it truly. As I lay in bed, the black room was a screen through which some part of my body traveled, leaving the rest behind. I thought I was a sun flying over a barge whose iron holds soaked me up until I became rust floating on a bright river.

A ferocious loneliness took hold of me. I felt spring-inspired de-sire, a sense of trajectory, but no interception was in sight. In fact, I wanted none. My body was a parenthetical dash laid against a landscape so spacious it defied space as we know it — space as a membrane — and curved out of time. That night a luscious, creamy fog rolled in, like a roll of fat, hugging me, but it was snow.

Recuperation is like spring: dormancy and vitality collide. In any year I'm like a bear, a partial hibernator. During January thaws I stick my nose out and peruse the frozen desolation as if reading a book whose language I don't know. In March I'm ramshackle, weak in the knees, giddy, dazzled by broken-backed clouds, the passing of Halley's comet, the on-and-off strobe of sun. Like a sheepherder I X out each calendar day as if time were a forest through which I could clear-cut a way to the future. My physicist friend straightens me out on this point too. The notion of "time passing," like a train through a landscape, is an illusion, he says. I hold the Big Ben clock taken from a dead sheepherder's wagon and look at it. The clock measures intervals of time, not the speed of time, and the calendar is a scaffolding we hang as if time were rushing water we could harness. Time-bound, I hinge myself to a linear bias — cause and effect all laid out in a neat row — and in this we learn two things: blame and shame.

Julius Caesar had a sense of humor about time. The Roman calendar with its calends, nones, and ides — counting days — changed according to who was in power. Caesar serendipitously added days, changed the names of certain months, and when he was through, the calendar was so skewed that January fell in autumn.

Einsteinian time is too big for even Julius Caesar to touch. It stretches and shrinks and dilates. In fact, it is the antithesis of the mechanistic concept we've imposed on it. Time, indecipherable from space, is not one thing but an infinity of space-times, overlapping, interfering, wavelike. There is no future that is not now, no past that is not now. Time includes every moment.

It's the ides of March today.

I've walked to a hill a mile from the house. It's not really a hill but a mountain slope that heaves up, turns sideways, and comes down again, straight down to a foot-wide creek. Everything I can see from here used to be a flatland covered with shallow water. "Used to be" means several hundred million years ago, and the land itself was not really "here" at all, but part of a continent floating near Bermuda. On top is a fin of rock, a marine deposition created during Jurassic times by small waves moving in and out slapping the shore.

I've come here for peace and quiet and to see what's going on in this secluded valley, away from ranch work and sorting corrals, but what I get is a slap on the ass by a prehistoric wave, gains and losses in altitude and aridity, outcrops of mud composed of rotting volcanic ash that fell continuously for ten thousand years a hundred million years ago. The soils are a geologic flag — red, white, green, and gray. On one side of the hill, mountain mahogany gives off a scent like orange blossoms; on the other, colonies of sagebrush root wide in ground the color of Spanish roof tiles. And it still looks like the ocean to me. "How much truth can a man stand, sitting by the ocean, all that perpetual motion," Mose Allison, the jazz singer, sings.

The wind picks up and blusters. Its fat underbelly scrapes the uneven ground, twisting like taffy toward me, slips up over the mountain, and showers out across the Great Plains. The sea smell it carried all the way from Seattle has long since been absorbed by pink gruss — the rotting granite that spills down the slopes of the Rockies. Somewhere over the Midwest the wind slows, tangling in the hair of hardwood forests, and finally drops into the corridors of the cities, past Manhattan's World Trade Center, ripping free again as it crosses the Atlantic's green swell.

Spring jitterbugs inside me. Spring *is* wind, symphonic and billowing. A dark cloud pops like a blood blister over me, letting hail down. It comes on a piece of wind that seems to have widened the sky, comes so the birds have something to fly on.

A message reports to my brain but I can't believe my eyes. The sheet of wind had a hole in it: an eagle just fell out of the sky. It fell as if down the chute of a troubled airplane. Landed, falling to one side as if a leg were broken. I was standing on the hill overlooking the narrow valley that had been a seashore 170 million years ago, whose sides had lifted like a medic's litter to catch up this eagle now.

She hops and flaps seven feet of wing and closes them down and sways. She had come down (on purpose?) near a dead fawn whose carcass had recently been feasted upon. When I walked closer, all I could see of the animal was a ribcage rubbed red with fine tissue and the decapitated head lying peacefully against sagebrush, eyes closed.

At twenty yards the eagle opened her wings halfway and rose up, her whole back lengthening and growing stiff. At forty feet she looked as big as a small person. She craned her neck, first to one side, then the other, and stared hard. She's giving me the eagle eye, I thought.

Friends who have investigated eagles' nests have literally feared for their lives. It's not that they were in danger of being pecked to death but, rather, grabbed. An eagle's talons are a powerful jaw. Their grip is so strong the talons can slice down through flesh to bone in one motion.

But I had come close only to see what was wrong, to see what I could do. An eagle with a bum leg will starve to death. Was it broken, bruised, or sprained? How could I get close enough to know? I approached again. She hopped up in the air, dashing the critical distance between us with her great wings. Best to leave her alone, I decided. My husband dragged a road-killed deer up the mountain slope so she could eat, and I brought a bucket of water. Then we turned toward home.

A golden eagle is not golden but black with yellow spots on the neck and wings. Looking at her, I had wondered how feathers came to be, how their construction — the rachis, vane, and quill — is unlike anything else in nature.

Birds are glorified flying lizards. The remarkable feathers that, positioned together, are like hundreds of smaller wings, evolved from reptilian scales. Ancestral birds had thirteen pairs of cone-shaped teeth that grew in separate sockets like a snake's, rounded ribs, and bony tails. Archaeopteryx was half bird, half dinosaur who glided instead of flying; ichthyornis was a fish-bird, a relative of the pelican; diatryma was a giant, seven feet tall with a huge beak and wings so absurdly small they must have been useless, though later the wingbone sprouted from them. *Aquila chrysaëtos,* the modern golden eagle, has seven thousand contour feathers, no teeth, and weighs about eight pounds.

I think about the eagle. How big she was, how each time she spread her wings it was like a thought stretching between two seasons.

Back at the house I relax with a beer. At 5:03 the vernal equinox occurs. I go outside and stand in the middle of a hayfield with my eyes closed. The universe is restless but I want to feel celestial equipoise: twelve hours of daylight, twelve of dark, and the earth ramrod straight on its axis. In celebration I straighten my posture in an effort to resist the magnetic tilt back into dormancy, spiritual and emotional reticence. Far to the south I imagine the equatorial sash, now nose to nose with the sun, sizzling like a piece of bacon, then the earth slowly tilting again.

In the morning I walk up to the valley again. I glass both hillsides, back and forth through the sagebrush, but the eagle isn't there. The hindquarters of the road-killed deer have been eaten. Coyote tracks circle the carcass. Did they have eagle for dinner too?

Afternoon. I return. Far up on the opposite hill I see her, flapping and hopping to the top. When I stop, she stops and turns her head. Her neck is the plumbline on which earth revolves. Even at two hundred yards, I can feel her binocular vision zeroing in; I can feel the heat of her stare.

Later, I look through my binoculars at all sorts of things. I'm seeing the world with an eagle eye. I glass the crescent moon. How jaded I've become, taking the moon at face value only, forgetting the charcoal, shaded backside, as if it weren't there at all.

That night I dream about two moons. One is pink and spins fast; the other is an eagle's head, farther away and spinning in the opposite direction. Slowly, both moons descend and then it is day.

At first light I clamber up the hill. Now the dead deer my husband brought is only a hoop of ribs, two forelegs, and hair. The eagle is not here or along the creek or on either hill. I go to the hill and sit. After a long time an eagle careens out from the narrow slit of the red-walled canyon whose creek drains into this valley. Surely it's the same bird. She flies by. I can hear the bone-creak and whoosh of air under her wings. She cocks her head and looks at me. I smile. What is a smile to her? Now she is not so much flying as lifting above the planet, far from me.

Late March. The emerald of the hayfields brightens. A flock of gray-capped rosy finches who overwintered here swarms a leafless apple tree, then falls from the smooth boughs like cut grass. The tree was planted by the Texan who homesteaded this ranch. As I walk past, one of the boughs, shaped like an undulating dragon, splits off from the trunk and falls.

Space is an arena in which the rowdy particles that are the building blocks of life perform their antics. All spring, things fall; the general law of increasing disorder is on the take. I try to think of what it is to be a cause without an effect, an effect without a cause. To abandon time-bound thinking, the use of tenses, the temporally related emotions of impatience, expectation, hope, and fear. But I can't. I go to the edge of the lake and watch the ducks. Like them, my thinking rises and falls on the same water.

Another day. Sometimes when I'm feeling small-minded I take a plane ride over Wyoming. As we take off I feel the plane's resistance to accepting air under its wings. Is this how an eagle feels? Ernst Mach's* principle tells me that an object's resistance against being accelerated is not the intrinsic property of matter, but a measure of its interaction with the universe; that matter has inertia only because it exists in relation to other matter.

*Ernst Mach: Austrian physicist and philosopher (1838–1916).

Airborne, then, I'm not aloof but in relation to everything —
like Wallace Stevens's floating eagle for whom the whole, intricate
Alps is a nest. We fly southeast from Heart Mountain across the Big
Horn River, over the long red wall where Butch Cassidy trailed
stolen horses, across the high plains to Laramie. Coming home
the next day, we hit clouds. Turbulence, like many forms of trouble, cannot always be seen. We bounce so hard my arms sail helplessly above my head. In evolution, wingbones became arms and
hands; perhaps I'm de-evolving.

From ten thousand feet I can see that spring is only half here:
the southern part of the state is white, the northern half is green.
Land is also time. The greening of time is a clock whose hands are
blades of grass moving vertically, up through the fringe of numbers, spreading across the middle of the face, sinking again as the
sun moves from one horizon to the other. Time doesn't go anywhere; the shadow of the plane, my shadow, moves across it.

To sit on a plane is to sit on the edge of sleep where the mind's
forge brightens into incongruities. Down there I see disparate
wholenesses strung together and the string dissolving. Mountains
run like rivers; I fly through waves and waves of chiaroscuro light.
The land looks bare but is articulate. The body of the plane is
my body, pressing into spring, pressing matter into relation with
matter. Is it even necessary to say the obvious? That spring brings
on surges of desire? From this disinterested height I say out loud
what Saint Augustine wrote: "My love is my weight. Because of it
I move."

Directly below us now is the fine old Wyoming ranch where Joel,
Mart, Dave, Hughy, and I have moved thousands of head of cattle.
Joel's father, Smokey, was one of two brothers who put the outfit
together. They worked hard, lived frugally, and even after Fred
died, Smokey did not marry until his late fifties. As testimony to a
long bachelorhood, there is no kitchen in the main house. The
cookhouse stands separate from all the other buildings. In back is
a bedroom and bath, which have housed a list of itinerant cooks
ten pages long.

Over the years I've helped during roundup and branding. We'd
rise at four. Smokey, now in his eighties, cooked flapjacks and
boiled coffee on the wood cookstove. There was a long table.
Joel and Smokey always sat at one end. They were lookalikes, both

skin-and-bones tall with tipped-up dark eyes set in narrow faces. Stern and vigilant, Smokey once threw a young hired hand out of the cookhouse because he hadn't grained his saddle horse after a long day's ride. "On this outfit we take care of our animals first," he said. "Then if there's time, we eat."

Even in his early twenties, Joel had his father's dignity and razor-sharp wit. They both wore white Stetsons identically shaped. Only their hands were different: Joel had eight fingers and one thumb — the other he lost while roping.

Eight summers ago my parents visited their ranch. We ate a hearty meal of homemade whiskey left over from Prohibition days, steaks cut from an Angus bull, four kinds of vegetables, watermelon, ice cream, and pie. Despite a thirteen-year difference in our ages, Smokey wanted Joel and me to marry. As we rose from the meal, he shook my father's hand. "I guess you'll be my son's father-in-law," he said. That was news to all of us. Joel's face turned crimson. My father threw me an astonished look, cleared his throat, and thanked his host for the fine meal.

One night Joel did come to my house and asked me if I would take him into my bed. It was a gentlemanly proposition — doffed hat, moist eyes, a smile almost grimacing with loneliness. "You're an older woman. Think of all you could teach me," he said jauntily, but with a blush. He stood ramrod straight waiting for an answer. My silence turned him away like a rolling wave and he drove to the home ranch, spread out across the Emblem Bench thirty-five miles away.

The night Joel died I was staying at a writer's farm in Missouri. I had fallen asleep early, then awakened suddenly, feeling claustrophobic. I jumped out of bed and stood in the dark. I wanted to get out of there, drive home to Wyoming, and I didn't know why. Finally, at seven in the morning, I was able to sleep. I dreamed about a bird landing, then lifting out of a tree along a river bank. That was the night Joel's pickup rolled. He was found five hours after the accident occurred — just about daylight — and died on the way to the hospital.

Now I'm sitting on a fin of Gypsum Springs rock looking west. The sun is setting. What I see are three gray cloud towers letting rain down at the horizon. The sky behind these massifs is gilded gold,

and long fingers of land — benches where the Hunt Oil Company's
Charolais cattle graze — are pink. Somewhere over Joel's grave the
sky is bright. The road where he died shines like a dash in a Paul
Klee painting. Over my head, it is still winter: snow so dry it feels
like Styrofoam when squeezed together, tumbles into my lap. I
think about flying and falling. The place in the sky where the eagle
fell is dark, as if its shadow had burned into the backdrop of
rock — Hiroshima style. Why does a wounded eagle get well and
fly away; why do the head wounds of a young man cut him down?
Useless questions.

Sex and death are the riddles thrown into the hopper, thrown
down on the planet like hailstones. Where one hits the earth, it
makes a crater and melts, perhaps a seed germinates, perhaps not.
If I dice life down into atoms, the trajectories I find are so wild, so
random, anything could happen: life or nonlife. But once we have
a body, who can give it up easily? Our own or others'? We check
our clocks and build our beautiful narratives, under which inde-
terminacy seethes.

Sometimes, lying in bed, I feel like a flounder with its two eyes
on one side pointing upward into nothingness. The casings of
thought rattle. Then I realize there are no casings at all. Is it possible that the mind, like space, is finite, but has no boundaries, no
center or edge? I sit cross-legged on old blankets. My bare feet
strain against the crotch of my knees. Time is between my toes, it
seems. Just as morning comes and the indigo lifts, the leaflessness
of the old apple tree looks ornate. Nothing in this world is plain.

"Every atom in your body was once inside a star," another physicist says, but he's only trying to humor me. Not all atoms in all
kinds of matter are shared. But who wouldn't find that idea appealing? Outside, shadows trade places with a sliver of sun that trades
places with shadow. Finally the lake ice goes and the water — pale
and slate blue — wears its coat of diamonds all day. The mallards
number twenty-six pairs now. They nest on two tiny islands and
squabble amicably among themselves. A Pacific storm blows in
from the south like a jibsail reaching far out, backhanding me
with a gust of something tropical. It snows into my mouth, between
my breasts, against my shins. Spring teaches me what space and
time teach me: that I am a random multiple; that the many fit together like waves; that my swell is a collision of particles. Spring is

a kind of music, a seething minor, a twelve-tone scale. Even the odd harmonies amassed only lift up to dissolve.

Spring passes harder and harder and is feral. The first thunder cracks the sky into a larger domain. Sap rises in obdurateness. For the first time in seven months, rain slants down in a slow pavane — sharp but soft — like desire, like the laying on of hands. I drive the highway that crosses the wild-horse range. Near Emblem I watch a black studhorse trot across the range all alone. He travels north, then turns in my direction as if trotting to me. Now, when I dream of Joel, he is riding that horse and he knows he is dead. One night he rides to my house, all smiles and shyness. I let him in.

Reflections and Responses

1. What does the author's physicist friend contribute to the essay? How does particle physics enter into Ehrlich's thinking? Would you say that she is scientific or nonscientific in her approach to nature?

2. Of what significance to Ehrlich's theme is the eagle with the "bum leg"? Consider carefully the passage in which she describes the eagle. What thoughts does the incident prompt? Why is it important that the eagle is hurt?

3. Much of Ehrlich's essay deals with time. Aside from her philosophical reflections on the subject, how does she mark the passage of time in the essay? Can you reconstruct her chronological outline? What is the time of the essay's opening, and how does it proceed? Of what importance is Wyoming's "three-part" spring to her structure?

IAN FRAZIER

A Lovely Sort of Lower Purpose

In the middle of the eighteenth century the great English essayist, Samuel Johnson, regularly published a series of essays known as The Idler. *The title was carefully chosen; from Montaigne on, essayists have traditionally cultivated a leisurely pace and written many pieces in praise of idleness or what in today's terms would be called "hanging out" and "fooling around."* *In "A Lovely Sort of Lower Purpose," Ian Frazier revisits this time-tested topic and, in his inimitable fashion, celebrates the virtues of doing nothing. Frazier warns us, however, that this virtue is rapidly declining as our restless society continually finds ways to make everything busy, useful, and purposeful. As Frazier suggests, the terrible question grown-ups often ask children, "What are you* doing*?" now haunts us all.*

Besides several collections of humorous essays and two award-winning books of nonfiction, Family *(1994) and* Great Plains *(1989), Ian Frazier is the author of* On the Rez *(1999), a look at life on a reservation. His writing has appeared in* The New Yorker, Outside, The Atlantic Monthly, *and many other magazines. Frazier was the guest editor of* The Best American Essays 1997. *"A Lovely Sort of Lower Purpose" originally appeared in* Outside *magazine and was selected by Edward Hoagland for* The Best American Essays 1999.

As kids, my friends and I spent a lot of time out in the woods. "The woods" was our part-time address, destination, purpose, and excuse. If I went to a friend's house and found him not at home, his mother might say, "Oh, he's out in the woods," with a tone of airy acceptance. It's similar to the tone people sometimes use nowadays to tell me that someone I'm looking for is on the golf course

or at the hairdresser's or at the gym, or even "away from his desk."
The combination of vagueness and specificity in the answer gives a
sense of somewhere romantically incommunicado. I once attended an awards dinner at which Frank Sinatra was supposed to
appear, and when he didn't, the master of ceremonies explained
that Frank had called to say he was "filming on location." Ten-year-
olds suffer from a scarcity of fancy-sounding excuses to do whatever they feel like for a while. For us, saying we were "out in the
woods" worked just fine.

We sometimes told ourselves that what we were doing in the
woods was exploring. Exploring was a more prominent idea back
then than it is today, History, for example, seemed to be mostly
about explorers, and the semirural part of Ohio where we lived
still had a faint recollection of being part of the frontier. At the
town's two high schools, the sports teams were the Explorers and
the Pioneers. Our explorations, though, seemed to have less system than the historic kind: something usually came up along the
way. Say we began to cross one of the little creeks plentiful in the
second-growth forests we frequented and found that all the creek's
moisture had somehow become a shell of milk-white ice about
eight inches above the now-dry bed. No other kind of ice is as satisfying to break. The search for the true meridian would be post-
poned while we spent the afternoon breaking the ice, stomping it
underfoot by the furlong, and throwing its bigger pieces like Fris-
bees to shatter in excellent, war-movie-type fragmentation among
the higher branches of the trees.

Stuff like that — throwing rocks at a fresh mudflat to make
craters, shooting frogs with slingshots, making forts, picking black-
berries, digging in what we were briefly persuaded was an Indian
burial mound — occupied much of our time in the woods. Our
purpose there was a higher sort of un-purpose, a free-form aim-
lessness that would be beyond me now. Once as we tramped for
miles along Tinker's Creek my friend Kent told me the entire plot
of two Bob Hope movies, *The Paleface* and *Son of Paleface*, which
he had just seen on a double bill. The joke-filled monotony of his
synopsis went well with the soggy afternoon, the muddy water,
the endless tangled brush. (Afterward, when I saw the movies
themselves, I found a lot to prefer in Kent's version.) The woods
were ideal for those trains of thought that involved tedium and

brooding. Often when I went by myself I would climb a tree and just sit.

I could list a hundred pointless things we did in the woods. Climbing trees, though, was a common one. Often we got "lost" and had to climb a tree to get our bearings. If you read a story in which someone does that successfully, be skeptical; the topmost branches are usually too skinny to hold weight, and we could never climb high enough to see anything except other trees. There were four or five trees that we visited regularly — tall beeches, easy to climb and comfortable to sit in. We spent hours at a time in trees, afflicting the best perches with so many carved-in names, hearts, arrows, and funny sayings from the comic strips that we ran out of room for more.

It was in a tree, too, that our days of fooling around in the woods came to an end. By then some of us had reached seventh grade and had begun the bumpy ride of adolescence. In March, the month when we usually took to the woods again after winter, two friends and I set out to go exploring. Right away, we climbed a tree, and soon were indulging in the spurious nostalgia of kids who have only short pasts to look back upon. The "remember whens" faltered, finally, and I think it occurred to all three of us at the same time that we really were rather big to be up in a tree. Some of us had started wearing unwoodsy outfits like short-sleeved madras shirts and penny loafers, even after school. Soon there would be the spring dances on Friday evenings in the high school cafeteria. We looked at the bare branches around us receding into obscurity, and suddenly there was nothing up there for us. Like Adam and Eve, we saw our own nakedness, and that terrible grown-up question "What are you *doing?*" made us ashamed.

We went back to the woods eventually — and when I say "we," I'm speaking demographically, not just of my friends and me. Millions of us went back, once the sexual and social business of early adulthood had been more or less sorted out. But significantly, we brought that same question with us. Now we had to be seriously doing — racing, strengthening, slimming, traversing, collecting, achieving, catching-and-releasing. A few parts per million of our concentrated purpose changed the chemistry of the whole outdoors. Even those rare interludes of actually doing nothing in the woods took on a certain fierceness as we reinforced them with personal dramas, usually of a social or sexual kind: the only way we could justify sitting motionless in an A-frame cabin in the north woods of Michigan, for example, was if we had just survived a really messy divorce.

"What are you *doing?*" The question pursues me still. When I go fishing and catch no fish, the idea that it's fun simply to be out on the river consoles me for not one second. I must catch fish; and if I do, I must then catch more and bigger fish. On a Sunday afternoon last summer I took my two young children fishing with me on a famous trout stream near my house. My son was four and my daughter was eight, and I kidded myself that in their company I would be able to fish with my usual single-minded mania. I suited up in my waders and tackle-shopful of gear and led my kids from the parking area down toward the water. On the way, however, we had to cross a narrow, shallow irrigation ditch dating from when this part of the valley had farms. Well, the kids saw that little ditch and immediately took off their shoes and waded in and splashed and floated pine cones. My son got an inexplicable joy from casting his little spinning rod far over the ditch into the woods and reeling the rubber casting weight back through the trees. My daughter observed many tent caterpillars — a curse of yard-owners that year — falling from bushes into the ditch and floating helplessly along, and she decided to rescue them. She kept watching the water carefully, and whenever she spotted a caterpillar she swooped down and plucked it out and put it carefully on the bank. I didn't have the heart to drag the kids away, and as I was sitting in all my fishing gear beside the unlikely trickle, a fly fisherman about my age and just as geared-up came along. He took me in at a glance, noticed my equipment and my idleness, and gave a small but unmistakable snort of derision. I was offended, but I understood how he felt as he and his purpose hurried on by.

Here, I'd like to consider a word whose meaning has begun to drift like a caterpillar on a stream. That word is *margin.* Originally its meaning — the blank space around a body of type or the border of a piece of ground — had neutral connotations. But its adjective form, *marginal,* now has a negative tinge. Marginal people or places or activities are ones that don't quite work out, don't sufficiently account of themselves in the economic world. From the adjective sprouted a far-fetched verb, *marginalize,* whose meaning is only bad. To be marginalized is to be a victim, and to marginalize someone else is an act of exclusion that can cost you tenure. Today's so-called marginal people are the exact equivalents, etymologically, of the old-time heathens. A heathen was a savage, wild, un-Christian person who lived out on a heath. The heath was the margin of Christendom. No one today would ever use the word *heathen* except ironically, but we call certain people and activities marginal without a hint of irony all the time.

I've never been on a heath, but to judge from accounts of coal-smogged London in the days when *heathen* was in vogue, a windswept place full of heather and salmon streams sounds like the better place to be. And if the modern version of the margin is somewhere in western Nebraska, and the un-margin, the coveted red-hot center, is a site like Rodeo Drive, I wouldn't know which to choose. We need both, but especially as the world gets more jammed up, we need margins. A book without margins is impossible to read. And marginal behavior can be the most important kind. Every purpose-filled activity we pursue in the woods began as just fooling around. The first person to ride his bicycle down a mountain trail was doing a decidedly marginal thing. The margin is where you can try out odd ideas that you might be afraid to admit to with people looking on. Scientists have a term for research carried on with no immediate prospects of economic gain: "blue-sky research." Marginal places are the blue-sky research zones of the outdoors.

Unfortunately, there are fewer and fewer of them every day. Now a common fate of a place on the margin is to have a convenience store or a windowless brick building belonging to a telephone company built on it. Across the country, endless miles of exurbia now overlap and spill into one another with hardly a margin at all. There's still a lot of open space out there, of course, but usually it's far enough from home that just getting to it requires purpose and premeditation. As the easy-to-wander-into hometown margins disappear, a certain kind of wandering becomes endangered too.

On the far west side of the small western city where I live, past the town-killer discount stores, is an open expanse of undeveloped ground. Its many acres border the Bitterroot River, and its far end

abuts a fence surrounding a commercial gravel pit. It is a classic
marginal, anything-goes sort of place, and at the moment I prefer
it to just about anywhere I know.

Army reservists sometimes drive tanks there on weekends. The
camouflaged behemoths slithering across the ground would make
my skin crawl if I didn't suspect that the kids driving them were
having such a good time. The dirt-bike guys certainly are, as they
zip all over, often dawn to dusk, exuberantly making a racket.
Dads bring their kids to this place to fly kites and model airplanes,
people in a converted school bus camp there for weeks on end,
coin-shooters cruise around with metal detectors, hunters just
in off the river clean game, college kids party and leave heaps
of cigarette butts and beer cans and occasionally pieces of underwear. I fish there, of course, but remarkably I don't always
feel I have to. Sometimes I also pick up the trash, and I pull
my kids around on a sled in the winter, and I bring friends just off
the plane to sit on the riverbank and drink wine and watch the
sunset.

Soon, I'm sure, Development will set its surveyor's tripod on this
ground and make it get with one program or another. Rumblings
of this have already begun to sound in the local newspaper. I foresee rows of condominiums, or an expansion of the gravel pit, or a
public park featuring hiking trails and grim pieces of exercise
equipment every twenty yards. That last choice, in all its worthy banality, somehow is the most disheartening of all. A plan will claim
the empty acres and erase the spotted knapweed and the tank
tracks and the beer-can heaps. The place's possibilities, which at
the moment are approximately infinite, will be reduced to merely
a few. And those of uncertain purpose will have to go elsewhere
when they feel like doing nothing in particular, just fooling
around.

Reflections and Responses

1. What do you think Frazier means by a "lower purpose"? What
would a higher purpose be? Give a few examples of lower-purpose
activities that appear in the essay.

2. What is Frazier opposed to in this essay? Do you think he opposes all kinds of purposeful activity? Explain in your own words what he objects to.

3. Why is the idea of margins important to the development of his essay? How has the term taken on negative meanings? Why does Frazier want to retain the word's other meanings? How do Frazier's final three paragraphs illustrate his use of the word *marginal*?

PATRICIA HAMPL

A Week in the Word

In recent years some of America's finest nonfiction authors have explored the concepts of religion and theology and helped introduce an exciting new type of spiritual essay. In its agile movement between abstract theological ideas and the particularities of an individual life, Patricia Hampl's "A Week in the Word" offers a superb example of this emerging new essay. Based on a week's retreat at a California monastery, the essay covers an astonishing amount of religious thought in a few pages. Its author considers the true meaning of human memory as we begin a new millennium: "I am launched by the Psalms into a memory to which I belong but which is not mine. I don't possess it; it possesses me."

Patricia Hampl is the author of two memoirs, A Romantic Education *(1981) and* Virgin Time *(1992). Her most recent book is* I Could Tell You Stories: Sojourns in the Land of Memory *(1999). She is Regents' Professor at the University of Minnesota and is a member of the permanent faculty of the Prague Summer Seminars. "A Week in the Word" originally appeared in* Image: A Journal of the Arts and Religion *and was selected by Edward Hoagland for* The Best American Essays *1999.*

If I neglect to take my flashlight up to the monastery chapel for Vespers, I will regret it later when, sloshing blindly through puddles left in the rutted dirt road by the recent downpours, I stumble back in the dark to my — hermitage. The word interrupts with a medieval hiccup this — how do we describe this culture of ours? — this *postmodern* world, this banquet of possibilities. Just as this weeklong retreat interrupts my own life "down there," as I already think of home. I'm on a mountain, praying, thinking my thoughts — or, rather, trying not to think them for once. I am living not simply "away," in a geographic sense, but out of time, out of modernity, in this California monastery.

Meanwhile, our postmodern culture still revs along, inside me too — so many choices all jumbled together, and just one stomach. We have chosen the name for ourselves: we are no longer souls, as we once were, not even citizens; we are consumers, grasping at the disorder of life, all the *stuff.* Order is not our thing. *Only connect,** great grandfather (who was a Modernist) instructed. A few generations of only connecting, and here we are.

And what a strange *fin de siècle†* it is. Not exuberant and brainy like the eighteenth century's mind bounding out of the Enlightenment looking for trouble, looking for progress, and not swooning like the nineteenth century, the Romantic heart sopping up sensibility with its Swinburne.‡ We're not sad like that; we're sated.

Maybe we don't need memory here either. Like order, memory is selective, too constrained. Besides, it is parochial and specific, terribly local. We don't want memories. We'd rather have theories, constructs, opinions *about* memory. The littleness of real memories is a burden, also an annoyance. No things but in ideas§ — that's how it is with us. Memories (as distinct from "memory") are the sorry consolation of those who finger their cache of lavender-scented old stuff, fuddling over the past which, if *not* fuddled over, would leave the poor souls scorched with the truth: they're toast.

We — Americans — hate to be lassoed to the particular like that, like Europeans stuck with their dripping medieval real estate, the grimy pastel villas set prettily on sienna hills, the cobbled corners where their inflamed youth hurtle back and forth on unmuffled motorcycles, rattling the stained glass in the badly caulked basilica embrasures. The kids are trying to get out of there. We understand. Our tradition is to mistrust tradition.

*****Only connect:** the author is alluding to the British novelist E. M. Forster (1879–1970) who used "Only connect . . ." as the epigraph to his 1910 novel *Howard's End.*

†**Fin de siècle:** French for "end of the century."

‡**Swinburne:** The British poet Algernon Charles Swinburne (1834–1896).

§**No things but in ideas:** Hampl is alluding to another Modernist, the American poet William Carlos Williams (1883–1963) whose line "No ideas but in things" runs through his epic poem *Paterson.*

The grotesqueries of leftover cathedrals, the doughty stone enclaves of ancient universities, armless statues, and Della Robbia* wreaths — this isn't our kind of Disneyland either. There is no abstraction to it, no illusion of possibility. Especially, there is no freedom *from* it. It is beautiful, beautiful! But where is the trapdoor to the future? That is, to abstraction, to imagining oneself, rather than knowing oneself. For knowing oneself, we seem to know, implies acquiescence to limitations. We aren't ready, not quite, to give in to that — why should we? We're in charge, aren't we? "The only superpower left," we say, claiming our tough-guy trophy with meaty hands. The vanity of the imperial glitter rubs off on us, a gold dust all the world longs for and fears. We can't help preening: we've created ourselves. We're nobody's memory.

Strangely, after all this time of being a country — a "great" country — Americans still prefer the idea of the future to the idea of history. In a way, the idea of the future is our history, or at least a version of our cultural history. The filmy future is a can-do place, our natural habitat. But the past is distressingly complete, full of our absence. We seem to know if you take history too seriously, you'll never get out. In the place of national memory we have substituted the only other possible story form: the dream. And the essential thing required of the American Dream has always been that it remain a dream, vivid, tantalizing, barely beyond reach. Just the dreaming of it — which costs nothing, absolutely nothing except every cent of our imaginative attention — inflates the soul. Fills it, rather than fulfills it.

The specificity of memory, on the other hand, is humiliating: you can buck that motorcycle up and down those *rues,* those *strasses* and *borgos,* and still you're caught in your cul de sac, the stained glass Madonna gazing down from the shuddering window with maddening calm. We bolt from the iron apron strings of history. We wish to be free — whatever that means — and we know that memory, personal or civic, does not promote freedom. Memory tethers.

*   *   *

Della Robbia: Andrea della Robbia (1435–1525) and his uncle Luca della Robbia (ca. 1400–1482) were Italian sculptors.

But I am living — one week, maybe two, tourist time — in a niche of memory. Cultural, not personal, memory. It is Lent, and I am on retreat. This is my hermitage. It is a small trailer. Prefab, wood paneled, snug. A cell, as the monks still call their own hexagonal hermitages, which surround the chapel farther up the steep hill. The idea is not prison cell but honeybee cell. The hive busy with the *opus Dei,** the life of prayer.

I am following a way of life, balanced on a pattern of worship trailing back to Saint Benedict and his sixth century Rule for monasteries. And still farther back, into the Syrian desert where the solitary weirdos starved and prayed themselves out of history their own mystic way. Benedict's Rule drew all that eccentric urgency into the social embrace. Into history. He took the savage hermitage of the Levant,† and gentled it into the European monastery. He made a center out of the raw margin the early desert recluses clawed toward. The convent, after all, says frankly what it is: a convention, part of the social compact which claims order as a minion of tradition.

The monastic day here in California at the end of the twentieth century, like the monastic day at Monte Casino early in the sixth century, is poised on a formal cycle of prayers that revolves with the seasons. It is called the Office of Hours or the Divine Office. It divides (or connects) the day (and night) by a series of communal prayer liturgies. This day, like all days, is a memory of the day that preceded it. The day is a habit, the hours reinscribed as ritual. Memory, habit, ritual — those qualities which do not perhaps sustain *life* (which is elemental, fiercely chaotic), but *a life*. A way of life, specific, bound to time with the silken ties of — what else? — words. The West murmurs, trying to locate itself; the East breathes, trying to lose itself.

A simplistic distinction, not entirely accurate. After all, the heart of Western contemplative life is silence, and the East, in at least one central practice, chews the word, the mantra. Still, Christianity is undeniably a wordy religion. *Lectio divino,* sacred reading,

---

*opus Dei: Latin for "the work of God."

†Levant: Historical term used to describe the lands bordering the eastern Mediterranean Sea.

the ancient practice laid down by the early patristic writers, is still alive today; it is part of the daily routine here.

Augustine, whose *Confessions* I've brought along on this retreat, is the most passionate exemplar of this practice. He is not simply one of the West's greatest writers, but its greatest reader. The year is 397, and he is composing the West's first autobiography, creating the genre which lies at the core of Western consciousness, substituting in place of the ancient idea of *a story*, the modern literary idea of *a life*. The omniscient authority of the tale told around the campfire turns to ash in the burning voice of the first person singular.

Augustine is, appropriately, hot with his subject, inflamed with the account of his fascinatingly bad life turned mysteriously good. But he only gives this story the first nine of the thirteen books of his *Confessions*. Then, without explanation or apology, as if it were the most natural thing in the world, the work elides smoothly into an extended meditation on the Book of Genesis as if this, too, were "his life."

In fact, the movement from his life to his reading is not smooth — it is ablaze. The narrative becomes more, not less, urgent. *His* story, for Augustine, is only part of the story. There is a clear logic dictating the form of the *Confessions*, which unites the account of his life with his reading of Genesis, though this is not a logic we in the late twentieth century see as readily as Augustine's late-fourth-century readers would have.

Having constructed himself in the first nine books of the *Confessions*, Augustine rushes on to investigate how God created the universe — how God, that is, created him. And all of us, all of *this*. Reading, therefore, is concentrated life, not a pastiche of life or an alternative to life. The soul, pondering, *is* experience. *Lectio* is not "reading" as we might think of it. It is for Augustine, as it was for Ambrose his teacher, and for these California monks in their late-twentieth-century cells, an acute form of *listening*. The method is reading — words on paper. But the endeavor is undertaken as a relationship, one filled with the pathos of the West: the individual, alone in a room, puts finger to page, following the Word, and attempts to touch the elusive Lord last seen scurrying down the rabbit hole of creation. *In the beginning God created . . .*

The voice of God is speaking on that page. Augustine, grappling with Genesis in his study, is no less heated — much more so — than Augustine struggling famously with "the flesh." He invents autobiography not to reveal his memory of his life, but to plumb the memory of God's creative act.

"My mind burns to solve this complicated enigma," he says with an anguish more intense than anything that accompanies his revelations about his own life. He understands his life as a model of the very creation that is beyond him — and of course in him. He writes and writes, he reads and reads his way through this double conundrum, the mystery of his own biography and the mystery of creation.

He makes the central, paradoxical, discovery of autobiography: memory is not in the service of the past; it is the future which commands its presence. It is not a reminiscence, but a quest.

Yet how bizarre the truncated modern notion of "seeking a self" would seem to Augustine. Autobiography, for him, does not seek a self, not even for its own "salvation." For Augustine, the memory work of autobiography creates a self as the right instrument to seek meaning. That is, to seek God. For what purpose? For praise, of course. For if God, the source, the creator, is found, what else is there to do but praise?

Augustine takes this a step further. On the first page of the *Confessions* he poses a problem that has a familiar modern ring: "it would seem clear that no one can call upon Thee without knowing Thee." There is, in other words, the problem of God's notorious absence. Augustine takes the next step West; he seeks his faith *with* his doubt: "May it be that a man must implore Thee before he can know Thee?" The assumption here is that faith is not to be confused with certainty; the only thing people can really count on is longing and the occult directives of desire. So, Augustine wonders, does that mean prayer must come *before* faith? Illogical as it is, perhaps not-knowing is the first condition of prayer, rather than its negation. Can that be?

He finds his working answer in Scripture: *How shall they call on Him in Whom they have not believed? . . . they shall praise the Lord that seek Him.* Praise, he decides, antedates certainty. Or rather, certainty resides in longing, that core of self from which praise unfurls its song. This is the same core from which streams the narrative impulse of memory: the wonder of a life lived. In the face (or, rather, in the embrace) of creation, there is no way to escape the instinct to cry out.

This is where the Psalms come in. They are praise. More: they are relation, full of the intensity of intimacy, the rage, petulance, and exaltation, the sheer delight and exasperation of intimate encounter. This is the spectrum of all emotion, all life. The Psalmist reaches with his lyric claw to fetch it all in words.

Words, words, words. They circle and spin around Western spiritual practice. They abide. They even sustain a way of life — this monastic one — which has careened down the centuries, creating families (the Benedictines, the Franciscans, the Carmelites, and others) with lineages longer and more unbroken than those of any royal house in Europe. The pattern of prayer, handed down generation to generation, has sustained this extraordinary lifeline.

Words have proven to be more protean than blood.

The monastic life of the West cleaves to the Psalms, claiming the ancient Jewish poetry as its real heart, more central to its day than the New Testament or even the sacraments. The Psalms keep this life going — the verbal engine running into the deepest recess of Christian social life, and beyond that back into the source of silence, the desert of the early hermits.

The idea here in this American monastery, based on a tenth-century reformation of the earlier Benedictine model, is to wed both traditions — the social monastery and the solitary hermitage, desert and city, public and private. It is a way of life based on a historical pattern.

Therefore, this life might be understood as a living memory. It is also a life lived, literally, within poetry. And as it happens, the name of this hermitage is Logos. The Word. The word made home. A week in the word.

Against one wall, the bed. I make it quickly like a good novice first thing every morning, pulling the dorm-room spread square. Suitcase stowed beneath — I'm here long enough to want to obscure the truth: I'm a visitor, passing through. I've never liked being a traveler: I take up residence. "I'm going home," I say instinctively, returning to my hotel the first day in a foreign city. So, here: Logos is my house.

Also here, a round table (eat, read, write, prop elbows on, sling leg over occasionally). Shelves niched in next to the tiny open closet space where I've installed my books, what I could lug on the plane: short stories by Harold Brodkey, a writer whose fiction I've sought out solely because of his searing AIDS memoir, drawn to the art by the life. Also a new novel by someone someone else said was good (not opened), poems I already love, one new book by Mark Doty, Augustine with his bookmark, Dawson's *Religion and the Rise of Western Culture*, plus a dictionary that didn't have the only word I've looked up so far, and Thich Nhat Hanh with yet another volume attempting to calm us Westerners down, out of ourselves: breathe, feel, exhale — there. And like everybody on a desert island, the Bible (the New Jerusalem version).

A rudimentary kitchen runs along another wall; bathroom beyond that, the only other room. And two windows, one to nowhere, hugged by two crowded eucalyptus trees and the vinca-covered curve of the steep eroded dirt road I alone seem to climb to the chapel. The other window, the window that counts, gives onto — paradise. The Western rind of America peels off far below into the extravagant white curl of Big Sur. Where the slant of the Santa Lucia range, where we are perched, cuts off the view of the coastline, the Pacific, blue as steel (it is overcast) or ultramarine (on sunny days), appears to be cantilevered below us, a blue platform leading to the end of the world. Sometimes, roughed up by wind and whitecaps, the ocean loses this quality of being architecture; it becomes expensive fabric, shimmering silver. Then, simply, what it is: the vast pool, brimming to the horizon.

This is where I have come. There was no crisis. No, at the moment, heartache or career impasse. No dark night except the usual ones. Doesn't everyone wake up maybe two nights a week, mind gunning, palms sweating? In the eyes-open misery of night, sensation gets mashed to a paste of meaninglessness — life's or one's own. No anguish beyond that to report. Every so often I just do this: go on retreat.

It is not uncommon in this supposedly secular age. Meditation, massage, monasteries, and spas — the postmodern stomach, if not its soul, knows it needs purging. Such places are even popular, booked months in advance. Down the coast the Buddhists are meditating, eating very intelligently. Esalen is nearby, too, and the place where Henry Miller discovered the hot tub. I could go to the

Buddhists, cleanse in the silence, approach the big Empty which is the great source: I believe that.

But I come here, and follow the Christian monastic day laid out like a garden plot by Benedict at the close of the Roman era. I am Western; I like my silence sung.

In any case, the day itself is silent. The only words are the chanted ones in the chapel, unless I call home. My thin voice sounds odd, insubstantial. My husband carefully recites all the messages from my office answering machine. I ask if he's OK. He is. You OK? I tell him I am. I love you. Me too — I love *you*. Touching base. The telephone receiver clicks back into its cradle, and the mirage of news and endearments melts. It doesn't disappear exactly — I leave the telephone room, a little booth by the monastery bookstore, smiling, his voice still in my ear. It's just that conversation has become a bare tissue of meaning, a funny human foible, but not something to take seriously for once. The midday bell is ringing, and there is something I'm trying to remember.

That's wrong. I am not trying "to remember" something. I want to get this right, this odd experience of praying all day. More like this: I am being remembered. Being remembered into a memory — beyond historic to the inchoate, still intense trace of feeling that first laid down this pattern. It is a memory which puts all personal memory in the shade, and with it, all other language. In my experience, it is unique, this sensation of being drawn out of language by language which the Divine Office occasions. Praying, chanting the Psalms, draws me out of whatever I might be thinking or remembering (for so much thinking *is* remembering, revisiting, rehearsing). I am launched by the Psalms into a memory to which I belong but which is not mine. I don't possess it; it possesses me. Possession understood not as ownership, but as embrace. The embrace of habitation. Hermitage of the word.

In recent years, I have gone on several Vipassana Buddhist retreats, also silent, where the practice has been sitting and walking meditation. I will do that again because it was what it promised: cleansing, insightful. It felt like the rarest air it is possible to breathe. And its substance was exactly that: breath and its entrance, its exit. Though it was difficult, it was gentle. More: it was a relief. Perhaps especially so for a contemporary Western mind, wracked with busyness. It was not a hive, the cells humming.

But here in this Benedictine monastery, even though the day is silent (conversation has been abducted somewhere), the hours murmur. The first morning bell rings at 5:30. I walk up to the chapel in the dead-night dark for Vigils, the first round of daily prayers. The chapel is stark, perhaps to some eyes severe. Not to me: the calm of the place is an invitation. I bow, as each of the monks does when he enters, toward the dark sanctuary. A candle burns there. The honey-colored chairs and benches, ranked on two sides, face each other. They form two barely curved lines, two choirs deftly passing the ball of chant back and forth across the arched room as, somewhere beyond us, the sun rises and the world begins to exist again.

It is important that this not sound ecstatic. I must leach the exaltation out of the description. Here is what happens in the chapel: old news is revisited, peeves and praise ritualized (the Psalms don't just exalt; they grunt and groan). The call to the elusive One, polished with plainchant, is handed back and forth across the ranks of the honey-colored chairs like an imaginary globe of blown glass passed by men wearing cream-colored habits over their jeans and work shirts, scuffed Reeboks visible below their chapel-robe hems. It sometimes seems improbable, ridiculous.

And my mind wanders. There are the monks, looking very much alike in their cream-colored robes, and yet I manage to wonder — is that one gay? The one with the clipped accent — from Boston maybe? The one on the left looks like a banker, could have been a CEO, why not? The guy over here looks like a truck driver. On and on it goes, my skittery mind. Meanwhile, the Psalms keep rolling. A line snags — *More than the watchman for daybreak, my whole being hopes in the Lord* — and I am pulled along.

It can also be boring. What happens in the chapel partakes of tedium. It must. The patterns repeat and return. Every four weeks the entire Book of Psalms, all 150 poems, is chanted. And then begun again, and again, and again. *Sing to the Lord a new song,* we have been saying since David was king. This new song rolls from the rise of monotheism, unbroken, across the first millennium, through the second, soon to enter the third, the lapidary waves of chant polishing the shore of history. There are men here — there are men and women in monasteries all over the world — repeating this pattern faithfully in antiphonal choirs, softly lobbing this same language back and forth to each other. What *is* this invisible globe they are passing across the space?

Worship, of course. But what is worship? It is the practice of the fiercest possible attention. And here, at the end of the millennium, the ancient globe of polished words, rubbed by a million anxious hands down the centuries, is also the filmy glass of memory. We touch it. But this is memory understood not as individual story, not as private fragment clutched to the heart, trusted only to the secret page. Even in the midst of high emotion, the rants and effusions that characterize the psalmist's wild compass, there is a curious nonpsychological quality to the voice. This is the voice of the intense anonymous self. It has no mother, no father. Or it borrows, finally, the human family as its one true relation. This is the memory of the world's longing. Desire so elemental that its shape can only be glimpsed in the incorruptible storehouse of poetic image —*he sends ice crystals like bread crumbs, and who can withstand that cold? Our days pass by like grass, our prime like a flower in bloom. A wind comes, the power goes . . .*

Paging through a picture book of Christian and Buddhist monasteries in the bookstore, stopped by this cutline accompanying a photograph of a beautiful Buddhist monastery, a remark by a dogen: "The only truth is we are here now." The humility of living in the present moment. The physical beauty of the place is eloquent, revealing the formal attentiveness of a supreme aesthetic: mindfulness. The human at its best. And the food is famous there. They are living their profound injunction, honoring the fleet moment, and the smallest life: Buddhist retreatants are asked not to kill the black flies that torment them. Here, when I told the monk at the bookstore that ants were streaming all over the kitchen counter of Logos, he handed me an aerosol canister, and I was glad. I sprayed, mopped, discarded the little poppy seeds of ant carcasses. I sat back satisfied, turning again to Augustine and the mind of the West, figuring, figuring. The sweetish spume of bug spray hung in the air for a day.

Lord, do we need the East. The bug spray has to stop, we know that. Contemplative nuns have told me that without the introduction of Buddhist meditation practice, they wouldn't be in the monastery anymore. "It's thanks to Buddhism that I'm a Catholic," one of them said. I have never been to an American Christian monastery that did not have Buddhist meditation mats and pillows somewhere in the chapel. The gentle missionary work of the East, its light, blessedly unecclesiastical heart, the absence of cultural imperialism, the poetry of its gestures: the bell is never "struck," never "hit." In the Buddhist monastery, it is invited to sound.

But still this handing down of words, still this Western practice I cannot abandon, would not wish myself out of. *The only truth is we are here now.* I don't believe we are *only* here. How could I, transfixed by memory as I am, believing in the surge of these particular words down the channel of the centuries? We are here — for now. My conception of this is not of a heaven (and hell) in the future, but rather of an understanding of existence which encompasses history as well as being.

I will ponder the story of your wonders. Imagine living one's life entirely around, within, through, over and under the chanting of poetry. Maybe it is another way, the West's way, of saying *we are here now.* Out of this recitation of the ancient words to reach the stillness of the present moment. The Psalms are an intricate web of human experience, reminding us that we live in history, and that history is the story of longing. Its pulse races.

We enter the dark sanctuary, bow to the flame, assemble in the honey-colored chairs again, two halves of the human choir. Some mornings at Vigils, before first light, it feels strangely as if our little band — fifteen monks, a handful of retreatants — are legion. The two facing choir lines curve slightly, two horizon lines, an embryonic globe forming anew.

We are greeting first light, we are entering dark night. It is all very old, a memory of a memory. And it is new as only the day can be new, over and over. The day is a paradox, and we enter it possessed by time's tricksy spirit, history and the present instant sublimely transposed.

We are here now, the East is chanting from its side of the monastery.

Oh yes, the West chants in response, the antiphon rising as it has all these short centuries, out of the endless memory we inhabit together, *Sing a new song, sing a new song to the Lord.*

Reflections and Responses

1. The author makes several references to literary and philosophical figures. How do these references indicate the level of audience she imagines for her writing? How do the references support her theme as suggested by the essay's title?

2. Consider Hampl's verbal style. How does she blend high-level diction with current slang or idiom? Provide a few examples of this technique. What is the effect of this mixture?

3. How does the idea of memory surface throughout the essay? In what sense does it "glue" together the various sections? Hampl's idea of what memory truly is and how it works is complex; try defining in your own words her concept of memory. Consider also how her idea of memory is related to language. Why, for example, does she title her essay "A Week *in* the Word" instead of "A Week *with* the Word"?

EDWARD HOAGLAND

Heaven and Nature

Speculation, says Edward Hoagland at the conclusion of this intensely reflective essay, is "a high-risk activity." Since speculation is at the heart of the genre, he might have added that to write essays is essentially to take risks. Intellectual, emotional, and literary security are not attractive goals for personal essayists like Hoagland, whose work often explores the outer edges of personality and social behavior. In "Heaven and Nature," he penetrates territory that most people would prefer to skirt around: the inclination to commit suicide. As usual, his approach is deeply personal and yet remarkably inclusive.

Hoagland, whom John Updike has called "the best essayist" of his generation, is the author of five books of fiction, two travel books, and seven essay collections, including The Courage of Turtles *(1971),* Walking the Dead Diamond River *(1973),* Red Wolves and Black Bears *(1976), and* The Tugman's Passage *(1982). In 1988, he published* Heart's Desire, *a collection of what he considered his best essays from twenty years of writing. Another collection of essays,* Balancing Acts, *appeared in 1992 and was followed by* Tigers and Ice *(1999). He is the general editor of the Penguin Nature Library and is a member of the American Academy of Arts and Letters. "Heaven and Nature" originally appeared in* Harper's Magazine *(1988) and was selected by Geoffrey Wolff for* The Best American Essays *1989.*

A friend of mine, a peaceable soul who has been riding the New York subways for thirty years, finds himself stepping back from the tracks once in a while and closing his eyes as the train rolls in. This, he says, is not only to suppress an urge to throw himself in front of it but because every couple of weeks an impulse rises in him to push a stranger onto the tracks, any stranger, thus ending his own life too. He blames this partly on apartment living, "pigeonholes without being able to fly."

It is profoundly startling not to trust oneself after decades of doing so. I don't dare keep ammunition in my country house for a small rifle I bought secondhand two decades ago. The gun had sat in a cupboard in the back room with the original box of .22 bullets under the muzzle all that time, seldom fired except at a few apples hanging in a tree every fall to remind me of my army training near the era of the Korean War, when I'd been considered quite a marksman. When I bought the gun I didn't trust either my professional competence as a writer or my competence as a father as much as I came to, but certainly believed I could keep myself alive. I bought it for protection, and the idea that someday I might be afraid of shooting myself with the gun would have seemed inconceivable — laughable.

One's fifties can be giddy years, as anybody fifty knows. Chest pains, back pains, cancer scares, menopausal or prostate complications are not the least of it, and the fidelities of a lifetime, both personal and professional, may be called into question. Was it a mistake to have stuck so long with one's marriage, and to have stayed with a lackluster well-paying job? (Or *not* to have stayed and stuck?) People not only lose faith in their talents and their dreams or values; some simply tire of them. Grow tired, too, of the smell of fried-chicken grease, once such a delight, and the cold glutinosity of ice cream, the boredom of beer, the stop-go of travel, the hiccups of laughter, and of two rush hours a day, then the languor of weekends, of athletes as well as accountants, and even the frantic birdsong of spring — red-eyed vireos that have been clocked singing twenty-two thousand times in a day. Life is a matter of cultivating the six senses, and an equilibrium with nature and what I think of as its subdivision, human nature, trusting no one completely but almost everyone at least a little; but this is easier said than done.

More than thirty thousand Americans took their own lives last year, men mostly, with the highest rate being among those older than sixty-five. When I asked a friend why three times as many men kill themselves as members of her own sex, she replied with sudden anger, "I'm not going to go into the self-indulgence of men." They won't bend to failure, she said, and want to make themselves memorable. Suicide is an exasperating act as often as it is pitiable. "Committing" suicide is in bad odor in our culture even among those who don't believe that to cash in your chips ahead of time and hand back to God his gifts to you is a blasphemous sin. We the living, in any case, are likely to feel accused by this person who "voted with his feet." It appears to cast a subversive judgment upon the social polity as a whole that what was supposed to work in life — religion, family, friendship, commerce, and industry — did not, and furthermore it frightens the horses in the street, as Shaw's friend Mrs. Patrick Campbell once defined wrongful behavior.

Many suicides inflict outrageous trauma, burning permanent injuries in the minds of their children, though they may have joked beforehand only of "taking a dive." And sometimes the gesture has a peevish or cowardly aspect, or seems to have been senselessly shortsighted as far as an outside observer can tell. There are desperate suicides and crafty suicides, people who do it to cause others trouble and people who do it to save others trouble, deranged exhibitionists who yell from a building ledge and close-mouthed, secretive souls who swim out into the ocean's anonymity. Suicide may in fact be an attempt to escape death, shortcut the dreadful deteriorating processes, abort one's natural trajectory, elude "the ruffian on the stairs," in A. E. Housman's phrase for a cruelly painful, anarchic death — make it neat and not messy. The deed can be grandiose or self-abnegating, vindictive or drably mousy, rationally plotted or plainly insane. People sidle toward death, intent upon outwitting their own bodies' defenses, or they may dramatize the chance to make one last, unambiguous, irrevocable decision, like a captain scuttling his ship — death before dishonor — leaping toward oblivion through a curtain of pain, like a frog going down the throat of a snake. One man I knew hosted a quietly affectionate evening with several unknowing friends on the night before he swallowed too many pills. Another waved an apologetic goodbye to a bystander on a bridge. Seldom shy ordinarily, and rarely considerate, he turned shy and apologetic in the last moment of life. Never physically inclined, he made a great vault toward the ice on the Mississippi.

In the army, we wore dog tags with a notch at one end by which these numbered pieces of metal could be jammed between our teeth, if we lay dead and nameless on a battlefield, for later sorting. As "servicemen" our job would be to kill people who were pointed out to us as enemies, or make "the supreme sacrifice" for a higher good than enjoying the rest of our lives. Life was very much a possession, in other words — not only God's, but the soldier's own to dispose of. Working in an army hospital, I frequently did handle dead bodies, but this never made me feel I would refuse to kill another man whose uniform was pointed out to me as being inimical, or value my life more tremulously and vigilantly. The notion of dying for my country never appealed to me as much as dying freelance for my ideas (in the unlikely event that I *could* do that), but I was ready. People were taught during the 1940s and 1950s that one should be ready to die for one's beliefs. Heroes were revered because they had deliberately chosen to give up their lives. Life would not be worth living under the tyranny of an invader and Nathan Hale apparently hadn't paused to wonder whether God might not have other uses for him besides being hung. Nor did the pilot Colin Kelly hesitate before plunging his plane into a Japanese battleship, becoming America's first well-publicized hero in World War II.

I've sometimes wondered why people who know that they are terminally ill, or who are headed for suicide, so very seldom have paused to take a bad guy along with them. It is lawless to consider an act of assassination, yet hardly more so, really, than suicide is regarded in some quarters (or death itself, in others). Government bureaucracies, including our own, in their majesty and as the executors of laws, regularly weigh the pros and cons of murdering foreign antagonists. Of course the answer is that most individuals are fortunately more timid as well as humbler in their judgment than government officialdom, but beyond that, when dying or suicidal, they no longer care enough to devote their final energies to doing good works of any kind — Hitler himself in their gunsights they would have passed up. Some suicides become so crushed and despairing that they can't recognize the consequences of anything they do, and it's not primarily vindictiveness that wreaks such havoc upon their survivors but their derangement from ordinary life.

Courting the idea is different from the real impulse. "When he begged for help, we took him and locked him up," another friend of mine says, speaking of her husband. "Not till then. Wishing to be out of the situation you are in — feeling helpless and unable to cope — is not the same as wishing to be dead. If I actually wished to be dead, even my children's welfare would have no meaning."

You might think the ready option of divorce available lately would have cut suicide rates, offering an escape to battered wives, lovelorn husbands, and other people in despair. But it doesn't work that way. When the number of choices people have increases, an entire range of possibilities opens up. Suicide among teenagers has almost quadrupled since 1950, although the standard of comfort that their families enjoy is up. Black Americans, less affluent than white Americans, have had less of a rise in suicides, and the rate among them remains about half of that for whites.

Still, if a fiftyish fellow with fine teeth and a foolproof pension plan, a cottage at the beach and the Fourth of July weekend coming up, kills himself, it seems truculent. We would look at him bafflingly if he told us he no longer likes the Sturm und Drang of banging fireworks.

Then stay at your hideaway! we'd argue with him.

"Big mouths eat little mouths. Nature isn't 'timeless.' Whole lives are squeezed into three months or three days."

What about your marriage?

"She's become more mannish than me. I loved women. I don't believe in marriage between men."

Remarry, then!

"I've gone impotent, and besides, when I see somebody young and pretty I guess I feel like dandling her on my knee."

Marriage is friendship. You can find someone your own age.

"I'm tired of it."

But how about your company?—a widows-and-orphans stock that's on the cutting edge of the silicon frontier? That's interesting.

"I know what wins. It's less and less appetizing."

You're not scared of death anymore?

"It interests me less than it did."

What are you so sick of? The rest of us keep going.

"I'm tired of weathermen and sportscasters on the screen. Of being patient and also of impatience. I'm tired of the president, whoever the president happens to be, and sleeping badly, with forty-eight half-hours in the day — of breaking two eggs every morning and putting sugar on something. I'm tired of the drone of my own voice, but also of us jabbering like parrots at each other — of all our stumpy ways of doing everything."

You're bored with yourself?

"That's an understatement. I'm maybe the least interesting person I know."

But to kill *yourself?*

"You know, it's a tradition, too," he remarks quietly, not making so bold as to suggest that the tradition is an honorable one, though his tone of voice might be imagined to imply this. "I guess I've always been a latent maverick."

Except in circumstances which are themselves a matter of life and death, I'm reluctant to agree with the idea that suicide is not the result of mental illness. No matter how reasonably the person appears to have examined his options, it goes against the grain of nature for him to destroy himself. And any illness that threatens his life changes a person. Suicidal thinking, if serious, can be a kind of death scare, comparable to suffering a heart attack or undergoing a cancer operation. One survives such a phase both warier and chastened. When — two years ago — I emerged from a bad dip into suicidal speculation, I felt utterly exhausted and yet quite fearless of ordinary dangers, vastly afraid of myself but much less scared of extraneous eventualities. The fact of death may not be tragic; many people die with a bit of a smile that captures their mouths at the last instant, and most people who are revived after a deadly accident are reluctant to be brought to life, resisting resuscitation, and carrying back confusing, beamish, or ecstatic memories. But the same impetuosity that made him throw himself out of the window might have enabled the person to love life all the more if he'd been calibrated somewhat differently at the time of the emergency. Death's edge is so abrupt and near that many people who expect a short and momentary dive may be astounded to find that it is bottomless and change their minds and start to scream when they are only halfway down.

Although my fright at my mind's anarchy superseded my fear of death in the conventional guise of automobile or airplane crashes, heart seizures, and so on, nightmares are more primitive and in my dreams I continued to be scared of a death not sought after — dying from driving too fast and losing control of the car, breaking through thin ice while skating and drowning in the cold, or falling off a cliff. When I am tense and sleeping raggedly, my worst nightmare isn't drawn from anxious prep school memories or my stint in the army or the bad spells of my marriages or any other of adulthood's vicissitudes. Nothing else from the past half century has the staying power in my mind of the elevated-train rides that my father and I used to take down Third Avenue to the Battery in New York City on Sunday afternoon when I was three or four or five so I could see the fish at the aquarium. We were probably pretty good companions in those years, but the wooden platforms forty feet up shook terribly as trains from both directions pulled in and out. To me they seemed worse than rickety — ready to topple. And the roar was fearful, and the railings left large gaps for a child to fall through, after the steep climb up the slat-sided, windy, shaking stairway from street level. It's a rare dream, but several times a year I still find myself on such a perch, without his company or anybody else's, on a boyish or a grown-up's mission, when the elevated platform begins to rattle desperately, seesaw, heel over, and finally come apart, disintegrate, while I cling to struts and trusses.

My father, as he lay dying at home of bowel cancer, used to enjoy watching Tarzan reruns on the children's hour of television. Like a strong green vine, they swung him far away from his deathbed to a world of skinny-dipping and friendly animals and scenic beauty linked to the lost realities of his adolescence in Kansas City. Earlier, when he had still been able to walk without much pain, he'd paced the house for several hours at night, contemplating suicide, I expect, along with other anguishing thoughts, regrets, remembrances, and yearnings, while the rest of us slept. But he decided to lie down and die the slower way. I don't know how much of that decision was for the sake of his wife and children, how much was because he didn't want to be a "quitter," as he sometimes put it, and how much was due to his believing that life belongs to God (which I'm not even sure he did). He was not a churchgoer after his thirties. He had belonged to J. P. Morgan's church, St. George's, on Stuyvesant Square — Morgan was a hero of his — but when things went a little wrong for him at the Wall Street law firm he worked for and he changed jobs and moved out to the suburbs, he became a skeptic on religious matters, and gradually, in the absence of faith of that previous kind, he adhered to a determined allegiance to the social order. Wendell Willkie or Dwight D. Eisenhower instead of J. P. Morgan became the sort of hero he admired, and suicide would have seemed an act of insurrection against the laws and conventions of the society, internationalist-Republican, that he believed in.

I was never particularly afraid that I might plan a suicide, swallowing a bunch of pills and keeping them down — only of what I think of as being Anna Karenina's kind of death. This most plausible self-killing in all of literature is frightening because it was unwilled, regretted at midpoint, and came as a complete surprise to Anna herself. After rushing impulsively, in great misery, to the Moscow railway station to catch a train, she ended up underneath another one, dismayed, astonished, and trying to climb out from under the wheels even as they crushed her. Many people who briefly verge on suicide undergo a mental somersault for a terrifying interval during which they're upside down, their perspective topsy-turvy, skidding, churning; and this is why I got rid of the bullets for my .22.

Nobody expects to trust his body overmuch after the age of fifty. Incipient cataracts or arthritis, outlandish snores, tooth-grinding, ankles that threaten to turn, are part of the game. But not to trust one's *mind*? That's a surprise. The single attribute that older people were sure to have (we thought as boys) was a stodgy dependability, a steady temperance or caution. Adults might be vain, unimaginative, pompous, and callous, but they did have their affairs tightly in hand. It was not till my thirties that I began to know friends who were in their fifties on equal terms, and I remember being amused, piqued, irritated, and slightly bewildered to learn that some of them still felt as marginal or rebellious or in a quandary about what to do with themselves for the next dozen years as my contemporaries were likely to. That close to retirement, some of them harbored a deep-seated contempt for the organizations they had been working for, ready to walk away from almost everybody they had known and the efforts and expertise of whole decades with very little sentiment. Nor did twenty years of marriage necessarily mean more than two or three — they might be just as ready to walk away from that also, and didn't really register it as twenty years at all. Rather, life could be about to begin all over again. "Bummish" was how one man described himself, with a raffish smile — "Lucky to have a roof over my head" — though he'd just put a child through Yale. He was quitting his job and claimed with exasperation that his wife still cried for her mother in her sleep, as if they'd never been married.

The great English traveler Richard Burton quoted an Arab proverb that speaks for many middle-aged men of the old-fashioned variety: "Conceal thy Tenets, thy Treasure, and thy Traveling." These are serious matters, in other words. People didn't conceal their tenets in order to betray them, but to fight for them more opportunely. And except for kings and princelings, concealing whatever treasure one had went almost without saying. As for travel, a man's travels were also a matter of gravity. Travel was knowledge, ambiguity, dalliances or misalliances, divided loyalty, forbidden thinking; and besides, someday he might need to make a run for it and go to ground someplace where he had made some secret friends. Friends of mine whose husbands or whose wives have died have been quite startled afterward to discover caches of money or traveler's checks concealed around the house, or a bundle of cash in a safe deposit box.

Burton, like any other desert adage-spinner and most individuals over fifty, would have agreed to an addition so obvious that it wasn't included to begin with: "Conceal thy Illnesses." I can remember how urgently my father worried that word would get out, after a preliminary operation for his cancer. He didn't want to be written off, counted out of the running at the corporation he worked for and in other enclaves of competition. Men often compete with one another until the day they die; comradeship consists of rubbing shoulders jocularly with a competitor. As breadwinners, they must be considered fit and sound by friend as well as foe, and so there's lots of truth to the most common answer I heard when asking why three times as many men as women kill themselves: "They keep their troubles to themselves"; "They don't know how to ask for help." Men greet each other with a sock on the arm, women with a hug, and the hug wears better in the long run.

I'm not entirely like that, and I discovered that when I confided something of my perturbation to a woman friend she was likely to keep telephoning me or mailing cheery postcards, whereas a man would usually listen with concern, communicate his sympathy, and maybe intimate that he had pondered the same drastic course of action himself a few years back and would end up respecting my decision either way. Open-mindedness seems an important attribute to a good many men, who pride themselves on being objective, hearing all sides of an issue, on knowing that truth and honesty do not always coincide with social dicta, and who may even cherish a subterranean outlaw streak that, like being ready to violently defend one's family, reputation, and country, is by tradition male.

Men, being so much freer than women in society, used to feel they had less of a stake in the maintenance of certain churchly conventions and enjoyed speaking irreverently about various social truisms, including even the principle that people ought to die on schedule, not cutting in ahead on their assigned place in line. Contemporary women, after their triumphant irreverence during the 1960s and 1970s, cannot be generalized about so easily, however. They turn as skeptical and saturnine as any man. In fact, women attempt suicide more frequently, but favor pills or other methods, whereas two-thirds of the men who kill themselves have used a gun. In 1985, 85 percent of suicides by means of firearms were done by men. An overdose of medication hasn't the same finality. It may be reversible if the person is discovered quickly, or be subject to benign miscalculation to start with. Even if it works, perhaps it can be fudged by a kindly doctor in the record-keeping. Like an enigmatic drowning or a single-car accident that baffles the suspicions of the insurance company, a suicide by drugs can be a way to avoid making a loud statement, and merely illustrate the final modesty of a person who didn't wish to ask for too much of the world's attention.

Unconsummated attempts at suicide can strike the rest of us as self-pitying and self-aggrandizing, or plaintive plea-bargaining — "childish," we say, though actually the suicide of children is ghastly beyond any stunt of self-mutilation an adult may indulge in because of the helplessness that echoes through the act. It would be hard to define chaos better than as a world where children decide that they don't want to live.

Love is the solution to all dilemmas, we sometimes hear, and in those moments when the spirit bathes itself in beneficence and manages to transcend the static of personalities rubbing fur off of each other, indeed it is. Without love nothing matters, Paul told the Corinthians, a mystery which, if true, has no ready Darwinian explanation. Love without a significant sexual component and for people who are unrelated to us serves little practical purpose. It doesn't help us feed our families, win struggles, thrive and prosper. It distracts us from the ordinary business of sizing people up and making a living, and is not even conducive to intellectual observation, because instead of seeing them, we see right through them to the bewildered child and dreaming adolescent who inhabited their bodies earlier, the now-tired idealist who fell in love and out of love, got hired and quit, hired and fired, bought cars and wore them out, liked black-eyed Susans, blueberry muffins, and roosters crowing — liked roosters crowing better than skyscrapers but now likes skyscrapers better than roosters crowing. As swift as thought, we select the details that we need to see in order to be able to love them.

Yet at other times we'll dispense with these same poignancies and choose only their grunginess to look at, their pinched mouths and shifty eyes, their thirst for gin at noon and indifference to their kids, their greed for the best tidbit on the buffet table and penchant for poking their penises up the excretory end of other human beings. I tend to gaze quite closely at the faces of priests I meet on the street to see if a lifetime of love has marked them noticeably. Real serenity or asceticism I no longer expect, and I take for granted the beefy calm that frequently goes with Catholic celibacy, but I am watching for the marks of love and often see mere resignation or tenacity.

Many men are romantics, likely to plunge, go for broke, take action in a spirit of exigency rather than waiting for the problem to resolve itself. Then, on the contrary, still as romantics, they may drift into despairing passivity, stare at the TV all day long, and binge with a bottle. Women too may turn frenetic for a while and then throw up their hands; but though they may not seem as grandiosely fanciful and romantic at the outset, they are more often believers — at least I think they tend to believe in God or in humanity, the future, and so on. We have above us the inviting eternity of "the heavens," if we choose to look at it, lying on our backs in the summer grass under starlight, some of which had left its source before mankind became man. But because we live in our heads more than in nature nowadays, even the summer sky is a mine field for people whose memories are mined. With the sky no longer humbling, the sunshine only a sort of convenience, and no godhead located anywhere outside our own heads, every problem may seem insolubly interlocked. When the telephone has become impossible to answer at home, sometimes it finally becomes impossible to stride down the gangplank of a cruise ship in Mombasa too, although no telephones will ring for you there.

But if escapist travel is ruled out in certain emergencies, surely you can *pray*? Pray, yes; but to whom? That requires a bit of preparation. Rarely do people obtain much relief from praying if they haven't stood in line awhile to get a visa. It's an appealing idea that you can just *go*, and in a previous era perhaps you could have, like on an old-fashioned shooting safari. But it's not so simple now. What do you believe in? Whom are you praying to? What are you praying for? There's no crèche on the courthouse lawn; you're not supposed to adhere exactly even to what your parents had believed. Like psychotherapy, praying takes time, even if you know which direction to face when you kneel.

Love is powerfully helpful when the roof falls in — loving other people with a high and hopeful heart and as a kind of prayer. Yet that feat too requires new and sudden insights or long practice. The beatitude of loving strangers as well as friends — loving them on sight with a leap of empathy and intuition — is a form of inspiration, edging, of course, in some cases toward madness, as other states of beatitude can do. But there's no question that a genuine love for the living will stymie suicidal depressions not chemical in origin. Love is an elixir, changing the life of the lover like no other. And many of us have experienced this — a temporary lightening of our leery, prickly disapproval of much of the rest of the world when at a wedding or a funeral of shared emotion, or when we have fallen in love.

Yet the zest for life of those unusual men and women who make a great zealous success of living is due more often in good part to the craftiness and pertinacity with which they manage to overlook the misery of others. You can watch them watch life beat the stuffing out of the faces of their friends and acquaintances, yet they themselves seem to outwit the dense delays of social custom, the tedious tick-tock of bureaucratic obfuscation, accepting loss and age and change and disappointment without suffering punctures in their stomach lining. Breathlessness or strange dull pains from their nether organs don't nonplus them. They fret and doubt in moderation, and love a lobster roast, squeeze lemon juice on living clams on the half shell to prove that the clams are alive, laugh

as robins tussle a worm out of the ground or a kitten flees a dog.
Like the problem drinkers, pork eaters, and chain smokers who
nevertheless finish out their allotted years, succumbing to a stroke
at a nice round biblical age when the best vitamin-eating vegetarian has long since died, their faces become veritable walnuts of
fine character, with the same smile lines as the rarer individual
whose grin has been affectionate all of his life.

We spend our lives getting to know ourselves, yet wonders never
cease. During my adolescent years my states of mind, though un-
dulant, seemed seamless; even when I was unhappy no cracks or
fissures made me wonder if I was a danger to myself. My confidence was such that I treaded the slippery lips of waterfalls, fought
forest fires, drove ancient cars cross-country night and day, and
scratched the necks of menagerie leopards in the course of various adventures which enhanced the joy of being alive. The chemistry of the mind, because unfathomable, is more frightening.
In the city, I live on the waterfront and occasionally will notice an
agitated-looking figure picking his way along the pilings and string-
pieces of the timbered piers nearby, staring at the sliding whorls
on the surface of the Hudson as if teetering over an abyss. Our
building, across the street, seems imposing from the water and
over the years has acted as a magnet for a number of suicides —
people who have dreaded the clammy chill, the onerous smother-
ing essential to their first plan. One woman climbed out after
jumping in and took the elevator to the roof (my neighbors remember how wringing wet she was) and leapt off, banging window
ledges on the way down, and hit with the whap of a sack of potatoes, as others have.

Yet what is more remarkable than that a tiny minority of souls
reach a point where they entrust their bodies to the force of gravity is that so few of the rest of us splurge an hour of a summer day
gazing at the trees and sky. How many summers do we *have?* One
sees prosperous families in the city who keep plants in their apartment windows that have grown so high they block the sunlight and
appear to be doing the living for the tenants who are bolted inside.
But beauty is nobody's sure salvation: not the beauty of a swimming hole if you get a cramp, and not the beauty of a woman if she
doesn't care for you. The swimming hole looks inviting under the
blue sky, with its amber bottom, green sedges sticking up in the

shallows, and curls of gentle current over a waterlogged basswood tree two feet beneath the surface near the brook that feeds it. Come back at dusk, however, and the pond turns black — as dark as death, or on the contrary, a restful dark, a dark to savor. Take it as you will.

People with sunny natures do seem to live longer than people who are nervous wrecks; yet mankind didn't evolve out of the animal kingdom by being unduly sunny-minded. Life was fearful and phantasmagoric, supernatural and preternatural, as well as encompassing the kind of clockwork regularity of our well-governed day. It had numerous superstitious (from the Latin, "standing over") elements, such as we are likely to catch a whiff of only when we're peering at a dead body. And it was not just our optimism but our pessimistic premonitions, our dark moments as a species, our irrational, frightful speculations, our strange mutations upon the simple theme of love, and our sleepless, obsessive inventiveness — our dread as well as our faith — that made us human beings. Staking one's life on the more general good came to include risking suicide also. Brilliant, fecund people sometimes kill themselves.

"Joy to the world . . . Let heaven and nature sing, and heaven and nature sing. . . Repeat the sounding joy . . ." The famous Christmas carol invokes not only glee but unity: heaven with nature, not always a Christian combination. It's a rapturous hymn, and no one should refuse to surrender to such a pitch of revelation when it comes. But the flip side of rapture can be a riptide of panic, of hysterical gloom. Our faces are not molded as if joy were a preponderant experience. (Nor is a caribou's or a thrush's.) Our faces in repose look stoic or battered, and people of the sunniest temperament sometimes die utterly unstrung, doubting everything they have ever believed in or have done.

Let heaven and nature sing! the hymn proclaims. But *is* there such harmony? Are God and Mother Nature really the same? Are they even compatible? And will we risk burning our wings if we mount high enough to try to see? I've noticed that woods soil in Italy smells the same as woods soil in New England when you pick up a handful of it and enjoy its aromas — but is God there the same? It can be precarious to wonder. I don't rule out suicide as being unthinkable for people who have tried to live full lives, and don't regard it as negating the work and faith and satisfaction and fun and even ecstasy they may have known before. In killing himself a person acknowledges his failures during a time span when perhaps heaven and earth had caught him like a pair of scissors — but not his life span. Man is different from animals in that he speculates, a high-risk activity.

Reflections and Responses

1. Hoagland's position on suicide is noticeably complex. Where do you think he ultimately stands on the issue? Do you think he would say, for example, that individuals have the moral right to take their own lives if they believe it is necessary to do so? Can you identify an instance in the essay in which you can pin down Hoagland's position? If not, why not?

2. Why do you think Hoagland devotes so much attention to the differences between men and women when it comes to suicide? Do you think those differences are significant? Would you say they are natural or cultural?

3. What do you make of the dialogue Hoagland reports on pages 183–184? Do you think it is a transcription of an actual dialogue? If so, who is the person being interviewed? If not, what is Hoagland's purpose in creating it?

ANN HODGMAN

No Wonder They Call Me a Bitch

Whether gently funny or savagely comic, the humorous essay has one of the longest traditions in the history of the essay genre. Decades ago, in the days of James Thurber, E. B. White, Robert Benchley, Dorothy Parker, and S. J. Perelman, the American essay thrived on an urbane wit and humor. For whatever reasons (political correctness? sensitivity? entrenched academic seriousness?), our era seems less accommodating to funny essays. There are far fewer humor magazines now, and the periodicals that ordinarily feature humor include less of it than they once did. Today's best-known humor writers usually work within the restrictions of 750-word newspaper columns and seldom expand the literary possibilities of humor as did S. J. Perelman, who died in 1979. Still, every now and then a humorous essay — like Ann Hodgman's deliciously comic tidbit — finds its way into The Best American Essays. *Reminiscent of Perelman's zany investigations, Hodgman's courageous essay pushes self-education past the point most of us would go.*

A former contributing editor to Spy *magazine, Ann Hodgman is the author of* Beat This! *(1993), a cookbook, several humor books, including* True Tiny Tales of Terror *(1982), and more than forty children's books, including a six-book series for middle schoolers called* My Babysitter Is a Vampire *(1991). Among her most recent books are* Hard Times for Cats *(1992),* Addams Family Values *(1993) and* Children of the Night: Dark Triumph *(1997). "No Wonder They Call Me a Bitch" originally appeared in* Spy *(1989) and was selected by Justin Kaplan for* The Best American Essays *1990.*

I've always wondered about dog food. Is a Gaines-burger really like a hamburger? Can you fry it? Does dog food "cheese" taste like real cheese? Does Gravy Train actually make gravy in the dog's bowl, or is that brown liquid just dissolved crumbs? And exactly what *are* by-products?

Having spent the better part of a week eating dog food, I'm sorry to say that I now know the answers to these questions. While my dachshund, Shortie, watched in agonies of yearning, I gagged my way through can after can of stinky, white-flecked mush and bag after bag of stinky, fat-drenched nuggets. And now I understand exactly why Shortie's breath is so bad.

Of course, Gaines-burgers are neither mush nor nuggets. They are, rather, a miracle of beauty and packaging — or at least that's what I thought when I was little. I used to beg my mother to get them for our dogs, but she always said they were too expensive. When I finally bought a box of cheese-flavored Gaines-burgers — after 20 years of longing — I felt deliciously wicked.

"Dogs love real beef," the back of the box proclaimed proudly. "That's why Gaines-burgers is the only beef burger for dogs with real beef and no meat by-products!" The copy was accurate: meat by-products did not appear in the list of ingredients. Poultry by-products did, though — right there next to preserved animal fat.

One Purina spokesman told me that poultry by-products consist of necks, intestines, undeveloped eggs and other "carcass remnants," but not feathers, heads or feet. When I told him I'd been eating dog food, he said, "Oh, you're kidding! Oh no!" (I came to share his alarm when, weeks later, a second Purina spokesman said that Gaines-burgers *do* contain poultry heads and feet — but *not* undeveloped eggs.)

Up close my Gaines-burger didn't much resemble chopped beef. Rather, it looked — and felt — like a single long, extruded piece of redness that had been chopped into segments and formed into a patty. You could make one at home if you had a Play-Doh Fun Factory.

I turned on the skillet. While I waited for it to heat up I pulled out a shred of cheese-colored material and palpated it. Again, like Play-Doh, it was quite malleable. I made a little cheese bird out of it; then I counted to three and ate the bird.

There was a horrifying rush of cheddar taste, followed immediately by the dull tang of soybean flour — the main ingredient in Gaines-burgers. Next I tried a piece of red extrusion. The main difference between the meat-flavored and cheese-flavored extrusions is one of texture. The "cheese" chews like fresh Play-Doh, whereas the "meat" chews like Play-Doh that's been sitting out on a rug for a couple of hours.

Frying only turned the Gaines-burger black. There was no melting, no sizzling, no warm meat smells. A cherished childhood illusion was gone. I flipped the patty into the sink, where it immediately began leaking rivulets of red dye.

As alarming as the Gaines-burgers were, their soy meal began to seem like an old friend when the time came to try some *canned* dog foods. I decided to try the Cycle foods first. When I opened them, I thought about how rarely I use can openers these days, and I was suddenly visited by a long-forgotten sensation of can-opener distaste. *This* is the kind of unsavory place can openers spend their time when you're not watching! Every time you open a can of, say, Italian plum tomatoes, you infect them with invisible particles of by-product.

I had been expecting to see the usual homogeneous scrapple inside, but each can of Cycle was packed with smooth, round, oily nuggets. As if someone at Gaines had been tipped off that a human would be tasting the stuff, the four Cycles really were different from one another. Cycle-1, for puppies, is wet and soyish. Cycle-2, for adults, glistens nastily with fat, but it's passably edible — a lot like some canned Swedish meatballs I once got in a care package at college. Cycle-3, the "lite" one, for fatties, had no specific flavor; it just tasted like dog food. But at least it didn't make me fat.

Cycle-4, for senior dogs, had the smallest nuggets. Maybe old dogs can't open their mouths as wide. This kind was far sweeter than the other three Cycles — almost like baked beans. It was also the only one to contain "dried beef digest," a mysterious substance that the Purina spokesman defined as "enzymes" and my dictionary defined as "the products of digestion."

Next on the menu was a can of Kal-Kan Pedigree with Chunky Chicken. Chunky chicken? There were chunks in the can, certainly — big, purplish-brown chunks. I forked one chunk out (by now I was becoming more callous) and found that while it had no discernible chicken flavor, it wasn't bad except for its texture — like meat loaf with ground-up chicken bones.

In the world of canned dog food, a smooth consistency is a

sign of low quality — lots of cereal. A lumpy, frightening, bloody, stringy horror is a sign of high quality — lots of meat. Nowhere in the world of wet dog foods was this demonstrated better than in the fanciest I tried — Kal Kan's Pedigree Select Dinners. These came not in a can but in a tiny foil packet with a picture of an imperious Yorkie. When I pulled open the container, juice spurted all over my hand, and the first chunk I speared was trailing a long gray vein. I shrieked and went instead for a plain chunk, which I was able to swallow only after taking a break to read some suddenly fascinating office equipment catalogs. Once again, though, it tasted no more alarming than, say, canned hash.

Still, how pleasant it was to turn to *dry* dog food! Gravy Train was the first I tried, and I'm happy to report that it really does make a "thick, rich, real beef gravy" when you mix it with water. Thick and rich, anyway. Except for a lingering rancid-fat flavor, the gravy wasn't beefy, but since it tasted primarily like tap water, it wasn't nauseating either.

My poor dachshund just gets plain old Purina Dog Chow, but Purina also makes a dry food called Butcher's Blend that comes in Beef, Bacon & Chicken flavor. Here we see dog food's arcane semiotics at its best: a red triangle with a *T* stamped into it is supposed to suggest beef; a tan curl, chicken; and a brown *S*, a piece of bacon. Only dogs understand these messages. But Butcher's Blend does have an endearing slogan: "Great Meaty Tastes — without bothering the Butcher!" *You know, I wanted to buy some meat, but I just couldn't bring myself to bother the butcher. . . .*

Purina O.N.E. ("Optimum Nutritional Effectiveness") is targeted at people who are unlikely ever to worry about bothering a tradesperson. "We chose chicken as a primary ingredient in Purina O.N.E. for several reasonings," the long, long essay on the back of the bag announces. Chief among these reasonings, I'd guess, is the fact that chicken appeals to people who are — you know — *like us.* Although our dogs do nothing but spend 18-hour days alone in the apartment, we still want them to be *premium* dogs. We want them to cut down on red meat, too. We also want dog food that comes in a bag with an attractive design, a subtle typeface and no kitschy pictures of slobbering golden retrievers.

Besides that, we want a list of the Nutritional Benefits of our dog food — and we get it on O.N.E. One thing I especially like about this list is its constant references to a dog's "hair coat," as in "Beef tallow is good for the dog's skin and hair coat." (On the other hand, beef tallow merely provides palatability, while the dried beef digest in Cycle provides palatability *enhancement.*)

I hate to say it, but O.N.E. was pretty palatable. Maybe that's because it has about 100 percent more fat than, say, Butcher's Blend. Or maybe I'd been duped by the packaging; that's been known to happen before.

As with people food, dog snacks taste much better than dog meals. They're better-looking too. Take Milk-Bone Flavor Snacks. The loving-hands-at-home prose describing each flavor is colorful; the writers practically choke on their own exuberance. Of bacon they say, "It's so good, your dog will think it's hot off the frying pan." Of liver: "The only taste your dog wants more than liver — is even more liver!" Of poultry: "All those farm fresh flavors deliciously mixed in one biscuit. Your dog will bark with delight!" And of vegetable: "Gardens of taste! Specially blended to give your dog that vegetable flavor he wants — but can rarely get!"

Well, I may be a sucker, but advertising *this* emphatic just doesn't convince me. I lined up all seven flavors of Milk-Bone Flavor Snacks on the floor. Unless my dog's palate is a lot more sensitive than mine — and considering that she steals dirty diapers out of the trash and eats them, I'm loath to think it is — she doesn't detect any more difference in the seven flavors than I did when I tried them.

I much preferred Bonz, the hard-baked, bone-shaped snack stuffed with simulated marrow. I liked the bone part, that is; it tasted almost exactly like the cornmeal it was made of. The mock-marrow inside was a bit more problematic: in addition to looking like the sludge that collects in the treads of my running shoes, it was bursting with tiny hairs.

I'm sure you have a few dog food questions of your own. To save us time, I've answered them in advance.

Q. Are those little cans of Mighty Dog actually branded with the sizzling word BEEF, *the way they show in the commercials?*

A. You should know by now that that kind of thing never happens.

Q. Does chicken-flavored dog food taste like chicken-flavored cat food?

A. To my surprise, chicken cat food was actually a little better — more chickeny. It tasted like inferior canned pâté.

Q. Was there any dog food that you just couldn't bring yourself to try?

A. Alas, it was a can of Mighty Dog called Prime Entree with Bone Marrow. The meat was dark, dark brown, and it was surrounded by gelatin that was almost black. I knew I would die if I tasted it, so I put it outside for the raccoons.

Reflections and Responses

1. What is Ann Hodgman making fun of? Is the essay a satire on dog food products alone or does she have other targets?

2. Of what importance is the "packaging" of dog food? How does Hodgman use the language of the packaging for comic effect?

3. Consider the advertising language that Hodgman cites. According to the ads, what similarities exist between the eating habits of dogs and people? What has Hodgman learned from her experiment?

DIANA KAPPEL-SMITH

Salt

*Take an ordinary, everyday item, like salt, and reflect upon it with atten-
tion and affection, and it will soon be transformed into something extraordinary, even mystical. At least that is what can happen when a talented
and observant writer is engaged in a meditation in which she finds that the
"chemistries of the planet and of our bodies are similar enough." For Diana
Kappel-Smith, salt becomes an all-encompassing metaphor for the mysterious ways the world and the body are tied together, all things, as she concludes, "mysteriously mixed." But to say that she can see the metaphorical
potential of her subject does not mean that she loses sight of its concrete reality. "Salt" offers readers and prospective writers a brilliant example of how
the mystical and the mundane — the abstract and the concrete — can be interwoven into a particular human experience.*

*Diana Kappel-Smith is the author and illustrator of three books of natu-
ral history essays:* Wintering *(1984),* Night Life: Nature from Dusk
to Dawn *(1996), and* Desert Time: A Journey Through the American Southwest *(1992). Her work has appeared in* New Woman, Orion
(where "Salt" originally appeared), and the Smithsonian, *among other
publications. She lives in Connecticut. "Salt" was selected by Jamaica Kincaid for* The Best American Essays 1995.

The first spring I spent in Utah there was too much rain in the
Wasach Range. Not having been west of Ohio before, I didn't know
those mountains one way or the other, though I knew that the
West was supposed to be dry, but not how dry, or how changeable,
or how much in the end it would change me.

I was going out there to work with sheep, and weather is the
number-one item of conversation for sheepherders anywhere. The

old man I worked for said that the whole winter had been wet — it was the first thing he told me when he picked me up at the airport in Salt Lake, just like that, not even "Hi" first. He was a fine, kind man, and good to work for, but like most people whose lives are made from the land he was obsessed. He needed to be. He had eight thousand ewes lambing in the hills above Spanish Fork. It was my job to solve obstetric problems and to bring any orphaned "dogies" into the compound for bottle feeding, and to carry a loaded rifle in case I got a shot at a coyote.

There were a lot of coyote problems, as usual. Lambing time is always the worst. In my first week there I saw enough eviscerated sheep and dead lambs and hind ends of coyotes escaping clean across the country to do me for life.

Even with the old man's sons and their wives working, we were short-handed. As the weeks passed exhaustion set in and my vision narrowed (or expanded, depends how you think of it) to the world of the animals. Everything hung on them and I ceased to matter. Any shepherd will recognize this as the way it always is at lambing time, and I was familiar with it, certainly, but not like this.

I knew a lot about sheep in those days, but my understanding of other things was primitive. I still saw myself as the center of the world with nature as a kind of backdrop, a beautiful backdrop in which I spent as much time as possible. It was also the raw heart-breaking place in which I worked. I had not begun to put these things together.

That spring I would be jolted out of these old notions. My ideas of what I was, and what the world was, just gradually . . . ceased; collapsed, emptied, ended by default. It wasn't just the drama of the animals, it was the landscape. To begin with it was the Wasach front and the Manti-La Sals, high white sugarcones gleaming rosily at dawn, streaked with impenetrable darkness. I breathed their breath. There they rose, always above the grubby fray. The distance between us was a lens of air, round and terrifying, like the palpable weight of distance one sees looking down from a height, suspended, miraculous. And all this landscape began to dictate, to sing in its own mineral voice, until any ideas I might have had about the primacy of People or the prettiness of Nature no longer held together by even as much as a thread of self-delusion or popular myth. It was rebirth; I was pushed, slithering and

exhausted by emotion, by the wide open question of the desert itself. I began a kind of journey in which my life would become
more insignificant and more wonderful than I could have ever
imagined. And — this was the odd thing — every step of the way
would taste of salt. Salt came in through my skin and my mouth,
left its mark on my hatband. It was part of the earth that moved
through me. Gradually, not looking for it, looking for coyotes, salt
became my teacher.

One day early that spring, before the lambing got too busy, the
old man took me with him when he went to Nevada to look at the
state of the winter range. It was a kind of holiday. We tooled along
in the pickup with the windows open and sunglasses on against
the blare of light. He took pleasure in pointing things out to me,
the greenhorn, and today it was the wonders of all this water.
Water is different in the desert than it is in other places. Here
there are no rivers, only washes; there are no lakes, only basins.
Water in the desert is temporary, yet can be destructive just when
you want it most.

Parts of the Great Salt Lake were levied with walls of sandbags so
the flood wouldn't inundate the highway. The sandbags were
sloppy looking, like melted bricks. After we'd passed miles and
miles of them I began to wonder if anything in the world stayed
put, if all our works were bound to be crudely kicked apart and
beaten down by the forces of nature. Rain or coyotes; both seemed
inhabited by the same pixie will. We stopped once and walked to
the sandbag wall and looked over at an expanse of filthy fluid that
stretched away to the rim of the universe.

The Great Salt Lake is a place where you can question the right-
ness of preconceived ideas. The water has the smell and color of a
pickle, the surrounding hills are red. There are salt mines — mechanical giants surrounded by piles of white that sear the eyes.
"Salt mines" is an archetypal image of banishment, imprisonment,
the opposite of what my own life was, riding green hills under
snow-decked mountains, surrounded by life — and death, too —
but death is part of life and any country person accepts this and
rolls with this as instinctively as he or she obeys the circular nature
of the year. Mines are something else again: they go down into
darkness and out of nature, like a kind of hell. They made me
shiver.

Southwest of the Great Salt Lake are the Bonneville Salt Flats, a hundred square miles of them as level all the way as the surface of water. Water brought the salt there, laid it down, vanished. Time is visible in the salt, as it is visible in the hands of a clock that seem motionless.

We crossed the Great Salt Desert south of the flats and on past Sevier Lake, heading for Nevada. The old man said that most of the time Sevier Lake was dry, but now it was a great wet mirror laid between the mountains. It was shallow and turbid and was filled with migrating waterbirds that rose as we passed with a massed roar of wings.

Even before the Nevada border the earth settled into basin and range, the sun grew hot, the land shrank down into itself, and the sky grew more immense. The old man pointed out the rocks where he'd seen a lion, a canyon where he sheltered the flock when a blizzard came, and another where he'd corralled mustangs to get himself a riding horse. Out here on the desert you never needed to give salt to the sheep. All grazing animals — and humans too if their diet is mostly grain — need salt as a necessary nutrient. Usually you have to give it to sheep by the hundred-pound sack — loose salt, not blocks, because they need so much of it in order to thrive.

But here all the minerals were in the feed. The old man gave me a leaf to chew and it was salt and bitter. He told me this was the best winter range that one could imagine. I believed him. The ewes I cared for had all wintered here. Their chunky lambs were the pure product of this Nevada brush. Now the range was rebounding: "Look at this here, look at that, well, well . . . ," he'd say, again and again. He would pluck a leaf here and there and chew it and then spit it out, nodding his head, pleased.

The red mountains thrusting up, the basins between them flat as glass, salt everywhere; it made me wonder what had happened here. I was new to the desert and to its nakedness and to how the earth is not hidden under anything, its history open to the air. I wanted to know everything about it at once. So on the way home I asked the old man about the salt. A Mormon, he stopped the truck and gave me an answer that had to do with God. This was not what I was after. It was the only time his Mormon-ness made me impatient, but I should have listened to him.

*   *   *

Since then I've found other answers to the questions of salt — the what of it, the how, the where, the how come — different answers from the one the old man gave me. I'm not sure they're any better, just different. And since that spring I've traveled all over the deserts: from the Wasach to the Sierras, from the valleys of eastern Oregon to the Owyhee hills of Idaho and south clear to the Mexican border, and across that into Sonora and Chihuahua. If anything, these dry landscapes grow more powerful with time and increased acquaintance. The answers to things get shorter, with more room for the unknown built into them, and the unknowable. They get more like the old man's answer, if you want to know the truth.

In the desert there aren't many people to get in the way of the earth's own mineral music, so one can hear it, after a while, without any mortal agendas in the way. Which is a fancy way of saying that I go to the desert for happiness, as other people go to concerts, or plays, or markets. Or churches.

I still go around tasting and smelling things the way I did when I was assaying the palatability of sheep feed; a handy skill, it turns out. There's the funky tang of sage — like rotted lavender — beautiful or foul depending; and the tarry marvel of creosote bush in the summer after a rain, in the darkness, thunder still drumming the air, while the snakes are emerging, and the spadefoot toads come out to sing and blurt from transient pools. A thousand scents: the sweet headiness of desert mistletoe in dry Mojave canyons in January, the piss smell of the tiny white night-blooming flower called desert snow, the cactus blooms that have a tang of tangerine or horehound, the mucilaginous beany taste of young *nopales,* and the scent of a salt spring, which is a little like death.

All that salt: vast white plains of it, cracked like ice floes. All through southern California the center of every valley is a pan of saline silt, flatter than any other place on earth, and dun colored, and cracked. If there's still a little water, then it's a salt marsh, with water so saturated it's caustic. Up around Pahrump and the Amargosa* there are plenty of salt springs in which one can soak naked and by moonlight, and everyone seems to have their favorite. There's a brittle whitish horn I carry in a plastic bag in my pack; I

*Amargosa is a Nevada river near Las Vegas; Pahrump is a nearby town. — Ed.

crush and sprinkle it as a sacrament on everything I eat when I'm living out there. I stole it from Badwater in Death Valley. One isn't supposed to do this. Robbery of anything from any National Monument is forbidden, but that salt has all the crunch and flavor of scofflaw freedom.

I'm eating what I love: the unendurable places, the bone-stuff, the ground. The same electrolytes that dance their vital dance in my blood — sodium, calcium, potassium, carbonate, chloride — are there in the evaporites at the fringe of desert marshes and ephemeral lakes: sulfates, carbonates, and chlorides crystallized on basin rims as white residues as though a pot had boiled dry. The chemistries of the planet and of our bodies are similar enough (why should we be amazed?). Our body fluids contain 0.9 percent salt, nowadays, very likely the exact salinity of whatever ancient sea we managed to crawl out of, a sea we could leave because we had learned, first of all, to contain it.

This is a marvel: that we still contain what once contained us. What is more marvelous is that we maintain it with exactitude. The concentration of electrolytes in our blood is regulated by the kidney, the kidney is in turn regulated by adrenal and pituitary hormones. Regulatory feedback loops operate constantly so that we run through natural cycles of ion concentration every eighteen days or so, our water content, and body weight, fluctuating, too, in tidal ripples of which we are largely unconscious. Emotional stress increases adrenal activity, and severe hormonal upsets or kidney disease can lead to edema: to swelling out of control, our cells drowning in a tidal wave of body fluids. When body salts are depleted below critical levels we get diarrhea, we vomit, we sweat, our blood pressure drops, we faint, our kidneys fail. Doctors have learned to treat the deadly phenomenon of shock with heavy doses of Ringer's solution: sodium chloride, potassium chloride, calcium chloride, and sodium bicarbonate, in the same concentration as blood plasma. When we are at the brink we can be pulled back into life by the renewal of our internal sea.

So I crush the white horn of Death Valley salt and sprinkle it on my food, and partake, of life, of my own life in which this salt moves, as it has moved through infinite numbers of others. The next day it will leave itself on my hat brim or dry on my shirt or sink with my urine into the soil in another place, attracting butterflies, who need the salts too. Until then it will dance in the most intimate machinery of my being.

It has been suggested that our almost universal religious concern with salvation, in one form or another, comes from our consciousness of time. The idea seems to be that if we understand the notion of *time,* then we are confronted slam-bang with the fact of our own mortality. Animals do not have time consciousness (so far as we know), so they don't suffer from the same need to be delivered from the *now* to the *eternal.* Knowing that we're mortal, we yearn for salvation, for release from the finitude of life and death.

That is one explanation, perhaps not the only one, but when you are in the desert it seems that one thinks of these things as easily as breathing. The grandeur of that space draws the mind beyond the present and beyond the self. The salt says this: our life is at one even with the stones. So after a few days in that country it becomes clear that one does live in the eternal all the time.

If there is good reason to preserve some desert untrammeled and unchanged, it is this: what the desert has to teach us is almost impossible to learn when we are surrounded by people. And if one scrawls all over those landscapes with the graffiti of dams and developments and mines and wells, then the sense of it and the singing of it vanish, chopped into a senseless confetti, sad little fragments of blowing paper, meaning nothing.

What becomes clear is that the world is tied together in wonderful ways, most of which are mysterious. For instance, when a wave breaks in the ocean it makes millions of bubbles and when the bubbles pop tiny droplets fly into the air, and they are carried up where the water itself is sucked away — leaving fragments of salt to whirl in the dry jet streams of the upper atmosphere. Later, encountering cloud, these become the nuclei of drops of rain.

In the desert in a wet year the runoff from winter storms may flow as far as the basins, the bolsones, the playa lakes, all names for the same things: the bowls of desert air surrounded by mountains, the place where all flow ends. There, spread shallow as if on a plate, water dries away.

Or, invisibly, it enters an underground river. A river no swifter than the seepage between pores of Jurassic sandstone. A subter-

ranean seep as long and brachiated as a system of nerves. The
water may surface hundreds of miles and thousands of years away.

In the Mojave just east of the Sierras, where the crust of the
earth has been crazed by active faults, there are lots of springs.
Many of them are hot and most of them are saline. These oases are
furred with crisp saltgrass and are surrounded by fan palms.
Where a pool overflows the salt makes a crust on the sand, a fragile glazing, like ice.

Nearby there is almost always a rock or two with petroglyphs* of
bighorn sheep: rams with immense headgear, flocks of ewes ca-
vorting over the rock with their tails in the air and their bellies as
round as bowls. People's passions and obsessions have not changed
much.

The springs welling up in the drought of the Mojave are a way to
see that the earth has a three-dimensional body, too, has creaking
bones, secret fluids. What I've also learned is that layers of salt
buried deep in it do strange things. Under pressure of gravity or
tectonics, salt becomes plastic and moves. Under pressure it can
flow and coalesce into a reverse-teardrop shape that punches upward like an immense fist: a *salt dome*. These domes come up from
as deep as 50,000 feet, piercing all the rock over themselves. They
can be as much as ten kilometers high and fifty kilometers long.
These domes are of astounding purity, so that when they're near
the surface they are often mined — for salt — and the surrounding rock layers are wonderful sources of oil. The dome acts like an
impervious plug. Oil migrating through rock layers reaches it and
stops.

Then near the Zuni Mountains in western New Mexico there is a
single cindercone filled with salt; this is one of the strangest things
I've ever seen. No geologist I've talked to knows where the salt has
come from — there's none of it anywhere near, not for hundreds
of miles. What must have happened is something like this: on its
way up from wherever volcanoes come from, this one tapped into
some very deep saline plumbing, and there was a gush, like the
bursting of a water main. After the cindercone blew, its crater was
filled by this spring of highly concentrated brine. Add a few millennia of evaporation, and now the cindercone is filled with a plug

*Petroglyphs are prehistoric drawings or carvings on rocks.

of pure lovely salt topped by a few feet of briny slush. The salt spring still springs, as heartily as ever. This white circular lake with its steep dark walls — strange place! — is called the Zuni Salt Lake. This is a sacred place to the Zuni people, the home of their Salt Mother, the place of their emergence from the previous World.

All life came from the sea, once, and this is one of the great mysteries, like the mystery of having been born once from the inside of one's mother. We were elsewhere, and in emerging we have been transformed. This is the truth of history, of biology, of myth, and of the spirit.

Nowadays I live by the sea, which is like the desert in many ways. It's spacious, and changeable, and dangerous, which means that when one travels on it one has to be keenly aware — of weather, tides, things that one cannot control.

One recent summer I was sailing with friends off New England when the wind picked up and blew a steady twenty-five, then thirty, and then thirty-five. By mid-afternoon everything was double-reefed and straining and still we clawed our way to windward, screaming at each other to be heard, wearing safety lines, our knuckles white where we gripped the wheel or the rails. The waves grew or we shrank — it was hard to tell — the sea became a landscape of wicked unpredictable hills.

I was at the helm when one wave came that was larger than the others. It rose up from the dark of the sea and turned green and finally silver as the tip of it came over the rail and flicked drops of water in my face. Then it went down, under the boat. The boat leapt up and slewed and hung a moment leaning in the air, then it plunged, and we were rudderless and beyond hope as we fell down the wave . . . until the wheel was solid again in my hands and the bows lifted, reluctant, toward the wind. Then the wave growled out under the leeward rail and ran away like an animal. I licked its salt from my mouth.

Then I understood something. Perhaps it's a matter of semantics, but to me the word "understand" means to possess physical knowledge; it means to have a corporeal grasp, a surety that the body owns. A purely cerebral construct is "not understanding." And — going back the other way — something that one has truly understood is so personal and visceral that it's almost impossible

to express in words. But this happened: the taste and feel of that
wave left me with something like terror but more like awe, an inhabiting whole-body awe.

The spring in Utah was my first taste of that. Though almost certainly not the very first. A saline flavor must have been on my
tongue when I was born, and before; the flavor of the eternal and
internal sea, from before we were conscious, before we were separate, before we emerged.

During those weeks above Spanish Fork I remember coming
back to the ranch house many mornings with half a dozen orphan
lambs hog-tied and draped over my saddlehorn. Some of the little
ones just got tucked into my jacket and zipped in and I would forget about them for hours, until they moved. Their mothers had
been half eaten by coyotes as they labored to give birth, or they
had cast themselves in a hollow, or had succumbed to one of those
diseases to do with birthing that can happen to any animal: masti-
tis or milk fever. For the most part the coyotes scorned the sick-
ened sheep and chose as prey the youngest and best fleshed. Or
they took lambs. And there were so many of these that they did not
bother to eat more of them than the liver. Every morning when I
came in with my harvest of dogies I left behind me frantically bel-
lowing ewes, calling for life, ignoring what life had become: those
punctured deflated scraps of gray hide.

Scenes of this nature are not pretty, but they are common. They
happen with the hyenas and the wild dogs and the wildebeest on
the Serengeti, with wolves and caribou on the North Slope, and
they have always happened. It can be said that predator and prey
are opposite halves of a single unity, a unity we belong to and always have. Here I had mixed myself into an ancient rite of birth
and death, and the mixing had the flavor of salt, so I began to
believe that this was the coin of the realm, the medium of life's
exchange.

I rode over the hills twelve hours a day, circling and circling
again. It was often raining. I wore a trash bag over my hat until the
old man took pity on me and gave me a plastic hat cover. Either
way the hat would dump gouts of water into my saddle at intervals.
Sometimes there was a difficult birth or an impossible one and I
would dismount and lie flat in the grass to turn the lamb or find

the front feet, which are supposed to be tucked under the nose as if the lamb were diving or praying. If they are swept back, the lamb gets jammed. Women seem to be better at sheep obstetrics than men; perhaps it's just because their hands are smaller. In any case, shepherds have noticed that when women do the work, more animals tend to survive. I would lie down and join the struggle. The birth mucus would mix with my streaming nose and the blood on my hands would mix — I couldn't help it — with tears, that were from rage or helplessness or finally relief. Sometimes when the birth took a long time the grass under me would turn to mud and the ewe would kick it up over me as we fought to do the thing. Afterward the ewe would lick mud and wet from its lamb with a frantic whickering delight and I would stand and wipe my face on my sleeve, which was salty with I don't know what. Pressing my face against my horse's neck, I tasted horse and horse sweat and rain. All things had become inextricably mixed. The medium of our common life began with this sea that flowed over us.

Reflections and Responses

1. Although the author's essay title is "salt," why do you think she concentrates on her experiences as a sheepherder? How is that personal experience related to her topic? Were you surprised by the way the essay opens? What sort of opening might you have expected given the title?

2. What does Kappel-Smith mean both literally and figuratively by "our internal sea"? What role does the sea play in her essay? In what ways is it connected to her announced topic?

3. The style of this essay is highly metaphorical. Take a close look at the author's use of metaphor. How do her metaphors reinforce her central theme? For example, how do her metaphors make you aware of how closely the world and the human body are "inextricably mixed"?

BARRY LOPEZ

The Stone Horse

Great works of art do not always hang in museums, accessible to anyone who cares to see them. When Barry Lopez wanted to see a mysterious stone horse carved perhaps some four hundred years ago by the Quechan people, his journey took him far off the beaten track. What he finds in the deserts of southern California near the Mexican border is the kind of large ground carving (an intaglio) that some think was intended as a sign to extraterrestrials. But, upon seeing the horse, Lopez does not believe it was "meant to be seen by gods in the sky above" nor does he think it can even be properly appreciated by an aerial photograph. How we see this work of art, Lopez suggests, is as important as what we see. And how we see it requires the journey to it.

One of America's most distinguished nonfiction writers, Lopez is the author of Arctic Dreams, *which won the National Book Award in 1986, and* Of Wolves and Men, *which won the John Burroughs Medal in 1979. His other publications include* Desert Notes *(1979),* River Notes *(1979),* Winter Count *(1981),* Crossing Open Ground *(1988),* Coyote Love *(1989),* The Rediscovery of North America *(1990),* Field Notes *(1994) and* Lessons from the Wolverine *(1997). He has also recently published* About This Life: Journeys on the Threshold of Memory *(1998). He received an award for fiction from the Friends of American Writers in 1982 and the Award in Literature from the American Academy and Institute of Arts and Letters in 1986. "The Stone Horse" originally appeared in* Antaeus *(1986) and was selected by Gay Talese for* The Best American Essays 1987.

I

The deserts of southern California, the high, relatively cooler and wetter Mojave and the hotter, dryer Sonoran to the south of it, carry the signatures of many cultures. Prehistoric rock drawings in the Mojave's Coso Range, probably the greatest concentration of petroglyphs in North America, are at least three thousand years old. Big-game-hunting cultures that flourished six or seven thousand years before that are known from broken spear tips, choppers, and burins left scattered along the shores of great Pleistocene lakes, long since evaporated. Weapons and tools discovered at China Lake may be thirty thousand years old; and worked stone from a quarry in the Calico Mountains is, some argue, evidence that human beings were here more than 200,000 years ago.

Because of the long-term stability of such arid environments, much of this prehistoric stone evidence still lies exposed on the ground, accessible to anyone who passes by — the studious, the acquisitive, the indifferent, the merely curious. Archaeologists do not agree on the sequence of cultural history beyond about twelve thousand years ago, but it is clear that these broken bits of chalcedony, chert, and obsidian, like the animal drawings and geometric designs etched on walls of basalt throughout the desert, anchor the earliest threads of human history, the first record of human endeavor here.

Western man did not enter the California desert until the end of the eighteenth century, 250 years after Coronado brought his soldiers into the Zuni pueblos in a bewildered search for the cities of Cibola. The earliest appraisals of the land were cursory, hurried. People traveled *through* it, en route to Santa Fe or the California coastal settlements. Only miners tarried. In 1823 what had been Spain's became Mexico's, and in 1848 what had been Mexico's became America's; but the bare, jagged mountains and dry lake beds, the vast and uniform plains of creosote bush and yucca plants, remained as obscure as the northern Sudan until the end of the nineteenth century.

Before 1940 the tangible evidence of twentieth-century man's passage here consisted of very little — the hard tracery of travel corridors; the widely scattered, relatively insignificant evidence of mining operations; and the fair expanse of irrigated fields at the desert's periphery. In the space of a hundred years or so the wagon roads were paved, railroads were laid down, and canals and high-tension lines were built to bring water and electricity across the desert to Los Angeles from the Colorado River. The dark

mouths of gold, talc, and tin mines yawned from the bony flanks of
desert ranges. Dust-encrusted chemical plants stood at work on
the lonely edges of dry lake beds. And crops of grapes, lettuce,
dates, alfalfa, and cotton covered the Coachella and Imperial valleys, north and south of the Salton Sea, and the Palo Verde Valley
along the Colorado.

These developments proceeded with little or no awareness of
earlier human occupations by cultures that preceded those of the
historic Indians — the Mojave, the Chemehuevi, the Quechan.
(Extensive irrigation began actually to change the climate of the
Sonoran Desert, and human settlements, the railroads, and farm-
ing introduced many new, successful plants into the region.)

During World War II, the American military moved into the
desert in great force, to train troops and to test equipment. They
found the clear weather conducive to year-round flying, the dry air
and isolation very attractive. After the war, a complex of training
grounds, storage facilities, and gunnery and test ranges was per-
manently settled on more than three million acres of military
reservations. Few perceived the extent or significance of the destruction of the aboriginal sites that took place during tank maneuvers and bombing runs or in the laying out of highways,
railroads, mining districts, and irrigated fields. The few who intu-
ited that something like an American Dordogne Valley lay exposed
here were (only) amateur archaeologists; even they reasoned that
the desert was too vast for any of this to matter.

After World War II, people began moving out of the crowded
Los Angeles basin into homes in Lucerne, Apple, and Antelope
valleys in the western Mojave. They emigrated as well to a stretch
of resort land at the foot of the San Jacinto Mountains that included Palm Springs, and farther out to old railroad and military
towns like Twentynine Palms and Barstow. People also began exploring the desert, at first in military-surplus jeeps and then with a
variety of all-terrain and off-road vehicles that became available in
the 1960s. By the mid-1970s, the number of people using such vehicles for desert recreation had increased exponentially. Most
came and went in innocent curiosity; the few who didn't wreaked
a havoc all out of proportion to their numbers. The disturbance
of previously isolated archaeological sites increased by an order
of magnitude. Many sites were vandalized before archaeologists,

themselves late to the desert, had any firm grasp of the bounds of human history in the desert. It was as though in the same moment an Aztec library had been discovered intact various lacunae had begun to appear.

The vandalism was of three sorts: the general disturbance usually caused by souvenir hunters and by the curious and the oblivious; the wholesale stripping of a place by professional thieves for black-market sale and trade; and outright destruction, in which vehicles were actually used to ram and trench an area. By 1980, the Bureau of Land Management estimated that probably 35 percent of the archaeological sites in the desert had been vandalized. The destruction at some places by rifles and shotguns, or by power winches mounted on vehicles, was, if one cared for history, demoralizing to behold.

In spite of public education, land closures, and stricter law enforcement in recent years, the BLM estimates that, annually, about 1 percent of the archaeological record in the desert continues to be destroyed or stolen.

II

A BLM archaeologist told me, with understandable reluctance, where to find the intaglio. I spread my Automobile Club of Southern California map of Imperial County out on his desk, and he traced the route with a pink felt-tip pen. The line crossed Interstate 8 and then turned west along the Mexican border.

"You can't drive any farther than about here," he said, marking a small X. "There's boulders in the wash. You walk up past them."

On a separate piece of paper he drew a route in a smaller scale that would take me up the arroyo to a certain point where I was to cross back east, to another arroyo. At its head, on higher ground just to the north, I would find the horse.

"It's tough to spot unless you know it's there. Once you pick it up . . ." He shook his head slowly, in a gesture of wonder at its existence.

I waited until I held his eye. I assured him I would not tell anyone else how to get there. He looked at me with stoical despair, like a man who had been robbed twice, whose belief in human beings was offered without conviction.

I did not go until the following day because I wanted to see it at

dawn. I ate breakfast at four A.M. in El Centro and then drove
south. The route was easy to follow, though the last section of road
proved difficult, broken and drifted over with sand in some spots.
I came to the barricade of boulders and parked. It was light
enough by then to find my way over the ground with little trouble.
The contours of the landscape were stark, without any masking
vegetation. I worried only about rattlesnakes.

I traversed the stone plain as directed, but, in spite of the frank-
ness of the land, I came on the horse unawares. In the first moment of recognition I was without feeling. I recalled later being
startled, and that I held my breath. It was laid out on the ground
with its head to the east, three times life size. As I took in its outline I felt a growing concentration of all my senses, as though my
attentiveness to the pale rose color of the morning sky and other
peripheral images had now ceased to be important. I was aware
that I was straining for sound in the windless air, and I felt the uneven pressure of the earth hard against my feet. The horse, out-
lined in a standing profile on the dark ground, was as vivid before
me as a bed of tulips.

I've come upon animals suddenly before, and felt a similar tension, a precipitate heightening of the senses. And I have felt the inexplicable but sharply boosted intensity of a wild moment in the
bush, where it is not until some minutes later that you discover the
source of electricity — the warm remains of a grizzly bear kill, or
the still moist tracks of a wolverine.

But this was slightly different. I felt I had stepped into an unoc-
cupied corridor. I had no familiar sense of history, the temporal
structure in which to think: this horse was made by Quechan people three hundred years ago. I felt instead a headlong rush of images: people hunting wild horses with spears on the Pleistocene
veld of southern California; Cortés riding across the causeway into
Montezuma's Tenochtitlán; a short-legged Comanche, astride his
horse like some sort of ferret, slashing through cavalry lines of
young men who rode like farmers; a hoof exploding past my face
one morning in a corral in Wyoming. These images had the weight
and silence of stone.

When I released my breath, the images softened. My initial feeling, of facing a wild animal in a remote region, was replaced with a
calm sense of antiquity. It was then that I became conscious, like

an ordinary tourist, of what was before me, and thought: this horse
was probably laid out by Quechan people. But when? I wondered.
The first horses they saw, I knew, might have been those that came
north from Mexico in 1692 with Father Eusebio Kino. But Cocopa
people, I recalled, also came this far north on occasion, to fight
with their neighbors, the Quechan. And *they* could have seen
horses with Melchior Díaz, at the mouth of the Colorado River in
the fall of 1540. So, it could be four hundred years old. (No one in
fact knows.)

I still had not moved. I took my eyes off the horse for a moment
to look south over the desert plain into Mexico, to look east past its
head at the brightening sunrise, to situate myself. Then, finally, I
brought my trailing foot slowly forward and stood erect. Sunlight
was running like a thin sheet of water over the stony ground and it
threw the horse into relief. It looked as though no hand had ever
disturbed the stones that gave it its form.

The horse had been brought to life on ground called desert
pavement, a tight, flat matrix of small cobbles blasted smooth by
sand-laden winds. The uniform, monochromatic blackness of the
stones, a patina of iron and magnesium oxides called desert var-
nish, is caused by long-term exposure to the sun. To make this type
of low-relief ground glyph, or intaglio, the artist either selectively
turns individual stones over to their lighter side or removes areas
of stone to expose the lighter soil underneath, creating a negative
image. This horse, about eighteen feet from brow to rump and
eight feet from withers to hoof, had been made in the latter way,
and its outline was bermed at certain points with low ridges of
stone a few inches high to enhance its three-dimensional qualities.
(The left side of the horse was in full profile; each leg was extended at 90 degrees to the body and fully visible, as though seen
in three-quarter profile.)

I was not eager to move. The moment I did I would be back in
the flow of time, the horse no longer quivering in the same way before me. I did not want to feel again the sequence of quotidian
events — to be drawn off into deliberation and analysis. A human
being, a four-footed animal, the open land. That was all that was
present — and a "thoughtless" understanding of the very old desires bearing on this particular animal: to hunt it, to render it, to
fathom it, to subjugate it, to honor it, to take it as a companion.

What finally made me move was the light. The sun now filled the shallow basin of the horse's body. The weighted line of the stone berm created the illusion of a mane and the distinctive roundness of an equine belly. The change in definition impelled me. I moved to the left, circling past its rump, to see how the light might flesh the horse out from various points of view. I circled it completely before squatting on my haunches. Ten or fifteen minutes later I chose another view. The third time I moved, to a point near the rear hooves, I spotted a stone tool at my feet. I stared at it a long while, more in awe than disbelief, before reaching out to pick it up. I turned it over in my left palm and took it between my fingers to feel its cutting edge. It is always difficult, especially with something so portable, to rechannel the desire to steal.

I spent several hours with the horse. As I changed positions and as the angle of the light continued to change I noticed a number of things. The angle at which the pastern carried the hoof away from the ankle was perfect. Also, stones had been placed within the image to suggest at precisely the right spot the left shoulder above the foreleg. The line that joined thigh and hock was similarly accurate. The muzzle alone seemed distorted — but perhaps these stones had been moved by a later hand. It was an admirably accurate representation, but not what a breeder would call perfect conformation. There was the suggestion of a bowed neck and an undershot jaw, and the tail, as full as a winter coyote's, did not appear to be precisely to scale.

The more I thought about it, the more I felt I was looking at an individual horse, a unique combination of generic and specific detail. It was easy to imagine one of Kino's horses as a model, or a horse that ran off from one of Coronado's columns. What kind of horses would these have been? I wondered. In the sixteenth century the most sought-after horses in Europe were Spanish, the offspring of Arabian stock and Barbary horses that the Moors brought to Iberia and bred to the older, eastern European strains brought in by the Romans. The model for this horse, I speculated, could easily have been a palomino, or a descendant of horses trained for lion hunting in North Africa.

A few generations ago, cowboys, cavalry quartermasters, and draymen would have taken this horse before me under consideration and not let up their scrutiny until they had its heritage fixed to their satisfaction. Today, the distinction between draft and harness horses is arcane knowledge, and no image may come to mind for a blue roan or a claybank horse. The loss of such refinement in everyday conversation leaves me unsettled. People praise the Eskimo's ability to distinguish among forty types of snow but forget the skill of others who routinely differentiate between overo and tobiano pintos. Such distinctions are made for the same reason. You have to do it to be able to talk clearly about the world.

For parts of two years I worked as a horse wrangler and packer in Wyoming. It is dim knowledge now; I would have to think to remember if a buckskin was a kind of dun horse. And I couldn't throw a double-diamond hitch over a set of panniers — the packer's basic tie-down — without guidance. As I squatted there in the desert, however, these more personal memories seemed tenuous in comparison with the sweep of this animal in human time. My memories had no depth. I thought of the Hittite cavalry riding against the Syrians 3,500 years ago. And the first of the Chinese emperors, Ch'in Shih Huang, buried in Shensi Province in 210 B.C. with thousands of life-size horses and soldiers, a terra-cotta guardian army. What could I know of what was in the mind of whoever made this horse? Was there some racial memory of it as an animal that had once fed the artist's ancestors and then disappeared from North America? And then returned in this strange alliance with another race of men?

Certainly, whoever it was, the artist had observed the animal very closely. Certainly the animal's speed had impressed him. Among the first things the Quechan would have learned from an encounter with Kino's horses was that their own long-distance runners — men who could run down mule deer — were no match for this animal.

From where I squatted I could look far out over the Mexican plain. Juan Bautista de Anza passed this way in 1774, extending El Camino Real into Alta California from Sinaloa. He was followed by others, all of them astride the magical horse; *gente de razón,* the people of reason, coming into the country of *los primitivos.* The horse, like the stone animals of Egypt, urged these memories upon me. And as I drew them up from some forgotten corner of my mind — huge horses carved in the white chalk downs of southern England by an Iron Age people; Spanish horses rearing and

wheeling in fear before alligators in Florida — the images seemed
tethered before me. With this sense of proportion, a memory of
my own — the morning I almost lost my face to a horse's hoof —
now had somewhere to fit.

I rose up and began to walk slowly around the horse again. I had
taken the first long measure of it and was now looking for a way to
depart, a new angle of light, a fading of the image itself before the
rising sun, that would break its hold on me. As I circled, feeling
both heady and serene at the encounter, I realized again how
strangely vivid it was. It had been created on a barren bajada between two arroyos, as nondescript a place as one could imagine.
The only plant life here was a few wands of ocotillo cactus. The
ground beneath my shoes was so hard it wouldn't take the print of
a heavy animal even after a rain. The only sounds I heard here
were the voices of quail.

The archaeologist had been correct. For all its forcefulness, the
horse is inconspicuous. If you don't care to see it you can walk
right past it. That pleases him, I think. Unmarked on this bleak
shoulder of the plain, the site signals to no one; so he wants no
protective fences here, no informative plaque, to act as beacons.
He would rather take a chance that no motorcyclist, no aimless
wanderer with a flair for violence and a depth of ignorance, will
ever find his way here.

The archaeologist had given me something before I left his
office that now seemed peculiar — an aerial photograph of the
horse. It is widely believed that an aerial view of an intaglio provides a fair and accurate depiction. It does not. In the photograph
the horse looks somewhat crudely constructed; from the ground it
appears far more deftly rendered. The photograph is of a single
moment, and in that split second the horse seems vaguely impotent. I watched light pool in the intaglio at dawn; I imagine you
could watch it withdraw at dusk and sense the same animation I
did. In those prolonged moments its shape and so, too, its general
character changed — noticeably. The living quality of the image,
its immediacy to the eye, was brought out by the light-in-time, not,
at least here, in the camera's frozen instant.

Intaglios, I thought, were never meant to be seen by gods in the
sky above. They were meant to be seen by people on the ground,
over a long period of shifting light. This could even be true of the

huge figures on the Plain of Nazca in Peru, where people could walk for the length of a day beside them. It is our own impatience that leads us to think otherwise.

This process of abstraction, almost unintentional, drew me gradually away from the horse. I came to a position of attention at the edge of the sphere of its influence. With a slight bow I paid my respects to the horse, its maker, and the history of us all, and departed.

III

A short distance away I stopped the car in the middle of the road to make a few notes. I could not write down what I was thinking when I was with the horse. It would have seemed disrespectful, and it would have required another kind of attention. So now I patiently drained my memory of the details it had fastened itself upon. The road I'd stopped on was adjacent to the All American Canal, the major source of water for the Imperial and Coachella valleys. The water flowed west placidly. A disjointed flock of coots, small, dark birds with white bills, was paddling against the current, foraging in the rushes.

I was peripherally aware of the birds as I wrote, the only movement in the desert, and of a series of sounds from a village a half-mile away. The first sounds from this collection of ramshackle houses in a grove of cottonwoods were the distracted dawn voices of dogs. I heard them intermingled with the cries of a rooster. Later, the high-pitched voices of children calling out to each other came disembodied through the dry desert air. Now, a little after seven, I could hear someone practicing on the trumpet, the same rough phrases played over and over. I suddenly remembered how as children we had tried to get the rhythm of a galloping horse with hands against our thighs, or by fluttering our tongues against the roofs of our mouths.

After the trumpet, the impatient calls of adults summoning children. Sunday morning. Wood smoke hung like a lens in the trees. The first car starts — a cold eight-cylinder engine, of Chrysler extraction perhaps, goosed to life, then throttled back to murmur through dual mufflers, the obbligato music of a shade-tree mechanic. The rote bark of mongrel dogs at dawn, the jagged outcries of men and women, an engine coming to life. Like a thousand villages from West Virginia to Guadalajara.

I finished my notes — where was I going to find a description of the horses that came north with the conquistadors? Did their manes come forward prominently over the brow, like this one's, like the forelocks of Blackfeet and Assiniboin men in nineteenth-century paintings? I set the notes on the seat beside me.

The road followed the canal for a while and then arced north, toward Interstate 8. It was slow driving and I fell to thinking how the desert had changed since Anza had come through. New plants and animals — the MacDougall cottonwood, the English house sparrow, the chukar from India — have about them now the air of the native-born. Of the native species, some — no one knows how many — are extinct. The populations of many others, especially the animals, have been sharply reduced. The idea of a desert impoverished by agricultural poisons and varmint hunters, by off-road vehicles and military operations, did not seem as disturbing to me, however, as this other horror, now that I had been those hours with the horse. The vandals, the few who crowbar rock art off the desert's walls, who dig up graves, who punish the ground that holds intaglios, are people who devour history. Their self-centered scorn, their disrespect for ideas and images beyond their ken, create the awful atmosphere of loose ends in which totalitarianism thrives, in which the past is merely curious or wrong.

I thought about the horse sitting out there on the unprotected plain. I enumerated its qualities in my mind until a sense of its vulnerability receded and it became an anchor for something else. I remembered that history, a history like this one, which ran deeper than Mexico, deeper than the Spanish, was a kind of medicine. It permitted the great breadth of human expression to reverberate, and it did not urge you to locate its apotheosis in the present.

Each of us, individuals and civilizations, has been held upside down like Achilles in the River Styx. The artist mixing his colors in the dim light of Altamira; an Egyptian ruler lying still now, wrapped in his byssus,* stored against time in a pyramid; the faded Dorset culture of the Arctic; the Hmong and Samburu and Walbiri of historic time; the modern nations. This great, imperfect stretch of human expression is the clarification and encouragement, the urging and the reminder, we call history. And it is inscribed

---

*byssus: Ancient cloth.

everywhere in the face of the land, from the mountain passes of the Himalayas to a nameless bajada in the California desert.

Small birds rose up in the road ahead, startled, and flew off. I prayed no infidel would ever find that horse.

Reflections and Responses

1. Lopez divides his essay into three parts. How does each of these parts differ? What purpose does each serve?

2. Examine Lopez's choice of words. When does he introduce technical terms into the essay? Go through the essay and identify the various technical terms. From what diverse disciplines are they drawn? How do these terms affect your response to both the author and his subject?

3. When this essay originally appeared, it included no photographs of the carving. Why do you think that decision was made? What distortions would photography introduce? What would a photograph *not* be able to show us? What is Lopez's attitude toward photography in this instance?

JOYCE CAROL OATES

They All Just Went Away

*The essay has long been the perfect form for the reflective mind. In the
hands of a great writer, the process of reflection can be stimulated by a single incident or image and then veer off in so many different directions that,
by the end of the essay, the reader is amazed at how much ground has been
covered. "They All Just Went Away" does everything a superb reflective
essay can do because it moves from the personal eccentricities of a lonely
young girl who finds herself drawn to abandoned houses and desolate families into a consideration of American art, class boundaries, sexual abuse,
and strange erotic attachments. It is not a cheerful or placid piece of writing, however. "As I am not drawn to art that makes me feel good, comfortable, or at ease," Joyce Carol Oates writes, "so I am not drawn to essays that
'smile,' except in the context of larger, more complex ambitions."*

*One of the country's most distinguished authors, Joyce Carol Oates has
published over two dozen novels and numerous collections of poems, plays,
short stories, criticism, and essays. Equipped with her work alone, the
scholar and essayist Henry Louis Gates, Jr., claimed, a future archaeologist
could "easily piece together the whole postwar America." The recipient of
countless literary awards, she was at thirty-one the youngest writer ever to
receive the prestigious National Book Award for fiction, when her novel*
them *was chosen in 1969. She currently teaches writing at Princeton University. Among her most recent works of fiction are* Man Crazy *(1997),*
The Collector of Hearts *(1998),* My Heart Laid Bare *(1998), and*
Broke Heart Blues *(1999). "They All Just Went Away" originally appeared in* The New Yorker *(1995) and was selected by Geoffrey C. Ward
for* The Best American Essays *1996.*

I must have been a lonely child. Until the age of twelve or thirteen,
my most intense, happiest hours were spent tramping desolate

fields, woods, and creek banks near my family's farmhouse in Millersport, New York. No one knew where I went. My father, working most of the day at Harrison's, a division of General Motors in Lockport, and at other times preoccupied, would not have asked; if my mother asked, I might have answered in a way that would deflect curiosity. I was an articulate, verbal child. Yet I could not have explained what drew me to the abandoned houses, barns, silos, corncribs. A hike of miles through fields of spiky grass, across outcroppings of shale as steeply angled as stairs, was a lark if the reward was an empty house.

Some of these houses had been inhabited as "homes" fairly recently — they had not yet reverted to the wild. Others, abandoned during the Depression, had long since begun to rot and collapse, engulfed by vegetation (trumpet vine, wisteria, rose of Sharon, willow) that elsewhere, on our property for instance, was kept neatly trimmed. I was drawn to both kinds of houses, though the more recently inhabited were more forbidding and therefore more inviting.

To push open a door into such silence: the absolute emptiness of a house whose occupants have departed. Often, the crack of broken glass underfoot. A startled buzzing of flies, hornets. The slithering, ticklish sensation of a garter snake crawling across floorboards.

Left behind, as if in haste, were remnants of a lost household. A broken toy on the floor, a baby's bottle. A rain-soaked sofa, looking as if it has been gutted with a hunter's skilled knife. Strips of wallpaper like shredded skin. Smashed crockery, piles of tin cans; soda, beer, whiskey bottles. An icebox, its door yawning open. Once, on a counter, a dirt-stiffened rag that, unfolded like precious cloth, revealed itself to be a woman's cheaply glamorous "see-through" blouse, threaded with glitter-strips of gold.

This was a long time ago, yet it is more vivid to me than anything now.

This was when I was too young to think *the house is the mother's body, you have been expelled and are forbidden now to reenter.*

Always, I was prepared to see a face at a high, empty window. A woman's hand uplifted in greeting, or in warning. *Hello! Come in! Stay away! Run! Who are you?* A movement in the corner of my eye: the blurred motion of a person passing through a doorway, or glimpsed through a window. There might be a single shriek of laughter from a barn — piercing as a bird's cry. Murmurous, teasing voices confused with wind rippling through tall, coarse, gone-to-seed grass. Voices that, when you pause to listen, fade immediately and are gone.

The sky in such places of abandonment was always of the hue and brightness of tin, as if the melancholy rural poverty of tin roofs reflected upward.

A house: a structural arrangement of space, geometrically laid out to provide what are called rooms, these divided from one another by verticals and horizontals called walls, ceilings, floors. The house contains the home but is not identical with it. The house antici-pates the home and will very likely survive it, reverting again sim-ply to house when home (that is, life) departs. For only where there is life can there be home.

I have never found the visual equivalent of these abandoned farmhouses of upstate New York, of northern Erie County, in the area of the long, meandering Tonawanda Creek and the Barge Canal. You think most immediately of the canvases of Edward Hopper: those dreamily stylized visions of a lost America, houses never depicted as homes, and human beings, if you look closer, never depicted as other than mannequins. For Hopper is not a re-alist but a surrealist. His dreams are of the ordinary, as if, even in imagination, the artist were trapped in an unyielding daylight consciousness. There seems almost a kind of rage, a revenge against such restraints, in Hopper's studied, endlessly repeated *simplicity*. By contrast, Charles Burchfield, with his numerous oils and watercolors — frequently of upstate New York landscapes, houses, and farms — rendered the real as visionary and luminous, suffused with a Blakean rapture and a kind of radical simplicity, too. Then there are the shimmering New England barns, fields, and skies of our contemporary Wolf Kahn — images evoked by memory, almost on the verge of dissolution. But the "real" — what assaults the eye before the eye begins its work of selection — is never on the verge of dissolution, still less of appropriation. The real is raw, jarring, unexpected, sometimes trashy, sometimes lu-minous. Above all, the real is arbitrary. For to be a realist (in art or in life) is to acknowledge that all things might be other than they are. That there is no design, no intention, no aesthetic or moral or teleological imprimatur but, rather, the equivalent of Darwin's great vision of a blind, purposeless, ceaseless evolutionary process that yields no "products"—only temporary strategies against extinction.

Yet, being human, we think, To what purpose these broken-off things, if not to be gathered up, at last, in a single ecstatic vision?

There is a strange and profound and unknowable reality to these abandoned houses where jealously guarded, even prized possessions have become mere trash: windowpanes long ago smashed, and the spaces where they had been festooned with cobwebs, and cobwebs brushing against your face, catching in your hair like caresses. The peculiar, dank smell of wood rot and mildew, in one of the houses I most recall that had partly burned down, the smell of smoke and scorch, in early summer pervading even the lyric smell of honeysuckle—these haunting smells, never, at the time of experiencing, given specific sources, names.

Where a house has been abandoned—unworthy of being sold to new tenants, very likely seized by the county for default on taxes and the property held in escrow—you can be sure there has been a sad story. There have been devastated lives. Lives to be spoken of pityingly. How they went wrong. Why did she marry him, why did she stay with him? Just desperate people. Ignorant. Poor white trash. Runs in the family. A wrong turn.

Shall I say for the record that ours was a happy, close-knit, and unextraordinary family for our time, place, and economic status? Yet what was vividly real in the solid-built old farmhouse that contained my home (my family consisted of my father, mother, younger brother, grandfather, and grandmother, who owned the property—a slow-failing farm whose principal crop had become Bartlett pears by the time I was a girl) was of far less significance to me than what was real elsewhere. A gone-to-seed landscape had an authority that seemed to me incontestable: the powerful authority of silence in houses from which the human voice had vanished. For the abandoned house contained the future of any house — the lilac tree pushing through the rotted veranda, hornets' nests beneath caves, windows smashed by vandals, human excrement left to dry on a parlor floor once scrubbed on hands and knees.

The abandoned, the devastated, was the profound experience, whereas involvement in family life — the fever, the bliss, the abrasions, the infinite distractions of human love — was so clearly temporary. Like a television screen upon which antic images (at this time, in the fifties, minimally varying gradations of gray) appear fleetingly and are gone.

I have seemed to suggest that the abandoned houses were all distant from our house, but in fact the one that had been partly gutted by fire — which I will call the Weidel house — was perhaps a half mile away. If you drove, turning right off Transit Road, which was our road, onto the old Creek Road, it would have been a distance of a mile or more, but if you crossed through our back potato field and through the marshy woods which no one seemed to own, it was a quick walk.

The Weidels' dog, Slossie, a mixed breed with a stumpy, energetic tail and a sweet disposition, sand-colored, rheumy-eyed, as hungry for affection as for the scraps we sometimes fed her, trotted over frequently to play with my brother and me. Though, strictly speaking, Slossie was not wanted at our house. None of the Weidels were wanted.

The "Weidel house," it would be called for years. The "Weidel property." As if the very land — which the family had not owned in any case, but only rented, partly with county-welfare support — were somehow imprinted with that name, a man's identity. Or infamy.

For tales were told of the father who drank, beat and terrorized his family, "did things to" his daughters, and finally set the house on fire and fled and was arrested, disappearing forever from the proper, decent life of our community. There was no romance in Mr. Weidel, whom my father knew only slightly and despised as a drinker, and as a wife- and child-beater. Mr. Weidel was a railway worker in Lockport, or perhaps an ex-railway worker, for he seemed to work only sporadically, though he always wore a railwayman's cap. He and his elder sons were hunters, owning a shotgun among them and one or two deer rifles. His face was broad, fair, vein-swollen, with a look of flushed, alcoholic reproach. He was tall and heavyset, with graying black whiskers that sprouted like quills. His eyes had a way of swerving in their sockets, seeking you out when you could not slip away quickly enough. *H'lo there, little*

Joyce! Joycie! Joycie Oates, h'lo! He wore rubber boots that flapped, un-buckled, about his feet.

Mrs. Weidel was a faded-pretty, apologetic woman with a body that seemed to have become bloated, as with a perpetual preg-nancy. Her bosom had sunk to her waist. Her legs were encased, sausagelike, in flesh-colored support hose. *How can that woman live with him? That pig.* There was disdain, disgust, in this frequent re-frain. *Why doesn't she leave him? Did you see that black eye? Did you hear them the other night? Take the girls away, at least.* It was thought that she could, for Mrs. Weidel was the only one in the family who seemed to work at all regularly. She was hired for seasonal canning in a tomato factory in lower Lockport and may have done house-cleaning in the city.

A shifting household of relatives and rumored "boarders" lived in the Weidel house. There were six Weidel children, four sons and two daughters. Ruth was a year older than I, and Dorothy two years younger. There was an older brother of Mr. Weidel's, who walked with a cane and was said to be an ex-convict, from Attica. The eldest Weidel son, Roy, owned a motorcycle, and friends of his often visited, fellow bikers. There were loud parties, frequent dis-putes, and tales of Mr. Weidel's chasing his wife with a butcher knife, a claw hammer, the shotgun, threatening to "blow her head off." Mrs. Weidel and the younger children fled outdoors in terror and hid in the hayloft. Sheriff's deputies drove out to the house, but no charges were ever pressed against Mr. Weidel. Until the fire, which was so public that it couldn't be denied.

There was the summer day — I was eleven years old — that Mr. Weidel shot Slossie. We heard the poor creature yelping and whim-pering for what seemed like hours. When my father came home from work, he went to speak to Mr. Weidel, though my mother begged him not to. By this time, the dog had dragged herself be-neath the Weidels' house to die. Mr. Weidel was furious at the in-trusion, drunk, defensive — Slossie was his goddam dog, he said, she'd been getting in the way, she was "old." But my father con-vinced him to put the poor dog out of her misery. So Mr. Weidel made one of his sons drag Slossie out from beneath the house, and he straddled her and shot her a second time, and a third, at close range. My father, who'd never hunted, who'd never owned a gun, backed off, a hand over his eyes.

Afterward, my father would say of that day that walking away from that drunken son of a bitch with a rifle in his hands was about the hardest thing he'd ever done. He'd expected a shot between his shoulders.

The fire was the following year, around Thanksgiving.

After the Weidels were gone from Millersport and the house stood empty, I discovered Slossie's grave. I'm sure it was Slossie's grave. It was beyond the dog hutch, in the weedy back yard, a sunken patch of earth measuring about three feet by four with one of Mrs. Weidel's big whitewashed rocks at the head.

Morning glories grew in clusters on the posts of the front porch. Mrs. Weidel had planted hollyhocks, sunflowers, and trumpet vine in the yard. Tough, weedlike flowers that would survive for years.

It had been said of Ruth and her sister Dorothy that they were "slow." Yet Ruth was never slow to fly into a rage when she was teased by neighborhood boys or by her older brothers. She waved her fists and stammered obscenities, words that stung like hail. Her face darkened with blood, and her full, thick lips quivered with a strange sort of pleasure. How you loved to see Ruth Weidel fly into one of her rages; it was like holding a lighted match to flammable material.

The Weidel house was like any other rundown woodframe house, said by my grandfather to have been "thrown up" in the 1920s. It had no cellar, only a concrete-block foundation — an emptiness that gradually filled with debris. It had an upstairs with several small bedrooms. There was no attic. No insulation. Steep, almost vertical stairs. The previous tenant had started to construct a front porch of raw planks, never completed or painted. (Though Mrs. Weidel added "touches" to the porch — chairs, a woven-rush rug, geraniums in flowerpots.) The roof of the house was made of sheets of tin, scarred and scabbed like skin, and the front was covered in simulated-brick asphalt siding pieced together from lumberyard scraps. All year round, a number of the windows were covered in transparent duct tape and never opened. From a distance, the house was the fading dun color of a deer's winter coat.

Our house had an attic and a cellar and a deep well and a solid cement foundation. My father did all the carpentry on our house, most of the shingling, the painting, the masonry. I would not know until I was an adult that he'd come from what's called a "broken home" himself — what an image, luridly visual, of a house literally broken, split in two, its secrets spilled out onto the ground for all to see, like entrails.

My mother, unlike Mrs. Weidel, had time to houseclean. It was a continuous task, a mother's responsibility. My mother planted vegetables, strawberries, beds of flowers. Petunias and pansies and zinnias. Crimson peonies that flowered for my birthday, in mid-June.

I remember the night of the fire vividly, as if it had been a festive affair to which I'd been invited.

There was the sound of a siren on the Creek Road. There were shouts, and an astonishing burst of flame in the night, in the direction of the Weidel house. The air was moist, and reflected and magnified the fire, surrounding it like a nimbus. My grandparents would claim there had never been such excitement in Millersport, and perhaps that was true. My father dressed hurriedly and went to help the firefighters, and my mother and the rest of us watched from upstairs windows. The fire began at about 1 A.M., and it would be past 4 A.M. before my seven-year-old brother and I got back to bed.

Yet what was so exciting an event was, in fact, an ending, with nothing to follow. Immediately afterward, the Weidels disappeared from Millersport and from our lives. It was said that Mr. Weidel fled "as a fugitive" but was captured and arrested the next day, in Buffalo. The family was broken up, scattered, the younger children placed in foster homes. That quickly, the Weidels were gone.

For a long time, the smell of wood smoke, scorch, pervaded the air of Millersport, the fresh, damp smell of earth sullied by its presence. Neighbors complained that the Weidel house should be razed at the county's expense, bulldozed over, and the property sold. But nothing was done for years. Who knows why? When I went away to college, the old falling-down house was still there.

How swiftly, in a single season, a human habitation can turn wild. The bumpy cinder driveway over which the eldest Weidel son had ridden his motorcycle was soon stippled with tall weeds.

What had happened to Roy Weidel? It was said he'd joined the navy. No, he had a police record and could not have joined the navy. He'd disappeared. Asked by the police to give a sworn statement about the night of his father's "arson," he'd panicked and fled.

Signs were posted — NO TRESPASSING, THIS PROPERTY CONDEMNED BY ERIE CO. — and they, too, over a period of months, became shabby and faded. My parents warned me never to wander onto the Weidel property. There was a well with a loose-fitting cover, among other dangers. As if *I* would fall into a well! I smiled to think how little my parents knew me. How little anyone knew me.

Have I said that my father never struck his children, as Mr. Weidel struck his? And did worse things to them, to the girls sometimes, it was whispered. Yes, and Mrs. Weidel, who seemed so soft and apologetic and sad, she too had beaten the younger children when she'd been drinking. County social workers came around to question neighbors, and spread the story of what they learned along the way.

In fact, I may have been disciplined, spanked, a few times. Like most children, I don't remember. I remember Mr. Weidel spanking his children until they screamed (though I wasn't a witness, was I?), but I don't remember being spanked by my parents, and in any case, if I was, it was no more than I deserved.

I'd seen Mr. Weidel urinating once at the roadside. The loose-flying skein of the kerosene he'd flung around the house before setting the fire must have resembled the stream of his urine, transparent and glittering. But they laughed, saying Mr. Weidel had been too drunk, or too careless, to have done an adequate job of sprinkling kerosene through the downstairs of the house. Wasn't it like him, such a slovenly job. Only part of the house had burned, a wall of the kitchen and an adjoining woodshed.

Had Mr. Weidel wanted to burn his family alive in their beds? Mrs. Weidel testified no, they'd all been awake, they'd run out into the yard before the fire began. They'd never been in any danger, she swore. But Mr. Weidel was indicted on several counts of attempted murder, along with other charges.

For so many years the Weidel house remained standing. There was something defiant about it, like someone who has been mortally wounded but will not die. In the weedy front yard, Mrs. Weidel's display of whitewashed rocks and plaster-of-Paris gnomes and the clay pedestal with the shiny blue glass ball disappeared from view within a year or so. Brambles grew everywhere. I forced myself to taste a small bitter red berry but spat it out, it made my mouth pucker so.

What did it mean that Erie County had "condemned" the Weidel property? The downstairs windows were carelessly boarded over, and both the front and rear doors were unlocked, collapsing on their hinges. Broken glass underfoot and a sickish stench of burn, mildew, decay. Yet there were "touches"—on what remained of a kitchen wall, a Holstein calendar from a local feed store, a child's crayon drawing. Upstairs, children's clothes, socks and old shoes heaped on the floor. I recognized with a thrill of repugnance an old red sweater of Ruth's, angora-fuzzy. There were broken Christmas tree ornaments, a naked pink plastic doll. Toppled bedsprings, filthy mattresses streaked with yellow and rust-colored stains. The mattresses looked as if they'd been gutted, their stuffing strewn about. The most terrible punishment, I thought, would be to be forced to lie down on such a mattress.

I thought of Mrs. Weidel, her swollen, blackened eyes, her bruised face. Shouts and sirens in the night, the sheriff's patrol car. But no charges filed. The social worker told my mother how Mrs. Weidel had screamed at the county people, insisting her husband hadn't done anything wrong and shouldn't go to jail. The names she'd called them! Unrepeatable.

She was the wife of that man, they'd had babies together. The law had no right to interfere. The law had nothing to do with them.

As a woman and as a writer, I have long wondered at the well-springs of female masochism. Or what, in despair of a more subtle, less reductive phrase, we can call the congeries of predilections toward self-hurt, self-erasure, self-repudiation in women. These predilections are presumably "learned"—"acquired"—but perhaps also imprinted in our genes, of biological necessity, neurophysiological fate, predilections that predate culture. Indeed, may shape culture. Do not say, "Yes, but these are isolated, peripheral examples. These are marginal Americans, uneducated. They tell us nothing about ourselves." They tell us everything about ourselves, and even the telling, the exposure, is a kind of cutting, an inscription in the flesh.

Yet what could possibly be the evolutionary advantage of self-hurt in the female? Abnegation in the face of another's cruelty? Acquiescence to another's will? This loathsome secret that women do not care to speak of, or even acknowledge.

Two or three years later, in high school, twelve miles away in a consolidated district school to which, as a sophomore, I went by school bus, Ruth Weidel appeared. She was living now with relatives in Lockport. She looked, at sixteen, like a woman in her twenties; big-breasted, with full, strong thighs and burnished-brown hair inexpertly bleached. Ruth's homeroom was "special education," but she took some classes with the rest of us. If she recognized me, in our home economics class, she was careful to give no sign.

There was a tacit understanding that "something had happened" to Ruth Weidel, and her teachers treated her guardedly. Ruth was special, the way a handicapped person is special. She was withdrawn, quiet; if still prone to violent outbursts of rage, she might have been on medication to control it. Her eyes, like her father's, seemed always about to swerve in their sockets. Her face was round, fleshy, like a pudding, her nose oily-pored. Yet she wore lipstick, she was "glamorous"—almost. In gym class, Ruth's large breasts straining against her T-shirt and the shining rippled muscles and fatty flesh of her thighs were amazing to us; we were so much thinner and less female, so much younger.

I believed that I should protect Ruth Weidel, so I told none of the other students about her family. Even to Ruth, for a long time I pretended not to know who she was. I can't explain how Ruth could have possibly believed me, yet this seems to have been so. Quite purposefully, I befriended Ruth. I thought her face would lose its sallow hardness if she could be made to smile, and so it became a kind of challenge to me to induce Ruth Weidel to smile. She was lonely and miserable at school, and flattered by my attention. For so few "normal" girls sought out "specialed" girls. At first she may have been suspicious, but by degrees she became trusting. I thought of Slossie: trust shows in the eyes.

I sat with Ruth at lunch in the school cafeteria and eventually I asked her about the house on the old Creek Road, and she lied bluntly, to my face, insisting that an uncle of hers had owned that house. She'd only visited a few times. She and her family. I asked,

"How did the fire start?" and Ruth said, slowly, each word sucked like a pebble in the mouth, "Lightning. Lightning hit it. One night in a storm." I asked, "Are you living with your mother now, Ruth?" and Ruth shrugged, and made a face, and said, "She's OK. I see her sometimes." I asked about Dorothy. I asked where Mrs. Weidel was. I said that my mother had always liked her mother, and missed her when she went away. But Ruth seemed not to hear. Her gaze had drifted. I said, "Why did you all move away?" Ruth did not reply, though I could hear her breathing hard. "Why did you abandon your house? It could have been fixed. It's still there. Your mom's hollyhocks are still there. You should come out and see it sometime. You could visit me." Ruth shrugged, and laughed. She gave me a sidelong glance, almost flirtatiously. It was startling to see how good-looking she could be, how sullen-sexy; to know how men would stare at her who would never so much as glance at a girl like me. Ruth said slowly, as if she'd come to a final, adamant conclusion to a problem that had long vexed her, "They all just went away."

Another time, after lunch with Ruth. I left a plastic change purse with a few coins in it on the ledge in one of the girls' lavatories, where Ruth was washing her hands. I don't recall whether I left it on purpose or not. But when I returned, after waiting for Ruth to leave the lavatory, the change purse was gone.

Once or twice, I invited Ruth Weidel to come home with me on the school bus some afternoon, to Millersport, to have supper with my family and stay the night. I must not have truly believed she might accept, for my mother would have been horrified and would have forced me to rescind the invitation. Ruth had hesitated, as if she wanted to say yes, wanted very badly to say yes, but finally she said, "No. I guess I better not."

Reflections and Responses

1. How does Joyce Carol Oates introduce the issue of class into the essay? How does her background differ from Ruth Weidel's? How would you describe her attitude toward the Weidel family? Why is she drawn to them? What does she find attractive about them?

2. How can you account for the abrupt introduction in the ninth paragraph of houses as the subject for famous American painters? Why do you think the author suddenly interjected this information? What does it contribute to the essay as a whole?

3. Where does the essay's title come from? Why do you think Joyce Carol Oates used this expression as the title? What does it suggest about the overall experience of the essay?

GAY TALESE

Ali in Havana

When one of America's leading journalists was assigned to profile one of the world's biggest celebrities on a humanitarian-aid visit to one of the world's most controversial political figures, the result was bound to be a fascinating piece of writing and disclosure. In "Ali in Havana," Gay Talese accompanies the great fighter Muhammad Ali as he travels with his wife and entourage, along with many other visitors, to a reception at the Palace of the Revolution in Havana to meet the aging communist leader, Fidel Castro. What ensues is both comic and poignant, as the magical Ali, stricken with Parkinson's disease, leaves Castro — who has been struggling to keep the small talk flowing — with a very odd parting token. A connoisseur of the unnoticed detail, Talese captures all of the humor, tension, and awkwardness of this nearly surrealistic scene.

Gay Talese is one of the founders of the New Journalism, a literary movement that irrevocably altered both the art of reporting and the art of the essay. He is the best-selling author of books about the New York Times (The Kingdom and the Power), *the inside story of a Mafia family* (Honor Thy Father), *the changing moral values of America* (Thy Neighbor's Wife), *and a historical memoir* (Unto the Sons). *Other nonfiction books include* The Bridge, New York: A Serendipiter's Journey, *and* Fame and Obscurity. *Talese served as guest editor of* The Best American Essays 1987. *"Ali in Havana" originally appeared in* Esquire *and was selected by Ian Frazier for the 1997 volume.*

It is a warm, breezy, palm-flapping winter evening in Havana, and the leading restaurants are crowded with tourists from Europe, Asia, and South America being serenaded by guitarists relentlessly singing *"Guan-tan-a-mera . . . guajira . . . Guan-tan-a-mera";* and at the

Café Cantante there are clamorous salsa dancers, mambo kings, grunting, bare-chested male performers lifting tables with their teeth, and turbaned women swathed in hip-hugging skirts, blowing whistles while gyrating their glistening bodies into an erotic frenzy. In the café's audience as well as in the restaurants, hotels, and other public places throughout the island, cigarettes and cigars are smoked without restraint or restriction. Two prostitutes are smoking and talking privately on the corner of a dimly lit street bordering the manicured lawns of Havana's five-star Hotel Nacional. They are copper-colored women in their early twenties wearing faded miniskirts and halters, and as they chat, they are watching attentively while two men — one white, the other black — huddle over the raised trunk of a parked red Toyota, arguing about the prices of the boxes of black-market Havana cigars that are stacked within.

The white man is a square-jawed Hungarian in his mid-thirties, wearing a beige tropical suit and a wide yellow tie, and he is one of Havana's leading entrepreneurs in the thriving illegal business of selling top-quality hand-rolled Cuban cigars below the local and international market price. The black man behind the car is a well-built, baldish, gray-bearded individual in his mid-fifties from Los Angeles named Howard Bingham; and no matter what price the Hungarian quotes, Bingham shakes his head and says, "No, no — that's too much!"

"You're crazy!" cries the Hungarian in slightly accented English, taking one of the boxes from the trunk and waving it in Howard Bingham's face. "These are Cohiba Esplendidos! The best in the world! You will pay one thousand dollars for a box like this in the States."

"Not me," says Bingham, who wears a Hawaiian shirt with a camera strapped around his neck. He is a professional photographer, and he is staying at the Hotel Nacional with his friend Muhammad Ali. "I wouldn't give you more than fifty dollars."

"You really are crazy," says the Hungarian, slicing through the box's paper seal with his fingernail, opening the lid to reveal a gleaming row of labeled Esplendidos.

"Fifty dollars," says Bingham.

"A hundred dollars," insists the Hungarian. "And hurry! The police could be driving around." The Hungarian straightens up and stares over the car toward the palm-lined lawn and stanchioned lights that glow in the distance along the road leading to the hotel's ornate portico, which is now jammed with people and vehicles; then he turns and flings a glance back toward the nearby public street, where he notices that the prostitutes are now blowing smoke in his direction. He frowns.

"Quick, quick," he says to Bingham, handing him the box. "One hundred dollars."

Howard Bingham does not smoke. He and Muhammad Ali and their traveling companions are leaving Havana tomorrow, after participating in a five-day American humanitarian-aid mission that brought a planeload of medical supplies to hospitals and clinics depleted by the United States' embargo, and Bingham would like to return home with some fine contraband cigars for his friends. But, on the other hand, one hundred is still too much.

"Fifty dollars," says Bingham determinedly, looking at his watch. He begins to walk away.

"O.K., O.K.," the Hungarian says petulantly. "Fifty."

Bingham reaches into his pocket for the money, and the Hungarian grabs it and gives him the Esplendidos before driving off in the Toyota. One of the prostitutes takes a few steps toward Bingham, but the photographer hurries on to the hotel. Fidel Castro is having a reception tonight for Muhammad Ali, and Bingham has only a half hour to change and be at the portico to catch the chartered bus that will take them to the government's headquarters. He will be bringing one of his photographs to the Cuban leader: an enlarged, framed portrait showing Muhammad Ali and Malcolm X walking together along a Harlem sidewalk in 1963. Malcolm X was thirty-seven at the time, two years away from an assassin's bullet; the twenty-one-year-old Ali was about to win the heavyweight title in a remarkable upset over Sonny Liston in Miami. Bingham's photograph is inscribed, TO PRESIDENT FIDEL CASTRO, FROM MUHAMMAD ALI. Under his signature, the former champion has sketched a little heart.

Although Muhammad Ali is now fifty-four and has been retired from boxing for more than fifteen years, he is still one of the most famous men in the world, being identifiable throughout five continents; and as he walks through the lobby of the Hotel Nacional toward the bus, wearing a gray sharkskin suit and a white cotton shirt buttoned at the neck without a tie, several guests approach him and request his autograph. It takes him about thirty seconds to write "Muhammad Ali," so shaky are his hands from the effects of Parkinson's syndrome; and though he walks without support, his movements are quite slow, and Howard Bingham and Ali's fourth wife, Yolanda, are following nearby.

Bingham met Ali thirty-five years ago in Los Angeles, shortly after the fighter had turned professional and before he discarded his "slave name" (Cassius Marcellus Clay) and joined the Black Muslims. Bingham subsequently became his closest male friend and has photographed every aspect of Ali's life: his rise and fall three times as the heavyweight champion; his three-year expulsion from boxing, beginning in 1967, for refusing to serve in the American military during the Vietnam War ("I ain't got no quarrel with them Vietcong"); his four marriages; his fatherhood of nine children (one adopted, two out of wedlock); his endless public appearances in all parts of the world — Germany, England, Egypt (sailing on the Nile with a son of Elijah Muhammad's), Sweden, Libya, Pakistan (hugging refugees from Afghanistan), Japan, Indonesia, Ghana (wearing a dashiki and posing with President Kwame Nkrumah), Zaire (beating George Foreman), Manila (beating Joe Frazier) . . . and now, on the final night of his 1996 visit to Cuba, he is en route to a social encounter with an aging contender he has long admired — one who has survived at the top for nearly forty years despite the ill will of nine American presidents, the CIA, the Mafia, and various militant Cuban Americans.

Bingham waits for Ali near the open door of the charter bus that is blocking the hotel's entrance; but Ali lingers within the crowd in the lobby, and Yolanda steps aside to let some people get closer to her husband.

She is a large and pretty woman of thirty-eight, with a radiant smile and a freckled, fair complexion that reflects her interracial ancestry. A scarf is loosely draped over her head and shoulders, her arms are covered by long sleeves, and her well-designed dress in vivid hues hangs below her knees. She converted to Islam from Catholicism when she married Ali, a man sixteen years her senior but one with whom she shared a familial bond dating back to her girlhood in their native Louisville, where her mother and Ali's mother were sisterly soul mates who traveled together to attend his fights. Yolanda had occasionally joined Ali's entourage, becoming acquainted with not only the boxing element but with Ali's female contemporaries who were his lovers, his wives, the mothers of his children; and she remained in touch with Ali throughout the 1970s, while she majored in psychology at Vanderbilt and later earned her master's degree in business at UCLA. Then — with the end of Ali's boxing career, his third marriage, and his vibrant health —Yolanda intimately entered his life as casually and naturally as she now stands waiting to reclaim her place at his side.

She knows that he is enjoying himself. There is a slight twinkle in his eyes, not much expression on his face, and no words forthcoming from this once most talkative of champions. But the mind behind his Parkinson's mask is functioning normally, and he is characteristically committed to what he is doing: he is spelling out his full name on whatever cards or scraps of paper his admirers are handing him. "Muhammad Ali." He does not settle for a time-saving "Ali" or his mere initials. He has never shortchanged his audience.

And in this audience tonight are people from Latin America, Canada, Africa, Russia, China, Germany, France. There are two hundred French travel agents staying at the hotel in conjunction with the Cuban government's campaign to increase its growing tourist trade (which last year saw about 745,000 visitors spending an estimated one billion dollars on the island). There is also on hand an Italian movie producer and his lady friend from Rome and a onetime Japanese wrestler, Antonio Inoki, who injured Ali's legs during a 1976 exhibition in Tokyo (but who warmly embraced him two nights ago in the hotel's lounge as they sat listening to Cuban pianist Chucho Valdes playing jazz on a Russian-made Moskva baby grand); and there is also in the crowd, standing taller than the rest, the forty-three-year-old, six-foot five-inch Cuban heavyweight hero Teófilo Stevenson, who was a three-time Olympic gold medalist, in 1972, 1976 and 1980, and who, on this island at least, is every bit as renowned as Ali or Castro.

Though part of Stevenson's reputation derives from his erstwhile power and skill in the ring (although he never fought Ali), it is also attributable to his not having succumbed to the offers of professional boxing promoters, stubbornly resisting the Yankee dollar — although Stevenson hardly seems deprived. He dwells among his countrymen like a towering Cuban peacock, occupying high positions within the government's athletic programs and gaining sufficient attention from the island's women to have garnered four wives so far, who are testimony to his eclectic taste.

His first wife was a dance instructor. His second was an industrial engineer. His third was a medical doctor. His fourth and present wife is a criminal attorney. Her name is Fraymari, and she is a girlishly petite olive-skinned woman of twenty-three who, standing next to her husband in the lobby, rises barely higher than the midsection of his embroidered guayabera — a tightly tailored, short-sleeved shirt that accentuates his tapered torso, his broad shoulders, and the length of his dark, muscular arms, which once prevented his opponents from doing any injustice to his winning Latin looks.

Stevenson always fought from an upright position, and he maintains that posture today. When people talk to him, his eyes look downward, but his head remains high. The firm jaw of his oval-shaped head seems to be locked at a right angle to his straight-spined back. He is a proud man who exhibits all of his height. But he does listen, especially when the words being directed up at him are coming from the perky little attorney who is his wife. Fraymari is now reminding him that it is getting late — everyone should be on the bus; Fidel may be waiting.

Stevenson lowers his eyes toward her and winks. He has gotten the message. He has been Ali's principal escort throughout this visit. He was also Ali's guest in the United States during the fall of 1995; and though he knows only a few words of English, and Ali no Spanish, they are brotherly in their body language.

Stevenson edges himself into the crowd and gently places his right arm around the shoulders of his fellow champion. And then, slowly but firmly, he guides Ali toward the bus.

The road to Fidel Castro's Palace of the Revolution leads through a memory lane of old American automobiles chugging along at about twenty-five miles an hour — springless, pre-embargo Ford coupes and Plymouth sedans, DeSotos and LaSalles, Nashes and Studebakers, and various vehicular collages created out of Cadillac grilles and Oldsmobile axles and Buick fenders patched with pieces of oil-drum metal and powered by engines interlinked with kitchen utensils and pre-Batista lawn mowers and other gadgets that have elevated the craft of tinkering in Cuba to the status of high art.

The relatively newer forms of transportation seen on the road are, of course, non-American products — Polish Fiats, Russian Ladas, German motor scooters, Chinese bicycles, and the glistening, newly imported, air-conditioned Japanese bus from which Muhammad Ali is now gazing through a closed window out toward the street. At times, he raises a hand in response to one of the waving pedestrians or cyclists or motorists who recognize the bus, which has been shown repeatedly on the local TV news conveying Ali and his companions to the medical centers and tourist sites that have been part of the busy itinerary.

On the bus, as always, Ali is sitting alone, spread out across the two front seats in the left aisle directly behind the Cuban driver. Yolanda sits a few feet ahead of him to the right; she is adjacent to the driver and within inches of the windshield. The seats behind her are occupied by Teófilo Stevenson, Fraymari, and the photographer Bingham. Seated behind Ali, and also occupying two seats, is an American screenwriter named Greg Howard, who weighs more than three hundred pounds. Although he has traveled with Ali for only a few months while researching a film on the fighter's life, Greg Howard has firmly established himself as an intimate sidekick, and as such is among the very few on this trip who have heard Ali's voice. Ali speaks so softly that it is impossible to hear him in a crowd, and as a result whatever public comments or sentiments he is expected to, or chooses to, express are verbalized by Yolanda, or Bingham, or Teófilo Stevenson, or even at times by this stout young screenwriter.

"Ali is in his Zen period," Greg Howard has said more than once, in reference to Ali's quiescence. Like Ali, he admires what he has seen so far in Cuba — "There's no racism here" — and as a black man he has long identified with many of Ali's frustrations and confrontations. His student thesis at Princeton analyzed the Newark race riots of 1967, and the Hollywood script he most recently completed focuses on the Negro baseball leagues of the pre–World War II years. He envisions his new work on Ali in the genre of *Gandhi.*

* * *

The two-dozen bus seats behind those tacitly reserved for Ali's inner circle are occupied by the secretary-general of the Cuban Red Cross and the American humanitarian personnel who have entrusted him with $500,000 worth of donated medical supplies; and there are also the two Cuban interpreters and a dozen members of the American media, including the CBS-TV commentator Ed Bradley and his producers and camera crew from *60 Minutes*.

Ed Bradley is a gracious but reserved individualist who has appeared on television for a decade with his left earlobe pierced by a small circular ring — which, after some unfavorable comment initially expressed by his colleagues Mike Wallace and Andy Rooney, prompted Bradley's explanation: "It's *my* ear." Bradley also indulges in his identity as a cigar smoker; and as he sits in the midsection of the bus next to his Haitian lady friend, he is taking full advantage of the Communist regime's laissez-faire attitude toward tobacco, puffing away on a Cohiba Robusto, for which he paid full price at the Nacional's tobacco shop — and which now exudes a costly cloud of fragrance that appeals to his friend (who occasionally also smokes cigars) but is not appreciated by the two California women who are seated two rows back and are affiliated with a humanitarian-aid agency.

Indeed, the women have been commenting about the smoking habits of countless people they have encountered in Havana, being especially disappointed to discover earlier this very day that the pediatric hospital they visited (and to which they committed donations) is under the supervision of three tobacco-loving family physicians. When one of the American women, a blonde from Santa Barbara, reproached one of the cigarette-smoking doctors indirectly for setting such a poor example, she was told in effect that the island's health statistics regarding longevity, infant mortality, and general fitness compared favorably with those in the United States and were probably better than those of Americans residing in the capital city of Washington. On the other hand, the doctor made it clear that he did not believe that smoking was good for one's health — after all, Fidel himself had given it up; but unfortunately, the doctor added, in a classic understatement, "Some people have not followed him."

Nothing the doctor said appeased the woman from Santa Barbara. She did not, however, wish to appear confrontational at the hospital's news conference, which was covered by the press; nor during her many bus rides with Ed Bradley did she ever request that he discard his cigar. "Mr. Bradley intimidates me," she confided to her California coworker. But he was of course living within the law on this island that the doctor had called "the cradle of the best tobacco in the world." In Cuba, the most available American periodical on the newsstands is *Cigar Aficionado*.

The bus passes through the Plaza de la Revolución and comes to a halt at a security checkpoint near the large glass doors that open onto the marble-floored foyer of a 1950s modern building that is the center of communism's only stronghold in the Western Hemisphere.

As the bus door swings open, Greg Howard moves forward in his seat and grabs the 235-pound Muhammad Ali by the arms and shoulders and helps him to his feet; and after Ali has made his way down to the metal step, he turns and stretches back into the bus to take hold of the extended hands and forearms of the 300-pound screenwriter and pulls him to a standing position. This routine, repeated at each and every bus stop throughout the week, is never accompanied by either man's acknowledging that he had received any assistance, although Ali is aware that some passengers find the pas de deux quite amusing, and he is not reluctant to use his friend to further comic effect. After the bus had made an earlier stop in front of the sixteenth-century Morro Castle — where Ali had followed Teófilo Stevenson up a 117-step spiral staircase for a rooftop view of Havana Harbor — he spotted the solitary figure of Greg Howard standing below in the courtyard. Knowing that there was no way the narrow staircase could accommodate Howard's wide body, Ali suddenly began to wave his arms, summoning Howard to come up and join him.

Castro's security guards, who know in advance the names of all the bus passengers, guide Ali and the others through the glass doors and then into a pair of waiting elevators for a brief ride that is followed by a short walk through a corridor and finally into a large white-walled reception room, where it is announced that Fidel Castro will soon join them. The room has high ceilings and potted palms in every corner and is sparsely furnished with modern tan leather furniture. Next to a sofa is a table with two telephones, one gray and the other red. Overlooking the sofa is an oil painting of the Viñales valley, which lies west of Havana; and among the primitive art displayed on a circular table in front of the sofa is a grotesque tribal figure similar to the one Ali had examined earlier in the week at a trinket stand while touring with the group in Havana's Old Square. Ali had then whispered into the ear of Howard Bingham, and Bingham had repeated aloud what Ali had said: "Joe Frazier."

Ali now stands in the middle of the room, next to Bingham, who carries under his arm the framed photograph he plans to give Castro. Teófilo Stevenson and Fraymari stand facing them. The diminutive and delicate-boned Fraymari has painted her lips scarlet and has pulled back her hair in a matronly manner, hoping no doubt to appear more mature than her twenty-three years suggest, but standing next to the three much older and heavier and taller men transforms her image closer to that of an anorexic teenager. Ali's wife and Greg Howard are wandering about within the group that is exchanging comments in muted tones, either in English or Spanish, sometimes assisted by the interpreters. Ali's hands are shaking uncontrollably at his sides; but since his companions have witnessed this all week, the only people who are now paying attention are the security guards posted near the door.

Also waiting near the door for Castro is the four-man CBS camera team, and chatting with them and his two producers is Ed Bradley, without his cigar. There are no ashtrays in this room! This is a most uncommon sight in Cuba. Its implications might be political. Perhaps the sensibilities of the blond woman from Santa Barbara were taken into account by the doctors at the hospital and communicated to Castro's underlings, who are now making a conciliatory gesture toward their American benefactress.

Since the security guards have not invited the guests to be seated, everybody remains standing — for ten minutes, for twenty minutes, and then for a full half hour. Teófilo Stevenson shifts his weight from foot to foot and gazes over the heads of the crowd toward the upper level of the portal through which Castro is expected to enter — if he shows up. Stevenson knows from experience that Castro's schedule is unpredictable. There is always a crisis of some sort in Cuba, and it has long been rumored on the

island that Castro constantly changes the location of where he
sleeps. The identity of his bed partners is, of course, a state secret.
Two nights ago, Stevenson and Ali and the rest were kept waiting
until midnight for an expected meeting with Castro at the Hotel
Biocaribe (to which Bingham had brought his gift photograph).
But Castro never appeared. And no explanation was offered.

Now in this reception room, it is already 9 P.M. Ali continues to
shake. No one has had dinner. The small talk is getting smaller: A
few people would like to smoke. The regime is not assuaging anyone in this crowd with a bartender. It is a cocktail party without
cocktails. There are not even canapés or soft drinks. Everyone is
becoming increasingly restless — and then suddenly there is a collective sigh. The very familiar man with the beard strides into the
room, dressed for guerrilla combat; and in a cheerful, high-
pitched voice that soars beyond his whiskers, he announces, *"Buenas noches!"*

In an even higher tone, he repeats, *"Buenas noches,"* this time
with a few waves to the group while hastening toward the guest of
honor; and then, with his arms extended, the seventy-year-old
Fidel Castro immediately obscures the lower half of Ali's expres-
sionless face with a gentle embrace and his flowing gray beard.

"I am glad to see you," Castro says to Ali, via the interpreter who
followed him into the room, a comely, fair-skinned woman with a
refined English accent. "I am very, very glad to see you," Castro
continues, backing up to look into Ali's eyes while holding on to
his trembling arms, "and I am thankful for your visit." Castro then
releases his grip and awaits a possible reply. Ali says nothing. His
expression remains characteristically fixed and benign, and his
eyes do not blink despite the flashbulbs of several surrounding
photographers. As the silence persists, Castro turns toward his
old friend Teófilo Stevenson, feigning a jab. The Cuban boxing
champion lowers his eyes and, with widened lips and cheeks, regis-
ters a smile. Castro then notices the tiny brunette standing beside
Stevenson.

"Stevenson, who is this young woman?" Castro asks aloud in a
tone of obvious approval. But before Stevenson can reply, Fraymari steps forward with a hint of lawyerly indignation: "You mean
you don't remember me?"

Castro seems stunned. He smiles feebly, trying to conceal his confusion. He turns inquiringly toward his boxing hero, but Stevenson's eyes only roll upward. Stevenson knows that Castro has met Fraymari socially on earlier occasions, but unfortunately the Cuban leader has forgotten, and it is equally unfortunate that Fraymari is now behaving like a prosecutor.

"You held my son in your arms before he was one year old!" she reminds him while Castro continues to ponder. The crowd is attentive; the television cameras are rolling.

"At a volleyball game?" Castro asks tentatively.

"No, no," Stevenson interrupts, before Fraymari can say anything more, "that was my former wife. The doctor."

Castro slowly shakes his head in mock disapproval. Then he abruptly turns away from the couple, but not before reminding Stevenson, "You should get name tags."

Castro redirects his attention to Muhammad Ali. He studies Ali's face.

"Where is your wife?" he asks softly. Ali says nothing. There is more silence and turning of heads in the group until Howard Bingham spots Yolanda standing near the back and waves her to Castro's side.

Before she arrives, Bingham steps forward and presents Castro with the photograph of Ali and Malcolm X in Harlem in 1963. Castro holds it up level with his eyes and studies it silently for several seconds. When this picture was taken, Castro had been in control of Cuba for nearly four years. He was then thirty-seven. In 1959, he defeated the U.S.-backed dictator Fulgencio Batista, overcoming odds greater than Ali's subsequent victory over the supposedly unbeatable Sonny Liston. Batista had actually announced Castro's death back in 1956. Castro, then hiding in a secret outpost, thirty years old and beardless, was a disgruntled Jesuit-trained lawyer who was born into a landowning family and who craved Batista's job. At thirty-two, he had it. Batista was forced to flee to the Dominican Republic.

During this period, Muhammad Ali was only an amateur. His greatest achievement would come in 1960, when he received a gold medal in Rome as a member of the United States Olympic boxing team. But later in the sixties, he and Castro would share the world stage as figures moving against the American establishment — and now, in the twilight of their lives, on this winter's

night in Havana, they meet for the first time: Ali silent and Castro
isolated on his island.

"*Que bien!*" Castro says to Howard Bingham before showing the
photograph to his interpreter. Then Castro is introduced by Bingham to Ali's wife. After they exchange greetings through the interpreter, he asks her, as if surprised, "You don't speak Spanish?"

"No," she says softly. She begins to caress her husband's left
wrist, on which he wears a $250 silver Swiss Army watch she
bought him. It is the only jewelry Ali wears.

"But I thought I saw you speaking Spanish on the TV news this
week," Castro continues wonderingly before acknowledging that
her voice had obviously been dubbed.

"Do you live in New York?"

"No, we live in Michigan."

"Cold," says Castro.

"Very cold," she repeats.

"In Michigan, don't you find many people that speak Spanish?"

"No, not many," she says. "Mostly in California, New York . . ."
and, after a pause, "Florida."

Castro nods. It takes him a few seconds to think up another
question. Small talk has never been the forte of this man who specializes in nonstop haranguing monologues that can last for hours;
and yet here he is, in a room crowded with camera crews and news
photographers — a talk-show host with a guest of honor who is
speechless. But Fidel Castro plods on, asking Ali's wife if she has a
favorite sport.

"I play a little tennis," Yolanda says, and then asks him, "Do you
play tennis?"

"Ping-Pong," he replies, quickly adding that during his youth he
had been active in the ring. "I spent hours boxing . . ." he begins to
reminisce, but before he finishes his sentence, he sees the slowly
rising right fist of Muhammad Ali moving toward his chin! Exuberant cheering and handclapping resound through the room, and
Castro jumps sideways toward Stevenson, shouting, "*Asesorame!*" —
"Help me!"

Stevenson's long arms land upon Ali's shoulders from behind,
squeezing him gently; and then, after he releases him, the two ex-
champions face each other and begin to act out in slow motion the
postures of competing prizefighters — bobbing, weaving, swing-

ing, ducking — all of it done without touching and all of it accompanied by three minutes of ongoing applause and the clicking of cameras, and also some feelings of relief from Ali's friends because, in his own way, he has decided to join them. Ali still says nothing, his face still inscrutable, but he is less remote, less alone, and he does not pull away from Stevenson's embrace as the latter eagerly tells Castro about a boxing exhibition that he and Ali had staged earlier in the week at the Balado gym, in front of hundreds of fans and some of the island's up-and-coming contenders.

Stevenson did not actually explain that it had been merely another photo opportunity, one in which they sparred openhanded in the ring, wearing their street clothes and barely touching each other's bodies and faces; but then Stevenson had climbed out of the ring, leaving Ali to the more taxing test of withstanding two abbreviated rounds against one and then another young bully of grade school age who clearly had not come to participate in a kiddie show. They had come to floor the champ. Their bellicose little bodies and hot-gloved hands and helmeted hell-bent heads were consumed with fury and ambition; and as they charged ahead, swinging wildly and swaggering to the roars of their teenage friends and relatives at ringside, one could imagine their future boastings to their grandchildren: On one fine day back in the winter of '96, I whacked Muhammad Ali! Except, in truth, on this particular day, Ali was still too fast for them. He backpedaled and shifted and swayed, stood on the toes of his black woven-leather pointed shoes, and showed that his body was made for motion — his Parkinson's problems were lost in his shuffle, in the thrusts of his butterfly sting that whistled two feet above the heads of his aspiring assailants, in the dazzling dips of his rope-a-dope that had confounded George Foreman in Zaire, in his ever-memorable style, which in this Cuban gym moistened the eyes of his ever-observant photographer friend and provoked the overweight screenwriter to cry out in a voice that few in this noisy Spanish crowd could understand, "Ali's on a high! Ali's on a high!"

Teófilo Stevenson raises Ali's right arm above the head of Castro, and the news photographers spend several minutes posing the three of them together in flashing light. Castro then sees Fraymari watching alone at some distance. She is not smiling. Castro nods toward her. He summons a photographer to take a picture of Fraymari and himself. But she relaxes only after her husband comes over to join her in the conversation, which Castro immediately directs to the health and growth of their son, who is not yet two years old.

"Will he be as tall as his father?" Castro asks.

"I assume so," Fraymari says, glancing up toward her husband. She also has to look up when talking to Fidel Castro, for the Cuban leader is taller than six feet and his posture is nearly as erect as her husband's. Only the six-foot three-inch Muhammad Ali, who is standing with Bingham on the far side of her husband — and whose skin coloring, oval-shaped head, and burr-style haircut are very similar to her husband's — betrays his height with the slope-shouldered forward slouch he has developed since his illness.

"How much does your son weigh?" Castro continues.

"When he was one year old, he was already twenty-six pounds," Fraymari says. "This is three above normal. He was walking at nine months."

"She still breast-feeds him," Teófilo Stevenson says, seeming pleased.

"Oh, that's very nourishing," agrees Castro.

"Sometimes the kid becomes confused and thinks my chest is his mother's breast," Stevenson says, and he could have added that his son is also confused by Ali's sunglasses. The little boy engraved teeth marks all over the plastic frames while chewing on them during the days he accompanied his parents on Ali's bus tour.

As a CBS boom pole swoops down closer to catch the conversation, Castro reaches out to touch Stevenson's belly and asks, "How much to you weigh?"

"Two hundred thirty-eight pounds, more or less."

"That's thirty-eight more than me," Castro says, but he complains, "I eat very little. Very little. The diet advice I get is never accurate. I eat around fifteen hundred calories — less than thirty grams of protein, less than that."

Castro slaps a hand against his own midsection, which is relatively flat. If he does have a potbelly, it is concealed within his well-tailored uniform. Indeed, for a man of seventy, he seems in fine health. His facial skin is florid and unsagging, his dark eyes dart around the room with ever-alert intensity, and he has a full head of lustrous gray hair not thinning at the crown. The attention he pays to himself might be measured from his manicured finger-nails down to his square-toed boots, which are unscuffed and smoothly buffed without the burnish of a lackey's spit shine. But his beard seems to belong to another man and another time. It is excessively long and scraggly. Wispy white hairs mix with the faded black and dangle down the front of his uniform like an old shroud, weather-worn and drying out. It is the beard from the hills. Castro strokes it constantly, as if trying to revive the vitality of its fiber.

Castro now looks at Ali.

"How's your appetite?" he asks, forgetting that Ali is not speaking.

"Where's your wife?" he then asks aloud, and Howard Bingham calls out to her. Yolanda has once more drifted back into the group.

When she arrives, Castro hesitates before speaking to her. It is as if he is not absolutely sure who she is. He has met so many people since arriving, and with the group rotating constantly due to the jostling of the photographers, Castro cannot be certain whether the woman at his side is Muhammad Ali's wife or Ed Bradley's friend or some other woman he has met moments ago who has left him with an unlasting impression. Having already committed a faux pas regarding one of the wives of the two multimarried ex-champions standing nearby, Castro waits for some hint from his interpreter. None is offered. Fortunately, he does not have to worry in this country about the women's vote — or any vote, for that matter — but he does sigh in mild relief when Yolanda reintroduces herself as Ali's wife and does so by name.

"Ah, Yolanda," Castro repeats, "what a beautiful name. That's the name of a queen somewhere."

"In our household," she says.

"And how is your husband's appetite?"

"Good, but he likes sweets."

"We can send you some of our ice cream to Michigan," Castro says. Without waiting for her to comment, he asks, "Michigan is very cold?"

"Oh, yes," she replies, not indicating that they had already discussed Michigan's winter weather.

"How much snow?"

"We didn't get hit with the blizzard," Yolanda says, referring to a storm in January, "but it can get three, four feet —"

Teófilo Stevenson interrupts to say that he had been in Michigan during the previous October.

"Oh," Castro says, raising an eyebrow. He mentions that during the same month he had also been in the United States (attending the United Nations' fiftieth-anniversary tribute). He asks Stevenson the length of his American visit.

"I was there for nineteen days," says Stevenson.

"Nineteen days!" Castro repeats. "Longer than I was."

Castro complains that he was limited to five days and prohibited from traveling beyond New York.

"Well, *comandante*," Stevenson responds offhandedly, in a slightly superior tone, "if you like, I will sometime show you my video."

Stevenson appears to be very comfortable in the presence of the Cuban leader, and perhaps the latter has habitually encouraged this; but at this moment, Castro may well be finding his boxing hero a bit condescending and worthy of a retaliatory jab. He knows how to deliver it.

"When you visited the United States," Castro asks pointedly, "did you bring your wife, the lawyer?"

Stevenson stiffens. He directs his eyes toward his wife. She turns away.

"No," Stevenson answers quietly. "I went alone."

Castro abruptly shifts his attention to the other side of the room, where the CBS camera crew is positioned, and he asks Ed Bradley, "What do you do?"

"We're making a documentary on Ali," Bradley explains, "and we followed him to Cuba to see what he was doing in Cuba and . . ."

Bradley's voice is suddenly overwhelmed by the sounds of laughter and handclapping. Bradley and Castro turn to discover that Muhammad Ali is now reclaiming everyone's attention. He is holding his shaky left fist in the air; but instead of assuming a boxer's pose, as he had done earlier, he is beginning to pull out from the top of his upraised fist, slowly and with dramatic delicacy, the tip of a red silk handkerchief that is pinched between his right index finger and thumb.

After he has pulled out the entire handkerchief, he dangles it in the air for a few seconds, waving it closer and closer to the forehead of the wide-eyed Fidel Castro. Ali seems bewitched. He continues to stare stagnantly at Castro and the others, surrounded by applause that he gives no indication he hears. Then he proceeds to place the handkerchief back into the top of his cupped left hand — pecking with the pinched fingers of his right — and then quickly opens his palms toward his audience and reveals that the handkerchief has disappeared.

"Where is it?" cries Castro, who seems to be genuinely surprised and delighted. He approaches Ali and examines his hands, repeating, "Where is it? Where have you put it?"

Everyone who has traveled on Ali's bus during the week knows where he has hidden it. They have seen him perform the trick repeatedly in front of some of the patients and doctors at the hospitals and clinics as well as before countless tourists who have recognized him in his hotel lobby or during his strolls through the town square. They have also seen him follow up each performance with a demonstration that exposes his method. He keeps hidden in his fist a flesh-colored rubber thumb that contains the handkerchief that he will eventually pull out with the fingers of his other hand; and when he is reinserting the handkerchief, he is actually shoving the material back into the concealed rubber thumb, into which he then inserts his own right thumb. When he opens his hands, the uninformed among his onlookers are seeing his empty palms and missing the fact that the handkerchief is tucked within the rubber thumb that is covering his outstretched right thumb. Sharing with his audience the mystery of his magic always earns him additional applause.

After Ali has performed and explained the trick to Castro, he gives Castro the rubber thumb to examine — and, with more zest than he has shown all evening, Castro says, "Oh, let me try it, I want to try — it's the first time I have seen such a wonderful thing!" And after a few minutes of coaching from Howard Bingham, who long ago learned how to do it from Ali, the Cuban leader performs with sufficient dexterity and panache to satisfy his magical ambitions and to arouse another round of applause from the guests.

Meanwhile, more than ten minutes have passed since Ali began his comic routine. It is already after 9:30 P.M., and the commentator Ed Bradley, whose conversation with Castro had been interrupted, is concerned that the Cuban leader might leave the room without responding to the questions Bradley has prepared for his show. Bradley edges close to Castro's interpreter, saying in a voice that is sure to be heard, "Would you ask him if he followed . . . was able to follow Ali when he was boxing professionally?"

The question is relayed and repeated until Castro, facing the CBS cameras, replies, "Yes, I recall the days when they were discussing the possibilities of a match between the two of them" — he nods toward Stevenson and Ali —"and I remember when he went to Africa."

"In Zaire," Bradley clarifies, referring to Ali's victory in 1974 over George Foreman. And he follows up: "What kind of impact did he have in this country, because he was a revolutionary as well as . . . ?"

"It was great," Castro says. "He was very much admired as a sportsman, as a boxer, as a person. There was always a high opinion of him. But I never guessed one day we would meet here, with this kind gesture of bringing medicine, seeing our children, visiting our polyclinics. I am very glad, I am thrilled, to have the opportunity to meet him personally, to appreciate his kindness. I see he is strong. I see he has a very kind face."

Castro is speaking as if Ali were not in the room, standing a few feet away. Ali maintains his fixed façade even as Stevenson whispers into his ear, asking in English, "Muhammad, Muhammad, why you no speak?" Stevenson then turns to tell the journalist who stands behind him, "Muhammad does speak. He speaks to me." Stevenson says nothing more because Castro is now looking at him while continuing to tell Bradley, "I am very glad that he and Stevenson have met." After a pause, Castro adds, "And I am glad that they never fought."

"He's not so sure," Bradley interjects, smiling in the direction of Stevenson.

"I find in that friendship something beautiful," Castro insists softly.

"There is a tie between the two of them," Bradley says.

"Yes," says Castro. "It is true." He again looks at Ali, then at Stevenson, as if searching for something more profound to say.

"And how's the documentary?" he finally asks Bradley.

"It'll be on *60 Minutes.*"

"When?"

"Maybe one month," Bradley says, reminding Castro's interpreter, "This is the program on which the *comandante* has been interviewed by Dan Rather a number of times in the past, when Dan
Rather was on *60 Minutes.*"

"And who's there now?" Castro wants to know.

"I am," Bradley answers.

"You," Castro repeats, with a quick glance at Bradley's earring.
"So you are there — the boss now?"

Bradley responds as a media star without illusions: "I'm a
worker."

Trays containing coffee, tea, and orange juice finally arrive, but
only in amounts sufficient for Ali and Yolanda, Howard Bingham,
Greg Howard, the Stevensons, and Castro — although Castro tells
the waiters he wants nothing.

Castro motions for Ali and the others to join him across the
room, around the circular table. The camera crews and the rest of
the guests follow, standing as near to the principals as they can.
But throughout the group there is a discernible restlessness. They
have been standing for more than an hour and a half. It is now approaching 10 P.M. There has been no food. And for the vast majority, it is clear that there will also be nothing to drink. Even among
the special guests, seated and sipping from chilled glasses or hot
cups, there is a waning level of fascination with the evening. Indeed, Muhammad Ali's eyes are closed. He is sleeping.

Yolanda sits next to him on the sofa, pretending not to notice.
Castro also ignores it, although he sits directly across the table,
with the interpreter and the Stevensons.

"How large is Michigan?" Castro begins a new round of questioning with Yolanda, returning for the third time to a subject they
had explored beyond the interest of anyone in the room except
Castro himself.

"I don't know how big the state is as far as demographics,"
Yolanda says. "We live in a very small village [Barrien Springs]
with about two thousand people."

"Are you going back to Michigan tomorrow?"

"Yes."

"What time?"

"Two-thirty."

"Via Miami?" Castro asks.

"Yes."

"From Miami, where do you fly?"

"We're flying to Michigan."

"How many hours' flight?"

"We have to change at Cincinnati—about two and a half hours."

"Flying time?" asks Castro.

Muhammad Ali opens his eyes, then closes them.

"Flying time," Yolanda repeats.

"From Miami to Michigan?" Castro continues.

"No," she again explains, but still with patience, "we have to go to Cincinnati. There are no direct flights."

"So you have to take two planes?" Castro asks.

"Yes," she says, adding for clarification, "Miami to Cincinnati— and then Cincinnati to South Bend, Indiana."

"From Cincinnati . . . ?"

"To South Bend," she says. "That's the closest airport."

"So," Fidel goes on, "it is on the outskirts of the city?"

"Yes."

"You have a farm?"

"No," Yolanda says, "just land. We let someone else do the growing."

She mentions that Teófilo Stevenson has traveled through this part of the Midwest. The mention of his name gains Stevenson's attention.

"I was in Chicago," Stevenson tells Castro.

"You were at their home?" Castro asks.

"No," Yolanda corrects Stevenson, "you were in Michigan."

"I was in the countryside," Stevenson says. Unable to resist, he adds, "I have a video of that visit. I'll show it to you sometime."

Castro seems not to hear him. He directs his attention back to Yolanda, asking her where she was born, where she was educated, when she became married, and how many years separate her age from that of her husband, Muhammad Ali.

After Yolanda acknowledges being sixteen years younger than Ali, Castro turns toward Fraymari and with affected sympathy says that she married a man who is twenty year her senior.

"Comandante!" Stevenson intercedes, "I am in shape. Sports

keep you healthy. Sports add years to your life and life to your years!"

"Oh, what conflict she has," Castro goes on, ignoring Stevenson and catering to Fraymari — and to the CBS cameraman who steps forward for a closer view of Castro's face. "She is a lawyer, and she does not put this husband in jail." Castro is enjoying much more than Fraymari the attention this topic is now getting from the group. Castro had lost his audience and now has it back and seemingly wants to retain it, no matter at what cost to Stevenson's harmony with Fraymari. Yes, Castro continues, Fraymari had the misfortune to select a husband "who can never settle down. . . . Jail would be an appropriate place for him."

"Comandante," Stevenson interrupts in a jocular manner that seems intended to placate both the lawyer who is his spouse and the lawyer who rules the country, "I might as well be locked up!" He implies that should he deviate from marital fidelity, his lawyer wife "will surely put me in a place where she is the only woman who can visit me!"

Everyone around the table and within the circling group laughs. Ali is now awake. The banter between Castro and Stevenson resumes until Yolanda, all but rising in her chair, tells Castro, "We have to pack."

"You're going to have dinner now?" he asks.

"Yes, sir," she says. Ali stands, along with Howard Bingham. Yolanda thanks Castro's interpreter directly, saying, "Be sure to tell him, 'You're always welcome in our home.'" The interpreter quotes Castro as again complaining that when he visits America, he is usually restricted to New York, but he adds, "Things change."

The group watches as Yolanda and Ali pass through, and Castro follows them into the hallway. The elevator arrives, and its door is held open by a security guard. Castro extends his final farewell with handshakes — and only then does he discover that he holds Ali's rubber thumb in his hand. Apologizing, he tries to hand it back to Ali, but Bingham politely protests. "No, no," Bingham says, "Ali wants you to have it."

Castro's interpreter at first fails to understand what Bingham is saying.

"He wants you to keep it," Bingham repeats.

Bingham enters the elevator with Ali and Yolanda. Before the door closes, Castro smiles, waves goodbye, and stares with curiosity at the rubber thumb. Then he puts it in his pocket.

Reflections and Responses

1. Read Gay Talese's comments "On Certain Magazine Interviews" and "Listening to People Think," (pages 25–26). How do you think his journalistic procedures in this essay compare to his comments about the art of interviewing?

2. How would you describe Talese's role in the essay? Where does he seem visible? Where does he seem almost invisible? How does he fit himself as a participant or as an observer into different situations?

3. Consider how Talese sets up the drama at the palace reception. How does he build tension? How does he mix both the leading and minor roles? Why do you think he focuses so closely on the different conversations? What do you think he wants the conversations to convey in general about the overall event? Consider, too, the strange gift Ali leaves with Castro. Do you think the gift can have any larger significance? Do you think Talese finds it significant? What exactly is it and what might it represent?

LEWIS THOMAS

Crickets, Bats, Cats, & Chaos

How do animals think? *Do they possess a consciousness like ours or is theirs entirely different? How can we enter into the mind of a cat or a cricket? In this insightful essay, a renowned medical researcher considers the mysterious world of animal awareness and discovers the important role that chaos and unpredictability play in the life and mind of nonhuman creatures. These biological considerations lead Dr. Lewis Thomas to a surprising idea about the human mind: If chaos is so important to a creature as lowly as the cricket, what might be its significance to more complex organisms? Chaos, he comes to believe, is not an occasional aspect of human thought but the norm: "Predictable, small-scale, orderly, cause-and-effect sequences are hard to come by and don't last long when they do turn up. Something else almost always turns up at the same time, and then another sequential thought intervenes alongside, and there come turbulence and chaos again." Out of this unpredictable jumble comes — when we are lucky — our insights and illuminations, our "good ideas."*

A celebrated physician, Lewis Thomas also wrote five outstanding collections of essays: The Lives of a Cell *(1974),* The Medusa and the Snail *(1979),* Late Night Thoughts on Listening to Mahler's Ninth Symphony *(1983),* Et Cetera, Et Cetera *(1990), and* The Fragile Species *(1992). Thomas's essays demonstrate an enormously wide range of interests as he roams expertly and entertainingly through biology, ecology, semantics, literature, and classical music. In addition to numerous scientific papers, he is also the author of a memoir,* The Youngest Science *(1983). Thomas died in 1993. "Crickets, Bats, Cats, & Chaos" originally appeared in* Audubon *(1992) and was selected by Joseph Epstein for* The Best American Essays *1993.*

I am not sure where to classify the mind of my cat Jeoffry. He is a small Abyssinian cat, a creature of elegance, grace, and poise, a piece of moving sculpture, and a total mystery. We named him Jeoffry after the eighteenth-century cat celebrated by the unpredictable poet Christopher Smart in a poem titled "Jubilate Agno," one section of which begins, "For I will consider my cat Jeoffry." The following lines are selected more or less at random:

> For he counteracts the powers of darkness by his electrical skin and glaring eyes.
> For he counteracts the Devil, who is death, by brisking about the life . . .
> For he is of the tribe of Tiger . . .
> For he purrs in thankfulness, when God tells him he's a good Cat . . .
> For he is an instrument for the children to learn benevolence upon . . .
> For he is a mixture of gravity and waggery . . .
> For there is nothing sweeter than his peace when at rest.
> For there is nothing brisker than his life when in motion.

I have not the slightest notion what goes on in the mind of my cat Jeoffry, beyond the conviction that it is a genuine mind, with genuine thoughts and a strong tendency to chaos, but in all other respects a mind totally unlike mine. I have a hunch, based on long moments of observing him stretched on the rug in sunlight, that his mind has more periods of geometric order, and a better facility for switching itself almost, but not quite, entirely off, and accordingly an easier access to pure pleasure. Just as he is able to hear sounds that I cannot hear, and smell important things of which I am unaware, and suddenly leap like a crazed gymnast from chair to chair, upstairs and downstairs through the house, flawless in every movement and searching for something he never finds, he has periods of meditation on matters I know nothing about.

While thinking about what nonhumans think is, in most biological quarters, an outlandish question, even an impermissible one, to which the quick and easy answer is nothing, or almost nothing, or certainly nothing like *thought* as we use the word, I still think about it. For while none of them may have real thoughts, foresee the future, regret the past, or be self-aware, most of us up here at the peak of evolution cannot manage the awareness of our own awareness, a state of mind only achieved when the mind succeeds in emptying itself of all other information and switches off all messages, interior and exterior. This is the state of mind for which the Chinese Taoists long ago used a term meaning, literally, no-knowledge. With no-knowledge, it is said, you get a different look at the world, an illumination.

Falling short of this, as I do, and dispossessed of anything I could call illumination, it has become my lesser satisfaction to learn secondhand whatever I can, and then to think, firsthand, about the behavior of other kinds of animals.

I think of crickets, for instance, and the thought of their unique, very small thoughts — principally about mating and bats — but also about the state of cricket society. The cricket seems to me an eminently suitable animal for sorting out some of the emotional issues bound to arise in any consideration of animal awareness. Nobody, so far as I know, not even an eighteenth-century minor poet, could imagine any connection between events in the mind of a cricket and those in the mind of a human. If there was ever a creature in nature meriting the dismissive description of a living machine, mindless and thoughtless, the cricket qualifies. So in talking about what crickets are up to when they communicate with each other, as they unmistakably do, by species-unique runs and rhythms of chirps and trills, there can be no question of *anthropomorphization,* that most awful of all terms for the deepest error a modern biologist can fall into.

If you reduce the temperature of a male cricket, the rate of his emission of chirping signals is correspondingly reduced. Indeed, some of the earlier naturalists used the technical term "thermometer crickets" because of the observation that you can make a close guess at the air temperature in a field by counting the rate of chirps of familiar crickets.

This is curious, but there is a much more curious thing going on when the weather changes. The female crickets in the same field, genetically coded to respond specifically to the chirp rhythm of their species, adjust their recognition mechanism to the same temperature change and the same new, slower rate of chirps. That is, as John Doherty and Ronald Hoy wrote on observing the phenomenon, "warm females responded best to the songs of warm males, and cold females responded best to the songs of cold males." The same phenomenon, known as temperature coupling, has been encountered in grasshoppers and tree frogs, and also in fireflies, with their flash communication system. The receiving mind of the female cricket, if you are willing to call it that, adjusts itself immediately to match the sending mind of the male. This has always struck me as one of the neatest examples of animals adjusting to a change in their environment.

But I started thinking about crickets with something quite different in mind, namely bats. It has long been known that bats feed voraciously on the nocturnal flights of crickets and moths, which they detect on the wing by their fantastically accurate ultrasound mechanism. What should have been guessed at, considering the ingenuity of nature, is that certain cricket species, green lacewings, and certain moths have ears that can detect the ultrasound emissions of a bat, and can analyze the distance and direction from which the ultrasound is coming. These insects can employ two separate and quite distinct defensive maneuvers for evading the bat's keen sonar.

The first is simply swerving away. This is useful behavior when the bat signal is coming from a safe distance, twenty to thirty meters away. At this range the insect can detect the bat, but the bat is too far off to receive the bounced ultrasound back to its own ears. So the cricket or moth needs to do nothing more, at least for the moment, than swing out of earshot.

But when the bat is nearby, three meters or less, the insect is in immediate and mortal danger, for now the bat's sonar provides an accurate localization. It is too late for swerving or veering; because of its superior speed the bat can easily track such simple evasions. What to do? The answer has been provided by Kenneth Roeder, who designed a marvelous laboratory model for field studies, including instruments to imitate the intensity and direction of bat signals.

The answer, for a cricket or moth or lacewing who hears a bat homing in close by, is *chaos*. Instead of swerving away, the insect launches into wild, totally erratic, random flight patterns, as unpredictable as possible. This kind of response tends to confuse the bat and results in escape for the insect frequently enough to have been selected by evolution as the final, stereotyped, "last-chance" response to the threat. It has the look of a very smart move, whether thought out or not.

So chaos is part of the useful, everyday mental equipment of a cricket or a moth, and that, I submit, is something new to think about. I don't wish to push the matter beyond its possible significance, but it seems to me to justify a modest nudge. The long debate over the problem of animal awareness is not touched by the observation, but it does bring up the opposite side of that argument, the opposite of anthropomorphization. It is this: Leaving aside the deep question as to whether the lower animals have anything going on in their mind that we might accept as conscious thought, are there important events occurring in our human minds that are matched by habits of the animal mind?

Surely chaos is a capacious area of common ground. I am convinced that my own mind spends much of its waking hours, not to mention its sleeping time, in a state of chaos directly analogous to that of the cricket hearing the sound of the nearby bat. But there is a big difference. My chaos is not induced by a bat; it is not suddenly switched on in order to facilitate escape; it is not an evasive tactic set off by any new danger. It is, I think, the normal state of affairs, and not just for my brain in particular but for human brains in general. The chaos that is my natural state of being is rather like the concept of chaos that has emerged in higher mathematical circles in recent years.

As I understand it, and I am quick to say that I understand it only quite superficially, chaos occurs when any complex, dynamic system is perturbed by a small uncertainty in one or another of its subunits. The inevitable result is an amplification of the disturbance and then the spread of unpredictable, random behavior throughout the whole system. It is the total unpredictability and randomness that makes the word "chaos" applicable as a technical term, but it is not true that the behavior of the system becomes disorderly. Indeed, as James P. Crutchfield and his associates have written, "There is order in chaos: underlying chaotic behavior there are elegant geometric forms that create randomness in the same way as a card dealer shuffles a deck of cards or a blender mixes cake batter." The random behavior of a turbulent stream of water, or of the weather, or of Brownian movement, or of the central nervous system of a cricket in flight from a bat, are all determined by the same mathematical rules. Behavior of this sort has been encountered in computer models of large cities: When a

small change was made in one small part of the city model, the amplification of the change resulted in enormous upheavals, none of
them predictable, in the municipal behavior at remote sites in the
models.

A moth or a cricket has a small enough nervous system to *seem*
predictable and orderly most of the time. There are not all that
many neurons, and the circuitry contains what seem to be mostly
simple reflex pathways. Laboratory experiments suggest that in a
normal day, one thing — the sound of a bat at a safe distance,
say — leads to another, predictable thing — a swerving off to one
side in flight. It is only when something immensely new and important happens — the bat sound at three meters away — that the
system is thrown into chaos.

I suggest that the difference with us is that chaos is the norm.
Predictable, small-scale, orderly, cause-and-effect sequences are
hard to come by and don't last long when they do turn up. Something else almost always turns up at the same time, and then another sequential thought intervenes alongside, and there come
turbulence and chaos again. When we are lucky, and the system
operates at its random best, something astonishing may suddenly
turn up, beyond predicting or imagining. Events like these we recognize as good ideas.

My cat Jeoffry's brain is vastly larger and more commodious
than that of a cricket, but I wonder if it is qualitatively all that different. The cricket lives with his two great ideas in mind, mating
and predators, and his world is a world of particular, specified
sounds. He is a tiny machine, I suppose, depending on what you
mean by "machine," but it is his occasional moments of randomness and unpredictability that entitle him to be called aware. In
order to achieve that feat of wild chaotic flight, and thus escape,
he has to make use, literally, of his brain. When Int 1, an auditory
interneuron, is activated by the sound of a bat closing in, the message is transmitted by an axon connected straight to the insect's
brain, and it is here, and only here, that the swerving is generated.
This I consider to be a thought, a very small thought, but still a
thought. Without knowing what to count as a thought, I figure that
Jeoffry, with his kind of brain, has a trillion thoughts of about the
same size in any waking moment. As for me, and my sort of brain, I
can't think where to begin.

We like to think of our minds as containing trains of thought, or streams of consciousness, as though they were orderly arrangements of linear events, one notion leading in a cause-and-effect way to the next notion. Logic is the way to go; we set a high price on logic, unlike E. M. Forster's elderly lady in *Aspects of the Novel*, who, when accused of being illogical, replied, "Logic? Good gracious! What rubbish! How can I tell what I think till I see what I say?"

But with regard to our own awareness of nature, I believe we've lost sight of, lost track of, lost touch with, and to some measurable degree lost respect for, the chaotic and natural in recent years — and during the very period of history when we humans have been learning more about the detailed workings of nature than in all our previous millennia. The more we learn, the more we seem to distance ourselves from the rest of life, as though we were separate creatures, so different from other occupants of the biosphere as to have arrived from another galaxy. We seek too much to explain, we assert a duty to run the place, to dominate the planet, to govern its life, but at the same time we ourselves seem to be less a part of it than ever before.

We leave it whenever we can, we crowd ourselves from open green countrysides onto the concrete surfaces of massive cities, as far removed from the earth as we can get, staring at it from behind insulated glass, or by way of half-hour television clips.

At the same time, we talk a great game of concern. We shout at each other in high virtue, now more than ever before, about the befoulment of our nest and about whom to blame. We have mechanized our lives so extensively that most of us live with the illusion that our only connection with nature is the nagging fear that it may one day turn on us and do us in. Polluting our farmlands and streams, even the seas, worries us because of what it may be doing to the food and water supplies necessary for human beings. Raising the level of CO_2, methane, and hydrofluorocarbons in the atmosphere troubles us because of the projected effects of climate upheaval on human habitats. These anxieties do not extend, really, to nature at large. They are not the result of any new awareness.

Nature itself, that vast incomprehensible meditative being, has come to mean for most of us nothing much more than odd walks in the nearby woods, or flowers in the rooftop garden, or the soap opera stories of the last giant panda or whooping crane, or curiosities like the northward approach, from Florida, of the Asiatic flying cockroach.

I will begin to feel better about us, and about our future, when we finally start learning about some of the things that are still mystifications. Start with the events in the mind of a cricket, I'd say, and then go on from there. Comprehend my cat Jeoffry and we'll be on our way. Nowhere near home, but off and dancing, getting within a few millennia of understanding why the music of Bach is what it is, ready at last for open outer space. Give us time, I'd say, the kind of endless time we mean when we talk about the real world.

Reflections and Responses

1. Consider Thomas's use of *anthropomorphization*. What does the term mean? Why does Thomas refer to it as "that most awful of all terms for the deepest error a modern biologist can fall into"? What is that error? How serious an "error" does Thomas consider it?

2. If biologists don't normally approve of attempting to understand animal consciousness in human terms, then what might they make of viewing human consciousness in terms of animals? Would it be a scientific error either way? Explain what you think Thomas's position is on this matter.

3. Note that Thomas breaks his essay into three (unnumbered) parts. How would you summarize and characterize each part? In what way is the third part of the essay related to the first two?

JOHN UPDIKE

The Disposable Rocket

We have already seen several selections that consider the human body from a woman's perspective, most notably Marcia Aldrich's "Hair," Lucy Grealy's "Mirrorings," Natalie Kusz's "Ring Leader," and Gretel Ehrlich's "Spring." In "The Disposable Rocket," John Updike, one of America's preeminent novelists, delivers his version of the male body. He states at the outset that it is quite different from the female body in that "it is a low-maintenance proposition." Men don't necessarily identify themselves with their bodies. In his characteristic metaphorical manner, Updike concludes, "A man and his body are like a boy and the buddy who has a driver's license and the use of his father's car for the evening; he goes along, gratefully, for the ride."

Updike was born in 1932 in Shillington, Pennsylvania. After graduation from Harvard in 1954 and a year at an English art school, he worked for the New Yorker's *"Talk of the Town" department for two years. Since 1957 he has lived in Massachusetts as a freelance writer. A novelist, poet, essayist, and reviewer, Updike is one of the nation's most distinguished authors. His fiction has won the Pulitzer Prize, the National Book Award, the American Book Award, and the National Book Critics Circle Award. He has published thirty-six books and collections; his most recent novel — his eighteenth — is* Toward the End of Time *(1998). "The Disposable Rocket" originally appeared in* Michigan Quarterly Review *and was selected by Tracy Kidder for* The Best American Essays *1994.*

Inhabiting a male body is much like having a bank account; as long as it's healthy, you don't think much about it. Compared to the female body, it is a low-maintenance proposition: a shower now and then, trim the fingernails every ten days, a haircut once a month. Oh yes, shaving — scraping or buzzing away at your face every morning. Byron, in *Don Juan,* thought the repeated nuisance of shaving balanced out the periodic agony, for females, of childbirth. Women are, his lines tell us,

> Condemn'd to child-bed, as men for their sins
> Have shaving too entail'd upon their chins, —
>
> A daily plague, which in the aggregate
> May average on the whole with parturition.

From the standpoint of reproduction, the male body is a delivery system, as the female is a mazy device for retention. Once the delivery is made, men feel a faint but distinct falling-off of interest. Yet against the enduring female heroics of birth and nurture should be set the male's superhuman frenzy to deliver his goods: he vaults walls, skips sleep, risks wallet, health, and his political future all to ram home his seed into the gut of the chosen woman. The sense of the chase lives in him as the key to life. His body is, like a delivery rocket that falls away in space, a disposable means. Men put their bodies at risk to experience the release from gravity.

When my tenancy of a male body was fairly new — of six or so years' duration — I used to jump and fall just for the joy of it. Falling — backwards, downstairs — become a specialty of mine, an attention-getting stunt I was practicing into my thirties, at suburban parties. Falling is, after all, a kind of flying, though of briefer duration than would be ideal. My impulse to hurl myself from high windows and the edges of cliffs belongs to my body, not my mind, which resists the siren call of the chasm with all its might; the interior struggle knocks the wind from my lungs and tightens my scrotum and gives any trip to Europe, with its Alps, castle parapets, and gargoyled cathedral lookouts, a flavor of nightmare. Falling, strangely, no longer figures in my dreams, as it often did when I was a boy and my subconscious was more honest with me. An airplane, that necessary evil, turns the earth into a map so quickly the brain turns aloof and calm; still, I marvel that there is no end of young men willing to become jet pilots.

Any accounting of male-female differences must include the male's superior recklessness, a drive not, I think, toward death, as the darker feminist cosmogonies would have it, but to test the limits, to see what the traffic will bear — a kind of mechanic's curiosity. The number of men who do lasting damage to their young bodies is striking; war and car accidents aside, secondary-school sports, with the approval of parents and the encouragement of brutish coaches, take a fearful toll of skulls and knees. We were made for combat, back in the post-simian, East African days, and the bumping, the whacking, the breathlessness, the pain-smothering adrenaline rush, form a cumbersome and unfashionable bliss, but bliss nevertheless. Take your body to the edge, and see if it flies.

The male sense of space must differ from that of the female, who has such interesting, active, and significant inner space. The space that interests men is outer. The fly ball high against the sky, the long pass spiraling overhead, the jet fighter like a scarcely visible pinpoint nozzle laying down its vapor trail at forty thousand feet, the gazelle haunch flickering just beyond arrow-reach, the uncountable stars sprinkled on their great black wheel, the horizon, the mountaintop, the quasar — these bring portents with them, and awaken a sense of relation with the invisible, with the empty. The ideal male body is taut with lines of potential force, a diagram extending outward; the ideal female body curves around centers of repose. Of course, no one is ideal, and the sexes are somewhat androgynous subdivisions of a species: Diana the huntress is a more trendy body-type nowadays than languid, overweight Venus, and polymorphous Dionysus poses for more underwear ads than Mars. Relatively, though, men's bodies, however elegant, are designed for covering territory, for moving on.

An erection, too, defies gravity, flirts with it precariously. It extends the diagram of outward direction into downright detachability — objective in the case of the sperm, subjective in the case of the testicles and penis. Men's bodies, at this juncture, feel only partly theirs; a demon of sorts has been attached to their lower torsos, whose performance is erratic and whose errands seem, at times, ridiculous. It is like having a (much) smaller brother toward whom you feel both fond and impatient; if he is you, it is you in curiously simplified and ignoble form. This sense, of the male body being two of them, is acknowledged in verbal love play and erotic writing, where the penis is playfully given its own name, an individuation not even the rarest rapture grants a vagina. Here, where maleness gathers to a quintessence of itself, there can be no insincerity, there can be no hiding; for sheer nakedness, there is nothing like a hopeful phallus; its aggressive shape is indivisible from its tender-skinned vulnerability. The act of intercourse, from the point of view of a consenting female, has an element of mothering, of enwrapment, of merciful concealment, even. The male body, for this interval, is tucked out of harm's way.

To inhabit a male body, then, is to feel somewhat detached from it. It is not an enemy, but not entirely a friend. Our essence seems to lie not in cells and muscles but in the traces our thoughts and actions inscribe on the air. The male body skims the surface of nature's deep, wherein the blood and pain and mysterious cravings of women perpetuate the species. Participating less in nature's processes than the female body, the male body gives the impression — false — of being exempt from time. Its powers of strength and reach descend in early adolescence, along with acne and sweaty feet, and depart, in imperceptible increments, after thirty or so. It surprises me to discover, when I remove my shoes and socks, the same paper-white hairless ankles that struck me as pathetic when I observed them on my father. I felt betrayed when, in some tumble of touch football twenty years ago, I heard my tibia snap; and when, between two reading engagements in Cleveland, my appendix tried to burst; and when, the other day, not for the first time, there arose to my nostrils out of my own body the musty attic smell my grandfather's body had.

A man's body does not betray its tenant as rapidly as a woman's. Never as fine and lovely, it has less distance to fall; what rugged beauty it has is wrinkle-proof. It keeps its capability of procreation indecently long. Unless intense athletic demands are made on it, the thing serves well enough to sixty, which is my age now. From here on, it's chancy. There are no breasts or ovaries to admit cancer to the male body, but the prostate, that awkwardly located little source of seminal fluid, shows the strain of sexual function with fits of hysterical cell replication, and all that beer and potato chips add up in the coronary arteries. A writer, whose physical equipment can be minimal, as long as it gets him to the desk, the lectern, and New York City once in a while, cannot but be grateful to his body, especially to his eyes, those tender and intricate sites where the brain extrudes from the skull, and to his hands, which hold the pen or tap the keyboard. His body has been, not himself exactly, but a close pal, pot-bellied and balding like most of his other pals now. A man and his body are like a boy and the buddy who has a driver's license and the use of his father's car for the evening; he goes along, gratefully, for the ride.

Reflections and Responses

1. Updike's essay is constructed around numerous points of comparison between the male and the female body. What are the essential differences? Do you agree with Updike about the different ways men and women perceive their bodies? Are there points about which you disagree?

2. What does the essay's title refer to? Why do you think Updike chose this particular metaphor? Why is the rocket "disposable"? In what ways is the essay's central metaphor of a rocket reinforced by other imagery Updike uses in the essay?

3. Do you think Updike believes the male body is superior to the female — or vice versa? Can you detect any hints of preference for either one, or do you think he takes a neutral position?

3

The Public Sphere: Advocacy, Argument, Controversy

JACOB COHEN

Yes, Oswald Alone
Killed Kennedy

Public personalities are most likely to be transformed into cultural icons only after they die. We have only to observe the careers of such celebrities as Marilyn Monroe and Elvis Presley or such public figures as Abraham Lincoln and John F. Kennedy. Kennedy is a good case in point; a president elected by one of the narrowest margins in American history, he struggled hard to earn popular approval. Yet after his assassination in Dallas, he became — almost overnight — one of our most loved and esteemed presidents. Kennedy's death not only elevated him to a martyr's stature, it spawned an entire assassination industry: Since the event, over two thousand books have been published on the subject and not a November 22 goes by without several television "specials" honoring the occasion by featuring yet another "theory" of what happened that day in Dallas. Almost all of these theories, of course, elaborate some version of conspiracy. One of the most recent and most publicized accounts of the assassination is Oliver Stone's three-hour 1991 film, JFK. The movie received an enormous amount of media attention and incited a flurry of articles attacking or defending the conspiracy theory. One of these responses came from Jacob Cohen, a scholar who for thirty years has seriously studied every facet of the assassination. In the following essay, he systematically reviews and assails every argument raised by the conspiracists.

Cohen is chairman of the American Studies Department at Brandeis University. He has written widely about allegations of government conspiracy throughout American history. "Yes, Oswald Alone Killed Kennedy" originally appeared in Commentary *(1992) and was selected by Joseph Epstein for* The Best American Essays *1993.*

Even the strongest supporters of *JFK*, Oliver Stone's notorious film on the assassination of President John F. Kennedy, concede that it is deceptive: fabricated footage gussied up as documentary fact; fictional characters and scenes offered as proof of perfidy; paranoid insinuations about the conscious involvement of the highest officials in the land; outright lies. Yet to an extraordinary number of often intelligent people, these characterizations seem utterly beside the point. "Don't trust anyone who says the movie is hogwash," writes a *Newsweek* critic, David Ansen, "and don't trust the movie either . . . [it] is a remarkable, a necessary, provocation." "One of the worst great movies ever made," declaims Norman Mailer. One wonders: how false, fanciful, and downright mendacious does a work purporting to portray and interpret historical events need to be before it is not just chided but discounted, disqualified, disgraced?

Those who defend the film's meta-purposes seem confident that if not all, then some and *certainly at least one* of its basal assertions of fact reflect what actually happened in Dallas: more than one person fired at the President. And if there was more than one gunman, there is *prima facie** evidence of a conspiracy of some sort or another.

Having spent a considerable part of my life over the last three decades studying and discussing the Kennedy assassination, I can testify to the tenacity of that basal assertion. Challenging the notion of multiple gunmen has become tantamount to suggesting that it was the United States which attacked Japan in 1941, Poland which attacked Germany in 1939. And yet, I will contend that for anyone who has seriously studied the original Warren Report on the assassination (and not just had it read to him by its critics); has gone over the materials produced in the reconsideration of that Report by the House of Representatives in 1977–78; and has familiarized himself with the many scientific studies over the years, including three separate reviews of the medical material, which have examined the testable bases of the single-assassin theory — to anyone who has done all this, the notion of multiple gunmen, on which nearly every conspiracy theory extant rests, is a demon-

---

***prima facie:** Latin, at first view; immediately clear. In law refers to evidence sufficient to establish a fact.

strable chimera. And if there was one and only one assassin, and if that assassin was Lee Harvey Oswald, then nearly every insinuation in *JFK*, and in the mountain of conspiracy literature which it summarizes, collapses.

II

The case for multiple assassins consists of four lines of argument: (1) there was not enough time for a single gunman to have done what the Warren Commission alleges Oswald did; (2) compelling eyewitness, photographic, and earwitness testimony place a second gunman on the fabled grassy knoll; (3) the evidence of Kennedy's wounds and the reaction of his body to the shots establishes the presence of assassins other than on the knoll; and (4) the so-called single-bullet theory, popularly known as the magic-bullet theory, the indispensable prerequisite of the notion that there was only one assassin, is a palpable absurdity.

These arguments are mutually reinforcing, but it is fair to say if any of them holds water, the single-assassin theory would be untenable. However, as we shall see, all four are baseless.

Consider the issue of timing. Repeatedly, like a mantra, *JFK*, and the critics it mimics, declare that the famous Zapruder film (a home movie taken of the assassination by a Dallas manufacturer, Abraham Zapruder) "established three shots in 5.6 seconds" and that such a feat would stretch the capacity of the most expert rifleman, and undoubtedly was beyond Oswald and his gun. In interviews and speeches Oliver Stone frequently refers to "the 5.6-second Zapruder film," as if that were all there was to it, 5.6 seconds, and many commentators on *JFK* dutifully repeat these data, usually in the movie's own tone of outraged incredulity.

Yet: (1) the Zapruder film, which is 30 seconds long in toto, firmly established only the final and unmistakable shot to Kennedy's head. (2) Even assuming that two hits occurred 5.6 seconds apart, nothing in Zapruder indicates that a possible third shot, which missed, had to have come *between* the two hits. The Warren Commission concluded only that there were probably three shots and that *the two hits*, not the three shots, came within 5.6 seconds of each other. The miss could have come first, or last, though it probably came first. That means the gunman had more than eight seconds to shoot, and more than five seconds — ample time —

between the two hits. (3) Even if the miss had come between the two hits, there would still have been 2.8 seconds to fire and refire — enough time even for an amateur used to handling guns, like Oswald. Stone and/or his advisers know this, as does everyone who has studied the case.

Were there shots from the grassy knoll by another assassin? Allegedly, eyewitness, photographic, and earwitness testimony placed a second gunman there. The knoll, I would remind the reader, was in front and to the right of the President's car when he was first struck, and directly to his right when he was fatally shot in the head. The Warren Commission placed the lone gunman above and behind the President in the Texas Book Depository building.

Surely, the most significant eye- and earwitnesses to the assassination were Abraham Zapruder himself and his secretary, Marilyn Sitzman, who was standing next to him as he took his famous home movie. The two of them were on the knoll, on a three-foot-high concrete pedestal overlooking the scene and directly overlooking the entire area behind a five-foot wooden fence at the top of the knoll from behind which, Stone and the other conspiracists say, an assassin shot at and killed the President.

But here is a point omitted by Stone and the conspiracists: Zapruder and Sitzman were within 50 feet, above, slightly *behind,* and in clear line of sight of the alleged assassin and (in Stone's recreation) his alleged "spotter." Fifty feet is ten feet less than the distance between home plate and the mound. Understand: Zapruder and Sitzman were on the mound facing the batter, as it were, and Stone would have us believe that they did not happen to hear or see two assassins to their right front halfway down the third base line, firing two explosive shots. They simply failed to glance that way during the shooting or to notice the gunman while he waited for the President to arrive.

Zapruder is now dead, but Sitzman was interviewed for a sensational five-part documentary produced by the Arts and Entertainment (A&E) Network on cable TV. Somehow, the interviewer did not ask her whether she noticed a man shooting the President just to her right front.

Those who have seen the A&E documentary will recall the gripping analysis of a black-and-white Polaroid snapshot of the knoll which was taken by one Mary Moorman just before the fatal head shot. In that picture, we are told, one may now see the clear image of "the badge man," a man in uniform, who, allegedly, fired at the President from the knoll. Yet while that image may leap out at the consultants to the A&E documentary, it was not clear to the panel of photographic experts who, in 1977, perused it for the House Assassinations Committee.

Of course, those experts were not privy to the blown-up, "colorized" enhancements of the photo developed by the A&E consultants, who claim to see in the photo not only a man (nothing remarkable in that, it's a free country and people were allowed to roam about the knoll) but a hatless man in uniform. They even claim to be able to see the label on his shirt and, "perhaps," a gun. Well, if "badge man" is an assassin, he fired from a spot right next to, at most fifteen feet below and to the right of, Zapruder and Sitzman. Again, they did not notice.

There are other pictures of the knoll — twenty-two persons were taking pictures in Dealey Plaza, the assassination site, that afternoon — and several are of the knoll at the time of the shooting. Over the years conspiracists have discerned in these pictures riflemen and rifles, only to have photographic expertise reveal the illusions created by light and shadow.

For example, in one set of photos purporting to show a rifleman in "the classic firing position," the rifleman, to be actual, would need to have been floating in the air nine feet above the ground. Another rifle, supposedly visible in Zapruder frame 413, turned out to be a small branch in a bush in front of the fence, and the head behind that bush, the one with a "tennis hat" on, would have to be the size of a lemon in order to have been where the critics say it is.

Notwithstanding Stone's insinuations, no one saw a gun on the knoll, though it would have been in the clear line of sight of hundreds of the 692 people who have been identified in Dealey Plaza. No one: not one of the eighteen people on the railroad bridge who, looking up Elm Street at the approaching President, could easily have spotted a gun about a hundred feet in front of them and slightly to their left; no one in the plaza, neither Zapruder nor Sitzman, who were on the knoll; none of the hundreds who, we presume, were following the presidential limousine with their eyes and need only have raised their gaze a few degrees to have seen the gun; not Lee Bowers, who surveyed the scene from a tower behind the alleged assassins; no one in the presidential caravan, including Secret Service men whom film and photos show scanning the surrounding scene. (Were they ordered not to see anything? Have they remained silent to this day about those criminal orders?) On the other hand, six people saw the rifle *inside* the sixth-floor, southeast corner window of the Book Depository: Oswald's rifle, the one that fired all the bullets that were recovered. Two people actually saw the rifle as it was fired, and two of them identified Oswald in a police lineup.

Those who have seen the Stone film, or the A&E documentary, or are familiar with the conspiracy literature, may now protest vehemently: what about Jean Hill, the woman in the Stone film who fervently claims she saw a "gunman" running? What about the others who swear passionately that the shots came from the knoll? What about the many, like A. J. Holland, who saw gunsmoke on the knoll, and the sheer weight of earwitness testimony that the shots came from the knoll? What about the deaf mute who for twenty-eight years has been trying to get someone to understand his signing message that, a few minutes before the assassination, from a distance of over a hundred yards, he saw men walking with rifles near the knoll?

And what about the lady who now claims to be the "babushka lady" visible in photos of the plaza, and who says she will go to her death believing there was a gunman on the knoll? And what of Gordon Arnold, who claims, after more than a quarter century of silence, that he filmed the assassination from in front of the fence on the knoll, that he sensed bullets whizzing past his ear, and that after the shooting a man with "dirty hands," in a uniform, came up to him, weeping, and threw him to the ground, physically forcing him to relinquish the incriminating film? Arnold's is one of several stories by people who claim they were roughed up and threatened because they had seen inadmissible things. Stone graphically depicts these alleged brutalities and the reign of terror which insiders to the asassination have been enduring.

Here are the answers. Jean Hill said she "saw a man running," not from the knoll but from the Depository. Stone has Hill say that the man was a "gunman." But a gunman, presumably, is a man holding a gun. Hill did not say that she saw a gun. It is possible that, as many witnesses do, she has fused two disparate facts — the

President is shot, a man is running — and created the saga she has made a career of telling?

Holland, who is the only one to say he saw a man with a submachine gun stand up in the back of the President's limousine, claims also to have seen smoke over the knoll. Others, too, saw smoke, and identified it with a shot. The Stone film shows a considerable puff of smoke wafting above the knoll, pretty much as Holland described it. But modern weapons do not make big puffs of smoke. Hot steam pipes do produce such cumulus effects, and there were hot steam pipes at the top of the knoll where the smoke was seen.

Beverly Oliver, the woman who claims to be the "babushka lady," not only swears "to her death" that the shots came from the knoll (although she saw no gun), but she also identifies herself as having been a nightclub singer in a club next to Jack Ruby's and has said that when Ruby, Oswald's eventual assassin, introduced her there to Oswald they casually identified themselves as "CIA agents." She says, too, that in 1968 she met for two hours with Richard Nixon, whom she ties to the killing. Stone knows all this detail, but omits much of it in order to create the character of a sympathetic nightclub singer terrified to tell the world about her certain knowledge of links between Oswald and Ruby. (No persuasive links between the two have ever been established.)

Was Gordon Arnold there? He does not appear in photos, though some find him in the Moorman photo right next to "badge man." (Apparently Arnold did not notice the "badge man" shooting the President.) As for the story that he was brutalized and his film removed — it is interesting that no one brutalized or even spoke to Zapruder and Sitzman, or removed them from the pivotal perch from which they filmed the assassination and, presumably, saw the assassins. And as for the deaf mute, whose twenty-eight years of silent frustration were ended when A&E finally found someone to read his signs and put him on television, is it indecorous to suggest that his story sounds like a routine on *Saturday Night Live*?

Stone and others would have us believe that on the knoll that day there was a platoon of conspirators, incognito, surveying every person's eyes, entering minds and cameras, knowing infallibly who had incriminating evidence and who did not. Like Santa Claus, they knew who had been bad or good, and they brutalized only those who saw or photographed the bad thing. And these people, in fear and trembling, agreed to be silent. Now, nearly three decades later, these same victims have agreed to take their ten minutes in the spotlight at the invitation of A&E and Oliver Stone.

And the earwitnesses? Undeniably, several people thought shots came from the knoll, said so freely to the Warren Commission, the FBI, the Secret Service, and the Dallas police, and were reported as having said so. Fourteen years later, in 1977, at the request of the House Assassinations Committee, a panel of acoustical scientists and psychologists examined all the earwitness evidence and then correlated it with observations they made at Dealey Plaza when rifles were test-fired from the knoll and the Book Depository. They discovered that of 178 earwitness accounts which they sampled, 132 thought there were three shots, 149 thought there were three or fewer. Six people thought there were four shots; one thought there were five, and one, Jean Hill, heard six. (Six is the number that Stone, and most conspiracists, say were fired.)

With regard to the source of the shots: 49 of the 178 thought it was the Depository, 21 thought it was the knoll, 30 gave other sources, 78 did not know. Crucially, however, only 4 of the 178 thought shots came from more than one direction. Since we know that at least some shots came from the Depository — the rifle, Oswald's, which fired all the recovered bullets and shells was found there, and six people saw a rifle in the window — shots would have needed to have come from two directions if there were also shots from the knoll. The panel concluded:

> It is hard to believe a rifle was fired from the knoll. . . . [D]espite the various sources of confusion in the locus of any single shot, a second shot from a different location should be distinctive and different enough to cause more than four witnesses to report multiple origins for the shots.*

Author's note — *One further comment on the matter of earwitness testimony. The House Assassinations Committee in 1979 concluded that a tape recording of police communications at the time of the assassination registered four, not three, shots, and specifically, three shots from the Depository and one from the knoll. Solely on the basis of that piece of evidence, the Committee decided that an unseen gunman shot an (unrecovered) bullet, and missed. In 1982 the National Academy of Science asked a blue ribbon panel of physicists and acoustical experts to review the recording and the accompanying studies which had persuaded the House Committee that there was a gunman on the knoll. The panel concluded unanimously and vigorously that the alleged sounds on the tape could not have been made at the time of the shooting, and also scoffed at the calculations and methodology of the House consultants.

According to *JFK,* there were ten to twelve assassins, firing six shots from three directions. No one heard it that way; no one. Nor do the conspiracists answer this question: if the idea (as Stone suggests) was to frame Oswald for having fired three shots, why fire six? Did the Conspiracy expect that no one would notice?

To take the full measure of what Stone and the others are suggesting, we must remember that this ingenious plot *intended* that the assassins on the knoll be invisible and escape unnoticed. But how could they have known where spectators would be, where cameras would be? Just behind the fence was a public parking lot, filled with cars. Anyone could have gone to retrieve his car at any time. And why does Stone not show us the (inevitably hilarious) planning session where it was decided that a feigned epileptic fit fifteen minutes before the shooting to distract attention from the gunman on the knoll, a diversionary shot from the Depository, and an omniscient goon squad to rough up awkward witnesses would be enough to provide anonymity and safe passage to assassins standing in broad daylight, in clear view?

There is a further reason to scoff at speculation of a shot from the knoll: the alleged gunman, one of the world's finest (according to Stone) or one of the Mafia's finest (in other versions), firing at point-blank range, missed the car and everyone in it with a bullet which was never recovered. The now decisively authenticated X-rays and photographs which were taken of the President's body the night of the assassination establish that no shots struck the President or Governor John Connally (who was with him in the motorcade) except shots fired from above and behind. There were no hits from the knoll.

Again, viewers of Stone's film will protest: what of the doctors at Dallas's Parkland Hospital, who for years after the shooting insisted that the small neat wound in Kennedy's throat was a wound of entry, inflicted from the front (hence, by another gunman)? What of their insistence, for years, that there was a massive wound of exit in the back, occipital region of his head, where the autopsy doctors had purported to find only a small wound of entry? And most memorably, what of the dramatic thrust of the President's body, backward and "to the left" — Kevin Costner, playing Stone's heroic protagonist, New Orleans District Attorney Jim Garrison, repeats the phrase "to the left" five times, while the gory Zapruder frames show the President, indeed, thrust backward and leftward — a movement consistent only with a hit from the right front?

It is true that several Dallas doctors once thought the throat wound was an entry wound, and said so at the time. And a few of them later recalled massive damage to the back of his head, not on the right side where the autopsy doctors placed the damage. The Dallas doctors agreed that there was no time for a proper "medical examination" of the President; all of their efforts were aimed at saving his life, not examining his wounds. So frenzied were their ministrations that they did not even notice at the time a small wound of entry in his back and a small wound of entry in the back of his head. Later, after the President was peremptorily removed from Dallas to the autopsy in Washington, to the considerable professional chagrin of the Dallas doctors, several of them came to insist that the wound in the throat "looked like" a wound of entry, and that there was a massive default in the rear, occipital, portion of the President's head, a glaring fact somehow missed by the official autopsy team.

Over and again, Stone and the conspiracists refer us to these incongruous comments by the Dallas doctors. What they do not tell us is that these doctors changed their minds when they reviewed the X-rays and the photos taken at the autopsy for a *Nova* documentary on public televison. The evidence in the X-rays and photos is of paramount importance. If the throat wound was an entry wound, that bullet, fired from the right front, would have torn into Kennedy's throat and probably out of the back or side of his neck. Or it would have lodged in the body, causing appropriate damage, all of which would be visible in X-rays and photos. Unless the photos and X-rays are fake, the throat wound is not a wound of entry. Every one of the by now more than twenty forensic pathologists who have examined those documents agrees there was no strike to the throat from the front.

Similarly with regard to the alleged massive wound of exit in the back of Kennedy's head — the result, according to Stone, of a bullet administered from the front right. The X-rays and photos clearly show that that massive wound of exit is on the right side of the head, not in the back, and was caused by a bullet entering in the rear of the skull where a small wound of entry was seen by the autopsy doctors.

Again, this is the conclusion of every one of the prominent forensic pathologists who have studied the photos and X-rays which show the location and nature of the wounds and the pattern of fracturing. Even Dr. Cyril Wecht, one of the stars of the A&E documentary, a frenetic critic of the official version, agreed on this point after examining the X-rays and photos over a two-day period. The Dallas doctors, too, examining these documents for the *Nova* program, agreed that their memory of the wound location had been erroneous.

Stone and the conspiracists, having spent hundreds of hours with the Zapruder film, examining it meticulously, frame by frame, must know all this. In frame 313, when Kennedy is struck in the head, and in subsequent frames, we see a large burst of pink — bone and brain matter — exploding out of the right side of his head, exactly where the X-rays and photos place it; the back of the head, clearly visible in these frames, is unruffled and completely intact. Where then is their theory of a massive rear exit? Robert Groden, one of Stone's technical advisers, has now taken to arguing that the Zapruder films too have been doctored, along with the X-rays and photos.

Well, are the X-rays and photos authentic? As to the photos, the analysis submitted to the House Assassinations Committee by a team of photographic experts found no evidence whatsoever of tampering. Far more important was the detailed report of the team of forensic anthropologists. Studying the photos of the President, fore and aft, the anthropologists meticulously measured the angle of his nasal septum, the lower third of the nose cavity, the nasal tip area, various features of his ear, the lip profile, facial creases, and the network of wrinkles across the back and side of his neck. All of them, when compared to previous, unquestionably valid photos, established that the wounded man in these photos was the dead President and no one else.

The authentication of the X-rays was equally decisive. X-rays are like fingerprints. Since every person has a unique bone structure, it is quite easy for forensic anthropologists to identify the mutilated remains of persons killed in combat or plane crashes. The only thing needed are previous X-rays for comparison; of course, many were available in this instance. Thus, the deviation in Kennedy's nasal septum was noted and compared with his other X-rays. The bony rims around his eyes, the honeycomb air cells of the mastoid bone, the saddle-shaped depressions at the base of his skull, the bony projections along the spine — all exactly matched the comparison X-rays, as did features in the X-rays of Kennedy's lower torso.

Furthermore, the damage in the photos matched the damage found in the X-rays. Let us be clear about what this means: these are X-rays and photos of the damaged President, taken the only time in his life that he was damaged in that way. If they are phony, whose body and face are in the fake X-rays and photos? The panel of experts did not argue that the government was incapable of contemplating forgery; they argued that such a forgery, even if contemplated, would be next to impossible: "There can be no doubt that they are the X-rays of John F. Kennedy, and no other person."

Why did President Kennedy lurch backward and to the left if he was struck from behind? Twice now, panels of experts examining the question — once for the Rockefeller Commission in 1972, yet again for the House Assassinations Committee — have concluded that no bullet, by itself, could have caused that physical reaction. Rather, the motion has been attributed to "a seizurelike neuromuscular reaction to major damage inflicted to nerve centers in the brain." The House panel even assassinated some live goats to demonstrate the effect.

Let us turn, finally, to the mother of all of Stone's and the other conspiracists' canards, their account of the so-called magic bullet, a term so deeply entrenched in discussions of the assassination that routine newspaper accounts of the latest conspiracy allegations refer to it, without quotation marks, as if it were the God-given name of the bullet. I have seen Stone's film three times, and each time Kevin Costner's derisive account of the Warren Commission's supposed position on the subject has brought gasps of incredulous, mutinous laughter from the audience:

> The magic bullet enters the President's back headed downward at an
> angle of 17 degrees; it then moves upward in order to leave Kennedy's

body from the front of his neck, wound number two, where it waits 1.6 seconds, presumably in midair, where it turns right then left [right then left, Costner repeats] and continues into Connally's body at the rear of his right armpit, wound number three. The bullet then heads downward at an angle of 27 degrees, shattering Connally's fifth rib, and exiting from the right side of his chest, wound number four. The bullet then turns right and reenters Connally's body at the right wrist, wound number five, shattering the radius bone. The bullet then exits Connally's wrist, wound number six, takes a dramatic U-turn and buries itself into Connally's left thigh, from which it later falls out and is found in almost pristine condition in a corridor of Parkland Hospital.

The Warren Commission, it should be unnecessary to say, argued no such thing. It contended that Kennedy and Connally were struck by the same bullet, somewhere between frames 207 and 223 of the Zapruder film. During that one-second period, the two men disappear behind a road sign. Just before Connally disappears behind the sign, and again a little less than a second — fifteen frames — later when he reappears, his right wrist is close to his lap, directly over his left thigh. He is holding the lid of a big Texas hat, knuckles up. His head has turned to the right — Connally has remembered doing this after hearing a shot (probably the first shot, the one that missed) — and in turning, his shoulders rotate rightward slightly, bringing his body into perfect alignment to receive all five of his wounds. It is only then, when the Commission held the two men were hit, that Connally could have been struck in a way to cause the scars which he indubitably has, to this day.

On three separate occasions in the last twenty years, panels of photographic experts analyzing the Zapruder frames and all the photographs have confirmed this analysis. Using the same evidence, and with the added help of wound locations established by X-rays and photographs, the panel of experts assembled by the House Committee showed that a line drawn through Connally and Kennedy's wounds leads right back, straight as an arrow, to the window from which someone fired Oswald's gun: no turns, no pauses.

Now consider Connally's position when Stone and other conspiracists say he was struck. (Costner: "Connally's turning here now, frame 238, the fourth shot, it misses Kennedy and takes Connally.") As I pointed out in *Commentary* seventeen years ago, in that frame Connally

has turned 90 degrees to the right and is facing out of the side of the car. A bullet striking Connally when the critics say he was hit would then have had to exit from the chest at a downward angle, to have taken two sharp turns upward, in midair — right and then left into the knuckle side of the wrist; and then, upon exiting on the palm side, further up in the air than the wound of entry, would have had to execute a very sharp U-turn into the thigh: plainly impossible.*

In other words, it is not the Warren Commission's account which requires these absurd zigs and zags, it is Stone's.

And the "almost pristine" bullet found "in a corridor" at Parkland Hospital? That bullet, unquestionably fired from Oswald's gun, was found next to Connally's stretcher in the basement of the hospital, exactly where it would be to support the single-bullet theory. It was not pristine; it lacked lead from its core in the amount found in Connally. It was also flattened at one end, and bent at its axis. In 1978, Professor Vincent Guinn, responding to a decade of demands by critics, employed recently improved neutron-activation techniques to compare the traces of antimony, silver, and copper in the lead from the "magic bullet" with the trace amounts of those metals in the lead recovered from Connally's wrist. He concluded that the wrist lead almost certainly came from lead missing from the "magic bullet."

Now, if the bullet found in the basement of Parkland Hospital next to Connally's stretcher, fired from Oswald's gun and missing the very lead found in Connally's wrist, is not the one which struck Connally, how did it get next to his stretcher? Stone suggests that someone from Assassination Central was sent over to drop a spare bullet somewhere in the hospital. Why the basement? Why Connally's stretcher and not Kennedy's? How could the Conspiracy have known where Connally's stretcher would be? How could it have known then that a bullet which had ended in the soft flesh of Connally's thigh needed to be placed with his stretcher in order to confirm a single-bullet theory which was not developed for another two months? And if this was not the bullet that hit Connally, what happened to the bullet that did?

In the film we see colonels and other gray eminences directing the autopsy like puppeteers, ordering doctors to lie about the

Author's note — *"Conspiracy Fever," *Commentary,* October 1975.

damage to the President, to silence their curiosity about dangerous matters, and forever. But at that point the Conspiracy could
not have known what directions to give. The single-bullet theory,
to repeat, was not developed until months later, and only an omniscient demon could have figured out so soon what precise changes
would be necessary in the autopsy report. When and how did the
Conspiracy brief its agents in the autopsy room, and who did the
briefing, and who briefed the briefers? It is a shame that Stone did
not invent scenes dramatizing all this; they too would have been
hilarious.

Similar objections may be raised to the theory developed by
David Lifton in a best-selling book and reiterated in the A&E documentary. Kennedy's body, we are told, was taken to a secret laboratory after its arrival in Washington while an elaborate ruse — empty
coffins, diversionary caravans — convinced the public that his
body was being taken directly to the Bethesda Naval Hospital. With
about forty minutes to do their work, the agents of the Conspiracy
completely altered the President's wounds to make it look as if he
had been hit by one assassin, firing from behind, disguising even
the signs of their intervention from the X-rays and photos, although not from Lifton and A&E.

In this version, then, the autopsy itself is honest, only the doctors are working on an altered body. But how could the Conspiracy have known what alterations to make? How could its agents be
sure forty minutes would be enough? Scores of people would need
to be involved: those who prepared the alternate route, those who
switched the body, those who performed the forty-minute surgical
miracle, those who carefully brought the body to Bethesda through
the back door, those who sent advance news of the nature of the
wounds from the Parkland Hospital or the President's plane. And
all have remained silent about the matter to this day.

There was, in sum, nothing magic about the "magic bullet." And
there was no need to alter the body, no need to fabricate an autopsy. The overwhelming burden of the evidence indicates that one
assassin shot the President, just as the Warren Commission said.

III

Was Lee Harvey Oswald that single assassin? Chief Justice Earl
Warren, who according to Stone was a perjurer and either a willing

or a moronic accomplice to a massive cover-up, said that in a life-time as a lawyer and judge he had never seen such a clear case of guilt. Here I can only sketch the outline of the case, but even a sketch is sufficient to demonstrate the absurdity of ubiquitous charges that Oswald did not shoot the President, that he was a "patsy" set up to deflect attention from other assassins.

First, there is this pivotal fact: Oswald worked in the building from which the President was shot and obtained the job there, un-suspiciously, three weeks before unsuspicious decisions were made (by Kenneth O'Donnell, Kennedy's friend) which occasioned the President's appearance in front of that building.

Stone tells us in the film that on the day of the assassination the Conspiracy "sent" Oswald to the building. But it did not have to; he reported for work as usual. What Stone does not tell us is that Oswald carried a gun to work that morning. A co-worker who drove him in (Oswald could not drive) reported that Oswald had a long object wrapped in paper which he held from below, cupped in his palm, military style. ("Curtain rods," was Oswald's answer to the obvious question.)

Paper that had been fashioned as a gun carrier was later found on the sixth floor, near the murder window. Oswald's fingerprints were on it, as was his palm print at the base where he would have cupped it in the manner described. Also on the bag were strands of wool from the blanket in which Oswald's rifle had been wrapped. There were no curtain rods. The murder rifle, Oswald's, which fired all the bullets and shells later recovered,* was also found on the sixth floor. On it were strands of wool from Oswald's shirt and Oswald's palm print.[†] Oswald's finger and palm prints were also on the card boxes used as a gun prop and on the brown bag. (Stone

Author's note — *One wonders how the conspirators recovered and disposed of the embarrassing bullets from the other alleged guns. They could not have known where they would end up. Scores of collaborators would have been needed, at the ready, in the plaza, in the car, in the hospital, to snatch away the damning missiles without being noticed.

Author's note — †Conspiracists make a good deal of the charge that there were no other prints on the gun. The charge is untrue. The FBI report did not say there were no other prints, it said there were no other "identifiable" prints, which is not unusual. As experts testified, the rough wood stock and poor-quality metal of the gun tended to absorb moisture from the skin, making a clear print unlikely.

mentions none of this.) In addition, two eyewitnesses who saw the gunman in the window identified Oswald as that gunman.

According to Stone and the conspiracists, the plotters went to extraordinary lengths to link Oswald to a rifle which they also claim was not used. But why not link him to the "real" gun? Viewers may remember very brief shots of a photograph of Oswald being altered. These shots are spliced into *JFK*, out of context and narrative sequence, in order to set the scene for Stone's later contention that a photograph of Oswald holding the murder rifle and pistol in his backyard was the crudest of forgeries. In that photo, the conspiracists say, two-thirds of Oswald's face has been pasted onto the chin and body of a stand-in. A distinct line across the chin shows the intervention clearly, and anyway the shadows cast by the nose are inconsistent with the shadows cast by the stand-in body.

What Stone does not tell us is that the photo was taken with Oswald's box camera, that his wife remembers taking it, that it is one of several taken of him with gun and pistol at that time, and that after exhaustive examination photographic experts employed by the House Assassinations Committee found even the challenged photo to be entirely unexceptionable, shadows and all. It also should be noted that this photo, found among Oswald's effects after the assassination, is superfluous to the proof that he possessed the gun: there are many other, superior, evidences of that.

Stone scoffs at the rifle, "the worst military weapon in the world." But the laugh is on him, for the neutron-activation analysis and ballistics findings prove that this supposedly defective rifle fired the bullet which deposited lead in Connally's wrist and also the bullet which hit Kennedy in the skull.* Someone used that rifle very effectively, and if it was not Oswald, Stone needs to explain why this brilliant Conspiracy, which used one world-class marksman, gave him the worst weapon in the world. He should also explain why, if the Conspiracy was framing Oswald, it would have wanted to link him to such a ridiculous weapon.

Author's note — *The traces of silver and antimony in the lead removed from Kennedy's brain were compared to traces in the lead found in bullet fragments, fired from Oswald's gun, which were recovered from the presidential limousine. Again, as was the case with Connally's wrist, the match was perfect.

Oswald left the building immediately after the shooting, retrieved a light-colored jacket and pistol from his rooming house, and about forty-five minutes after the assassination was seen shooting a Dallas policeman named Tippit. Twelve eyewitnesses identify Oswald as Tippit's assailant — although, to be sure, a few others, the ones presented by Stone and the A&E documentary, do not. The shells expended at the scene and the bullets in Tippit match the pistol found on Oswald when he was arrested. His jacket was found nearby. When the eyewitnesses reported the shooting to the police, using the radio in Tippit's car, police swarmed to the area. After a phoned report to them that a man had been seen ducking into a theater without paying, they rushed to the theater and arrested Oswald, who resisted, for the murder of Tippit. On him was the murder pistol; he had ordered it by mail, ten months earlier.

Astonishingly, Stone and many other conspiracists even question the contention that Oswald shot Tippit. Citing inconsistencies in eyewitness reports, which are to be expected in nearly all such reports, they imply that the bullets and shells were a plant, that the real ones were removed, that the jacket was a plant, and that the narrative by which the police traced Oswald to the theater was a contrived fiction.

What may have happened, according to Stone and the others, is that the Dallas police were expecting Oswald at the theater. They would murder someone in the neighbohood, a Dallas policeman murdered with the cooperation of Dallas policemen, and they would blame it on Oswald, presumably to prove that he was a murdering sort. The reader is invited to recapitulate the planning which would need to go into this part of the Conspiracy, involving now new bullet-snatchers and -replacers in the Dallas police, the elimination of anyone who could prove that Oswald was elsewhere than next to Tippit's car when the officer was shot, etc. Of course, all parties to this part of the Conspiracy have remained silent ever since.

It is often asked why Oswald denied having killed the President, as though guilty people do not deny things all the time. The fact is that Oswald denied everything. He himself was the first to insist that the backyard photo of him with the gun was a forgery. Shown it during his interrogation, he dismissed it at a glance. He denied having hunted in this country; he denied possessing the rifle, any rifle; he denied ever using the pseudonym Alec Hidell, which he had used to order the guns and on several identification documents; he made up an easily contradicted story that the manager of the Depository brought a rifle to the building; he denied the curtain rod tale, saying he carried only his lunch to work that morning; he denied killing Tippit; when asked his reason for visiting his estranged wife and children on Thursday, assassination eve, rather than his usual Friday, he made up a story about a birthday party; he denied using an alias at his rooming house. He also refused to take a polygraph test. The law familiarly says that lies of this sort indicate a "consciousness of guilt," especially if they are explicable only by the hypothesis that the accused knows he is guilty.

To sum up: Oswald (1) worked in the building which was the only source of shots; (2) owned and possessed the one and only murder rifle; (3) brought it to work with him the morning of the murder; (4) was at the murder window at the time the President was shot; (5) left the scene immediately after the shooting; (6) shot an officer who attempted to question him and then forcibly resisted arrest; (7) lied about crucial matters of fact when interrogated.

There is an eighth reason to believe he was the killer: this was not his first assassination attempt. Among the photographs in Oswald's effects were several of a house and adjoining driveway. Weeks after the assassination, the FBI discovered that the house in the photo was that of General Edwin Walker, a right-wing, anti-Castro, anti-civil rights fanatic. The G-men irrefutably established the exact date the photo was taken, which turned out to be just before someone unsuccessfully tried to assassinate Walker on April 10, 1963. The photo was taken with Oswald's camera; Oswald had a collection of news stories about the assassination attempt; bullets that had slammed into Walker's wall were consistent with Oswald's gun; a note written to his wife at the time, and her suspicions voiced then as well, indicate that he was Walker's would-be assassin. In the Marines he had twice been court-martialed, once for threatening a superior officer. Needless to say, Oliver Stone tells us nothing of this.

Why would Oswald try to kill a right-wing general? An obvious hypothesis, the one Stone and the critics feverishly try to silence, is that the attempt had something to do with Oswald's intense left-wing sympathies. Stone's campaign to transform him into a long-term right-winger, in league with Castro-hating activists, involves biographical surgery even more radical than the surgery which allegedly transformed the President's wounds the night of the assassination.

Oswald was already a left-winger at the age of thirteen when he distributed pro-Rosenberg material in New York. He defected to the Soviet Union and attempted to commit suicide when, notwithstanding his offer of radar data, the land of his dreams refused him citizenship. Disillusioned with the Soviet Union, he returned to the United States and transferred his fantasies to a new hero, Castro, whose picture he kept by his bed. He monitored radio broadcasts from Havana on his shortwave radio.

Oswald subscribed to the Communist *Daily Worker* and the Trotskyist *Militant*; these are the newspapers he holds in the authentic photos of him with gun and pistol taken in his backyard. He formed a one-person chapter of the pro–Castro Fair Play for Cuba Committee (FPCC), handed out FPCC leaflets, which he himself printed, and spoke on the radio in its behalf. Imagining himself a Castro operative, and acting alone, as always, he briefly attempted to infiltrate an anti-Castro group in New Orleans but then immediately revealed his pro-Castro sympathies, to the group's considerable dismay. He composed a schmaltzy and horrifically spelled "historic diary," as he called it, and several paeans to Marxism. He visited the Cuban and Russian embassies in Mexico City in October 1963, seeking a visa to Cuba, and reacted in fury when denied his request.

This recital only scratches the surface of Oswald's left-wing record and his unstable, lone-wolf personality. But it is enough to sustain at least the possibility that the sole assassin of John F. Kennedy was a left-wing fantasist who found himself working in a building in front of which would come the President of the United States, the man whom Castro had publicly named as responsible for assassination attempts on his, Castro's, life. The same fantasist who went to the Soviet Union expecting to be accepted as a hero (and told his Russian wife that someday he would be "president of the world") now thought, incoherently, stupidly, that he would become a hero in Cuba as the assassin of Castro's enemies: General Walker and President Kennedy. Character, as the Greeks said, is fate.

IV

If there was only one assassin and he was Lee Harvey Oswald, if there was no massive frame-up or cover-up, then Stone's and every other conspiracy theory currently before the public are fatally wounded. The government's allegedly ubiquitous hand disappears. Absent that hand, what other grand conspirators — military industrialists, mafiosi — would use so unlikely a killer, stage so unlikely a killing?

For nearly thirty years, platoons of conspiracists have concertedly scavenged the record, floating their appalling and thrilling might-have-beens, unfazed by the contradictions and absurdities in their own wantonly selective accounts, often consciously, cunningly deceitful. They have refused to let go of any shred of their earliest suspicions, even when these have been demolished by decisive scientific findings. And the media have patronized them, for journalists love their thrilling insinuations and share many of their philosophical and political assumptions; and with regard to the assassination, they remain stone ignorant. Small wonder that 85 percent of the American public thinks there was a conspiracy of some sort.

Recently, thirteen thousand copies of a new study guide, sympathetic to *JFK*, were sent to American high school teachers. Our students know nothing about the case or the times. Their teachers remember little, and many of them, especially the most "liberated," hold the view that to *question* any official version of anything is important in and of itself, even if the questions are based on palpable falsehoods. I do not think we should rejoice that our children ask questions in this manner. I think we should weep; and scold the scurrilous.

Reflections and Responses

1. Note that Cohen refers to Oliver Stone's *JFK* in his opening sentence as "notorious." What other terms might he have used? Why did he not write "famous" or "controversial"?

2. According to Cohen, what does "nearly every conspiracy theory extant" have in common? How important is this commonality to

Cohen's argument? Can you think of any theory of the assassination that would substantially differ from the commonly held theories?

3. Oliver Stone's film represents just one of a multitude of conspiracist theories. Why do you think Cohen devotes so much of his attention to it? What elements of the film disturb him the most?

ப

FRANK CONROY

Think About It

Though educators don't like to think so, education is very often a mysterious process. How we come to understand something — both in and out of school — can be far less direct and systematic than methodically minded teachers might acknowledge. Illumination sometimes takes time: "The light bulb may appear over your head," Frank Conroy writes, "but it may be a while before it actually goes on." In this brief but deeply intriguing essay, Conroy explores several episodes from his younger years and shows how some puzzling things he couldn't quite understand at first finally revealed their meaning to him long afterward. But not every such illumination came with "a resolving kind of click." Conroy also recalls a series of enigmatic meetings with two of America's most famous legal minds and how they led to the strange satisfaction of an unresolved problem.

Conroy, director of the prestigious Iowa Writers' Workshop, is the author of Stop-Time *(1967) and* Midair *(1985). His stories and essays have appeared in* The New Yorker, Esquire, Harper's Magazine, GQ, *and many other publications. He has worked as a jazz pianist and has often written about American music. Music is the theme of his latest novel,* Body & Soul *(1993). "Think About It" originally appeared in* Harper's Magazine *(1988) and was selected by Geoffrey Wolff for* The Best American Essays *1989.*

When I was sixteen I worked selling hot dogs at a stand in the Fourteenth Street subway station in New York City, one level above the trains and one below the street, where the crowds continually flowed back and forth. I worked with three Puerto Rican men who could not speak English. I had no Spanish, and although we understood each other well with regard to the tasks at hand, sensing and adjusting to each other's body movements in the extremely confined space in which we operated, I felt isolated with no one to talk to. On my break I came out from behind the counter and passed the time with two old black men who ran a shoeshine stand in a dark corner of the corridor. It was a poor location, half hidden by columns, and they didn't have much business. I would sit with my back against the wall while they stood or moved around their ancient elevated stand, talking to each other or to me, but always staring into the distance as they did so.

As the weeks went by I realized that they never looked at anything in their immediate vicinity — not at me or their stand or anybody who might come within ten or fifteen feet. They did not look at approaching customers once they were inside the perimeter. Save for the instant it took to discern the color of the shoes, they did not even look at what they were doing while they worked, but rubbed in polish, brushed, and buffed by feel while looking over their shoulders, into the distance, as if awaiting the arrival of an important person. Of course there wasn't all that much distance in the underground station, but their behavior was so focused and consistent they seemed somehow to transcend the physical. A powerful mood was created, and I came almost to believe that these men could see through walls, through girders, and around corners to whatever hyperspace it was where whoever it was they were waiting and watching for would finally emerge. Their scattered talk was hip, elliptical, and hinted at mysteries beyond my white boy's ken, but it was the staring off, the long, steady staring off, that had me hypnotized. I left for a better job, with handshakes from both of them, without understanding what I had seen.

Perhaps ten years later, after playing jazz with black musicians in various Harlem clubs, hanging out uptown with a few young artists and intellectuals, I began to learn from them something of the extraordinarily varied and complex riffs and rituals embraced by different people to help themselves get through life in the ghetto. Fantasy of all kinds — from playful to dangerous — was in the very air of Harlem. It was the spice of uptown life.

Only then did I understand the two shoeshine men. They were trapped in a demeaning situation in a dark corner in an underground corridor in a filthy subway system. Their continuous staring off was a kind of statement, a kind of dance. Our bodies are here, went the statement, but our souls are receiving nourishment from distant sources only we can see. They were powerful magic dancers, sorcerers almost, and thirty-five years later I can still feel the pressure of their spell.

The light bulb may appear over your head, is what I'm saying, but it may be a while before it actually goes on. Early in my attempts to learn jazz piano, I used to listen to recordings of a fine player named Red Garland, whose music I admired. I couldn't quite figure out what he was doing with his left hand, however; the chords eluded me. I went uptown to an obscure club where he was playing with his trio, caught him on his break, and simply asked him. "Sixths," he said cheerfully. And then he went away.

I didn't know what to make of it. The basic jazz chord is the seventh, which comes in various configurations, but it is what it is. I was a self-taught pianist, pretty shaky on theory and harmony, and when he said sixths I kept trying to fit the information into what I already knew, and it didn't fit. But it stuck in my mind — a tantalizing mystery.

A couple of years later, when I began playing with a bass player, I discovered more or less by accident that if the bass played the root and I played a sixth based on the fifth note of the scale, a very interesting chord involving both instruments emerged. Ordinarily, I suppose I would have skipped over the matter and not paid much attention, but I remembered Garland's remark and so I stopped and spent a week or two working out the voicings, and greatly strengthened my foundations as a player. I had remembered what I hadn't understood, you might say, until my life caught up with the information and the light bulb went on.

I remember another, more complicated example from my sophomore year at the small liberal-arts college outside Philadelphia. I seemed never to be able to get up in time for breakfast in the dining hall. I would get coffee and a doughnut in the Coop instead — a basement area with about a dozen small tables where students could get something to eat at odd hours. Several mornings in a row I noticed a strange man sitting by himself with a cup of coffee. He was in his sixties, perhaps, and sat straight in his chair with very little extraneous movement. I guessed he was some sort of distinguished visitor to the college who had decided to put in some time at a student hangout. But no one ever sat with him. One morning I approached his table and asked if I could join him.

"Certainly," he said. "Please do." He had perhaps the clearest eyes I had ever seen, like blue ice, and to be held in their steady gaze was not, at first, an entirely comfortable experience. His eyes gave nothing away about himself while at the same time creating in me the eerie impression that he was looking directly into my soul. He asked a few quick questions, as if to put me at my ease, and we fell into conversation. He was William O. Douglas from the Supreme Court, and when he saw how startled I was he said, "Call me Bill. Now tell me what you're studying and why you get up so late in the morning." Thus began a series of talks that stretched over many weeks. The fact that I was an ignorant sophomore with literary pretensions who knew nothing about the law didn't seem to bother him. We talked about everything from Shakespeare to the possibility of life on other planets. One day I mentioned that I was going to have dinner with Judge Learned Hand. I explained that Hand was my girlfriend's grandfather. Douglas nodded, but I could tell he was surprised at the coincidence of my knowing the chief judge of the most important court in the country save the Supreme Court itself. After fifty years on the bench Judge Hand had become a famous man, both in and out of legal circles — a living legend, to his own dismay. "Tell him hello and give him my best regards," Douglas said.

Learned Hand, in his eighties, was a short, barrel-chested man with a large, square head, huge, thick, bristling eyebrows, and soft brown eyes. He radiated energy and would sometimes bark out remarks or questions in the living room as if he were in court. His humor was sharp, but often leavened with a touch of self-mockery. When something caught his funny bone he would burst out with explosive laughter — the laughter of a man who enjoyed laughing. He had a large repertoire of dramatic expressions involving the use of his eyebrows — very useful, he told me conspiratorially, when looking down on things from behind the bench. (The court stenographer could not record the movement of his eyebrows.) When I told him I'd been talking to William O. Douglas, they first shot up in exaggerated surprise, and then lowered and moved forward in a glower.

"*Justice* William O. Douglas, young man," he admonished. "Justice

Douglas, if you please." About the Supreme Court in general, Hand insisted on a tone of profound respect. Little did I know that in private correspondence he had referred to the Court as "The Blessed Saints, Cherubim and Seraphim," "The Jolly Boys," "The Nine Tin Jesuses," "The Nine Blameless Ethiopians," and my particular favorite, "The Nine Blessed Chalices of the Sacred Effluvium."

Hand was badly stooped and had a lot of pain in his lower back. Martinis helped, but his strict Yankee wife approved of only one before dinner. It was my job to make the second and somehow slip it to him. If the pain was particularly acute he would get out of his chair and lie flat on the rug, still talking, and finish his point without missing a beat. He flattered me by asking for my impression of Justice Douglas, instructed me to convey his warmest regards, and then began talking about the Dennis case, which he described as a particularly tricky and difficult case involving the prosecution of eleven leaders of the Communist party. He had just started in on the First Amendment and free speech when we were called in to dinner.

William O. Douglas loved the outdoors with a passion, and we fell into the habit of having coffee in the Coop and then strolling under the trees down toward the duck pond. About the Dennis case, he said something to this effect: "Eleven Communists arrested by the government. Up to no good, said the government; dangerous people, violent overthrow, etc. First Amendment, said the defense, freedom of speech, etc." Douglas stopped walking. "Clear and present danger."

"What?" I asked. He often talked in a telegraphic manner, and one was expected to keep up with him. It was sometimes like listening to a man thinking out loud.

"Clear and present danger," he said. "That was the issue. Did they constitute a clear and present danger? I don't think so. I think everybody took the language pretty far in Dennis." He began walking, striding along quickly. Again, one was expected to keep up with him. "The FBI was all over them. Phones tapped, constant surveillance. How could it be clear and present danger with the FBI watching every move they made? That's a ginkgo," he said suddenly, pointing at a tree. "A beauty. You don't see those every day. Ask Hand about clear and present danger."

I was in fact reluctant to do so. Douglas's argument seemed to me to be crushing — the last word, really — and I didn't want to embarrass Judge Hand. But back in the living room, on the second martini, the old man asked about Douglas. I sort of scratched my nose and recapitulated the conversation by the ginkgo tree.

"What?" Hand shouted. "Speak up, sir, for heaven's sake."

"He said the FBI was watching them all the time so there couldn't be a clear and present danger," I blurted out, blushing as I said it.

A terrible silence filled the room. Hand's eyebrows writhed on his face like two huge caterpillars. He leaned forward in the wing chair, his face settling, finally, into a grim expression. "I am astonished," he said softly, his eyes holding mine, "at Justice Douglas's newfound faith in the Federal Bureau of Investigation." His big, granite head moved even closer to mine, until I could smell the martini. "I had understood him to consider it a politically corrupt, incompetent organization, directed by a power-crazed lunatic." I realized I had been holding my breath throughout all of this, and as I relaxed, I saw the faintest trace of a smile cross Hand's face. Things are sometimes more complicated than they first appear, his smile seemed to say. The old man leaned back. "The proximity of the danger is something to think about. Ask him about that. See what he says."

I chewed the matter over as I returned to campus. Hand had pointed out some of Douglas's language about the FBI from other sources that seemed to bear out his point. I thought about the words "clear and present danger," and the fact that if you looked at them closely they might not be as simple as they had first appeared. What degree of danger? Did the word "present" allude to the proximity of the danger, or just the fact that the danger was there at all — that it wasn't an anticipated danger? Were there other hidden factors these great men were weighing of which I was unaware?

But Douglas was gone, back to Washington. (The writer in me is tempted to create a scene here — to invent one for dramatic purposes — but of course I can't do that.) My brief time as a messenger boy was over, and I felt a certain frustration, as if, with a few more exchanges, the matter of *Dennis* v. *United States* might have been resolved to my satisfaction. They'd left me high and dry. But, of course, it is precisely because the matter did not resolve that has caused me to think about it, off and on, all these years. "The Constitution," Hand used to say to me flatly, "is a piece of paper. The Bill of Rights is a piece of paper." It was many years before I understood what he meant. Documents alone do not keep democracy alive, nor maintain the state of law. There is no particular safety in them. Living men and women, generation after generation, must continually remake democracy and the law, and that involves an ongoing state of tension between the past and the present which will never completely resolve.

Education doesn't end until life ends, because you never know when you're going to understand something you hadn't understood before. For me, the magic dance of the shoeshine men was the kind of experience in which understanding came with a kind of click, a resolving kind of click. The same with the experience at the piano. What happened with Justice Douglas and Judge Hand was different, and makes the point that understanding does not always mean resolution. Indeed, in our intellectual lives, our creative lives, it is perhaps those problems that will never resolve that rightly claim the lion's share of our energies. The physical body exists in a constant state of tension as it maintains homeostasis, and so too does the active mind embrace the tension of never being certain, never being absolutely sure, never being done, as it engages the world. That is our special fate, our inexpressibly valuable condition.

Reflections and Responses

1. How does Conroy finally come to understand the reason the two shoeshine men always seemed to be looking into the distance? What has Conroy learned that illuminates their behavior? Can you think of other explanations?

2. What connections can you see between Conroy's insight into the behavior of the shoeshine men and his later understanding of

the elusive jazz chords? In what ways does the insight go beyond music?

3. Consider the conclusion of the episode involving William O. Douglas and Learned Hand. How does it end? Conroy says: "The writer in me is tempted to create a scene here — to invent one for dramatic purposes — but of course I can't do that." What do you think he means by the "writer in me"? Why is the refusal to "create a scene" significant to both Conroy's theme and his technique?

ALAN M. DERSHOWITZ

Shouting "Fire!"

Artists and performers are not the only ones who explore the boundaries of free expression. Lawyers and judges, too, frequently find themselves struggling to ascertain the limits of free speech. In the following essay, one of America's best-known trial lawyers, Alan M. Dershowitz, takes a close look at one of the most commonly used arguments against free speech, the idea that some speech should be suppressed because it is "just like" falsely shouting fire in a crowded theater. In his investigation into the source of this famous analogy, Dershowitz demonstrates how it has been widely misused and abused by proponents of censorship. Indeed, it was an "inapt analogy even in the context in which it was originally offered." As an expression to suppress expression, the "shouting fire" analogy, Dershowitz maintains, has been "invoked so often, by so many people, in such diverse contexts, that it has become part of our national folk language."

Alan M. Dershowitz is Felix Frankfurter professor of law at Harvard Law School. He is the author of many books, including The Best Defense *(1982),* Taking Liberties *(1988),* Chutzpah *(1991),* Contrary to Public Opinion *(1992),* The Abuse Excuse *(1994),* Reasonable Doubts *(1996), and* Sexual McCarthyism *(1998). In addition to his teaching and writing, Professor Dershowitz is an active criminal defense and civil liberties lawyer. "Shouting Fire!" originally appeared in* The Atlantic *(1989) and was selected by Justin Kaplan for* The Best American Essays 1990.

When the Reverend Jerry Falwell learned that the Supreme Court had reversed his $200,000 judgment against *Hustler* magazine for the emotional distress that he had suffered from an outrageous parody, his response was typical of those who seek to censor speech:

"Just as no person may scream 'Fire!' in a crowded theater when there is no fire, and find cover under the First Amendment, likewise, no sleazy merchant like Larry Flynt should be able to use the First Amendment as an excuse for maliciously and dishonestly attacking public figures, as he has so often done."

Justice Oliver Wendell Holmes's classic example of unprotected speech — falsely shouting "Fire!" in a crowded theater — has been invoked so often, by so many people, in such diverse contexts, that it has become part of our national folk language. It has even appeared — most appropriately — in the theater: in Tom Stoppard's play *Rosencrantz and Guildenstern Are Dead* a character shouts at the audience, "Fire!" He then quickly explains: "It's all right — I'm demonstrating the misuse of free speech." Shouting "Fire!" in the theater may well be the only jurisprudential analogy that has assumed the status of a folk argument. A prominent historian recently characterized it as "the most brilliantly persuasive expression that ever came from Holmes' pen." But in spite of its hallowed position in both the jurisprudence of the First Amendment and the arsenal of political discourse, it is and was an inapt analogy, even in the context in which it was originally offered. It has lately become — despite, perhaps even because of, the frequency and promiscuousness of its invocation — little more than a caricature of logical argumentation.

The case that gave rise to the "Fire!"-in-a-crowded-theater analogy, *Schenck* v. *United States*, involved the prosecution of Charles Schenck, who was the general secretary of the Socialist party in Philadelphia, and Elizabeth Baer, who was its recording secretary. In 1917 a jury found Schenck and Baer guilty of attempting to cause insubordination among soldiers who had been drafted to fight in the First World War. They and other party members had circulated leaflets urging draftees not to "submit to intimidation" by fighting in a war being conducted on behalf of "Wall Street's chosen few."

Schenck admitted, and the Court found, that the intent of the pamphlets' "impassioned language" was to "influence" draftees to resist the draft. Interestingly, however, Justice Holmes noted that nothing in the pamphlet suggested that the draftees should use unlawful or violent means to oppose conscription: "In form at least [the pamphlet] confined itself to peaceful measures, such as a petition for the repeal of the act" and an exhortation to exercise "your right to assert your opposition to the draft." Many of its most impassioned words were quoted directly from the Constitution.

Justice Holmes acknowledged that "in many places and in ordinary times the defendants, in saying all that was said in the circular, would have been within their constitutional rights." "But," he added, "the character of every act depends upon the circumstances in which it is done." And to illustrate that truism he went on to say:

> The most stringent protection of free speech would not protect a man in falsely shouting fire in a theater, and causing a panic. It does not even protect a man from an injunction against uttering words that may have all the effect of force.

Justice Holmes then upheld the convictions in the context of a wartime draft, holding that the pamphlet created "a clear and present danger" of hindering the war effort while our soldiers were fighting for their lives and our liberty.

The example of shouting "Fire!" obviously bore little relationship to the facts of the Schenck case. The Schenck pamphlet contained a substantive political message. It urged its draftee readers to *think* about the message and then — if they so chose — to act on it in a lawful and nonviolent way. The man who shouts "Fire!" in a crowded theater is neither sending a political message nor inviting his listener to think about what he has said and decide what to do in a rational, calculated manner. On the contrary, the message is designed to force action *without* contemplation. The message "Fire!" is directed not to the mind and the conscience of the listener but, rather, to his adrenaline and his feet. It is a stimulus to immediate *action,* not thoughtful reflection. It is — as Justice Holmes recognized in his follow-up sentence — the functional equivalent of "uttering words that may have all the effect of force."

Indeed, in that respect the shout of "Fire!" is not even speech, in any meaningful sense of that term. It is a *clang* sound, the equivalent of setting off a nonverbal alarm. Had Justice Holmes been more honest about his example, he would have said that freedom of speech does not protect a kid who pulls a fire alarm in the absence of a fire. But that obviously would have been irrelevant to the case at hand. The proposition that pulling an alarm is not protected speech certainly leads to the conclusion that shouting the word "fire" is also not protected. But the core analogy is the nonverbal alarm, and the derivative example is the verbal shout. By cleverly substituting the derivative shout for the core alarm, Holmes made it possible to analogize one set of words to another — as he could not have done if he had begun with the self-evident proposition that setting off an alarm bell is not free speech.

The analogy is thus not only inapt but also insulting. Most Americans do not respond to political rhetoric with the same kind of automatic acceptance expected of schoolchildren responding to a fire drill. Not a single recipient of the Schenck pamphlet is known to have changed his mind after reading it. Indeed, one draftee, who appeared as a prosecution witness, was asked whether reading the pamphlet asserting that the draft law was unjust would make him "immediately decide that you must erase that law." Not surprisingly, he replied, "I do my own thinking." A theatergoer would probably not respond similarly if asked how he would react to a shout of "Fire!"

Another important reason why the analogy is inapt is that Holmes emphasizes the factual falsity of the shout "Fire!" The Schenck pamphlet, however, was not factually false. It contained political opinions and ideas about the causes of the war and about appropriate and lawful responses to the draft. As the Supreme Court recently reaffirmed (in *Falwell* v. *Hustler*), "The First Amendment recognizes no such thing as a 'false' idea." Nor does it recognize false opinions about the causes of or cures for war.

A closer analogy to the facts of the Schenck case might have been provided by a person's standing outside a theater, offering the patrons a leaflet advising them that in his opinion the theater was structurally unsafe, and urging them not to enter but to complain to the building inspectors. That analogy, however, would not have served Holmes's argument for punishing Schenck. Holmes needed an analogy that would appear relevant to Schenck's political speech but that would invite the conclusion that censorship was appropriate.

Unsurprisingly, a war-weary nation — in the throes of a know-nothing hysteria over immigrant anarchists and socialists — welcomed the comparison between what was regarded as a seditious political pamphlet and a malicious shout of "Fire!" Ironically, the

"Fire!" analogy is nearly all that survives from the Schenck case; the ruling itself is almost certainly not good law. Pamphlets of the kind that resulted in Schenck's imprisonment have been circulated with impunity during subsequent wars.

Over the past several years I have assembled a collection of instance — cases, speeches, arguments — in which proponents of censorship have maintained that the expression at issue is "just like" or "equivalent to" falsely shouting "Fire!" in a crowded theater and ought to be banned, "just as" shouting "Fire!" ought to be banned. The analogy is generally invoked, often with self-satisfaction, as an absolute argument-stopper. It does, after all, claim the high authority of the great Justice Oliver Wendell Holmes. I have rarely heard it invoked in a convincing, or even particularly relevant, way. But that, too, can claim lineage from the great Holmes.

Not unlike Falwell, with his silly comparison between shouting "Fire!" and publishing an offensive parody, courts and commentators have frequently invoked "Fire!" as an analogy to expression that is not an automatic stimulus to panic. A state supreme court held that "Holmes' aphorism . . . applies with equal force to pornography" — in particular to the exhibition of the movie *Carmen Baby* in a drive-in theater in close proximity to highways and homes. Another court analogized "picketing . . . in support of a secondary boycott" to shouting "Fire!" because in both instances "speech and conduct are brigaded." In the famous Skokie case one of the judges argued that allowing Nazis to march through a city where a large number of Holocaust survivors live "just might fall into the same category as one's 'right' to cry fire in a crowded theater."

Outside court the analogies become even more badly stretched. A spokesperson for the New Jersey Sports and Exposition Authority complained that newspaper reports to the effect that a large number of football players had contracted cancer after playing in the Meadowlands — a stadium atop a landfill — were the "journalistic equivalent of shouting fire in a crowded theater." An insect researcher acknowledged that his prediction that a certain amusement park might become roach-infested "may be tantamount to shouting fire in a crowded theater." The philosopher Sidney Hook, in a letter to the *New York Times* bemoaning a Supreme Court decision that required a plaintiff in a defamation action to prove that the offending statement was actually false, argued that the First Amendment does not give the press carte blanche to accuse innocent persons "anymore than the First Amendment protects the right of someone falsely to shout fire in a crowded theater."

Some close analogies to shouting "Fire!" or setting off an alarm are, of course, available: calling in a false bomb threat; dialing 911 and falsely describing an emergency; making a loud, gunlike sound in the presence of the President; setting off a voice-activated sprinkler system by falsely shouting "Fire!" In one case in which the "Fire!" analogy was directly to the point, a creative defendant tried to get around it. The case involved a man who calmly advised an airline clerk that he was "only here to hijack the plane." He was charged, in effect, with shouting "Fire!" in a crowded theater, and his rejected defense — as quoted by the court — was as follows: "If we built fire-proof theaters and let people know about this, then the shouting of 'Fire!' would not cause panic."

Here are some more-distant but still related examples: the recent incident of the police slaying in which some members of an onlooking crowd urged a mentally ill vagrant who had taken an officer's gun to shoot the officer; the screaming of racial epithets during a tense confrontation; shouting down a speaker and preventing him from continuing his speech.

Analogies are, by their nature, matters of degree. Some are closer to the core example than others. But any attempt to analogize political ideas in a pamphlet, ugly parody in a magazine, offensive movies in a theater, controversial newspaper articles, or any of the other expressions and actions catalogued above to the very different act of shouting "Fire!" in a crowded theater is either self-deceptive or self-serving.

The government does, of course, have some arguably legitimate bases for suppressing speech which bear no relationship to shouting "Fire!" It may ban the publication of nuclear-weapon codes, of information about troop movements, and of the identity of undercover agents. It may criminalize extortion threats and conspiratorial agreements. These expressions may lead directly to serious harm, but the mechanisms of causation are very different from that at work when an alarm is sounded. One may also argue — less persuasively, in my view — against protecting certain forms of public obscenity and defamatory statements. Here, too, the mechanisms of causation are very different. None of these exceptions to the First Amendment's exhortation that the government "shall make no law . . . abridging the freedom of speech, or of the press" is anything like falsely shouting "Fire!" in a crowded theater; they all must be justified on other grounds.

A comedian once told his audience, during the stand-up routine, about the time he was standing around a fire with a crowd of people and got in trouble for yelling "Theater, theater!" That, I think, is about as clever and productive a use as anyone has ever made of Holmes's flawed analogy.

Reflections and Responses

1. Consider Dershowitz's analysis of Justice Holmes's decision in the Schenck case. What does Dershowitz find wrong with Holmes's reasoning? In what ways is Holmes's analogy "flawed"?

2. To what kinds of expression does Dershowitz find Holmes's analogy applicable? Go through Dershowitz's examples of protected and unprotected speech. Why is the "falsely shouting fire" analogy appropriate in some instances and not in others?

3. Consider Dershowitz's anecdote in the last paragraph about the comedian who yells "Theater, theater!" What was the comedian expressing? Why does Dershowitz find this response to Holmes's analogy "clever and productive"?

DEBRA DICKERSON

Who Shot Johnny?

On July 27, 1995, Debra Dickerson's sixteen-year-old nephew was shot in the back for no apparent reason and paralyzed. Although relatives kept trying to find out why ("Being black, male and shot, he must, apparently, be gang- or drug-involved"), his story held up and there was no way for anyone to make sense of the shooting. In this brief, tough, and unforgettable essay, Dickerson introduces us to her hospitalized nephew and angrily confronts his unknown assailant, whom she feels she knows all too well: "We rarely wonder about or discuss the brother who shot him because we already know everything about him."

Debra Dickerson is a contributing editor of US News & World Report. *Her articles have appeared in* The New Republic, Slate, Good House-keeping, *the* Washington Post Book World, Allure, The Christian Science Monitor Report, The Nation, Underwire, Boston Review, *and* Reconstruction. *She is a graduate of the Harvard Law School and is at work on a memoir about social and political conflict within the black community. "Who Shot Johnny?," which originally appeared in* The New Republic *(1996), was selected by Ian Frazier for* The Best American Essays 1997.

Given my level of political awareness, it was inevitable that I would come to view the everyday events of my life through the prism of politics and the national discourse. I read *The Washington Post, The New Republic, The New Yorker, Harper's, The Atlantic Monthly, The Nation, National Review, Black Enterprise,* and *Essence* and wrote a weekly column for the Harvard Law School *Record* during my three years just ended there. I do this because I know that those of us who are not well-fed white guys in suits must not yield the debate to them, however well-intentioned or well-informed they may be. Accordingly, I am unrepentant and vocal about having gained admittance to Harvard through affirmative action; I am a feminist, stoic about my marriage chances as a well-educated, thirty-six-year-old black woman who won't pretend to need help taking care of herself. My strength flags, though, in the face of the latest role assigned to my family in the national drama. On July 27, 1995, my sixteen-year-old nephew was shot and paralyzed.

Talking with friends in front of his house, Johnny saw a car he thought he recognized. He waved boisterously — his trademark — throwing both arms in the air in a full-bodied, hip-hop Y. When he got no response, he and his friends sauntered down the walk to join a group loitering in front of an apartment building. The car followed. The driver got out, brandished a revolver, and fired into the air. Everyone scattered. Then he took aim and shot my running nephew in the back.

Johnny never lost consciousness. He lay in the road, trying to understand what had happened to him, why he couldn't get up. Emotionlessly, he told the story again and again on demand, remaining apologetically firm against all demands to divulge the missing details that would make sense of the shooting but obviously cast him in a bad light. Being black, male, and shot, he must apparently be involved with gangs or drugs. Probably both. Witnesses corroborate his version of events.

Nearly six months have passed since that phone call in the night and my nightmarish headlong drive from Boston to Charlotte. After twenty hours behind the wheel, I arrived haggard enough to reduce my mother to fresh tears and to find my nephew reassuring well-wishers with an eerie sang-froid.

I take the day shift in his hospital room; his mother and grandmother, a clerk and cafeteria worker, respectively, alternate nights there on a cot. They don their uniforms the next day, gaunt after hours spent listening to Johnny moan in his sleep. How often must his subconscious replay those events and curse its host for saying hello without permission, for being carefree and young while a would-be murderer hefted the weight of his uselessness and failure like Jacob Marley's* chains? How often must he watch

*Jacob Marley: The doomed ghost in Charles Dickens's *A Christmas Carol.*

himself lying stubbornly immobile on the pavement of his nightmares while the sound of running feet syncopate his attacker's
taunts?

I spend these days beating him at gin rummy and Scrabble,
holding a basin while he coughs up phlegm and crying in the corridor while he catheterizes himself. There are children here much
worse off than he. I should be grateful. The doctors can't, or won't,
say whether he'll walk again.

I am at once repulsed and fascinated by the bullet, which remains lodged in his spine (having done all the damage it can do,
the doctors say). The wound is undramatic — small, neat, and perfectly centered — an impossibly pink pit surrounded by an otherwise undisturbed expanse of mahogany. Johnny has asked me
several times to describe it but politely declines to look in the mirror I hold for him.

Here on the pediatric rehab ward, Johnny speaks little, never
cries, never complains, works diligently to become independent.
He does whatever he is told; if two hours remain until the next pain
pill, he waits quietly. Eyes bloodshot, hands gripping the bed rails.
During the week of his intravenous feeding, when he was tormented
by the primal need to masticate, he never asked for food. He just
listened while we counted down the days for him and planned his
favorite meals. Now required to dress himself unassisted, he does
so without demur, rolling himself back and forth valiantly on the
bed and shivering afterward, exhausted. He "ma'am"s and "sir"s
everyone politely. Before his "accident," a simple request to take
out the trash could provoke a firestorm of teenage attitude. We,
the women who have raised him, have changed as well; we've finally come to appreciate those boxer-baring, oversized pants we
used to hate — it would be much more difficult to fit properly
sized pants over his diaper.

He spends a lot of time tethered to rap music still loud enough
to break my concentration as I read my many magazines. I hear
him try to soundlessly mouth the obligatory "mothafuckers" over-
laying the funereal dirge of the music tracks. I do not normally tolerate disrespectful music in my or my mother's presence, but if it
distracts him now . . .

"Johnny," I ask later, "do you still like gangster rap?" During the
long pause I hear him think loudly, I'm paralyzed Auntie, not

stupid. "I mostly just listen to hip-hop," he says evasively into his *Sports Illustrated.*

Miserable though it is, time passes quickly here. We always seem to be jerking awake in our chairs just in time for the next pill, his every-other-night bowel program, the doctor's rounds. Harvard feels a galaxy away — the world revolves around Family Members Living with Spinal Cord Injury class, Johnny's urine output, and strategizing with my sister to find affordable, accessible housing. There is always another long-distance uncle in need of an update, another church member wanting to pray with us, or Johnny's little brother in need of some attention.

We Dickerson women are so constant a presence the ward nurses and cleaning staff call us by name and join us for cafeteria meals and cigarette breaks. At Johnny's birthday pizza party, they crack jokes and make fun of each other's husbands (there are no men here). I pass slices around and try not to think, Seventeen with a bullet.

Oddly, we feel little curiosity or specific anger toward the man who shot him. We have to remind ourselves to check in with the police. Even so, it feels pro forma, like sending in those $2 rebate forms that come with new pantyhose: you know your request will fall into a deep, dark hole somewhere, but still, it's your duty to try. We push for an arrest because we owe it to Johnny and to ourselves as citizens. We don't think about it otherwise — our low expectations are too ingrained. A Harvard aunt notwithstanding, for people like Johnny, Marvin Gaye was right that only three things are sure: taxes, death, and trouble. At least it wasn't the second.

We rarely wonder about or discuss the brother who shot him because we already know everything about him. When the call came, my first thought was the same one I'd had when I'd heard about Rosa Parks's beating: a brother did it. A non-job-having, middle-of-the-day malt-liquor-drinking, crotch-clutching, loud-talking brother with many neglected children born of many forgotten women. He lives in his mother's basement with furniture rented at an astronomical interest rate, the exact amount of which he does not know. He has a car phone, an $80 monthly cable bill, and every possible phone feature but no savings. He steals Social Security numbers from unsuspecting relatives and assumes their identities to acquire large TV sets for which he will never pay. On the slim chance that he is brought to justice, he will have a colorful criminal history and no coherent explanation to offer for his act. His family will raucously defend him and cry cover-up. Some liberal lawyer just like me will help him plea-bargain his way to yet another short stay in a prison pesthouse that will serve only to add another layer to the brother's sociopathology and formless, mindless nihilism. We know him. We've known and feared him all our lives.

As a teenager, he called, "Hey, baby, gimme somma that boodie!" at us from car windows. Indignant at our lack of response, he followed up with, "Fuck you, then, 'ho!" He called me a "white-boy-lovin' nigger bitch oreo" for being in the gifted program and loving it. At twenty-seven, he got my seventeen-year-old sister pregnant with Johnny and lost interest without ever informing her that he was married. He snatched my widowed mother's purse as she waited in predawn darkness for the bus to work and then broke into our house while she soldered on an assembly line. He chased all the small entrepreneurs from our neighborhood with his violent thievery and put bars on our windows. He kept us from sitting on our own front porch after dark and laid the foundation for our periodic bouts of self-hating anger and racial embarrassment. He made our neighborhood a ghetto. He is the poster fool behind the maddening community knowledge that there are still some black mothers who raise their daughters but merely love their sons. He and his cancerous carbon copies eclipse the vast majority of us who are not sociopaths and render us invisible. He is the Siamese twin who has died but cannot be separated from his living, vibrant sibling; which of us must attract more notice? We despise and disown this anomalous loser, but for many he *is* black America. We know him, we know that he is outside the fold, and we know that he will only get worse. What we didn't know is that, because of him, my little sister would one day be the latest hysterical black mother wailing over a fallen child on TV.

Alone, lying in the road bleeding and paralyzed but hideously conscious, Johnny had lain helpless as he watched his would-be murderer come to stand over him and offer this prophecy: "Betch'ou won't be doin' nomo' wavin', mothafucker."

Fuck you, asshole. He's fine from the waist up. You just can't do anything right, can you?

Reflections and Responses

1. Why do you think the author begins her essay by telling us about herself? What does her introductory paragraph establish? Does it predispose you in any way to the events she narrates?

2. Consider the essay's final line. What criticism is Dickerson making of Johnny's assailant? How effective do you find it?

3. How would you answer the question posed by the essay's title? Do we really know who shot Johnny? Whom do you hold responsible?

GERALD EARLY

Understanding Afrocentricism: Why Blacks Dream of a World Without Whites

Writing essays can be very risky business. When Gerald Early recently wrote an essay critical of Malcolm X for Harper's Magazine, *he received three death threats. In the following essay he takes on a similarly controversial subject: the rise of Afrocentrism. Although he is not in sympathy with the political goals or the scholarly methods of the Afrocentric movement — in either its academic or popular manifestations — he nevertheless tries to understand its appeal, especially among young, middle-class African Americans. "Afrocentrism," Early concludes, "may be wrong in many respects, and it certainly can be stifling and restrictive, but some of its impulses are right." Early's essay is complex and contains many historical and literary references, but these are often explained in context.*

Gerald Early is the Merle S. Kling Professor of Modern Letters and director of Afro-American Studies at Washington University in St. Louis. He is the author of Tuxedo Junction: Essays on American Culture *and the editor of numerous books, including* Lure and Loathing: Essays on Race, Identity, and the Ambivalence of Assimilation. *He won the 1994 National Book Critics Circle Award in Criticism for* The Culture of Bruising: Essays on Prizefighting, Literature, and Modern American Culture. *Other books include* Daughters: On Family and Fatherhood *(1994) and* One Nation Under a Groove: Motown and American Culture *(1995). His personal and critical essays have appeared in numerous magazines and literary journals, including* The Kenyon Review, Hungry Mind Review, *and* Civilization, *where*

"Understanding Afrocentrism" originally appeared in 1995. Civilization is sponsored by the Library of Congress, which is why much of Early's essay centers around key books in the field of Afrocentrism. The essay won several awards and was selected by Geoffrey C. Ward for The Best American Essays 1996.

> The White man will never admit his real references. He will steal everything you have and still call you those names.
>
> — Ishmael Reed, *Mumbo Jumbo* (1972)

> Furthermore, no one can be thoroughly educated until he learns as much about the Negro as he knows about other people.
>
> — Carter G. Woodson, *The Mis-Education of the Negro* (1933)

> [Alexander] Crummell's black nationalism was marked by certain inconsistencies, but they derived from the inconsistencies and hypocrisy of American racism, rather than from any intellectual shortcomings on his part. It was impossible to create an ideology that responded rationally to an irrational system.
>
> — Wilson Jeremiah Moses, *Alexander Crummell: A Study of Civilization and Discontent* (1989)

In a span of three weeks during the early spring semester of 1995, Angela Davis and bell hooks, two notable black leftist, feminist thinkers, visited the camp of Washington University in St. Louis, invited by different student groups. They were generally well received, indeed, enthusiastically so. But there was, for each of them during these visits, something of a jarring note, both involving black students.

Professor Davis, entertaining questions during a panel session after having spoken earlier on the subject of prison reform, was asked by a black woman student what she had to offer black people as a solution to their problems. The student went on to explain that she did not consider herself an African American. She was simply an African, wishing to have nothing to do with being an American or with America itself. She wanted black people to separate themselves entirely from "Europeans," as she called white Americans, and wanted to know what Davis could suggest to further that aim.

Davis answered that she was not inclined to such stringent race separation. She was proud of being of African descent but wished to be around a variety of people, not just people like herself. Davis felt further that blacks should not isolate themselves but accept in partnership anyone who was sincerely interested in the cause of overthrowing capitalism, a standard and reasonable Marxist response to the "essentializing" of race in a way that would divert true political engagement "against the system." The student was visibly annoyed with the answer, which presumably smacked of "white" intellectualism.

Professor bell hooks, after her address on ending racism and sexism in America — love, I think, was the answer — was asked by a black woman student how feminism was relevant to black women. Hooks explained that feminism was not only for white women, that black women needed to read more feminist texts, even if some of them were racist. After all, Karl Marx was racist, but he did give the world a brilliant analysis of capitalism. She had said in her speech how disappointed she was that her black women students at City College of New York were not inclined to embrace feminism, rejecting it as something white. She felt that these black women were unduly influenced by black male rappers who bashed feminism. The answer did not persuade or please the student.

Later that day, I heard many black undergraduates dismiss hooks's talk as not addressing the needs of black people, as being too geared to the white feminists in the audience. Some were disturbed that hooks would feel that they formed their opinions on the basis of listening to rap records. None of this was said, necessarily, with hostility, but rather with regret and a shade of condescension that only the young can so keenly and innocently express when speaking about the foolishness of their elders.

I recall a fairly recent incident where a black student, a very bright young woman, asked if, when doing research, one had to acknowledge racist books. I told her that a certain amount of objectivity was part of the discipline of being a scholar. Anger at unjust or inaccurate statements and assessments was understandable, but personalizing everything often caused a kind of tunnel vision where crude self-affirmation seemed to be the only fit end of scholarship. She responded that she would refuse to acknowledge racist sources, that if the book was racist, then everything it said was tainted and should be disregarded.

The attitudes of these students have been shaped by Afrocentrism, an insistence by a growing number of black Americans on seeing the world from an "African-centered" perspective in response to the dominant "European-centered" perspective, to which they feel they have been subjected throughout their lives. Afrocentrism is many things and has many degrees of advocacy. It can range from the commercialism and pretense of the shallow holiday called Kwanza (no shallower, it should be said, than the commercialized celebration of Christmas) to the kente-cloth ads and nationalist talk that one finds in most black publications these days; from talk about racist European scholarship to a view that world culture is essentially African in origin and that Europeans are usurpers, thieves, and generally inferior. On the one hand, we have the recent cover story "Is Jesus Black?" in *Emerge,* an Afrocentric-tinged news magazine for the black middle class. The answer in this instance, of course, is clearly yes. (Obviously, this is grounds for competing claims between blacks and Jews; whatever can be said about Jesus' skin color or the religious movement that bears his name, there is no question that he was a Jew.) On the other hand, we have the first explicitly Afrocentric Hollywood western in Mario Van Peebles's 1993 film *Posse,* a jumbled multi-cultural critique of white fin-de-siècle imperialism and the myth of how the West was won.

No doubt, Afrocentrists specifically and black folk generally found it to be a signal victory that in the recent television dramatization of the love affair between Solomon and Sheba, Sheba was played by a black actress and Solomon by a swarthy Hispanic. In the 1959 Hollywood film version of *Solomon and Sheba,* directed by King Vidor — who, incidentally, made the first all-black Hollywood film —Solomon was played by Yul Brynner and Sheba by Gina Lollobrigida. It is safe to say that the real Solomon and the real Sheba, if they ever existed, did not look remotely like any of the actors who ever played them. But whom we want them to look like is very important. The Afrocentrists will feel their triumph to be complete when black actors portray Beethoven, Joseph Haydn, Warren G. Harding, Alexander Hamilton, Hannibal, Abraham Lincoln, Dwight Eisenhower, Cleopatra, Moses, Jesus Christ, and Saint Augustine. Many African Americans are inclined to believe that any noted white with ambiguous ancestry must be black. They are also inclined to believe that any white with dark skin tones, one who hangs around blacks or who "acts black" in some way is truly black. At various times in my life, I have heard blacks argue vehemently that Madonna, Phoebe Snow, Keith Jarrett, Mae West, Ava Gardner, and Dorothy Parker were black, even though they did not have a shred of evidence to support the claims. Blacks have always been fascinated by "passing," by the possibility that some whites are really black — "fooling old massa," so to speak.

Afrocentrism is an intellectual movement, a political view, a historically traceable evolution, a religious orthodoxy. It derives in part from Negritude and Pan-Africanism,* which stressed the culture and achievements of Africans. Both movements were started by Africans, West Indians, and African Americans in response to European colonialism and the worldwide oppression of African-descended people. But Afrocentrism is also a direct offshoot of earlier forms of black nationalism, in which blacks around the world believed they had a special destiny to fulfill and a special consciousness to redeem. More important, Afrocentrism is a mood that has largely erupted in the past ten to fifteen years in response to integration, or, perhaps more precisely, to the failure of integration. Many blacks who have succeeded in the white world tend to feel most Afrocentric, although I think it would be a mistake to see Afrocentrism purely as middle class, since significant numbers of working-class blacks are attracted to some elements of it. The bourgeois, "midcult" element of Afrocentrism, nonetheless, is very strong. "Integrated" middle-class blacks see it as a demonstration of their race loyalty and solidarity with their brothers and sisters throughout the world, whether in American cities or on African farms. (It is worth noting the economic clout of the black middle class, which can be seen in the growing number of black Hollywood films and filmmakers, in new black magazines ranging from *Body and Soul* to *The Source* to *Upscale,* and in the larger audience for black books. It is the market power of this class that has given Afrocentrism its force as a consumer ideology.)

So the middle-class black, having had more contact with whites

---

*Negritude and Pan-Africanism:** A protest against French assimilationist policies, the Negritude movement of the 1930s and 1940s was an early assertion of African cultural value. Pan-Africanism refers to the organization of African unity that dates back to the beginning of the twentieth century; the movement became politically influential in the 1950s with the formation of new African states demanding independence.

and their institutions, is expected to speak for and to other blacks. Afrocentrism, like Negritude and Pan-Africanism, is meant to be an ideological glue to bring black people together, not just on the basis of color but as the expression of a cultural and spiritual will that crosses class and geographical lines. As W.E.B. Du Bois wrote in 1940: "Since the fifteenth century these ancestors of mine and their other descendants have had a common history; have suffered a common disaster and have one long memory. . . . The real essence of this kinship is its social heritage of slavery; the discrimination and insults; and this heritage binds together not simply the children of Africa, but extends through yellow Asia and into the South Seas. It is this unity that draws me to Africa."

Louis H. Farrakhan, the head of the Nation of Islam, is probably the most familiar figure associated with Afrocentrism. (Muhammad Ali introduced Islamic conversion to an even bigger public, suffering greatly for his religious and political beliefs and becoming the most noted and charismatic dissident of his era. Ali's prodigious athletic abilities and his genial temperament succeeded in endearing him to the American public despite his religion. He never became a member of Farrakhan's sect.) Farrakhan is a fiery preacher, prone to making extreme statements, with a militant flair and a racist edge, that have the conviction of truth among some blacks. He especially exploits the idea that he is a heroic black man at grave risk for daring to tell the truth about the white man. (Malcolm X used this device effectively, too.) He is also a master demagogue who exploits the paranoia of his audience. But then, as a friend once said to me, "What black person isn't justified in being at least half paranoid?"

Farrakhan has found three effective lines of entry among blacks, particularly young blacks, that draw on the Afrocentric impulse: First, that Islam is the true religion of black people. (This has led to a move among black Christian leaders to point out with great vehemence the African origins of Christianity, to make it, in effect, a black religion.) Second, that black people need business enterprise in their community in order to liberate themselves (an old belief among blacks, going back to at least the early part of the nineteenth century). And third, that Jews of European descent (whom he calls "false Jews") are not to be trusted, a charge that exploits the current tension between blacks and Jews — and that

Farrakhan has used to move into the black civil rights establishment. All three positions enjoy remarkable support within the
black middle class, a situation that has helped Farrakhan tap
people's insecurities for his own purposes. The Nation of Islam
may be famous for converting addicts and criminals, but above all,
it wants, as all religions do, to win over the middle class, with its
money, its respectability, and its organizational know-how.

Whatever might be said of Farrakhan's importance as a political
figure in the black community or in the United States, he is a
minor figure in the development of Afrocentrism. His position in
the history of Afrocentrism is similar to that of, say, Rush Limbaugh in the development of American conservatism. He is, like
Limbaugh, a figure the media can use to give a sellable face and
voice to a unique temper among a group of people. For both Limbaugh and Farrakhan represent an intense sentimentality in American life, a yearning for a fantasized, idealized past of racial
grandeur and simplicity. This sentimentality appeals powerfully to
the black middle class, which yearns for a usable, untainted past.
This partly explains why Farrakhan and the Muslims can often be
found speaking to black college students.

In thinking about the connection between class and nationalistic feelings, it should be recalled that in Harriet Beecher Stowe's
1852 novel *Uncle Tom's Cabin*, the most light-complexioned blacks,
the ones with the greatest skills, George, Eliza, and Cassy, return to
Africa at the novel's end to retrieve their degraded patrimony. It
might be said that this is purely Stowe's own perverse vision, since
some of the fiercest advocates for returning to Africa have been
Martin Delany, Alexander Crummell, and Marcus Garvey, all very
dark men. Yet there is more than a little truth to the idea that
class, caste, and race consciousness are closely interwoven. Nationalism of whatever sort has almost always been an affair of a disaf-
fected middle class. And until the 1920s, the black middle class in
America was disproportionately made up of light-skinned people.

The paradox of the bourgeois aspect of Afrocentrism is that it
rejects cosmopolitanism* as being "white" or "Eurocentric." Yet
Afrocentrism has no other way of seeing cosmopolitanism except

---

*Cosmopolitanism: a political perspective that tries to be free of local or national
biases; it literally refers to a citizen of the world.

on the "Eurocentric" model, so it tries to make Africa for black Americans the equivalent of what Europe is for white Americans: the source of civilization. Indeed, by trying to argue that Africa is the source of Western civilization, the Afrocentric sees the African, symbolically, as the mother of white Europe (just as the black mother, the mammy, is the mythic progenitor of the white South, or so Langston Hughes seemed to believe, in his famous short story "Father and Son," which became his even more famous play *Mulatto*). The African becomes, in this view, the most deeply cultured person on the planet, which matches his status as the oldest person on the planet, with the longest and deepest genetic history. In short, Afrocentrism becomes another form of the American apologizing for being American to people he imagines are his cultural superiors. Afrocentrism tries to mask a quest for American filiopiety* behind a façade of African ancestor and culture worship.

It would be easy, on one level, to dismiss Afrocentrism as an expression, in white workplaces and white colleges, of intimidated black folk who are desperately trying to find a space for themselves in what they feel to be alien, unsympathetic environments. Seen this way, Afrocentrism becomes an expression of the low self-esteem and inferiority that blacks feel most intensely when they are around whites; their response is to become more "black," estranged from the environment that they find so unaccepting of them. The greatest psychic burden of the African American is that he must not only think constantly about being different but about what his difference means. And it might be suggested that Afrocentrism does not solve this problem but merely reflects it in a different mirror. There is a certain amount of truth to this, especially at a time when affirmative action, which promotes group identification and group difference, tends to intensify black self-consciousness. And black people, through no fault of their own, are afflicted with a debilitating sense of self-consciousness when around whites. When whites are in the rare situation of being a minority in a sea of blacks, they often exhibit an abject self-consciousness as well, but the source of that self-consciousness is quite different. The

*__Filiopiety:__ A reverence, usually excessive, for ancestors and tradition.

white is used to traveling anywhere in the world and having his cultural inclinations accommodated. The black is neither used to this nor does he realistically expect it. The European exults in his culture, while the African is utterly degraded by his. That blacks should want to free themselves from the white gaze seems not merely normal but essential to the project of reconstructing themselves as a people on their own terms. And the history of blacks in the United States has been an ongoing project — tragic, pathetic, noble, heroic, misguided, sublime — of self-reconstruction.

> When it comes to black folk in America, the white man wants to say that if you have a ⅟₃₂ portion of black blood, a mere drop of black blood, then you are black, no matter what your skin color. But when it comes to the ancient Egyptians, it doesn't matter if they have a drop of black blood — and we know that they had at least ⅟₃₂ portion of African blood. It doesn't matter how much African blood they have, they are still white. The white man wants to have his cake and eat it too. When it's convenient he wants you to be black, and when it's convenient he wants you to be white. Either you're a nigger, because he thinks you're nothing. Or you're white, if you have done anything he's bound to respect. The white man wants to control all the definitions of blackness.
>
> — A conversation with an Afrocentric friend

Afrocentrism, like a good many nationalistic ideologies, might be called the orthodoxy of the book, or, more precisely, the orthodoxy of the books. Afrocentrism is an attempt to wed knowledge and ideology. Movements like Afrocentrism, which feels both its mission and its authority hinge on the revelation of a denied and buried truth, promote a fervent scholasticism, a hermeneutical ardor among true believers for compilations of historical minutiae on the one hand, and for grand philosophical tracts on the other. The former might be best represented by George G. M. James's *Stolen Legacy*, published in 1954, the latter by Mustafa El-Amin's *Al-Islam, Christianity, and Freemasonry* and *Freemasonry, Ancient Egypt, and the Islamic Destiny*. These books were not written by professional historians or by college professors. The fact that several classic Afrocentric texts have been written by amateurs gives Afrocentrism its powerful populist appeal, its legitimacy as an expression of "truth" that white institutional forces hide or obscure. At the same time, this leaves it vulnerable to charges of being homemade, unprofessional, theoretically immature, and the like. It is

one of the striking aspects of Afrocentrism that within the last
twenty years it has developed a cadre of academics to speak for it,
to professionalize it, to make it a considerable insurgency movement on the college campus.

There are several texts that might be considered the literary and
intellectual cornerstones of the Afrocentrism movement. Molefi K
Asante, professor and chair of African American studies at Temple
University in Philadelphia, is credited with inventing the name
"Afrocentrism" or "Afrocentricity" (although currently the term
"Africentrism" is on the rise in certain quarters, probably because
there is a group of black folk who, for some reason, despise the
prefix "Afro," as if the word "Africa" itself were created by the people of the continent rather than by Europeans). Asante's very short
books, including *The Afrocentric Idea,* published in 1987, and *Afrocentricity: The Theory of Social Change,* published in 1980, are frequently the starting points for people seeking a basic explanation
of this ideology. As defined by Asante, Afrocentrism seems to take
the terms and values of Eurocentrism — intense individualism,
crass greed, lack of spirituality, warlike inclinations, dominance
and racism, dishonesty and hypocrisy — and color their opposites
black, giving us a view of black people not terribly different from
the romantic racism of Harriet Beecher Stowe and other whites
like her in the nineteenth and twentieth centuries. I cannot re-
count the number of "race sensitivity" meetings I have attended
where blacks begin to describe themselves (or those they perceive
to be Africans) as more spiritual, more family-oriented, more
community-oriented, more rhythmic, more natural, and less com-
bative than whites. All of which is, of course, a crock of nonsense,
largely the expression of wishes for qualities that blacks see as absent from their community life now. But, thanks to Asante, this has
become the profile of the African in the Afrocentric vision.

Martin Bernal's massively researched two-volume *Black Athena*
(published in 1987 and 1991) is a popular title in Afrocentric circles, in large measure because Bernal, a professor at Cornell, is
one of the few white scholars to take Afrocentrism seriously —
William Piersen, Robert Farris Thompson, and Andrew Hacker, in
decidedly different ways, are others — and one of the few to write
an academic treatise in its defense that forces whites to take it seriously too. (The irony that blacks still need whites, in some measure,

to sell their ideas and themselves to other whites is not entirely lost on those who have thought about this.)

Black Athena supports three major contentions of the Afrocentrists: 1) ancient Egypt was a black civilization; 2) the Greeks derived a good deal, if not all, of their philosophy and religion from the Egyptians; 3) European historiography has tried strenuously and with clear political objectives to deny both. Bernal's book provoked a scathing attack by Mary R. Lefkowitz, a professor at Wellesley, who characterizes Afrocentrism as a perversion of the historiography of antiquity and a degradation of academic standards for political ends. Lefkowitz has also battled with Tony Martin, a cultural historian, barrister, and Marcus Garvey specialist, who began using and endorsing the Nation of Islam's anti-Semitic *The Secret Relationship Between Blacks and Jews* (Volume 1) in his classes on slavery at Wellesley. Martin responded in 1993 with his own account of the dispute, *The Jewish Onslaught: Despatches from the Wellesley Battlefront,* which elaborates his claims of Jewish racism and the hypocrisy of academic freedom.

Maulana Karenga, professor and chair of black studies at California State University at Long Beach, created the black philosophical code called the Kawaida, which was the inspiration for Kwanza and the seven principles (Nguzo Saba) that the holiday celebrates. The code contains a bit of Marxism to create a "theoretical" ambiance. Karenga is also author of the popular *Introduction to Black Studies,* used by many colleges in their introductory courses, despite its rather tendentious manner, which he tries to pass off as sharp-minded Marxism, and the fact that the book is weak on a good many aspects of African American life and culture.

Perhaps the most popular Afrocentric text is Chancellor Williams's *The Destruction of Black Civilization: Great Issues of a Race from 4500 B.C. to 2000 A.D.* (published in 1987), an account of his exhaustive research trips to Africa. Although not directly trained in the study of African history, Williams studied under William Leo Hansberry, a history professor at Howard University and probably the leading black American authority on Africa during the 1930s, 1940s, and 1950s. Hansberry did path-breaking work in an utterly neglected field, eventually becoming known as "the father of African studies" in the United States. (Scholars, until recently, did not think Africa had a "history." The continent, especially its sub-Saharan regions, had an "anthropology" and an "archaeology," folkways to be discovered and remains to be unearthed, but never a record of institutions, traditions, political ideologies, and complex societies.) Williams also did research on African history at Oxford and at the University of London, where, because of colonialism, interest in the nature of African societies was far keener than in the United States. His book *The Re-Birth of African Civilization*, an account of his 1953–1957 research project investigating the nature of education in Europe and Africa, calls for Pan-African education of blacks in Africa and around the world. Williams concluded that "European" and "Eurocentric" education was antithetical, both politically and intellectually, to African interests, a common refrain in Afrocentrist thought.

Most Afrocentric scholars at universities today genuflect at the intellectual altar of Cheikh Anta Diop, a Senegalese humanist and scientist who began his research into African history in 1946, as the battle against European colonialism in Africa was beginning. Diop saw his mission as undermining European colonialism by destroying the Europeans' claim to a superior history. He was tenacious in demonstrating that Africa had a "real" history that showed that Africans were the product of civilizations and not of the jungle. This claim to history was a sign to the African that he was an equal player in the family of man, and was essential to any demand for independence.

For Diop, it was not enough to reconstruct African history; it was also necessary to depict a unified Africa, an idea that, whether myth or fact, was considered ideologically crucial by the Pan-African movement to overthrow European imperialism. Like every other oppressed people, the African could face the future only if he could hark back to some version of his past, preferably a past touched with greatness. This could be done only by running African history and civilization through Egypt, the only African civilization that impressed European intellectuals. As jazz and cultural critic Stanley Crouch suggested, Egypt is the only African civilization that has monuments, a physical legacy that indicates history as understood in European terms. Thus, for black people in Africa to be unified, for black people around the world to feel unified, ancient Egypt had to be a "black" civilization and serve as the origin of all blackness and, even more important, all whiteness. We know from scientific evidence that Africa is the place of origin for human life. If it is also true that Egypt is the oldest civilization from which Europeans borrowed freely (Bernal makes a persuasive argument for the influence of Egypt on European intellectuals through the nineteenth century), then Africans helped shape Western culture and were major actors in history, not bit players in the unfolding drama of European dominance.

Diop's doctoral dissertation, based on the idea that Egypt was African and that European civilization was largely built on Egyptian ideas, was rejected at the University of Paris in 1951. The story goes that he was able to defend his dissertation successfully only in 1960 when he was accompanied into the examination room by an army of historians, sociologists, and anthropologists who supported his views, or at least his right as a responsible scholar to express them. By then, with African independence in full swing, his ideas had a political currency in Africa as an expression of Pan-Africanism. And no one supported the idea of a unified Africa more than Egypt's then president, Gamal Abdel Nasser, probably the most powerful independent leader on the continent. Like Gandhi, Nasser called himself a black man, and he envisioned an Africa united in opposition to Israel and South Africa. It was a good moment for Diop to be saying what he was saying. At the 1956 Conference of Negro-African Writers and Artists in Paris, Diop was one of the most popular speakers, although black American James Baldwin was not much impressed with his thesis. (Admittedly, for Baldwin this was pretty new stuff.) For his part, Diop, a Marxist, thought the American delegation was blindly anti-Communist and naively committed to the integrationist policies of the civil rights movement.

Diop produced a number of volumes translated into English, some based on his dissertation. They include *The African Origin of Civilization: Myth or Reality; Civilization or Barbarism: An Authentic Anthropology;* and *The Cultural Unity of Negro Africa.* For Diop, everything turned on establishing that ancient Egypt was a black civilization: "The history of Black Africa will remain suspended in air and cannot be written correctly until African historians dare to connect it with the history of Egypt." Moreover, Diop felt that the African could not remove the chains of colonialism from his psyche until he had a fully reconstructed history — in other words, until he had a usable past. Diop was brilliant and clearly obsessed. His importance in the formation of African American intellectual history does not depend on whether his historical theories are correct. (Although there is considerable debate about ancient Egypt — not surprising, since there is no documentation of the claim in the language of the people who lived there at the time — it is now conceded by virtually everyone that the Egyptians were a mixed-race people.) Diop's work transcends questions of historical accuracy and enters the realm of "belief." Much of what Diop wrote may be true (he had vast amounts of evidence to support his claims), but, as a Marxist, he was not motivated simply by the quest for positivistic, objective "truth." He wanted to use the supposed objectivity of scientific research for political ends.

Diop brought together three important elements in understanding the origins of Afrocentrism: first, the tradition of professional, politically motivated historical research that buttresses the claims of untrained, amateur historians; second, the explicit connection between knowledge of one's "proper" history and one's psychological and spiritual well-being; third, the connection between "proper" knowledge of one's history and the realization of a political mission and purpose. If European history functioned as an ideological and political justification for Europe's place in the world and its hope for its future, why shouldn't African history function in the same manner? This is the reasoning of the Pan-Africanists and Afrocentrists who see "proper" history as the version that is most ideologically and politically useful to their group. Diop's research supports the idea of a conspiracy among white historians to discredit or ignore black civilization. Without a "proper" knowledge of African history, Diop argues, blacks will remain politically impotent and psychologically crippled. These ideas have become the uncritical dogma of Afrocentrism. By the time Diop died in 1986, he had been virtually canonized by an important set of black American scholars who identified themselves as Afrocentric.

Diop is useful for Afrocentrism today not only because of his monumental research but because he was an African, thus linking Afrocentrism to Africa itself and permitting the black American to kneel before the perfect intellect of the "purer" African. But Diop's ideas about ancient black civilization in Egypt and the importance of fuller knowledge of its history had been advanced earlier by several African American intellectuals, including W.E.B. Du Bois in his momentous book *Black Folk, Then and Now: An Essay in the History and Sociology of the Negro Race*, which appeared in 1939. Du Bois said he was inspired to write about the glories of the Negro past after hearing a lecture in 1906 at Atlanta University by the preeminent white anthropologist Franz Boas, debunker of racism and mentor of Zora Neale Hurston. Du Bois's work remains, despite the more richly researched efforts of Diop, Bernal, and St. Clair Drake in *Black Folk Here and There* (published in two volumes in 1987 and 1990), the best and most readable examination of the subject. Indeed, his work must be seen in a larger historical context, dating back to the founding of the American Negro Academy in 1897, when he and other black intellectuals tried to organize themselves for the purpose of producing scholarship that defended the race and promoted race consciousness. Yet Du Bois's book is not the central work of the Afrocentric movement by a black American writer.

That book would be Carter G. Woodson's *The Mis-Education of the Negro*, originally published in 1933. Woodson, a Harvard Ph.D. in history who launched both the Association for the Study of Negro Life and History (1915) and Negro History Week (1926), was as obsessed with the reconstruction of the Negro past as Diop or Du Bois. He churned out dozens of books on virtually every aspect of African and African American history. Some were wooden, opaque, or just plain sloppy, and several are unreadable (even in the opinion of his assistant, the late, brilliant black historian Lorenzo Greene), indicating the haste with which they were composed. Even so, Woodson was a serious and demanding scholar. Greene thought of him, at times, as having the pious devotion of a Franciscan friar and the crotchety temper of an eccentric intellectual consumed by his work.

The Mis-Education of the Negro, although written by a man who endorsed Booker T. Washington and the Tuskegee method, was generally critical of black education. Black people, Woodson argued, were not being educated in a way that would encourage them to press their own political and economic interests or make them a viable social group in the United States. They were, in fact, being educated against their own interests, largely because their education was controlled by whites who saw advantage in giving blacks an inferior education. Moreover, Woodson made the explicit connection between "improper" education, including a lack of knowledge about the black past, and the psychological degradation of the Negro, his internalized sense of inferiority. In short, a white-controlled education led to Uncle Tomism and black sellouts, to a defective Negro who suffered from false consciousness, or, more precisely, "white" consciousness. Some of this argument was restated in black sociologist E. Franklin Frazier's seminal 1957 work, *Black Bourgeoisie.* The black middle class was almost exclusively the target of this indictment — a fact that prompted that class to romanticize certain aspects of black lower-class life, particularly its antisocial and criminal elements, in an effort to demonstrate its solidarity with "authentic" black experience. This was true with the Black Panthers in the late 1960s and it continues with rap music today. Another consequence is that the black middle class insists on a degree of race loyalty that sometimes thwarts any critical inquiry that does not promote race unity.

Much of Woodson's argument resonates with blacks today because it seems to endorse the idea of Afrocentric schools and especially the idea that knowledge of a glorious African past would give black youngsters self-esteem, reduce violence and criminality in black neighborhoods, and lead to the spiritual and political uplift of black people. This is why history is actually a less important discipline to the rise of Afrocentrism than psychology. After all, the reconstruction of black history was always connected with the reconstruction of the black mind, a mind that existed before the coming of the white man — or at least a mind that could be free of the white man and his image of what black people were.

In some ways, the rise of Afrocentrism is related to the rise of "black psychology" as a discipline. The Association of Black Psychologists was organized in 1968, a time when a number of black professional offshoots were formed in political and ideological protest against the mainstream, white-dominated versions of their organizations. Somewhat later came the *Journal of Black Psychology,* given impetus by the initial assaults against black intelligence or pointed suggestions of black genetic inferiority by Richard Herrnstein, Arthur Jensen, and others in the early 1970s; this was also the time of the first wave of court challenges against affirmative action. The black psychology movement argued for new modes of treatment for black mental illness, the medical efficacy of using black history to repair a collectively damaged black psyche, and the destruction of "Eurocentrism" and the values it spawned — from the idealization of white standards of beauty to the scientific measurement of intelligence — as totally inimical to the political and psychological interests of black people. Rationality, order, individualism, dominance, sexual repression as well as sexual license, aggression, warmaking, moneymaking, capitalism itself — all soon became "white values."

That all of this happened during the era of Vietnam War protests, when white Western civilization was coming under withering intellectual attack from the radical left, is not without significance. Radical white intellectuals, who otherwise had no more use for a black epic history than a white one, found the black version useful as a weapon against "Eurocentrism," which, as a result of the Vietnam War, they held in utter contempt. In short, Jean-Paul Sartre and Susan Sontag* were as instrumental, albeit indirectly, in the formation of Afrocentrism as, say, the Black Power movement of the late 1960s or the writings of African psychiatrist Frantz Fanon, whose *The Wretched of the Earth* became the revolutionary psychological profile of the oppressed black diaspora. Also occurring at this time was the movement on white college campuses to establish black studies programs, which provided a black intellectual wedge into the white academy. These programs, largely multidisciplinary, required an ideological purpose and mission to bind together the various disciplines, which is why many began to articulate some kind of Afrocentrism or, as it was called in the 1970s, "black aesthetic" — in other words, an ideological framework to give black studies a reason for being. When used to challenge the dominance of Western thought, Afrocentrism becomes part of a multicultural wave of complaint and resentment against the white man by a number of groups that feel they have been oppressed.

In an age of dysfunction and psychotherapy, no one can have greater claim to having been made dysfunctional by political oppression than the African American, who was literally a slave; and

---

*For more information on Susan Sontag, see p. 388.

no one can have a greater need for recourse to psychotherapy in the form of Afrocentrism. But what made the black psychology movement possible was the rise of the Nation of Islam, particularly the rise of Malcolm X.

The charismatic Muslim minister did two things. First, he forced the white mainstream press to take notice of black nationalism, Pan-Africanism, and the concept of African unity. Previously these ideas had been marginalized as ridiculous or even comic expressions of black nationalism, to be read by blacks in black barbershops and beauty salons as they thumbed through the Ripley's-Believe-It-or-Not-type work of the self- taught black historian J. A. Rogers *(One Hundred Amazing Facts about the Negro, Five Negro Presidents,* and the like). Malcolm X revitalized the ideas of Marcus Garvey, the great black nationalist leader of the 1910s and 1920s, whose Universal Negro Improvement Association became, for a time, one of the most popular black political groups in America. Malcolm, like Garvey, felt that the Negro still needed to be "improved," but unlike Garveyites, the Muslims did not offer costumes and parades but sober suits, puritanical religion, dietary discipline, and no-nonsense business practices. Malcolm himself was also, by his physical appearance alone, a figure who would not be dismissed as a buffoon, as Garvey often was by both blacks and whites. According to Malcolm's *Autobiography,* his father had been a Garveyite as well as a wife beater who favored his lighter-skinned children. Malcolm's Islamic-based black nationalism, his sexual abstinence, which lasted from his religious conversion until his marriage a decade later, and his triumph over his own preference for lighter-skinned blacks and whites were all meant to demonstrate vividly how he superseded his father as a nationalist and how the Nation of Islam had superseded Garveyism.

Malcolm enlisted a body of enforcers, the feared Fruit of Islam, grim-faced men who, one imagines, were supposed to personify the essence of an unbowed yet disciplined black manhood. In this way, he dramatically associated black nationalism with a new type of regenerated black male. It was said in the black community, and may still be, that no one bothers a Muslim for fear of retribution from the Fruit of Islam. Certainly, there was a point in the development of the Fruit of Islam and the Nation itself in the 1960s and early 1970s (Malcolm was assassinated in 1965) when both were closely associated with racketeering and gangster activity. During this period, many East Coast mosques were among the most terrifying organizations in the black community.

Second, Malcolm, in his *Autobiography*, also managed to link the psychological redemption of the Negro with his reacquaintance with his history. The prison chapters of the *Autobiography* have become nearly mythic as a paradigm of black reawakening. Malcolm's religious conversion became, in a sense, the redemption of the black male and the rehabilitation of black masculinity itself. Lately, we have seen two major black male public figures who were incarcerated for serious crimes, Marion Barry and Mike Tyson, use the Malcolm paradigm to resuscitate their standing with the black public. The martyrdom of Malcolm gave this paradigm a blood-endorsed political heroism that has virtually foreclosed any serious criticism of either its origins or its meaning.

It is extraordinary to contemplate how highly regarded Malcolm X is in the black community today, especially in comparison with Martin Luther King. (When I wrote an article for *Harper's Magazine* that was critical of Malcolm X, I received three death threats.) Despite the fact that King's achievements were enormous — and that Malcolm left really nothing behind other than a book — King's association with integration, with nonviolence, even with Christianity has reduced him in the eyes of many blacks. When blacks in major cities, inspired by figures like Malcolm X and the romanticization of Africa that Malcolm's nationalism wrought, began to organize African-oriented celebrations, such as my aunts did in Philadelphia with the creation of the Yoruba-inspired Odunde festival in 1975, then Afrocentrism has succeeded not only in intellectual spheres but on the grassroots level as well. Its triumph as the legitimation of the black mind and the black aesthetic vision was complete.

Afrocentrism may eventually wane in the black community, but probably not very soon. Moreover, a certain type of nationalistic mood, a kind of racial preoccupation, will always exist among blacks. It always has, in varying degrees. Homesickness is strong among black Americans, although it is difficult to point to a homeland. What Afrocentrism reflects is the inability of a large number of black people to deal with the reality of being American and with the meaning of their American experience.

Stanley Crouch is right in pointing out that the Afrocentrist is similar to the white Southerner after the Civil War. To black nationalists, the lost war was the "war of liberation" led by black "revolutionaries" in the late 1960s, which in their imagination was modeled on the struggles against colonialism then taking place around the world. (The enslavement of the Africans, of course, was an earlier lost war, and it also weighs heavily on the Afrocentrist. He, like the white Southerner, hates the idea of belonging to a defeated people.) This imaginative vision of a restored and indomitable ethnicity is not to be taken lightly. In a culture as driven by the idea of redemption and as corrupted by racism as this one, race war is our Armageddon. It can be seen in works as various as Thomas Jefferson's *Notes on the State of Virginia,* David Walker's *Appeal to the Colored Citizens of the World,* Joseph Smith's *Book of Mormon,* D. W. Griffith's *Birth of a Nation,* and Mario Van Peebles's *Posse.*

Today, Afrocentrism is not a mature political movement but rather a cultural style and a moral stance. There is a deep, almost lyrical poignancy in the fantasy of the Afrocentrist, as there is in the white Southerner's. What would I have been had I not lost the war? The Afrocentrist is devoted to his ancestry and his blood, fixated on the set of traditions that define his nobility, preoccupied with an imagined lost way of life. What drives the Afrocentrist and the white Southerner is not the expression of a group self-interest but concern with pride and honor. One group's myth is built on the surfeit of honor and pride, the other on the total absence of them.

Like the white Southerner, the Afrocentrist is in revolt against liberalism itself, against the idea of individual liberty. In a way, the Afrocentrist is right to rage against it, because liberalism set free the individual but did not encourage the development of a community within which the individual could flower. This is what the Afrocentrist wishes to retrieve, a place for himself in his own community. Wilson Jeremiah Moses, a black historian, is right: Afrocentrism is a historiography of decline, like the mythic epic of the South. The tragedy is that black people fail to see their "Americanization" as one of the great human triumphs of the past five hundred years. The United States is virtually the only country where the ex-masters and the ex-slaves try to live together as equals, not only by consent of the ex-masters but by the demand of the ex-slaves. Ironically, what the Afrocentrist can best hope for is precisely what multiculturalism offers: the idea that American culture is a blend of many white and nonwhite cultures. In the end, although many Afrocentrists claim they want this blending, multiculturalism will not satisfy. For if the Euro-American is reminded through this that he is not European or wholly white, the African American will surely be reminded that he is not African or wholly black. The Afrocentrist does not wish to be a mongrel. He wants, like the Southerner, to be pure.

Afrocentrism is intense now because blacks are in a special period of social development in a nation going through a period of fearsome transition. Social development, by its nature, is ambivalent, characterized by a sense of exchange, of gaining and losing. Afrocentrism, in its conservatism, is opposed to this ambivalence and to this sense of exchange. What blacks desire during these turbulent times is exactly what whites want: the security of a golden past that never existed. A significant number of both blacks and whites want, strangely, to go back to an era of segregation, a fantasy time between 1920 and 1955, when whites felt secure in a stable culture and when blacks felt unified and strong because black people were forced to live together. Afrocentrism wants social change without having to pay the psychic price for it. Perhaps many black folk feel that they have paid too much already, and who is to say they are not right.

The issue raised by Afrocentrism is the meaning and formation of identity, which is the major fixation of the American, especially the black American. In a country that relentlessly promotes the myth of self-reliance because it is unable to provide any sense of security in a cauldron of capitalistic change, identity struggle is so acute because so much is at stake. Afrocentrism may be wrong in many respects, and it certainly can be stifling and restrictive, but some of its impulses are right. In a culture where information and resources of knowledge are the main levers for social and economic advancement, psychological well-being has become increasingly important as, in the words of one scholar, "a social resource," just as "social networks of care and community support [have become] central features of a dynamic economy." Black folk know, and rightly so, that their individual identities are tied to the strength of their community. The struggle over black identity in the United States has been the struggle over the creation of a true black community here. What integration has done to the individual black mind in the United States is directly related to what it has done to the black community. This is the first lesson we must learn. The second is that perhaps many black folk cling to Afrocentrism because the black *American* experience still costs more, requires more courage, than white Americans — and black Americans — are willing to admit.

Reflections and Responses

1. Why does Early refer to Afrocentrism as "bourgeois"? What evidence does he offer for this evaluation? Do you think that those who endorse the Afrocentric movement would agree with Early's assessment?

2. Why is ancient Egypt so important for the theory and ideology of Afrocentrism? What does Egypt provide that other African nations do not? What did Cheikh Anta Diop contribute to the Afrocentric movement? Why does Early believe that Diop's contributions are extremely significant?

3. How would you assess Early's overall attitude toward the Afrocentric movement? What aspects of the movement and which publications does he appear to have the least respect for? Can you discern which elements and studies of Afrocentrism he does respect?

STEPHEN JAY GOULD

The Creation Myths
of Cooperstown

*Why are we so easily drawn to and persuaded by myths of beginnings? Why
do we need a heroic story to explain origins—whether it's of humankind or
baseball? This is the central question posed by one of America's most famous scientists and essayists, Stephen Jay Gould. In "The Creation Myths
of Cooperstown," Gould artfully weaves together his knowledge of paleontol-
ogy and baseball to demonstrate the stubborn power of myth over fact. "By
contrasting the myth of Cooperstown," Gould argues, "with the fact of evolution, we can learn something about our cultural practices and their frequent disrespect for truth." His essay is not so much about baseball as it is
about our deep-seated resistance to complex modes of explanation and our
attraction to fuzzy thinking in general.*

*Stephen Jay Gould is the Alexander Agassiz Professor of zoology and
professor of geology at Harvard as well as curator for invertebrate paleon-
tology at the university's Museum of Comparative Zoology. He is also a visiting professor of biology at New York University. Gould is the author of
numerous scientific books and essay collections, including* Ever Since
Darwin *(1977),* The Panda's Thumb *(1980),* The Mismeasure of
Man *(1982),* Hen's Teeth and Horse's Toes *(1983),* The Flamingo's
Smile *(1985),* An Urchin in the Storm *(1987),* Bully for Bron-
tosaurus *(1991),* Dinosaur in a Haystack *(1996), and* Questioning
the Millennium *(1997). A MacArthur Prize Fellow, he writes a monthly
scientific essay for* Natural History *magazine and is a regular contributor
to* The New York Review of Books, *where he frequently writes about two
of his favorite subjects, biology and baseball. "The Creation Myths of Cooperstown" originally appeared in* Natural History *and was selected by
Justin Kaplan for* The Best American Essays *1990.*

You may either look upon the bright side and say that hope springs eternal or, taking the cynic's part, you may mark P. T. Barnum as an astute psychologist for his proclamation that suckers are born every minute. The end result is the same: you can, Honest Abe notwithstanding, fool most of the people all of the time. How else to explain the long and continuing compendium of hoaxes — from the medieval shroud of Turin to Edwardian Piltdown Man to an ultramodern array of flying saucers and astral powers — eagerly embraced for their consonance with our hopes or their resonance with our fears?

Some hoaxes make a sufficient mark upon history that their products acquire the very status initially claimed by fakery — legitimacy (although as an object of human or folkloric, rather than natural, history. I once held the bones of Piltdown Man and felt that I was handling an important item of Western culture).

The Cardiff Giant, the best American entry for the title of paleontological hoax turned into cultural history, now lies on display in a shed behind a barn at the Farmer's Museum in Cooperstown, New York. This gypsum man, more than ten feet tall, was "discovered" by workmen digging a well on a farm near Cardiff, New York, in October 1869. Eagerly embraced by a gullible public, and ardently displayed by its creators at fifty cents a pop, the Cardiff Giant caused quite a brouhaha around Syracuse, and then nationally, for the few months of its active life between exhumation and exposure.

The Cardiff Giant was the brainchild of George Hull, a cigar manufacturer (and general rogue) from Binghamton, New York. He quarried a large block of gypsum from Fort Dodge, Iowa, and shipped it to Chicago, where two marble cutters fashioned the rough likeness of a naked man. Hull made some crude and minimal attempts to give his statue an aged appearance. He chipped off the carved hair and beard because experts told him that such items would not petrify. He drove darning needles into a wooden block and hammered the statue, hoping to simulate skin pores. Finally, he dumped a gallon of sulfuric acid all over his creation to simulate extended erosion. Hull then shipped his giant in a large box back to Cardiff.

Hull, as an accomplished rogue, sensed that his story could not hold for long and, in that venerable and alliterative motto, got out while the getting was good. He sold a three-quarter interest in the Cardiff Giant to a consortium of highly respectable businessmen, including two former mayors of Syracuse. These men raised the statue from its original pit on November 5 and carted it off to Syracuse for display.

The hoax held on for a few more weeks, and Cardiff Giant fever swept the land. Debate raged in newspapers and broadsheets between those who viewed the giant as a petrified fossil and those who regarded it as a statue wrought by an unknown and wondrous prehistoric race. But Hull had left too many tracks — at the gypsum quarries in Fort Dodge, at the carver's studio in Chicago, along the roadways to Cardiff (several people remembered seeing an awfully large box passing on a cart just days before the supposed discovery). By December, Hull was ready to recant, but held his tongue a while longer. Three months later, the two Chicago sculptors came forward, and the Cardiff Giant's brief rendezvous with fame and fortune ended.

The common analogy of the Cardiff Giant with Piltdown Man works only to a point (both were frauds passed off as human fossils) and fails in one crucial respect. Piltdown was cleverly wrought and fooled professionals for forty years, while the Cardiff Giant was preposterous from the start. How could a man turn to solid gypsum while preserving all his soft anatomy, from cheeks to toes to penis? Geologists and paleontologists never accepted Hull's statue. O. C. Marsh, later to achieve great fame as a discoverer of dinosaurs, echoed a professional consensus in his unambiguous pronouncement: "It is of very recent origin and a decided humbug."

Why, then, was the Cardiff Giant so popular, inspiring a wave of interest and discussion as high as any tide in the affairs of men during its short time in the sun? If the fraud had been well executed, we might attribute this great concern to the dexterity of the hoaxers (just as we grant grudging attention to a few of the most accomplished art fakers for their skills as copyists). But since the Cardiff Giant was so crudely done, we can only attribute its fame to the deep issue, the raw nerve, touched by the subject of its fakery — human origins. Link an absurd concoction to a noble and mysterious subject and you may prevail, at least for a while. My opening reference to P. T. Barnum was not meant sarcastically; he

was one of the great practical psychologists of the nineteenth century — and his motto applies with special force to the Cardiff
Giant: "No humbug is great without truth at bottom." (Barnum
made a copy of the Cardiff Giant and exhibited it in New York
City. His mastery of hype and publicity assured that his model far
outdrew the "real" fake when the original went on display at a rival
establishment in the same city.)

For some reason (to be explored but not resolved in this essay),
we are powerfully drawn to the subject of beginnings. We yearn to
know about origins, and we readily construct myths when we do
not have data (or we suppress data in favor of legend when a truth
strikes us as too commonplace). The hankering after an origin
myth has always been especially strong for the closest subject of
all — the human race. But we extend the same psychic need to our
accomplishments and institutions — and we have origin myths
and stories for the beginning of hunting, of language, of art, of
kindness, of war, of boxing, bowties, and brassieres. Most of us
know that the Great Seal of the United States pictures an eagle
holding a ribbon reading *e pluribus unum*. Fewer would recognize
the motto on the other side (check it out on the back of a dollar
bill): *annuit coeptis*— "he smiles on our beginnings."

Cooperstown may house the Cardiff Giant, but the fame of this
small village in central New York does not rest upon its celebrated
namesake, author James Fenimore, or its lovely Lake Otsego or the
Farmer's Museum. Cooperstown is "on the map" by virtue of a different origin myth — one more parochial but no less powerful for
many Americans than the tales of human beginnings that gave life
to the Cardiff Giant. Cooperstown is the sacred founding place in
the official myth about the origin of baseball.

Origin myths, since they are so powerful, can engender enormous practical problems. Abner Doubleday, as we shall soon see,
most emphatically did not invent baseball at Cooperstown in 1839
as the official tale proclaims; in fact, no one invented baseball at
any moment or in any spot. Nonetheless, this creation myth made
Cooperstown the official home of baseball, and the Hall of Fame,
with its associated museum and library, set its roots in this small
village, inconveniently located near nothing in the way of airports
or accommodations. We all revel in bucolic imagery on the field of
dreams, but what a hassle when tens of thousands line the roads,
restaurants, and port-a-potties during the annual Hall of Fame

weekend, when new members are enshrined and two major league teams arrive to play an exhibition game at Abner Doubleday field, a sweet little ten-thousand-seater in the middle of town. Put your compass point at Cooperstown, make your radius at Albany — and you'd better reserve a year in advance if you want any accommodation within the enormous resulting circle.

After a lifetime of curiosity, I finally got the opportunity to witness this annual version of forty students in a telephone booth or twenty circus clowns in a Volkswagen. Since Yaz (former Boston star Carl Yastrzemski to the uninitiated) was slated to receive baseball's Nobel in 1989, and his old team was playing in the Hall of Fame game, and since I'm a transplanted Bostonian (although still a New Yorker and not-so-secret Yankee fan at heart), Tom Heitz, chief of the wonderful baseball library at the Hall of Fame, kindly invited me to join the sardines in this most lovely of all cans.

The silliest and most tendentious of baseball writing tries to wrest profundity from the spectacle of grown men hitting a ball with a stick by suggesting linkages between the sport and deep issues of morality, parenthood, history, lost innocence, gentleness, and so on, seemingly ad infinitum. (The effort reeks of silliness because baseball is profound all by itself and needs no excuses; people who don't know this are not fans and are therefore unreachable anyway.) When people ask me how baseball imitates life, I can only respond with what the more genteel newspapers used to call a "barnyard epithet," but now, with growing bravery, usually render as "bullbleep." Nevertheless, baseball is a major item of our culture, and it does have a long and interesting history. Any item or institution with those two properties must generate a set of myths and stories (perhaps even some truths) about its beginnings. And the subject of beginnings is the bread and butter of this column on evolution in the broadest sense. I shall make no woolly analogies between baseball and life; this is an essay on the origins of baseball, with some musings on why beginnings of all sorts hold such fascination for us. (I thank Tom Heitz not only for the invitation to Cooperstown at its yearly acme but also for drawing the contrast between creation and evolution stories of baseball, and for supplying much useful information from his unparalleled storehouse.)

Stories about beginnings come in only two basic modes. An entity either has an explicit point of origin, a specific time and place of creation, or else it evolves and has no definable moment of entry into the world. Baseball provides an interesting example of this contrast because we know the answer and can judge received wisdom by the two chief criteria, often opposed, of external fact and internal hope. Baseball evolved from a plethora of previous stick-and-ball games. It has no true Cooperstown and no Doubleday. Yet we seem to prefer the alternative model of origin by a moment of creation — for then we can have heroes and sacred places. By contrasting the myth of Cooperstown with the fact of evolution, we can learn something about our cultural practices and their frequent disrespect for truth.

The official story about the beginning of baseball is a creation myth, and a review of the reasons and circumstances of its fabrication may give us insight into the cultural appeal of stories in this mode. A. G. Spalding, baseball's first great pitcher during his early career, later founded the sporting goods company that still bears his name and became one of the great commercial moguls of America's gilded age. As publisher of the annual *Spalding's Official Base Ball Guide,* he held maximal power in shaping both public and institutional opinion on all facets of baseball and its history. As the sport grew in popularity, and the pattern of two stable major leagues coalesced early in our century, Spalding and others felt the need for clarification (or merely for codification) of opinion on the hitherto unrecorded origins of an activity that truly merited its common designation as America's "national pastime."

In 1907, Spalding set up a blue ribbon committee to investigate and resolve the origins of baseball. The committee, chaired by A. G. Mills and including several prominent businessmen and two senators who had also served as presidents of the National League, took much testimony but found no smoking gun for a beginning. Then, in July 1907, Spalding himself transmitted to the committee a letter from an Abner Graves, then a mining engineer in Denver, who reported that Abner Doubleday had, in 1839, interrupted a marbles game behind the tailor's shop in Cooperstown, New York, to draw a diagram of a baseball field, explain the rules of the game, and designate the activity by its modern name of "base ball" (then spelled as two words).

Such "evidence" scarcely inspired universal confidence, but the commission came up with nothing better — and the Doubleday myth, as we shall soon see, was eminently functional. Therefore, in 1908, the Mills Commission reported its two chief findings: first, "that base ball had its origins in the United States"; and second, "that the first scheme for playing it, according to the best evidence available to date, was devised by Abner Doubleday, at Coopers-town, New York, in 1839." This "best evidence" consisted only of "a circumstantial statement by a reputable gentleman" — namely, Graves's testimony as reported by Spalding himself.

When cited evidence is so laughably insufficient, one must seek motivations other than concern for truth value. The key to under-lying reasons stands in the first conclusion of Mills's committee: hoopla and patriotism (cardboard version) decreed that a national pastime must have an indigenous origin. The idea that baseball had evolved from a wide variety of English stick-and-ball games — although true — did not suit the mythology of a phenomenon that had become so quintessentially American. In fact, Spalding had long been arguing, in an amiable fashion, with Henry Chadwick, another pioneer and entrepreneur of baseball's early years. Chad-wick, born in England, had insisted for years that baseball had de-veloped from the British stick-and-ball game called rounders; Spalding had vociferously advocated a purely American origin, cit-ing the Colonial game of "one old cat" as a distant precursor, but holding that baseball itself represented something so new and ad-vanced that a pinpoint of origin — a creation myth — must be sought.

Chadwick considered the matter of no particular importance, arguing (with eminent justice) that an English origin did not "de-tract one iota from the merit of its now being unquestionably a thoroughly American field sport, and a game too, which is fully adapted to the American character." (I must say that I have grown quite fond of Mr. Chadwick, who certainly understood evolution-ary change and its chief principle that historical origin need not match contemporary function.) Chadwick also viewed the commit-tee's whitewash as a victory for his side. He labeled the Mills report as "a masterful piece of special pleading which lets my dear old friend Albert [Spalding] escape a bad defeat. The whole matter was a joke between Albert and myself."

We may accept the psychic need for an indigenous creation myth, but why Abner Doubleday, a man with no recorded tie to the game and who, in the words of Donald Honig, probably "didn't know a baseball from a kumquat"? I had wondered about this for years, but only ran into the answer serendipitously during a visit to Fort Sumter in the harbor of Charleston, South Carolina. There, an exhibit on the first skirmish of the Civil War points out that Abner Doubleday, as captain of the Union artillery, had personally sighted and given orders for firing the first responsive volley following the initial Confederate attack on the fort. Doubleday later commanded divisions at Antietam and Fredericksburg, became at least a minor hero at Gettysburg, and retired as a brevet major general. In fact, A. G. Mills, head of the commission, had served as part of an honor guard when Doubleday's body lay in state in New York City, following his death in 1893.

If you have to have an American hero, could anyone be better than the man who fired the first shot (in defense) of the Civil War? Needless to say, this point was not lost on the members of Mills's committee. Spalding, never one to mince words, wrote to the committee when submitting Graves's dubious testimony: "It certainly appeals to an American pride to have had the great national game of base ball created and named by a Major General in the United States Army." Mills then concluded in his report: "Perhaps in the years to come, in view of the hundreds of thousands of people who are devoted to base ball, and the millions who will be, Abner Doubleday's fame will rest evenly, if not quite as much, upon the fact that he was its inventor . . . as upon his brilliant and distinguished career as an officer in the Federal Army."

And so, spurred by a patently false creation myth, the Hall of Fame stands in the most incongruous and inappropriate locale of a charming little town in central New York. Incongruous and inappropriate, but somehow wonderful. Who needs another museum in the cultural maelstroms (and summer doldrums) of New York, Boston, or Washington? Why not a major museum in a beautiful and bucolic setting? And what could be more fitting than the spatial conjunction of two great American origin myths — the Cardiff Giant and the Doubleday Fable? Thus, I too am quite content to treat the myth gently, while honesty requires fessing up. The exhibit on Doubleday in the Hall of Fame Museum sets just the right tone in its caption: "In the hearts of those who love baseball, he is remembered as the lad in the pasture where the game was invented. Only cynics would need to know more." Only in the hearts; not in the minds.

Baseball evolved. Since the evidence is so clear (as epitomized below), we must ask why these facts have been so little appreciated for so long, and why a creation myth like the Doubleday story ever gained a foothold. Two major reasons have conspired: first, the positive block of our attraction to creation stories; second, the negative impediment of unfamiliar sources outside the usual purview of historians. English stick-and ball games of the nineteenth century can be roughly classified into two categories along social lines. The upper and educated classes played cricket, and the history of this sport is copiously documented because the literati write about their own interests, and because the activities of men in power are well recorded (and constitute virtually all of history, in the schoolboy version). But the ordinary pastimes of rural and urban working people can be well nigh invisible in conventional sources of explicit commentary. Working people played a different kind of stick-and-ball game, existing in various forms and designated by many names, including "rounders" in western England, "feeder" in London, and "base ball" in southern England. For a large number of reasons, forming the essential difference between cricket and baseball, cricket matches can last up to several days (a batsman, for example, need not run after he hits the ball and need not expose himself to the possibility of being put out every time he makes contact). The leisure time of working people does not come in such generous gobs, and the lower-class stick-and-ball games could not run more than a few hours.

Several years ago, at the Victoria and Albert Museum in London, I learned an important lesson from an excellent exhibit on the late-nineteenth-century history of the British music hall. This is my favorite period (Darwin's century, after all), and I consider myself tolerably well informed on cultural trends of the time. I can sing any line from any of the Gilbert and Sullivan operas (a largely middle-class entertainment), and I know the general drift of high cultural interests in literature and music. But here was a whole world of entertainment for millions, a world with its heroes, its stars, its top forty songs, its gaudy theaters — and I knew nothing, absolutely nothing, about it. I felt chagrined, but my ignorance had an explanation beyond personal insensitivity (and the exhibit had been mounted explicitly to counteract the selective invisibility of certain important trends in history). The music hall was the chief entertainment of Victorian working classes, and the history of working people is often invisible in conventional written sources. It must be rescued and reconstituted from different sorts of data; in this case, from posters, playbills, theater accounts, persistence of some songs in the oral tradition (most were never published as sheet music), recollections of old-timers who knew the person who knew the person . . .

The early history of baseball — the stick-and-ball game of working people — presents the same problem of conventional invisibility — and the same promise of rescue by exploration of unusual sources. Work continues and intensifies as the history of sport becomes more and more academically respectable, but the broad outlines (and much fascinating detail) are not well established. As the upper classes played a codified and well-documented cricket, working people played a largely unrecorded and much more diversified set of stick-and-ball games ancestral to baseball. Many sources, including primers and boys' manuals, depict games recognizable as precursors to baseball well into the early eighteenth century. Occasional references even spill over into high culture. In *Northanger Abbey,* written at the close of the eighteenth century, Jane Austen remarks: "It was not very wonderful that Catherine . . . should prefer cricket, base ball, riding on horseback, and running about the country, at the age of fourteen, to books." As this quotation illustrates, the name of the game is no more Doubleday's than the form of play.

These ancestral styles of baseball came to America with early settlers and were clearly well established by Colonial times. But they were driven ever further underground by Puritan proscriptions of sport for adults. They survived largely as children's games and suffered the double invisibility of location among the poor and the young. But two major reasons brought these games into wider repute and led to a codification of standard forms quite close to modern baseball between the 1820s and the 1850s. First, a set of social reasons, from the decline of Puritanism to increased concern about health and hygiene in crowded cities, made sport an acceptable activity for adults. Second, middle-class and professional people began to take up these early forms of baseball, and with this upward social drift came teams, leagues, written rules, uniforms, stadiums, guidebooks: in short, all the paraphernalia of conventional history.

I am not arguing that these early games could be called baseball with a few trivial differences (evolution means substantial change, after all), but only that they stand in a complex lineage, better called a nexus, from which modern baseball emerged, eventually in a codified and canonical form. In those days before instant communication, every region had its own version, just as every set of outdoor steps in New York City generated a different form of stoopball in my youth, without threatening the basic identity of the game. These games, most commonly called town ball, differed from modern baseball in substantial ways. In the Massachusetts Game, a codification of the late 1850s drawn up by ballplayers in New England towns, four bases and three strikes identify the genus, but many specifics are strange by modern standards. The bases were made of wooden stakes projecting four feet from the ground. The batter (called the striker) stood between first and fourth base. Sides changed after a single out. One hundred runs (called tallies), not higher score after a specified number of innings, spelled victory. The field contained no foul lines, and balls hit in any direction were in play. Most importantly, runners were not tagged out but were retired by "plugging," that is, being hit with a thrown ball while running between bases. Consequently, since baseball has never been a game for masochists, balls were soft — little more than rags stuffed into leather covers — and could not be hit far. (Tom Heitz has put together a team of Cooperstown worthies to re-create town ball for interested parties and prospective opponents. Since few other groups are well schooled in this lost art, Tom's team hasn't been defeated in ages, if ever. "We are the New York Yankees of town ball," he told me. His team is called, quite appropriately in general but especially for this essay, the Cardiff Giants.)

Evolution is continual change, but not insensibly gradual transition; in any continuum, some points are always more interesting than others. The conventional nomination for most salient point in this particular continuum goes to Alexander Joy Cartwright, leader of a New York team that started to play in lower Manhattan, eventually rented some changing rooms and a field in Hoboken (just a quick ferry ride across the Hudson), and finally drew up a set of rules in 1845, later known as the New York Game. Cartwright's version of town ball is much closer to modern baseball, and many clubs followed his rules — for standardization became ever more vital as the popularity of early baseball grew and opportunity for play between regions increased. In particular, Cartwright introduced two key innovations that shaped the disparate forms of town ball into a semblance of modern baseball. First, he eliminated plugging and introduced tagging in the modern sense; the ball could now be made harder, and hitting for distance became an option. Second, he introduced foul lines, again in the modern sense, as his batter stood at a home plate and had to hit the ball within lines defined from home through first and third bases. The game could now become a spectator sport because areas close to the field but out of action could, for the first time, be set aside for onlookers.

The New York Game may be the highlight of a continuum, but it provides no origin myth for baseball. Cartwright's rules were followed in various forms of town ball. His New York Game still included many curiosities by modern standards (twenty-one runs, called aces, won the game, and balls caught on one bounce were outs). Moreover, our modern version is an amalgam of the New York Game plus other town ball traditions, not Cartwright's baby grown up by itself. Several features of the Massachusetts Game entered the modern version in preference to Cartwright's rules. Balls had to be caught on the fly in Boston, and pitchers threw overhand, not underhand as in the New York Game (and in professional baseball until the 1880s).

Scientists often lament that so few people understand Darwin and the principles of biological evolution. But the problem goes deeper. Too few people are comfortable with evolutionary modes of explanation in any form. I do not know why we tend to think so fuzzily in this area, but one reason must reside in our social and psychic attraction to creation myths in preference to evolutionary stories — for creation myths, as noted before, identify heroes and sacred places, while evolutionary stories provide no palpable, particular thing as a symbol for reverence, worship, or patriotism. Still, we must remember — and an intellectual's most persistent and nagging responsibility lies in making this simple point over and over again, however noxious and bothersome we render ourselves thereby — that truth and desire, fact and comfort, have no necessary, or even preferred, correlation (so rejoice when they do coincide).

To state the most obvious example in our current political turmoil. Human growth is a continuum, and no creation myth can define an instant for the origin of an individual life. Attempts by anti-abortionists to designate the moment of fertilization as the beginning of personhood make no sense in scientific terms (and also violate a long history of social definitions that traditionally focused on the quickening, or detected movement, of the fetus in the womb). I will admit — indeed, I emphasized as a key argument of this essay — that not all points on a continuum are equal. Fertilization is a more interesting moment than most, but it no more provides a clean definition of origin than the most interesting moment of baseball's continuum — Cartwright's codification of the New York Game — defines the beginning of our national pastime. Baseball evolved and people grow; both are continua without definable points of origin. Probe too far back and you reach absurdity, for you will see Nolan Ryan on the hill when the first ape hit a bird with a stone; or you will define both masturbation and menstruation as murder — and who will then cast the first stone? Look for something in the middle, and you find nothing but continuity — always a meaningful "before," and always a more modern "after." (Please note that I am not stating an opinion on the vexatious question of abortion — an ethical issue that can only be decided in ethical terms. I only point out that one side has rooted its case in an argument from science that is not only entirely irrelevant to the proper realm of resolution but also happens to be flat-out false in trying to devise a creation myth within a continuum.)

And besides, why do we prefer creation myths to evolutionary stories? I find all the usual reasons hollow. Yes, heroes and shrines are all very well, but is there not grandeur in the sweep of continuity? Shall we revel in a story for all humanity that may include the sacred ball courts of the Aztecs, and perhaps, for all we know, a group of *Homo erectus* hitting rocks or skulls with a stick or a femur? Or shall we halt beside the mythical Abner Doubleday, standing behind the tailor's shop in Cooperstown, and say "behold the man" — thereby violating truth and, perhaps even worse, extinguishing both thought and wonder?

Reflections and Responses

1. Where in the essay does the reader first become aware that Gould's topic is baseball? Why do you think he covers the story of the Cardiff Giant before introducing his main topic? What connection helps him make the transition? Why is the Cardiff Giant important to his main point?

2. According to Gould, if the official version of the origin of baseball (the Abner Doubleday story) is so sketchy and dubious, why does it command such authority? What advantages does it have over the origins Gould prefers?

3. How does Gould's central dichotomy between creation and continuum apply to other issues? Do you think his argument is applicable to the biblical story of Genesis, say, or to the invention of the lightbulb? Can you think of a creation story that would be historically accurate?

VICKI HEARNE

What's Wrong with
Animal Rights

*When people argue for the rights of animals, what exactly do they mean by
"rights"? Does their definition of animal rights take into account the "certain unalienable rights" that Thomas Jefferson wrote into the Declaration
of Independence — the right to "life, liberty and the pursuit of happiness"?
In the following essay, Vicki Hearne skillfully combines personal and professional experience with philosophical reflections on happiness as she
builds a case against the reductive view of animals that typifies the animal-
rights movement. In Hearne's opinion, the problem with animal-rights advocates is not that they take their position too far; "it's that they've got it all
wrong."*

*An active professional dog trainer and Yale University professor,
Hearne is the author of three volumes of poetry,* Nervous Horses *(1980),*
In the Absence of Horses *(1983), and* Parts of Light *(1994), and
two books of essays,* Adam's Task: Calling Animals by Name *(1986)
and* Bandit: Dossier of a Dangerous Dog *(1992). A collection of prose,*
Animal Happiness, *was published in 1994. "What's Wrong with Animal Rights" originally appeared in* Harper's Magazine *in 1991 and
was selected by Susan Sontag for* The Best American Essays 1992.

Not all happy animals are alike. A Doberman going over a hurdle
after a small wooden dumbbell is sleek, all arcs of harmonious
power. A basset hound cheerfully performing the same exercise exhibits harmonies of a more lugubrious nature. There are chimpan-
zees who love precision the way musicians or fanatical housekeepers
or accomplished hypochondriacs do; others for whom happiness
is a matter of invention and variation — chimp vaudevillians. There

is a rhinoceros whose happiness, as near as I can make out, is in needing to be trained every morning, all over again, or else he "forgets" his circus routine, and in this you find a clue to the slow, deep, quiet chuckle of his happiness and to the glory of the beast. Happiness for Secretariat is in his ebullient bound, that joyful length of stride. For the draft horse or the weight-pull dog, happiness is of a different shape, more awesome and less obviously intelligent. When the pulling horse is at its most intense, the animal goes into himself, allocating all of the educated power that organizes his desire to dwell in fierce and delicate intimacy with that power, leans into the harness, and MAKES THAT SUCKER MOVE.

If we are speaking of human beings and use the phrase "animal happiness," we tend to mean something like "creature comforts." The emblems of this are the golden retriever rolling in the grass, the horse with his nose deep in the oats, the kitty by the fire. Creature comforts are important to animals — "Grub first, then ethics" is a motto that would describe many a wise Labrador retriever, and I have a pit bull named Annie whose continual quest for the perfect pillow inspires her to awesome feats. But there is something more to animals, a capacity for satisfactions that come from work in the fullest sense — what is known in philosophy and in this country's Declaration of Independence as "happiness." This is a sense of personal achievement, like the satisfaction felt by a good wood-carver or a dancer or a poet or an accomplished dressage horse. It is a happiness that, like the artist's, must come from something within the animal, something trainers call "talent." Hence, it cannot be imposed on the animal. But it is also something that does not come *ex nihilo*.* If it had not been a fairly ordinary thing, in one part of the world, to teach young children to play the pianoforte, it is doubtful that Mozart's music would exist.

Happiness is often misunderstood as a synonym for pleasure or as an antonym for suffering. But Aristotle associated happiness with ethics — codes of behavior that urge us toward the sensation of getting it right, a kind of work that yields the "click" of satisfaction upon solving a problem or surmounting an obstacle. In his *Ethics*, Aristotle wrote, "If happiness is activity in accordance with

thess

ex nihilo: Latin, "out of nothing."

excellence, it is reasonable that it should be in accordance with the highest excellence." Thomas Jefferson identified the capacity for happiness as one of the three fundamental rights on which all others are based: "life, liberty, and the pursuit of happiness."

I bring up this idea of happiness as a form of work because I am an animal trainer, and work is the foundation of the happiness a trainer and an animal discover together. I bring up these words also because they cannot be found in the lexicon of the animal-rights movement. This absence accounts for the uneasiness toward the movement of most people, who sense that rights advocates have a point but take it too far when they liberate snails or charge that goldfish at the county fair are suffering. But the problem with the animal-rights advocates is not that they take it too far; it's that they've got it all wrong.

Animal rights are built upon a misconceived premise that rights were created to prevent us from unnecessary suffering. You can't find an animal-rights book, video, pamphlet, or rock concert in which someone doesn't mention the Great Sentence, written by Jeremy Bentham* in 1789. Arguing in favor of such rights, Bentham wrote: "The question is not, Can they *reason?* nor, can they *talk?* but, can they suffer?"

The logic of the animal-rights movement places suffering at the iconographic center of a skewed value system. The thinking of its proponents — given eerie expression in a virtually sadoporno-graphic sculpture of a tortured monkey that won a prize for its compassionate vision — has collapsed into a perverse conundrum. Today the loudest voices calling for — demanding — the destruc-tion of animals are the humane organizations. This is an inevitable consequence of the apotheosis of the drive to relieve suffering: death is the ultimate release. To compensate for their contradic-tions, the humane movement has demonized, in this century and the last, those who made animal happiness their business: veteri-narians, trainers, and the like. We think of Louis Pasteur as the man whose work saved you and me and your dog and cat from ra-bies, but antivivisectionists of the time claimed that rabies in-creased in areas where there were Pasteur Institutes.

*Jeremy Bentham: British philosopher and social reformer (1748–1832) whose *Introduction to the Principles of Morals and Legislation* appeared in 1789.

An anti-rabies public relations campaign mounted in England in the 1880s by the Royal Society for the Prevention of Cruelty to Animals and other organizations led to orders being issued to club any dog found not wearing a muzzle. England still has her cruel and unnecessary law that requires an animal to spend six months in quarantine before being allowed loose in the country. Most of the recent propaganda about pit bulls — the crazy claim that they "take hold with their front teeth while they chew away with their rear teeth" (which would imply, incorrectly, that they have double jaws) — can be traced to literature published by the Humane Society of the United States during the fall of 1987 and earlier. If your neighbors want your dog or horse impounded and destroyed because he is a nuisance — say the dog barks, or the horse attracts flies — it will be the local Humane Society to whom your neighbors turn for action.

In a way, everyone has the opportunity to know that the history of the humane movement is largely a history of miseries, arrests, prosecutions, and death. The Humane Society is the pound, the place with the decompression chamber or the lethal injections. You occasionally find worried letters about this in Ann Landers's column.

Animal-rights publications are illustrated largely with photographs of two kinds of animals — "Helpless Fluff" and "Agonized Fluff," the two conditions in which some people seem to prefer their animals, because any other version of an animal is too complicated for propaganda. In the introduction to his book *Animal Liberation,* Peter Singer says somewhat smugly that he and his wife have no animals and, in fact, don't much care for them. This is offered as evidence of his objectivity and ethical probity. But it strikes me as an odd, perhaps obscene underpinning for an ethical project that encourages university and high school students to cherish their ignorance of, say, great bird dogs as proof of their devotion to animals.

I would like to leave these philosophers behind, for they are inept connoisseurs of suffering who might revere my Airedale for his capacity to scream when subjected to a blowtorch but not for his wit and courage, not for his natural good manners that are a gentle rebuke to ours. I want to celebrate the moment not long ago when, at his first dog show, my Airedale, Drummer, learned that there can be a public place where his work is respected. I want to celebrate his meticulousness, his happiness upon realizing at the dog show that no one would swoop down upon him and swamp him with the goo-goo excesses known as the "teddy-bear complex" but that people actually got out of his way, gave him room to work. I want to say, "There can be a six-and-a-half-month-old puppy who can care about accuracy, who can be fastidious, and whose fastidiousness will be a foundation for courage later." I want to say, "Leave my puppy alone!"

I want to leave the philosophers behind, but I cannot, in part because the philosophical problems that plague academicians of the animal-rights movement are illuminating. They wonder, do animals have rights or do they have interests? Or, if these rightists lead particularly unexamined lives, they dismiss that question as obvious (yes, of course animals have rights, prima facie) and proceed to enumerate them, James Madison style. This leads to the issuance of bills of rights — the right to an environment, the right not to be used in medical experiments — and other forms of trivialization.

The calculus of suffering can be turned against the philosophers of festering flesh, even in the case of food animals, or exotic animals who perform in movies and circuses. It is true that it hurts to be slaughtered by man, but it doesn't hurt nearly as much as some of the cunningly cruel arrangements meted out by "Mother Nature." In Africa, 75 percent of the lions cubbed do not survive to the age of two. For those who make it to two, the average age at death is ten years. Asali, the movie and TV lioness, was still working at age twenty-one. There are fates worse than death, but twenty-one years of a close working relationship with Hubert Wells, Asali's trainer, is not one of them. Dorset sheep and polled Herefords would not exist at all were they not in a symbiotic relationship with human beings.

A human being living in the "wild"— somewhere, say, without the benefits of medicine and advanced social organization — would probably have a life expectancy of from thirty to thirty-five years. A human being living in "captivity"— in, say, a middle-class neighborhood of what the Centers for Disease Control call a Metropolitan Statistical Area — has a life expectancy of seventy or more years. For orangutans in the wild in Borneo and Malaysia, the life expectancy is thirty-five years; in captivity, fifty years. The wild is not a suffering-free zone or all that frolicsome a location.

The questions asked by animal-rights activists are flawed, because they are built on the concept that the origin of rights is in the avoidance of suffering rather than in the pursuit of happiness. The question that needs to be asked — and that will put us in closer proximity to the truth — is not, do they have rights? or, what are those rights? but rather, what is a right?

Rights originate in committed relationships and can be found, both intact and violated, wherever one finds such relationships — in social compacts, within families, between animals, and between people and nonhuman animals. This is as true when the nonhuman animals in question are lions or parakeets as when they are dogs. It is my Airedale whose excellencies have my attention at the moment, so it is with reference to him that I will consider the question, what is a right?

When I imagine situations in which it naturally arises that A defends or honors or respects B's rights, I imagine situations in which the relationship between A and B can be indicated with a possessive pronoun. I might say, "Leave her alone, she's my daughter" or "That's what she wants, and she is my daughter. I think I am bound to honor her wants." Similarly, "Leave her alone, she's my mother." I am more tender of the happiness of my mother, my father, my child, than I am of other people's family members; more tender of my friends' happinesses than your friends' happinesses, unless you and I have a mutual friend.

Possession of a being by another has come into more and more disrepute, so that the common understanding of one person possessing another is slavery. But the important detail about the kind of possessive pronoun that I have in mind is reciprocity: if I have a friend, she has a friend. If I have a daughter, she has a mother. The possessive does not bind one of us while freeing the other; it cannot do that. Moreover, should the mother reject the daughter, the word that applies is "disown." The form of disowning that most often appears in the news is domestic violence. Parents abuse children; husbands batter wives.

Some cases of reciprocal possessives have built-in limitations, such as "my patient/my doctor" or "my student/my teacher" or "my agent/my client." Other possessive relations are extremely limited but still remarkably binding: "my neighbor" and "my country" and "my president."

The responsibilities and the ties signaled by reciprocal possession typically are hard to dissolve. It can be as difficult to give up an enemy as to give up a friend, and often the one becomes the other, as though the logic of the possessive pronoun outlasts the forms it chanced to take at a given moment, as though we were stuck with one another. In these bindings, nearly inextricable, are found the origin of our rights. They imply a possessiveness but also recognize an acknowledgment by each side of the other's existence.

The idea of democracy is dependent on the citizens' having knowledge of the government; that is, realizing that the government exists and knowing how to claim rights against it. I know this much because I get mail from the government and see its "representatives" running about in uniforms. Whether I actually have any rights in relationship to the government is less clear, but the idea that I do is symbolized by the right to vote. I obey the government, and, in theory, it obeys me, by counting my ballot, reading the *Miranda* warning to me, agreeing to be bound by the Constitution. My friend obeys me as I obey her; the government "obeys" me to some extent, and, to a different extent, I obey it.

What kind of thing can my Airedale, Drummer, have knowledge of? He can know that I exist and through that knowledge can claim his happinesses, with varying degrees of success, both with me and against me. Drummer can also know about larger human or dog communities than the one that consists only of him and me. There is my household — the other dogs, the cats, my husband. I have had enough dogs on campuses to know that he can learn that Yale exists as a neighborhood or village. My older dog, Annie, not only knows that Yale exists but can tell Yalies from townies, as I learned while teaching there during labor troubles.

Dogs can have elaborate conceptions of human social structures, and even of something like their rights and responsibilities within them, but these conceptions are never elaborate enough to construct a rights relationship between a dog and the state, or a dog and the Humane Society. Both of these are concepts that depend on writing and memoranda, officers in uniform, plaques and seals of authority. All of these are literary constructs, and all of them are beyond a dog's ken, which is why the mail carrier who doesn't also happen to be a dog's friend is forever an intruder — this is why dogs bark at mailmen.

It is clear enough that natural rights relations can arise between people and animals. Drummer, for example, can insist, "Hey, let's go outside and do something!" if I have been at my computer several days on end. He can both refuse to accept various of my suggestions and tell me when he fears for his life — such as the time when the huge, white flapping flag appeared out of nowhere, as it seemed to him, on the town green one evening when we were working. I can (and do) say to him either, "Oh, you don't have to worry about that" or, "Uh oh, you're right, Drum, that guy looks dangerous." Just as the government and I— two different species of organism — have developed improvised ways of communicating, such as the vote, so Drummer and I have worked out a number of ways to make our expressions known. Largely through obedience, I have taught him a fair amount about how to get responses from me. Obedience is reciprocal; you cannot get responses from a dog to whom you do not respond accurately. I have enfranchised him in a relationship to me by educating him, creating the conditions by which he can achieve a certain happiness specific to a dog, maybe even specific to an Airedale, inasmuch as this same relationship has allowed me to plumb the happiness of being a trainer and writing this article.

Instructions in this happiness are given terms that are alien to a culture in which liver treats, fluffy windup toys, and miniature sweaters are confused with respect and work. Jack Knox, a sheepdog trainer originally from Scotland, will shake his crook at a novice handler who makes a promiscuous move to praise a dog, and will call out in his Scottish accent, "Eh! Eh! Get back, get BACK! Ye'll no be abusin' the dogs like that in my clinic." America is a nation of abused animals, Knox says, because we are always swooping at them with praise, "no gi'ing them their freedom." I am reminded of Rainer Maria Rilke's* account in which the Prodigal Son leaves — has to leave — because everyone loves him, even the dogs love him, and he has no path to the delicate and fierce

*Rainer Maria Rilke: Austrian lyric poet (1875–1926).

truth of himself. Unconditional praise and love, in Rilke's story, disenfranchise us, distract us from what truly excites our interest.

In the minds of some trainers and handlers, praise is dishonesty. Paradoxically, it is a kind of contempt for animals that masquerades as a reverence for helplessness and suffering. The idea of freedom means that you do not, at least not while Jack Knox is nearby, helpfully guide your dog through the motions of, say, herding over and over — what one trainer calls "explainy-wainy." This is rote learning. It works tolerably well on some handlers, because people have vast unconscious minds and can store complex preprogrammed behaviors. Dogs, on the other hand, have almost no unconscious minds, so they can learn only by thinking. Many children are like this until educated out of it.

If I tell my Airedale to sit and stay on the town green, and someone comes up and burbles, "What a pretty thing you are," he may break his stay to go for a caress. I pull him back and correct him for breaking. Now he holds his stay because I have blocked his way to movement but not because I have punished him. (A correction blocks one path as it opens another for desire to work; punishment blocks desire and opens nothing.) He holds his stay now, and — because the stay opens this possibility of work, new to a heedless young dog — he watches. If the person goes on talking, and isn't going to gush with praise, I may heel Drummer out of his stay and give him an "Okay" to make friends. Sometimes something about the person makes Drummer feel that reserve is in order. He responds to an insincere approach by sitting still, going down into himself, and thinking, "This person has no business pawing me. I'll sit very still, and he will go away." If the person doesn't take the hint from Drummer, I'll give the pup a little backup by saying, "Please don't pet him, he's working," even though he was not under any command.

The pup reads this, and there is a flicker of a working trust now stirring in the dog. Is the pup grateful? When the stranger leaves, does he lick my hand, full of submissive blandishments? This one doesn't. This one says nothing at all, and I say nothing much to him. This is a working trust we are developing, not a mutual congratulation society. My backup is praise enough for him; the use he makes of my support is praise enough for me.

Listening to a dog is often praise enough. Suppose it is just after dark and we are outside. Suddenly there is a shout from the house. The pup and I both look toward the shout and then toward each other: "What do you think?" I don't so much as cock my head, because Drummer is growing up, and I want to know what he thinks. He takes a few steps toward the house, and I follow. He listens again and comprehends that it's just Holly, who at fourteen is much given to alarming cries and shouts. He shrugs at me and goes about his business. I say nothing. To praise him for this performance would make about as much sense as praising a human being for the same thing. Thus:

A. What's that?
B. I don't know. [Listens] Oh, it's just Holly.
A. What a gooooooood human being!
B. Huh?

This is one small moment in a series of like moments that will culminate in an Airedale who on a Friday will have the discrimination and confidence required to take down a man who is attacking me with a knife and on Saturday clown and play with the children at the annual Orange Empire Dog Club Christmas party.

People who claim to speak for animal rights are increasingly devoted to the idea that the very keeping of a dog or a horse or a gerbil or a lion is in and of itself an offense. The more loudly they speak, the less likely they are to be in a rights relation to any given animal, because they are spending so much time in airplanes or transmitting fax announcements of the latest Sylvester Stallone anti-fur rally. In a 1988 *Harper's* forum, for example, Ingrid Newkirk, the national director of People for the Ethical Treatment of Animals, urged that domestic pets be spayed and neutered and ultimately phased out. She prefers, it appears, wolves — and wolves someplace else — to Airedales and, by a logic whose interior structure is both emotionally and intellectually forever closed to Drummer, claims thereby to be speaking for "animal rights."

She is wrong. I am the only one who can own up to my Airedale's inalienable rights. Whether or not I do it perfectly at any given moment is no more refutation of this point than whether I am perfectly my husband's mate at any given moment refutes the fact of marriage. Only people who know Drummer, and whom he can know, are capable of this relationship. PETA and the Humane Society and the ASPCA and the Congress and NOW— as institutions — do have the power to affect my ability to grant rights to Drummer but are otherwise incapable of creating conditions or laws or rights that would increase his happiness. Only Drummer's owner has the power to obey him — to obey who he is and what he is capable of — deeply enough to grant him his rights and open up the possibility of happiness.

Reflections and Responses

1. How does Hearne define happiness? What is its relation to work? Why, in her opinion, are the interrelated concepts of happiness and work not "in the lexicon of the animal-rights movement"?

2. Why does Hearne bring up the life-expectancy statistics of animals living "in the wild"? In what way do these statistics reinforce her argument? How might an animal-rights advocate respond to her use and interpretation of these statistics?

3. The Declaration of Independence reads: "We hold these truths to be self-evident, that all men are created equal, that they are endowed by their Creator with certain unalienable rights, that among these are life, liberty and the pursuit of happiness." Do you think Hearne legitimately or illegitimately extends Jefferson's words to apply to nonhumans? Explain your position.

JAMAICA KINCAID

On Seeing England
for the First Time

One of the most sinister sides of imperialism is the way it promotes the ruling nation's culture and rejects the colony's. The effect of this on an impressionable young person is vividly described in Jamaica Kincaid's sensitive and angry autobiographical essay about growing up in Antigua with the dark shadow of England continually looming over her. England and a reverence for things English invaded every aspect of her daily life and education. Yet it was not until adulthood that she finally journeyed to England and really saw it for the first time. "The space between the idea of something and its reality," Kincaid writes, "is always wide and deep and dark." The real England she finally sees is far different from the other England, whose maps and history she was made to memorize as a schoolgirl in Antigua.

Kincaid is the author of At the Bottom of the River *(1983),* Annie John *(1985),* A Small Place *(1988),* Lucy *(1990),* The Autobiography of My Mother *(1996), and* My Brother *(1997). A staff writer for* The New Yorker, *her stories and essays have also appeared in* Rolling Stone, Paris Review, *and other literary periodicals. She was born in Antigua and currently lives in Vermont. "On Seeing England for the First Time" originally appeared in* Transition *(1991) and was selected by Susan Sontag for* The Best American Essays *1992.*

When I saw England for the first time, I was a child in school sitting at a desk. The England I was looking at was laid out on a map gently, beautifully, delicately, a very special jewel; it lay on a bed of sky blue — the background of the map — its yellow form mysterious, because though it looked like a leg of mutton, it could not really look like anything so familiar as a leg of mutton because it was England — with shadings of pink and green, unlike any shadings of pink and green I had seen before, squiggly veins of red running in every direction. England was a special jewel all right, and only special people got to wear it. The people who got to wear England were English people. They wore it well and they wore it everywhere: in jungles, in deserts, on plains, on top of the highest mountains, on all the oceans, on all the seas, in places where they were not welcome, in places they should not have been. When my teacher had pinned this map up on the blackboard, she said, "This is England" — and she said it with authority, seriousness, and adoration, and we all sat up. It was as if she had said, "This is Jerusalem, the place you will go to when you die but only if you have been good." We understood then — we were meant to understand then — that England was to be our source of myth and the source from which we got our sense of reality, our sense of what was meaningful, our sense of what was meaningless — and much about our own lives and much about the very idea of us headed that last list.

At the time I was a child sitting at my desk seeing England for the first time, I was already very familiar with the greatness of it. Each morning before I left for school, I ate a breakfast of half a grapefruit, an egg, bread and butter and a slice of cheese, and a cup of cocoa; or half a grapefruit, a bowl of oat porridge, bread and butter and a slice of cheese, and a cup of cocoa. The can of cocoa was often left on the table in front of me. It had written on it the name of the company, the year the company was established, and the words "Made in England." Those words, "Made in England," were written on the box the oats came in too. They would also have been written on the box the shoes I was wearing came in; a bolt of gray linen cloth lying on the shelf of a store from which my mother had bought three yards to make the uniform that I was wearing had written along its edge those three words. The shoes I wore were made in England; so were my socks and cotton undergarments and the satin ribbons I wore tied at the end of two plaits of my hair. My father, who might have sat next to me at breakfast, was a carpenter and cabinet maker. The shoes he wore to work would have been made in England, as were his khaki shirt and trousers, his underpants and undershirt, his socks and brown felt hat. Felt was not the proper material from which a hat that was expected to provide shade from the hot sun should be made, but my father must have seen and admired a picture of an Englishman wearing such a hat in England, and this picture that he saw must have been so compelling that it caused him to wear the wrong hat for a hot climate most of his long life. And this hat — a brown felt hat — became so central to his character that it was the first thing he put on in the morning as he stepped out of bed and the last thing he took off before he stepped back into bed at night. As we sat at breakfast a car might go by. The car, a Hillman or a Zephyr, was made in England. The very idea of the meal itself, breakfast, and its substantial quality and quantity was an idea from England; we somehow knew that in England they began the day with this meal called breakfast and a proper breakfast was a big breakfast. No one I knew liked eating so much food so early in the day; it made us feel sleepy, tired. But this breakfast business was Made in England like almost everything else that surrounded us, the exceptions being the sea, the sky, and the air we breathed.

At the time I saw this map — seeing England for the first time — I did not say to myself, "Ah, so that's what it looks like," because there was no longing in me to put a shape to those three words that ran through every part of my life, no matter how small; for me to have had such a longing would have meant that I lived in a certain atmosphere, an atmosphere in which those three words were felt as a burden. But I did not live in such an atmosphere. My father's brown felt hat would develop a hole in its crown, the lining would separate from the hat itself, and six weeks before he thought that he could not be seen wearing it — he was a very vain man — he would order another hat from England. And my mother taught me to eat my food in the English way: the knife in the right hand, the fork in the left, my elbows held still close to my side, the food carefully balanced on my fork and then brought up to my mouth. When I had finally mastered it, I overheard her saying to a friend, "Did you see how nicely she can eat?" But I knew then that I enjoyed my food more when I ate it with my bare hands, and I continued to do so when she wasn't looking. And when my teacher showed us the map, she asked us to study it carefully, because no test we would ever take would be complete without this statement: "Draw a map of England."

I did not know then that the statement "Draw a map of England" was something far worse than a declaration of war, for in fact a flat-out declaration of war would have put me on alert, and again in fact, there was no need for war — I had long ago been conquered. I did not know then that this statement was part of a process that would result in my erasure, not my physical erasure, but my erasure all the same. I did not know then that this statement was meant to make me feel in awe and small whenever I heard the word "England": awe at its existence, small because I was not from it. I did not know very much of anything then — certainly not what a blessing it was that I was unable to draw a map of England correctly.

After that there were many times of seeing England for the first time. I saw England in history. I knew the names of all the kings of England. I knew the names of their children, their wives, their disappointments, their triumphs, the names of people who betrayed them, I knew the dates on which they were born and the dates they died. I knew their conquests and was made to feel glad if I figured in them; I knew their defeats. I knew the details of the year 1066 (the Battle of Hastings, the end of the reign of the Anglo-Saxon kings) before I knew the details of the year 1832 (the year slavery was abolished). It wasn't as bad as I make it sound now; it was worse. I did like so much hearing again and again how Alfred the Great, traveling in disguise, had been left to watch cakes, and because he wasn't used to this the cakes got burned, and Alfred burned his hands pulling them out of the fire, and the woman who had left him to watch the cakes screamed at him. I loved King Alfred. My grandfather was named after him; his son, my uncle, was named after King Alfred; my brother is named after King Alfred. And so there are three people in my family named after a man they have never met, a man who died over ten centuries ago. The first view I got of England then was not unlike the first view received by the person who named my grandfather.

This view, though — the naming of the kings, their deeds, their disappointments — was the vivid view, the forceful view. There were other views, subtler ones, softer, almost not there — but these were the ones that made the most lasting impression on me, these

were the ones that made me really feel like nothing. "When morning touched the sky" was one phrase, for no morning touched the
sky where I lived. The mornings where I lived came on abruptly,
with a shock of heat and loud noises. "Evening approaches" was
another, but the evenings where I lived did not approach; in fact, I
had no evening — I had night and I had day and they came and
went in a mechanical way: on, off; on, off. And then there were
gentle mountains and low blue skies and moors over which people
took walks for nothing but pleasure, when where I lived a walk was
an act of labor, a burden, something only death or the automobile
could relieve. And there were things that a small turn of a head
could convey — entire worlds, whole lives would depend on this
thing, a certain turn of a head. Everyday life could be quite tiring,
more tiring than anything I was told not to do. I was told not to
gossip, but they did that all the time. And they ate so much food,
violating another of those rules they taught me: do not indulge in
gluttony. And the foods they ate actually: if only sometime I could
eat cold cuts after theater, cold cuts of lamb and mint sauce, and
Yorkshire pudding and scones, and clotted cream, and sausages
that came from upcountry (imagine, "up-country"). And having
troubling thoughts at twilight, a good time to have troubling
thoughts, apparently; and servants who stole and left in the middle
of a crisis, who were born with a limp or some other kind of defor-
mity, not nourished properly in their mother's womb (that last
part I figured out for myself; the point was, oh to have an untrust-
worthy servant); and wonderful cobbled streets onto which solid
front doors opened; and people whose eyes were blue and who had
fair skins and who smelled only of lavender, or sometimes sweet
pea or primrose. And those flowers with those names: delphini-
ums, foxgloves, tulips, daffodils, floribunda, peonies; in bloom, a
striking display, being cut and placed in large glass bowls, crystal,
decorating rooms so large twenty families the size of mine could fit
in comfortably but used only for passing through. And the weather
was so remarkable because the rain fell gently always, only occasionally in deep gusts, and it colored the air various shades of gray,
each an appealing shade for a dress to be worn when a portrait was
being painted; and when it rained at twilight, wonderful things
happened: people bumped into each other unexpectedly and that
would lead to all sorts of turns of events — a plot, the mere weather

caused plots. I saw that people rushed: they rushed to catch trains, they rushed toward each other and away from each other; they rushed and rushed and rushed. That word: rushed! I did not know what it was to do that. It was too hot to do that, and so I came to envy people who would rush, even though it had no meaning to me to do such a thing. But there they are again. They loved their children; their children were sent to their own rooms as a punishment, rooms larger than my entire house. They were special, everything about them said so, even their clothes; their clothes rustled, swished, soothed. The world was theirs, not mine; everything told me so.

If now as I speak of all this I give the impression of someone on the outside looking in, nose pressed up against a glass window, that is wrong. My nose was pressed up against a glass window all right, but there was an iron vise at the back of my neck forcing my head to stay in place. To avert my gaze was to fall back into something from which I had been rescued, a hole filled with nothing, and that was the word for everything about me, nothing. The reality of my life was conquests, subjugation, humiliation, enforced amnesia. I was forced to forget. Just for instance, this: I lived in a part of St. John's, Antigua, called Ovals. Ovals was made up of five streets, each of them named after a famous English seaman — to be quite frank, an officially sanctioned criminal: Rodney Street (after George Rodney), Nelson Street (after Horatio Nelson), Drake Street (after Francis Drake), Hood Street, and Hawkins Street (after John Hawkins). But John Hawkins was knighted after a trip he made to Africa, opening up a new trade, the slave trade. He was then entitled to wear as his crest a Negro bound with a cord. Every single person living on Hawkins Street was descended from a slave. John Hawkins's ship, the one in which he transported the people he had bought and kidnapped, was called *The Jesus*. He later became the treasurer of the Royal Navy and rear admiral.

Again, the reality of my life, the life I led at the time I was being shown these views of England for the first time, for the second time, for the one-hundred-millionth time, was this: the sun shone with what sometimes seemed to be a deliberate cruelty; we must have done something to deserve that. My dresses did not rustle in the evening air as I strolled to the theater (I had no evening, I had no theater; my dresses were made of a cheap cotton, the weave of which would give way after not too many washings). I got up in the morning, I did my chores (fetched water from the public pipe for my mother, swept the yard), I washed myself, I went to a woman to have my hair combed freshly every day (because before we were allowed into our classroom our teachers would inspect us, and children who had not bathed that day, or had dirt under their fingernails, or whose hair had not been combed anew that day, might not be allowed to attend class). I ate that breakfast. I walked to school. At school we gathered in an auditorium and sang a hymn, "All Things Bright and Beautiful," and looking down on us as we sang were portraits of the Queen of England and her husband; they wore jewels and medals and they smiled. I was a Brownie. At each meeting we would form a little group around a flagpole, and after raising the Union Jack, we would say, "I promise to do my best, to do my duty to God and the Queen, to help other people every day and obey the scouts' law."

Who were these people and why had I never seen them, I mean really seen them, in the place where they lived? I had never been to England. No one I knew had ever been to England, or I should say, no one I knew had ever been and returned to tell me about it. All the people I knew who had gone to England had stayed there. Sometimes they left behind them their small children, never to see them again. England! I had seen England's representatives. I had seen the governor general at the public grounds at a ceremony celebrating the Queen's birthday. I had seen an old princess and I had seen a young princess. They had both been extremely not beautiful, but who of us would have told them that? I had never seen England, really seen it, I had only met a representative, seen a picture, read books, memorized its history. I had never set foot, my own foot, in it.

The space between the idea of something and its reality is always wide and deep and dark. The longer they are kept apart — idea of thing, reality of thing — the wider the width, the deeper the depth, the thicker and darker the darkness. This space starts out empty, there is nothing in it, but it rapidly becomes filled up with obsession or desire or hatred or love — sometimes all of these things, sometimes some of these things, sometimes only one of these things. The existence of the world as I came to know it was a

result of this: idea of thing over here, reality of thing way, way over there. There was Christopher Columbus, an unlikable man, an un- pleasant man, a liar (and so, of course, a thief) surrounded by maps and schemes and plans, and there was the reality on the other side of that width, that depth, that darkness. He became ob- sessed, he became filled with desire, the hatred came later, love was never a part of it. Eventually, his idea met the longed-for real- ity. That the idea of something and its reality are often two com- pletely different things is something no one ever remembers; and so when they meet and find that they are not compatible, the weaker of the two, idea or reality, dies. That idea Christopher Columbus had was more powerful than the reality he met, and so the reality he met died.

And so finally, when I was a grown-up woman, the mother of two children, the wife of someone, a person who resides in a powerful country that takes up more than its fair share of a continent, the owner of a house with many rooms in it and of two automobiles, with the desire and will (which I very much act upon) to take from the world more than I give back to it, more than I deserve, more than I need, finally then, I saw England, the real England, not a picture, not a painting, not through a story in a book, but Eng- land, for the first time. In me, the space between the idea of it and its reality had become filled with hatred, and so when at last I saw it I wanted to take it into my hands and tear it into little pieces and then crumble it up as if it were clay, child's clay. That was impossi- ble, and so I could only indulge in not-favorable opinions.

There were monuments everywhere; they commemorated victo- ries, battles fought between them and the people who lived across the sea from them, all vile people, fought over which of them would have dominion over the people who looked like me. The monuments were useless to them now, people sat on them and ate their lunch. They were like markers on an old useless trail, like a piece of old string tied to a finger to jog the memory, like old dec- oration in an old house, dirty, useless, in the way. Their skins were so pale, it made them look so fragile, so weak, so ugly. What if I had the power to simply banish them from their land, send boat after boatload of them on a voyage that in fact had no destination, force them to live in a place where the sun's presence was a con- stant? This would rid them of their pale complexion and make

them look more like me, make them look more like the people I
love and treasure and hold dear, and more like the people who occupy the near and far reaches of my imagination, my history, my
geography, and reduce them and everything they have ever known
to figurines as evidence that I was in divine favor, what if all this
was in my power? Could I resist it? No one ever has.

And they were rude, they were rude to each other. They didn't
like each other very much. They didn't like each other in the way
they didn't like me, and it occurred to me that their dislike for me
was one of the few things they agreed on.

I was on a train in England with a friend, an English woman.
Before we were in England she liked me very much. In England
she didn't like me at all. She didn't like the claim I said I had on
England, she didn't like the views I had of England. I didn't like
England, she didn't like England, but she didn't like me not liking
it too. She said, "I want to show you my England, I want to show
you the England that I know and love." I had told her many times
before that I knew England and I didn't want to love it anyway. She
no longer lived in England; it was her own country, but it had not
been kind to her, so she left. On the train, the conductor was rude
to her; she asked something, and he responded in a rude way. She
became ashamed. She was ashamed at the way he treated her;
she was ashamed at the way he behaved. "This is the new England,"
she said. But I liked the conductor being rude; his behavior
seemed quite appropriate. Earlier this had happened: we had
gone to a store to buy a shirt for my husband; it was meant to be a
special present, a special shirt to wear on special occasions. This
was a store where the Prince of Wales has his shirts made, but the
shirts sold in this store are beautiful all the same. I found a shirt I
thought my husband would like and I wanted to buy him a tie to go
with it. When I couldn't decide which one to choose, the salesman
showed me a new set. He was very pleased with these, he said, because they bore the crest of the Prince of Wales, and the Prince of
Wales had never allowed his crest to decorate an article of clothing
before. There was something in the way he said it; his tone was
slavish, reverential, awed. It made me feel angry; I wanted to hit
him. I didn't do that. I said, my husband and I hate princes, my
husband would never wear anything that had a prince's anything
on it. My friend stiffened. The salesman stiffened. They both drew
themselves in, away from me. My friend told me that the prince

was a symbol of her Englishness, and I could see that I had caused offense. I looked at her. She was an English person, the sort of English person I used to know at home, the sort who was nobody in England but somebody when they came to live among the people like me. There were many people I could have seen England with; that I was seeing it with this particular person, a person who reminded me of the people who showed me England long ago as I sat in church or at my desk, made me feel silent and afraid, for I wondered if, all these years of our friendship, I had had a friend or had been in the thrall of a racial memory.

I went to Bath — we, my friend and I, did this, but though we were together, I was no longer with her. The landscape was almost as familiar as my own hand, but I had never been in this place before, so how could that be again? And the streets of Bath were familiar, too, but I had never walked on them before. It was all those years of reading, starting with Roman Britain. Why did I have to know about Roman Britain? It was of no real use to me, a person living on a hot, drought-ridden island, and it is of no use to me now, and yet my head is filled with this nonsense, Roman Britain. In Bath, I drank tea in a room I had read about in a novel written in the eighteenth century. In this very same room, young women wearing those dresses that rustled and so on danced and flirted and sometimes disgraced themselves with young men, soldiers, sailors, who were on their way to Bristol or someplace like that, so many places like that where so many adventures, the outcome of which was not good for me, began. Bristol, England. A sentence that began "That night the ship sailed from Bristol, England" would end not so good for me. And then I was driving through the countryside in an English motorcar, on narrow winding roads, and they were so familiar, though I had never been on them before; and through little villages the names of which I somehow knew so well though I had never been there before. And the countryside did have all those hedges and hedges, fields hedged in. I was marveling at all the toil of it, the planting of the hedges to begin with and then the care of it, all that clipping, year after year of clipping, and I wondered at the lives of the people who would have to do this, because wherever I see and feel the hands that hold up the world, I see and feel myself and all the people who look like me. And I said, "Those hedges" and my friend said that someone, a woman named Mrs. Rothchild, worried that the hedges weren't being taken care of properly; the farmers couldn't afford or find the help to keep up the hedges, and often they replaced them with wire fencing. I might have said to that, well if Mrs. Rothchild doesn't like the wire fencing, why doesn't she take care of the hedges herself, but I didn't. And then in those fields that were now hemmed in by wire fencing that a privileged woman didn't like was planted a vile yellow flowering bush that produced an oil, and my friend said that Mrs. Rothchild didn't like this either; it ruined the English countryside, it ruined the traditional look of the English countryside.

It was not at that moment that I wished every sentence, everything I knew, that began with England would end with "and then it all died; we don't know how, it just all died." At that moment, I was thinking, who are these people who forced me to think of them all the time, who forced me to think that the world I knew was incomplete, or without substance, or did not measure up because it was not England; that I was incomplete, or without substance, and did not measure up because I was not English. Who were these people? The person sitting next to me couldn't give me a clue; no one person could. In any case, if I had said to her, I find England ugly, I hate England; the weather is like a jail sentence, the English are a very ugly people, the food in England is like a jail sentence, the hair of English people is so straight, so dead looking, the English have an unbearable smell so different from the smell of people I know, real people of course, she would have said that I was a person full of prejudice. Apart from the fact that it is I — that is, the people who look like me — who made her aware of the unpleasantness of such a thing, the idea of such a thing, prejudice, she would have been only partly right, sort of right: I may be capable of prejudice, but my prejudices have no weight to them, my prejudices have no force behind them, my prejudices remain opinions, my prejudices remain my personal opinion. And a great feeling of rage and disappointment came over me as I looked at England, my head full of personal opinions that could not have public, my public, approval. The people I come from are powerless to do evil on grand scale.

The moment I wished every sentence, everything I knew, that began with England would end with "and then it all died, we don't know how, it just all died" was when I saw the white cliffs of Dover.

I had sung hymns and recited poems that were about a longing to
see the white cliffs of Dover again. At the time I sang the hymns
and recited the poems, I could really long to see them again because I had never seen them at all, nor had anyone around me at
the time. But there we were, groups of people longing for something we had never seen. And so there they were, the white cliffs,
but they were not that pearly majestic thing I used to sing about,
that thing that created such a feeling in these people that when
they died in the place where I lived they had themselves buried
facing a direction that would allow them to see the white cliffs of
Dover when they were resurrected, as surely they would be. The
white cliffs of Dover, when finally I saw them, were cliffs, but they
were not white; you would only call them that if the word "white"
meant something special to you; they were dirty and they were
steep; they were so steep, the correct height from which all my
views of England, starting with the map before me in my classroom and ending with the trip I had just taken, should jump and
die and disappear forever.

compare
contrast.

Reflections and Responses

1. Note that Kincaid opens her essay with various images of England. What do these images have in common? How do they reflect colonialism? How do they reflect literature? Why do you think
Kincaid begins by placing the images in the context of a classroom?

2. Consider Kincaid's account of her father's hat. In what ways
does the "brown felt hat" represent England? How does Kincaid
view the hat?

3. When Kincaid finally visits England, what aspects of the country does she dislike the most? What does she mean when she says
toward the end of her essay that "I may be capable of prejudice,
but my prejudices have no weight to them"? Do you find her opinions prejudiced? In your opinion has she or has she not "pre-
judged" England?

THOMAS PALMER

The Case for Human Beings

Are human beings a plague on the planet? Are we a species whose sole pur-
pose appears to be the destruction of all other species? Unfortunately, ac-
cording to Thomas Palmer, many people today think this way: "In the past
twenty years this argument has conquered much of the world; it may soon
become part of the thinking of nearly every schoolchild." In "The Case for
Human Beings," Palmer carefully constructs a counterargument to this
pessimistic view, demonstrating that once human beings entered the scene
about a half million years ago the natural world was irrevocably changed,
though contemporary biologists and ecologists are reluctant to acknowledge
that fact. "Maybe it's time," Palmer argues, "to give up the notion of human
beings as intruders, tramplers, and destroyers."

Thomas Palmer is the author of several novels, including The Transfer
(1983) and Dream Science *(1990). "The Case for Human Beings," he*
writes, "is an attempt to come to terms intellectually with the emotional tur-
moil anyone with 'green' sympathies must suffer as the old disappears and
the new takes its place." The essay, which originally appeared in The Atlantic Monthly, *is adapted from* Landscape with Reptile: Rattlesnakes
in an Urban World *(1992), a natural and cultural history of the Boston*
area's last timber rattlesnakes. The essay was selected by Joseph Epstein for
The Best American Essays 1993.

An argument, a human argument, maintains that we ought to be
concerned about the disappearance of individual animal species.
If it could be directed at the objects of its solicitude, it would go
approximately as follows: "You lesser beasts had better watch your
step—*we'll* decide when you can leave." It recognizes that once
chromosome patterns combine at the species level, they become

unique and irreplaceable — one cannot make a rattlesnake, for instance, out of anything but more rattlesnakes. It looks at the speed at which such patterns are disappearing and shudders to think how empty our grandchildren's world might become, patternwise.

In the past twenty years this argument has conquered much of the world; it may soon become part of the thinking of nearly every schoolchild.

Perhaps because we ourselves are a species, we regard the species level as that at which deaths become truly irreversible. Populations, for instance, can and do fade in and out; when a species dies, however, we call it extinct and retire its name forever, being reasonably certain that it will not reappear in its old form.

Students of evolution have shown that species death, or extinction, is going on all the time, and that it is an essential feature of life history. Species are adapted to their environments; as environments change, some species find themselves in the position of islanders whose islands are washing away, and they go under. Similarly, new islands (or environments) are appearing all the time, and they almost invariably produce new species.

What alarms so many life historians is not that extinctions are occurring but that they appear to be occurring at a greater rate than they have at all but a few times in the past, raising the specter of the sort of wholesale die-offs that ended the reign of the dinosaurs. Do we want, they ask, to exile most of our neighbors to posterity? Exactly how much of our planet's resources do we mean to funnel into people-making? Such questions are serious; they involve choosing among futures, and some of these futures are already with us, in the form of collapsing international fisheries, rich grasslands gnawed and trampled into deserts, forests skeletonized by windborne acids, and so forth. Thus high rates of extinction are seen as a symptom of major problems in the way our species operates — problems that may, if we're not careful, be solved for us. A new word has been coined to define the value most threatened by these overheated rates: "biodiversity." As species disappear, biodiversity declines, and our planet's not-quite-limitless fund of native complexities — so some argue — declines with it.

The process described above is indeed occurring. Human beings tend to change environments; when they do, species vanish. The Puritans, for example, though famous for their efforts to discipline

sexuality, imposed upon Massachusetts an orgy of ecological licen-
tiousness: they introduced dozens of microbes, weeds, and pests
foreign to the region, some of which played havoc with the natives.
Human beings tend to travel everywhere, and to bring their cats,
rats, and fleas with them, so that hardly any environment is truly
isolated today, and creatures that evolved in isolated environments
have paid a high price. Of the 171 species and subspecies of birds
that have become extinct in the past three years, for example, 155
were island forms.

Since extinction is a particularly final and comprehensive form
of death, species preservation and its corollary, habitat protection,
are now seen as the most important means available to stem the
erosion of biodiversity. So far, so good — but I wonder if these
ideas, which emphasize diversity at the species level, fail to give an
adequate picture of recent biological history. If, for instance, biodiversity is regarded as the chief measure of a landscape's richness,
then the American continents reached their peak of splendor on
the day after the first Siberian spearmen arrived, and have been
deteriorating ever since. More recent developments — such as the
domestication of maize, the rise of civilizations in Mexico and
Peru, and the passage of the U.S. Bill of Rights — are neutral at
best, and are essentially invisible, since they are the work of a single species, a species no more or less weighty than any other, and
already present at the start of the interval. But what kind of yard-
stick measures a handful of skinclad hunters against Chicago, Los
Angeles, and Caracas, and finds one group no more "diverse" than
the other?

A considerable amount of pessimism is built into this species-
based notion of diversity. Nearly all change on such a scale is change
for the worse — especially human-mediated change. Change involves stress, and stress causes extinctions; each extinction is another pock in the skin of an edenic original. This original is frozen
in time; more often than not, it is defined as the blissful instant
just prior to the arrival of the first human being. In fact, the only
way to re-create this instant, and restore biodiversity to its greatest
possible richness, would be to arrange for every human being on
earth to drop dead tomorrow.

This is not to say that cities are better than coral reefs, or that
binary codes are an improvement on genetic ones, but only that

"biodiversity" cannot adequately account for the phenomenon of *Homo sapiens.*

Maybe it's time to give up the notion of human beings as intruders, tramplers, and destroyers. We are all of these, there's no doubt about it, but they are not all we are. And yet the same mind-set that interprets human history as little more than a string of increasingly lurid ecological crimes also insists that our species represents the last, best hope of "saving" the planet. Is it any wonder that the future looks bleak?

Here we have the essential Puritan outlook disguised as science — human beings, the sinners, occupy center stage, and cannot move a muscle without risking the direst consequences in a cosmic drama. At stake is the fate of the world; thousands of innocents (other species) rely on the shaky powers of human foresight. One false step — and our ancestors, as we know, have taken almost nothing but false steps — and our dwelling place may be mutilated beyond redemption.

This outlook is realistic in its recognition that our species is different in kind from all others, as any visitor from outer space would admit; it is obnoxious in the limits it places on the organic experiment. Human consciousness — whether in the form of Bach chorales, three-masted schooners, or microwave communications — cannot, in this view, contribute to biodiversity, except by staying as far out of the picture as possible, so as to avoid tainting still-intact landscapes with unnatural influences. The possibility that chorales and schooners might represent positive contributions to biotic richness — that they might, just as much as any rain forest orchid, embody the special genius of this planet — is never admitted. Somehow an agreement has been reached to exclude whatever is human from the sum of biodiversity — as if the Apollo landings, for example, do not represent an astonishing breakthrough *in strictly biological terms.*

This view has a certain legitimacy as long as its definition of diversity is narrowly chromosomal, or species-based. Those environments richest in species — the tropical forests and the warmwater seas — are, from its perspective, the most diverse and complex. But I would argue that this definition, though accurate enough for most of the history of life, became obsolete about a half million years ago, when *Homo sapiens* came on the scene. This creature released organic change from its age-old dependence on genetic recombination and harnessed it to new energies — culture, symbolic language, and imagination. As is becoming more and more evident, nothing has been the same since.

Being reluctant to acknowledge this fact, ecologists, biologists, and environmentalists have had fits trying to introduce our species into their models of the natural world. These models are based on the idea of balance, or equilibrium, wherein each variety of plant or animal plays a limited, genetically prescribed role in the cycling of materials and energy. The roles are not absolutely fixed — natural selection, by sorting and resorting chromosomes, can adapt lines of descent to new ones — but change, by and large, is assumed to be gradual, and millions of years can pass without any notable restructuring of communities.

Human beings cannot be worked into such models. One cannot look at human beings and predict what they will eat, or where they will live, or how many of their children a given landscape will support. If they inhabit a forest, they may burn it down and raise vegetables, or flood it and plant rice, or sell it to a pulp and paper manufacturer. They may think of anything; the life their parents led is not a reliable blueprint, but merely a box with a thousand exits. Moralists in search of instructive contrasts will sometimes idealize primitive societies, claiming that they deliberately live "in balance" with their environments, but these examples don't stand up to scrutiny. The Massachuset Indians, for instance, though sometimes presented as sterling conservationists, were the descendants of aboriginal American hunters who appear to have pursued a whole constellation of Ice Age mammals to extinction (including several species of horses). When in historical times, they were offered metal fishhooks, knives, and firearms, they didn't say, "Thanks, but we prefer rock-chipping."

The revelation that we are not like other creatures in certain crucial respects is an ancient one, and may be nearly as old as humanity; it probably contributed to the idea, central to several major religions, that we inhabit a sort of permanent exile. Until recently, however, we could still imagine ourselves encompassed by, if not entirely contained in, landscapes dominated by non-human forces — weather, infectious illness, growing seasons, light and darkness, and so forth. This is no longer so; today most human beings live in artificial wildernesses called cities, and don't raise the food they eat, or know where the water they drink fell as rain. A sort of vertigo has set in — a feeling that a rhythm has been upset, and that soon nothing will be left of the worlds that made us. This feeling is substantiated by population curves, ocean pollution, chemical changes in the earth's atmosphere, vanishing wildlife, mountains of garbage, and numerous other signs that anyone can read. The nineteenth-century conservation movement, which sought to preserve landscapes for largely aesthetic reasons, has become absorbed in the twentieth-century environmental movement, which insists that more is at stake than postcard views. We are, it argues, near to exceeding the carrying capacity of our planet's natural systems, systems whose importance to us will become very obvious when they begin to wobble and fail.

These are not empty warnings. Human communities can and occasionally do self-destruct by overstraining their resource bases. Historical examples include the Easter Islanders, the lowland Maya, and some of the classical-era city-dwellers of the Middle East and North Africa. But if we set aside the equilibrium-based models of the ecologists and do not limit ourselves to species-bound notions of diversity — in other words, if we seek to include human beings in the landscape of nature, rather than make them outcasts — what sort of picture do we get of the phenomenon of life?

The difference between life and nonlife, according to the biologists, is a matter of degree. A glass of seawater, for instance, contains many of the same materials as a condor (or a green turtle). What makes one alive and the other not are the varying chemical pathways those materials follow. The glass of water contains few internal boundaries, and gases diffuse freely across its surface. In the condor, in contrast, a much more complex array of reactions is in progress, reactions that maintain certain molecular-energy potentials in an oddly elevated state, even though the bird as a whole shows a net energy loss. In other words, both the condor and the glass of water cycle energy, but in the condor the energy goes to support a level of complexity not present in the water.

Perhaps the condor is more like a candle flame — both burn energy, and that burning keeps certain patterns intact. The condor, like the candle, can burn out. But although one can relight the candle, one cannot relight the condor — it is too delicately tuned, too dependent on various internal continuities.

As useful as these distinctions are, they tend to blur under increased magnification. A virus, for instance, is more condorlike than flamelike, because the energy and materials it draws from its surroundings reappear not primarily as heat, light, and simple oxides but as viral protein and nucleic acids — complex substances that the flame cannot construct but only disassemble. And yet most students agree that viruses are not alive, because they cannot build these substances without the aid of the machineries inside a living cell. A certain level of independence is necessary — living things, according to this definition, not only must transform simple compounds into more varied and characteristic ones but also must be able to do so in an atmosphere of nonlife.

Life, for the biologists, is an uphill or retrograde process — it adds order and complexity to environments whose overall tendency is toward diffusion and disorder. It captures energies released by decay and exploits them for growth and rebirth. It is startlingly anomalous in this respect: so far as we know, it occurs nowhere but on the surface of this planet, and even here its appearance seems to have been a one-time-only event; though many lifelike substances have been produced inside sterile glassware, none has ever quickened into veritable beasthood.

The evidence suggests that life continued to fructify and elaborate itself for several billion years after its appearance. The milestones along the way — the nucleated cell, photosynthesis, sexual reproduction, multicellularity, the internal skeleton, the invasion of the land and sky, and so forth — are usually interpreted as advances, because they added additional layers of complexity, interconnection, and ordered interaction to existing systems. This drama did not proceed without crises — photosynthesis, for instance, probably wiped out entire ecosystems by loading the atmosphere with a deadly poison, free oxygen — but life as a whole laughed at such insults, and continued on its protean way.

If we believe that all life — in contrast to rocks and gases — shares a certain quality of sensitivity, or self-awareness, then *Homo sapiens* was an astonishing and wholly unpredictable leap forward in this respect, because human beings manifested an idea of personhood never before achieved. The exact moment of this discovery is of course problematic, as are most events in evolution, but I would date it from early summer about sixty thousand years ago, when a group of Neanderthals living in present-day Iraq lost one of their members, dug a grave for him in the Shanidar Cave of the Zagros Mountain highlands, placed his body inside, and covered it with yarrow blossoms, cornflowers, hyacinths, and mallows. Here, in a gesture of remarkable grace, a group of living creatures betrayed an awareness that creatureliness is a pose, a pose that can't be held forever.

The poignancy of this moment is profound. Though the idea is startling to consider, all the evidence suggests that most of life's history has unfolded unobserved, so to speak. I would bet that the dinosaurs, for instance, did not know that they were reptiles, or that they had faces like their neighbors, or that they once hatched from eggs like their offspring.

Consciousness. Mind. Insight. Here are qualities that, if not exclusively human, seem appallingly rudimentary elsewhere. Primitive peoples distributed them throughout their worlds; we moderns hold to stricter standards of evidence. Does a cloud yearn, for instance, to drop rain? Is a seed eager to sprout?

The irruption of thoughtfulness that our species represents is not inexplicable in Darwinian terms. Once our apelike and erect ancestors began using weapons, hunting large animals, and sharing the spoils, the ability to develop plans and communicate them acquired considerable survival value, and was genetically enhanced. This ability, and the tripling in brain weight that accompanied it, turned out to be one of the most revolutionary experiments in the history of gene-sorting. It was as if Nature, after wearing out several billion years tossing off new creatures like nutshells, looked up to see that one had come back, and was eyeing her strangely.

The distance between that moment and today is barely a hiccup, geologically speaking. We are genetically almost indistinguishable from those bear-roasters and mammoth-stickers. But the world is a different place now. Grad students in ecology, for instance, are expected to do a certain amount of "fieldwork," and many of them have to travel hundreds and even thousands of miles before they consider themselves far enough from classrooms to be in the field.

Plainly, our planet contained vast opportunities for creatures willing to shape it consciously toward their ends. The way was clear; we know of no other species that has divined what we've been up to or has a mind to object. What seems simple to us is far beyond them; it's almost as if we move so fast that we are invisible, and they are still trying to pretend — without much success — that the world is the same as it was before we arrived.

This speed on the uptake appears to be the chief advantage that cultural adaptation has over genetic. When human beings encounter new circumstances, adaptation rarely depends on which individuals are genetically best suited to adjust, passing on their abilities more successfully than others and producing subsequent generations better adapted to the new order. No, human beings tend to cut the loop short by noticing the new, puzzling over it, telling their friends, and attempting to find out immediately whether it is edible, combustible, domesticable, or whatever. In this way we develop traditions that are immaterial, so to speak, in that they evolve on a track largely disengaged from the double helix.

This talent for endless jabber and experiment, and the pooling of useful knowledge it makes possible, means that human beings, unlike orangutans or condors, operate not primarily as individuals scattered over a landscape but as shareholders in a common fund of acquired skills, many of them the work of previous generations. This fund is extraordinarily deep and sophisticated, even among the most isolated bands of hunter-gatherers; when, as in recent times, it has included experience accumulated by thousands or even millions of forebears, it has enabled our species to become the quickest-acting agent of change in life's history. In fact, we might sensibly think of the human species not as five billion distinct selves but as five billion nodes in a single matrix, just as the human body is more commonly considered a unit than an accumulation of cells.

If life, as before noted, is a paradoxical chemical process by which order arises from disorder, and a movement toward uniformity produces more complex local conditions, then human enterprise, though full of disasters for other species, is clearly not outside the main line of development. Equatorial rain forests, for instance, are probably the most diverse and multifaceted communities of species on earth. But are they more densely stuffed with highly refined codes and labels than, say, the Library of Congress? Long ago certain moths learned to communicate over as much as two miles of thick woods by releasing subtle chemicals that prospective mates could detect at levels measured in parts per million; today a currency broker in Tokyo can pick up a phone and hear accurate copies of sounds vocalized a split second earlier by a counterpart on the other side of the world. Which system of signals is more sensitive and flexible?

I am concerned, as is obvious, with an image — the image of our species as a vast, featureless mob of yahoos mindlessly trampling this planet's most ancient and delicate harmonies. This image, which is on its way to becoming an article of faith, is not a completely inaccurate description of present conditions in some parts of the world, but it portrays the human presence as a sort of monolithic disaster, when in fact *Homo sapiens* is the crown of creation, if by creation we mean the explosion of earthly vitality and particularity long ago ignited by a weak solution of amino acids mixing in sunlit waters. Change — dramatic, wholesale change — is one of the most reliable constants of this story. To say that the changes we have brought, and will continue to bring, are somehow alien to the world, and are within a half inch of making its "natural" continuance impossible, displays some contempt, I think, for the forces at work, along with a large dose of inverted pride. Who are we, for instance, to say what's possible and what isn't? Have we already glimpsed the end? Where exactly did things go awry? It's useful to remember that just yesterday our main concern was finding something to eat.

I prefer to suppose that we will be here awhile, and that such abilities as we have, though unprecedented in certain respects, are not regrettable. The human mind, for instance, could never have set itself the task of preserving rare species if earlier minds had not learned how to distinguish light from darkness, or coordinate limbs, or identify mates. Now that we think we know something about our immediate neighborhood, we are beginning to realize what a rare quality life is, and if we think of its multibillion-year history on earth as a sort of gradual awakening of matter, we must conclude that the dawning of human consciousness represents one of the most extraordinary sunrises on record. Is it any wonder, then, that the world is changing?

Perhaps because we have become so expert at interrogating our surroundings, we tremble a little at our own shadows. God, for instance, has become almost a fugitive. We have disassembled the atom; we have paced off the galaxies; He doesn't figure in our equations.

Maybe it would be useful at this point to compare our common birthplace to a fertile hen's egg. Nearly everyone has seen the delicate tracery of blood vessels that begins to spread across the yolk of such an egg within a few hours of laying. Before long a tiny pump starts to twitch rhythmically, and it drives a bright scarlet fluid through these vessels. The egg doesn't know that it is on its way to becoming a chicken. Chickens, for the egg, lie somewhere on the far side of the beginning of time. And yet the egg couldn't be better equipped to make a chicken out of itself.

I would argue that our planet, like the egg, is on a mission of sorts. We don't know what that mission is any more than the nascent nerve cells in the egg know why they are forming a network. All we know is that things are changing rapidly and dramatically.

Today many believe that these changes are often for the worse, and represent a fever or virus from which the body of life will emerge crippled and scarred. We look back with longing on a time, only a moment ago, when the human presence barely dimpled the landscaped — when the yolk, so to speak, was at its creamiest, and no angry little eye spots signaled an intent to devour everything.

I'm not persuaded by this picture — I think it arises from a mistaken belief that the outlines of earthly perfection are already evident. It has inspired a small army of doomsayers — if we burn the forests of the Amazon, we are told, our planet's lungs will give out, and we will slowly asphyxiate. Surely we have better, more practical reasons for not burning them than to stave off universal catastrophe. I can easily imagine similar arguments that would have required the interior of North America to remain empty of cities — and yet I don't think this continent is a poorer place now than it was twenty thousand years ago. The more convinced we are that our species is a plague, the more we are obliged to yearn for disasters.

Students of historical psychology have noticed that the end of the world is always at hand. For the Puritan preachers it was to take the form of divine wrath, and they warned that the Wampanoag war was only a foretaste. The Yankees saw it coming in the flood of nineteenth-century immigrants, who meant to drown true Americanism. Today we are more likely to glimpse it in canned aerosols, poisoned winds, and melting ice caps.

Curiously enough, the end of the world always *is* at hand — the world dies and is reborn on a daily basis. A fertile hen's egg is never today what it was yesterday, or will be tomorrow. Few would deny that the effort to preserve and protect as many as possible of the millions of species now existing represents a fresh and heartening expansion of human ambitions. But to suppose that earthly diversity is past its prime, and that a strenuous program of self-effacement is the best contribution our species has left to offer, is neither good biology nor good history.

Reflections and Responses

1. Palmer believes that those who "emphasize diversity at the species level" do not provide an adequate picture of the natural life of the planet. What is "a species-based notion of diversity" and why does Palmer focus on this view in his essay?

2. According to Palmer, why don't human beings fit into the "species-based diversity" model? What happened in present-day Iraq one early summer day some sixty thousand years ago? Why does Palmer find that moment profound? How does it support his argument?

3. Throughout his essay Palmer associates current ecological notions with pessimism and doomsaying. What is the basis for his perspective? Why does he consider his own argument about human beings as more optimistic? Do you agree or disagree with his conclusions?

SUSAN SONTAG

A Century of Cinema

*If you enjoy today's movies, be prepared to argue with Susan Sontag, who
sees the recent history of film as "an ignominious, irreversible decline." The
main reason for this decline, Sontag suggests, is that the film industry is
now more of an "industry" than ever before; given the enormous costs of
production, movie makers today seek out only products that will be commer-
cially successful. Thus, film-making, she argues, is derivative and engaged
mainly in the business of "reproducing past successes." And if original
film-making is nearly dead, so, too, is cinephilia — "the name of the very
specific kind of love that cinema inspired." In the following essay, she maps
out a brief history of cinema's 100 years and provides us with a sense of
what it meant at one time (not so long ago) to be a cinephile — someone who
"wanted to be kidnapped by the movie." A noted cinephile herself, she refers
throughout the essay to many distinguished and innovative film-makers,
both foreign and American. Although a number of these will be unfamiliar
to most readers, to gloss each of them with a biographical footnote would interrupt the flow of the essay and diminish its spirit. I have therefore kept the
glosses to a minimum.*

    Susan Sontag is the author of three novels, The Benefactor, Death
Kit, *and* The Volcano Lover; *a collection of stories,* I, etcetera; *a play,*
Alice in Bed; *and five books of essays, including* On Photography, Ill-
ness as Metaphor, *and* Under the Sign of Saturn. *She has also writ-
ten and directed four feature-length films and directed plays in the United
States and Europe, her most recent theatre work being a staging of Beckett's*
Waiting for Godot *in besieged Sarajevo. Her new novel,* In America,
will be published in 2000.

Cinema's hundred years seem to have the shape of a life cycle: an
inevitable birth, the steady accumulation of glories, and the onset

in the last decade of an ignominious, irreversible decline. This doesn't mean that there won't be any more new films that one can admire. But such films will not simply be exceptions; that's true of great achievement in any art. They will have to be heroic violations of the norms and practices that now govern moviemaking every-where in the capitalist and would-be capitalist world — which is to say, everywhere. And ordinary films, films made purely for enter-tainment (that is, commercial) purposes, will continue to be aston-ishingly witless; already the vast majority fail resoundingly to appeal to their cynically targeted audiences. While the point of a great film is now, more than ever, to be a one-of-a-kind achieve-ment, the commercial cinema has settled for a policy of bloated, derivative filmmaking, a brazen combinatory or recombinatory art, in the hope of reproducing past successes. Every film that hopes to reach the largest possible audience is designed as some kind of remake. Cinema, once heralded as *the* art of the twentieth century, seems now, as the century closes numerically, to be a decadent art.

Perhaps it is not cinema that has ended, but only cinephilia, the name of the very specific kind of love that cinema inspired. Each art breeds its fanatics. The love that cinema inspired, however, was special. It was born of the sense that cinema was an art unlike any other: quintessentially modern, distinctively accessible, poetic and mysterious and erotic and moral — all at the same time. Cinema had apostles (it was like religion). Cinema was a crusade. Cinema was a world-view. Lovers of poetry or opera or dance don't think there is *only* poetry or opera or dance. But lovers of cinema could think there was only cinema. That the movies encapsulated every-thing — and they did. It was both the book of art and the book of life.

As many people have noted, the start of moviemaking a hun-dred years ago was, conveniently, a double start. In that first year, 1895, two kinds of films were made, proposing two modes of what cinema could be: cinema as the transcription of real, unstaged life (the Lumière brothers) and cinema as invention, artifice, illusion, fantasy (Méliès). But this was never a true opposition. For those first audiences watching the Lumière brothers' *The Arrival of a Train at La Ciotat Station,* the camera's transmission of a banal sight was a fantastic experience. Cinema began in wonder, the wonder that reality can be transcribed with such magical immediacy. All of cinema is an attempt to perpetuate and to reinvent that sense of wonder.

Everything begins with that moment, one hundred years ago, when the train pulled into the station. People took movies into themselves, just as the public cried out with excitement, actually ducked, as the train seemed to move toward *them*. Until the advent of television emptied the movie theaters, it was from a weekly visit to the cinema that you learned (or tried to learn) how to walk, to smoke, to kiss, to fight, to suffer. Movies gave you tips about how to be attractive, such as: it looks good to wear a raincoat even when it isn't raining. But whatever you took home from the movies was only a part of the larger experience of losing yourself in faces, in lives that were *not* yours — which is the more inclusive form of desire embodied in the movie experience. The strongest experience was simply to surrender to, to be transported by, what was on the screen. You wanted to be kidnapped by the movie.

The first prerequisite of being kidnapped was to be overwhelmed by the physical presence of the image. And the conditions of "going to the movies" were essential to that. To see a great film only on TV isn't to have really seen that film. (This is equally true of those made for TV, like Fassbinder's *Berlin Alexanderplatz* and the two *Heimat* films of Edgar Reitz.) It's not only the difference of dimensions: the superiority of the larger-than-you image in the theater to the little image on the box at home. The conditions of paying attention in a domestic space are radically disrespectful of film. Since film no longer has a standard size, home screens *can* be as big as living room or bedroom walls. But you are still in a living room or a bedroom, alone or with familiars. To be kidnapped, you have to be in a movie theater, seated in the dark among anonymous strangers.

No amount of mourning will revive the vanished rituals — erotic, ruminative — of the darkened theater. The reduction of cinema to assaultive images and the unprincipled manipulation of images (faster and faster cutting) to be more attention-grabbing have produced a disincarnated, lightweight cinema that doesn't demand anyone's full attention. Images now appear in any size and on a variety of surfaces: on a screen in a theater, on home screens as small as the palm of your hand or as big as a wall, on disco walls and megascreens hanging above sports arenas and the outsides of tall public buildings. The sheer ubiquity of moving images has steadily undermined the standards people once had both for cinema as art at its most serious and for cinema as popular entertainment.

In the first years there was essentially no difference between cinema as art and cinema as entertainment. And all films of the silent era — from the masterpieces of Feuillade, D. W. Griffith, Djiga Vertov, Pabst, Murnau, King Vidor to the most formula-ridden melodramas and comedies — are on a very high artistic level compared with most of what was to follow. With the coming of sound, the image-making lost much of its brilliance and poetry, and commercial standards tightened. This way of making movies — the Hollywood system — dominated filmmaking for about twenty-five years (roughly from 1930 to 1955). The most original directors, like Erich von Stroheim and Orson Welles, were defeated by the system and eventually went into artistic exile in Europe — where more or less the same quality-defeating system was now in place, with lower budgets; only in France were a large number of superb films produced throughout this period. Then, in the mid-1950s, vanguard ideas took hold again, rooted in the idea of cinema as a craft pioneered by the Italian films of the immediate postwar period. A dazzling number of ambitious, passionate, artisanally* crafted films of the highest seriousness got made with new actors and tiny crews, went to film festivals (of which there were more and more), and from there, garlanded with festival prizes, into movie theaters around the world. This golden age actually lasted as long as twenty years.

It was at this specific moment in the hundred-year history of cinema that going to movies, thinking about movies, talking about movies, became a passion among university students and other young people. You fell in love not just with actors but with cinema itself. Cinephilia had first become visible in the 1950s in France: its forum was the legendary film magazine *Cahiers du Cinéma* (followed by similarly fervent magazines in Germany, Italy, Great Britain, Sweden, the United States, Canada). Its temples, as it spread throughout Europe and the Americas, were the many cinematheques and film clubs specializing in films from the past and directors' retrospectives that sprang up. The 1960s and early

---

*Artisanally: Skillfully in an applied art; from the word *artisan*.

1970s were the feverish age of moviegoing, with the full-time cinephile always hoping to find a seat as close as possible to the big screen, ideally the third row center. "One can't live without Rossellini,"* declares a character in Bertolucci's *Before the Revolution* (1964)— and means it.

Cinephilia — a source of exultation in the films of Godard and Truffaut and the early Bertolucci and Syberberg; a morose lament in some recent films of Nanni Moretti — was mostly a Western European affair. The great directors of "the other Europe" (Zanussi in Poland, Angelopoulos in Greece, Tarkovsky and Sokurov in Russia, Jancso and Tarr in Hungary) and the great Japanese directors (Ozu, Mizoguchi, Kurosawa, Oshima, Imamura) have tended not to be cinephiles, perhaps because in Budapest or Moscow or Tokyo or Warsaw or Athens there wasn't a chance to get a cinémathèque education. The distinctive thing about cinephile taste was that it embraced both "art" films and popular films. Thus, European cinephilia had a romantic relation to the films of certain directors in Hollywood at the apogee of the studio system: Godard for Howard Hawks, Fassbinder for Douglas Sirk. Of course, this moment — when cinephilia emerged — was also the moment when the Hollywood studio system was breaking up. It seemed that moviemaking had rewon the right to experiment; cinephiles could *afford* to be passionate (or sentimental) about the old Hollywood genre films. A host of new people came into cinema, including a generation of young film critics from *Cahiers du Cinéma;* the towering figure of that generation, indeed of several decades of filmmaking anywhere, was Jean-Luc Godard. A few writers turned out to be wildly talented filmmakers: Alexander Kluge in Germany, Pier Paolo Pasolini in Italy. (The model for the writer who turns to filmmaking actually emerged earlier, in France, with Pagnol in the 1930s and Cocteau in the 1940s; but it was not until the 1960s that this seemed, at least in Europe, normal.) Cinema seemed reborn.

For some fifteen years there were new masterpieces every month, and one allowed oneself to imagine that this would go on forever. How far away that era seems now. To be sure, there was always a conflict between cinema as an industry and cinema as an art, cinema as routine and cinema as experiment. But the conflict was not

Rossellini: Roberto Rossellini (1906–1977) was one of Italy's major film directors.

such as to make impossible the making of wonderful films, sometimes within and sometimes outside of mainstream cinema. Now
the balance has tipped decisively in favor of cinema as an industry.
The great cinema of the 1960s and 1970s has been thoroughly re-
pudiated. Already in the 1970s Hollywood was plagiarizing and ba-
nalizing the innovations in narrative method and editing of
successful new European and ever-marginal independent American films. Then came the catastrophic rise in production costs in
the 1980s, which secured the worldwide reimposition of industry
standards of making and distributing films on a far more coercive,
this time truly global scale. The result can be seen in the melancholy fate of some of the greatest directors of the last decades.
What place is there today for a maverick like Hans Jürgen Syberberg, who has stopped making films altogether, or for the great
Godard, who now makes films about the history of film, on video?
Consider some other cases. The internationalizing of financing
and therefore of casts was a disaster for Andrei Tarkovsky in the
last two films of his stupendous, tragically abbreviated career. And
these conditions for making films have proved to be as much an
artistic disaster for two of the most valuable directors still working:
Krzysztof Zanussi *(The Structure of Crystals, Illumination, Spiral, Contract)* and Theo Angelopoulos *(Reconstruction, Days of '36, The Traveling Players)*. And what will happen now to Bela Tarr *(Damnation,
Satantango)*? And how will Aleksandr Sokurov *(Save and Protect,
Days of Eclipse, The Second Circle, Stone, Whispering Pages)* find the
money to go on making films, his sublime films, under the rude
conditions of Russian capitalism?

Predictably, the love of cinema has waned. People still like going
to the movies, and some people still care about and expect something special, necessary from a film. And wonderful films are still
being made: Mike Leigh's *Naked,* Gianni Amelio's *Lamerica,* Fred
Keleman's *Fate,* Abbas Kiarostami's *Through the Olive Trees.* But one
hardly finds anymore, at least among the young, the distinctive
cinephilic love of movies, which is not simply love of but a certain
taste in films (grounded in a vast appetite for seeing and reseeing
as much as possible of cinema's glorious past). Cinephilia itself has
come under attack, as something quaint, outmoded, snobbish. For
cinephilia implies that films are unique, unrepeatable, magic
experiences. Cinephilia tells us that the Hollywood remake of

Godard's *Breathless** cannot be as good as the original. Cinephilia
has no role in the era of hyperindustrial films. For cinephilia cannot help, by the very range and eclecticism of its passions, but
sponsor the idea of the film as, first of all, a poetic object, and cannot help but incite those outside the movie industry, like painters
and writers, to want to make films, too. It is precisely this conception of movies that must be defeated. That has been defeated.

   If cinephilia is dead, then movies are dead too — no matter how
many movies, even very good ones, go on being made. If cinema
can be resurrected, it will only be through the birth of a new kind
of cine-love.

Reflections and Responses

1. What is cinephilia? What were its origins? Why does Susan Sontag consider it very different from other kinds of fanatic interest in
the arts?

2. Why are movie theaters so important to cinephiles? What do
they contribute to the art of film? How have various types of home
video equipment figured in the decline of film as an art form?

3. Susan Sontag concludes her essay with the comment that "one
hardly finds anymore, at least among the young, the distinctive
cinephilic love of movies. . . ." Do you agree with this observation?
Would you say, for example, that young people fixated on the *Star
Wars* or the *Die Hard* films are cinephiles? Explain your answer
within the context of Susan Sontag's definition of cinephilia.

***Godard's *Breathless:** The renowned French director Jean-Luc Godard's (b. 1930)
Breathless was released in 1960 and became one of the cinephile's all-time favorite
films. In 1983, Richard Gere starred in a flop remake of the film.

SHELBY STEELE

On Being Black
and Middle Class

One of the most controversial selections to have appeared in The Best
American Essay *series, Shelby Steele's 1988 essay disturbed readers who
saw it not as a black writer's candid account of his divided identity but
rather as an assimilationist endorsement of white America. In refusing to
define himself solely along racial lines, Steele appeared to be turning his
back on his own people. His essay, however, calls into question this very
dilemma: Steele wonders why black middle-class Americans are somehow expected to celebrate the black underclass as the "purest" representation of
African American identity. While maintaining that he has more in common with middle-class Americans than with underclass blacks, Steele con-
fesses that he often finds himself contriving to be black, aligning himself
with a "victim-focused black identity." He concludes his essay with a distinction he believes African Americans must make if they are to enjoy the opportunities open to them: they must learn, he says, to distinguish between
"actual victimization" and "identification with the victim's status." In his
resistance to that kind of "identification," Steele establishes his own "identity" as a writer and individual.*

*Shelby Steele is a professor of English at San Jose State University. His
collection of essays,* The Content of Our Character, *won the National
Book Critics Circle Award for general nonfiction in 1991. His essays have
appeared in a wide variety of periodicals, including* Harper's, The American Scholar, Commentary, The New Republic, Confrontation,
Black World, *and* The New York Times Magazine. *His most recent
book is* A Dream Deferred: The Second Betrayal of Black Freedom
in America *(1998). "On Being Black and Middle Class" originally*

appeared in Commentary *(1988) and was selected by Geoffrey Wolff for* The Best American Essays 1989.

Not long ago, a friend of mine, black like myself, said to me that the term "black middle class" was actually a contradiction in terms. Race, he insisted, blurred class distinctions among blacks. If you were black, you were just black and that was that. When I argued, he let his eyes roll at my naiveté. Then he went on. For us, as black professionals, it was an exercise in self-flattery, a pathetic pretension, to give meaning to such a distinction. Worse, the very idea of class threatened the unity that was vital to the black community as a whole. After all, since when had white America taken note of anything but color when it came to blacks? He then reminded me of an old Malcolm X line that had been popular in the sixties. Question: What is a black man with a Ph.D.? Answer: A nigger.

For many years I had been on my friend's side of this argument. Much of my conscious thinking on the old conundrum of race and class was shaped during my high school and college years in the race-charged sixties, when the fact of my race took on an almost religious significance. Progressively, from the mid-sixties on, more and more aspects of my life found their explanation, their justification, and their motivation in race. My youthful concerns about career, romance, money, values, and even styles of dress became a subject to consultation with various oracular sources of racial wisdom. And these ranged from a figure as ennobling as Martin Luther King, Jr., to the underworld elegance of dress I found in jazz clubs on the South Side of Chicago. Everywhere there were signals, and in those days I considered myself so blessed with clarity and direction that I pitied my white classmates who found more embarrassment than guidance in the fact of *their* race. In 1968, inflated by my new power, I took a mischievous delight in calling them culturally disadvantaged.

But now, hearing my friend's comment was like hearing a priest from a church I'd grown disenchanted with. I understood him, but my faith was weak. What had sustained me in the sixties sounded monotonous and off the mark in the eighties. For me, race had lost much of its juju, its singular capacity to conjure meaning. And today, when I honestly look at my life and the lives of many other middle-class blacks I know, I can see that race never fully explained our situation in American society. Black though I may be, it is impossible for me to sit in my single-family house with two cars in the driveway and a swing set in the back yard and *not* see the role class has played in my life. And how can my friend, similarly raised and similiarly situated, not see it?

Yet despite my certainty I felt a sharp tug of guilt as I tried to explain myself over my friend's skepticism. He is a man of many comedic facial expressions and, as I spoke, his brow lifted in extreme moral alarm as if I were uttering the unspeakable. His clear implication was that I was being elitist and possibly (dare he suggest?) anti-black — crimes for which there might well be no redemption. He pretended to fear for me. I chuckled along with him, but inwardly I did wonder at myself. Though I never doubted the validity of what I was saying, I felt guilty saying it. Why?

After he left (to retrieve his daughter from a dance lesson) I realized that the trap I felt myself in had a tiresome familiarity and, in a sort of slow-motion epiphany, I began to see its outline. It was like the suddenly sharp vision one has at the end of a burdensome marriage when all the long-repressed incompatibilities come undeniably to light.

What became clear to me is that people like myself, my friend, and middle-class blacks generally are caught in a very specific double bind that keeps two equally powerful elements of our identity at odds with each other. The middle-class values by which we were raised — the work ethic, the importance of education, the value of property ownership, of respectability, of "getting ahead," of stable family life, of initiative, of self-reliance, etc. — are, in themselves, raceless and even assimilationist. They urge us toward participation in the American mainstream, toward integration, toward a strong identification with the society — and toward the entire constellation of qualities that are implied in the word "individualism." These values are almost rules for how to prosper in a democratic, free-enterprise society that admires and rewards individual effort. They tell us to work hard for ourselves and our families and to seek our opportunities whenever they appear, inside or outside the confines of whatever ethnic group we may belong to.

But the particular pattern of racial identification that emerged in the sixties and that still prevails today urges middle-class blacks (and all blacks) in the opposite direction. This pattern asks us to see ourselves as an embattled minority, and it urges an adversarial stance toward the mainstream, an emphasis on ethnic consciousness over individualism. It is organized around an implied separatism.

The opposing thrust of these two parts of our identity results in the double bind of middle-class blacks. There is no forward movement on either plane that does not constitute backward movement on the other. This was the familiar trap I felt myself in while talking with my friend. As I spoke about class, his eyes reminded me that I was betraying race. Clearly, the two indispensable parts of my identity were a threat to each other.

Of course when you think about it, class and race are both similar in some ways and also naturally opposed. They are two forms of collective identity with boundaries that intersect. But whether they clash or peacefully coexist has much to do with how they are defined. Being both black and middle class becomes a double bind when class and race are defined in sharply antagonistic terms, so that one must be repressed to appease the other.

But what is the "substance" of these two identities, and how does each establish itself in an individual's overall identity? It seems to me that when we identify with any collective we are basically identifying with images that tell us what it means to be a member of that collective. Identity is not the same thing as the fact of membership in a collective; it is, rather, a form of self-definition, facilitated by images of what we wish our membership in the collective to mean. In this sense, the images we identify with may reflect the aspirations of the collective more than they reflect reality, and their content can vary with shifts in those aspirations.

But the process of identification is usually dialectical. It is just as necessary to say what we are *not* as it is to say what we are — so that finally identification comes about by embracing a polarity of positive and negative images. To identify as middle class, for example, I must have both positive and negative images of what being middle class entails; then I will know what I should and should not be doing in order to be middle class. The same goes for racial identity.

In the racially turbulent sixties the polarity of images that came to define racial identification was very antagonistic to the polarity that defined middle-class identification. One might say that the positive images of one lined up with the negative images of the other, so that to identify with both required either a contortionist's flexibility or a dangerous splitting of the self. The double bind of the black middle class was in place. . . .

The black middle class has always defined its class identity by means of positive images gleaned from middle- and upper-class white society, and by means of negative images of lower-class blacks. This habit goes back to the institution of slavery itself, when "house" slaves both mimicked the whites they served and held themselves above the "field" slaves. But in the sixties the old bourgeois impulse to dissociate from the lower classes (the "we-they" distinction) backfired when racial identity suddenly called for the celebration of this same black lower class. One of the qualities of a double bind is that one feels it more than sees it, and I distinctly remember the tension and strange sense of dishonesty I felt in those days as I moved back and forth like a bigamist between the demands of class and race.

Though my father was born poor, he achieved middle-class standing through much hard work and sacrifice (one of his favorite words) and by identifying fully with solid middle-class values — mainly hard work, family life, property ownership, and education for his children (all four of whom have advanced degrees). In his mind these were not so much values as laws of nature. People who embodied them made up the positive images in his class polarity. The negative images came largely from the blacks he had left behind because they were "going nowhere."

No one in my family remembers how it happened, but as time went on, the negative images congealed into an imaginary character named Sam, who, from the extensive service we put him to, quickly grew to mythic proportions. In our family lore he was sometimes a trickster, sometimes a boob, but always possessed of a catalogue of sly faults that gave up graphic images of everything we should not be. On sacrifice: "Sam never thinks about tomorrow. He wants it now or he doesn't care about it." On work: "Sam doesn't favor it too much." On children: "Sam likes to have them but not to raise them." On money: "Sam drinks it up and pisses it out." On fidelity: "Sam has to have two or three women." On clothes: "Sam features loud clothes. He likes to see and be seen." And so on. Sam's persona amounted to a negative instruction manual in class identity.

I don't think that any of us believed Sam's faults were accurate representations of lower-class black life. He was an instrument of self-definition, not of sociological accuracy. It never occurred to us that he looked very much like the white racist stereotype of blacks, or that he might have been a manifestation of our own racial self-hatred. He simply gave us a counterpoint against which to express our aspirations. If self-hatred was a factor, it was not, for us, a matter of hating lower-class blacks but of hating what we did not want to be.

Still, hate or love aside, it is fundamentally true that my middle-class identity involved a dissociation from images of lower-class black life and a corresponding identification with values and patterns of responsibility that are common to the middle class everywhere. These values sent me a clear message: be both an individual and a responsible citizen; understand that the quality of your life will approximately reflect the quality of effort you put into it; know that individual responsibility is the basis of freedom and that the limitations imposed by fate (whether fair or unfair) are no excuse for passivity.

Whether I live up to these values or not, I know that my acceptance of them is the result of lifelong conditioning. I know also that I share this conditioning with middle-class people of all races and that I can no more easily be free of it than I can be free of my race. Whether all this got started because the black middle class modeled itself on the white middle class is no longer relevant. For the middle-class black, conditioned by these values from birth, the sense of meaning they provide is as immutable as the color of his skin.

I started the sixties in high school feeling that my class-conditioning was the surest way to overcome racial barriers. My racial identity was pretty much taken for granted. After all, it was obvious to the world that I was black. Yet I ended the sixties in graduate school a little embarrassed by my class background and with an almost desperate need to be "black." The tables had turned. I knew very clearly (though I struggled to repress it) that my aspirations and my sense of how to operate in the world came from my class background, yet "being black" required certain attitudes and stances that made me feel secretly a little duplicitous. The inner compatibility of class and race I had known in 1960 was gone.

For blacks, the decade between 1960 and 1969 saw racial identification undergo the same sort of transformation that national identity undergoes in times of war. It became more self-conscious, more narrowly focused, more prescribed, less tolerant of opposition. It spawned an implicit party line, which tended to disallow competing forms of identity. Race-as-identity was lifted from the relative slumber it knew in the fifties and pressed into service in a social and political war against oppression. It was redefined along sharp adversarial lines and directed toward the goal of mobilizing the great mass of black Americans in this warlike effort. It was imbued with a strong moral authority, useful for denouncing those who opposed it and for celebrating those who honored it as a positive achievement rather than as a mere birthright.

The form of racial identification that quickly evolved to meet this challenge presented blacks as a racial monolith, a singular people with a common experience of oppression. Differences within the race, no matter how ineradicable, had to be minimized. Class distinctions were one of the first such differences to be sacrificed, since they not only threatened racial unity but also seemed to stand in contradiction to the principle of equality which was the announced goal of the movement for racial progress. The discomfort I felt in 1969, the vague but relentless sense of duplicity, was the result of a historical necessity that put my race and class at odds, that was asking me to cast aside the distinction of my class and identify with a monolithic view of my race.

If the form of this racial identity was the monolith, its substance was victimization. The civil rights movement and the more radical splinter groups of the late sixties were all dedicated to ending racial victimization, and the form of black identity that emerged to facilitate this goal made blackness and victimization virtually synonymous. Since it was our victimization more than any other variable that identified and unified us, moreover, it followed logically that the purest black was the poor black. It was images of him that clustered around the positive pole of the race polarity; all other blacks were, in effect, required to identify with him in order to confirm their own blackness.

Certainly there were more dimensions to the black experience than victimization, but no other had the same capacity to fire the indignation needed for war. So, again out of historical necessity, victimization became the overriding focus of racial identity. But this only deepened the double bind for middle-class blacks like me. When it came to class we were accustomed to defining ourselves against lower-class blacks and identifying with at least the values of middle-class whites; when it came to race we were now being asked to identify with images of lower-class blacks and to see whites, middle class or otherwise, as victimizers. Negative lining up with positive, we were called upon to reject what we had previously embraced and to embrace what we had previously rejected. To put it still more personally, the Sam figure I had been raised to define myself against had now become the "real" black I was expected to identify with.

The fact that the poor black's new status was only passively earned by the condition of his victimization, not by assertive, positive action, made little difference. Status was status apart from the means by which it was achieved, and along with it came a certain power — the power to define the terms of access to that status, to say who was black and who was not. If a lower-class black said you were not really "black" — a sellout, an Uncle Tom — the judgment was all the more devastating because it carried the authority of his status. And this judgment soon enough came to be accepted by many whites as well.

In graduate school I was once told by a white professor, "Well, but . . . you're not really black. I mean, you're not disadvantaged." In his mind my lack of victim status disqualified me from the race itself. More recently I was complimented by a black student for speaking reasonably correct English, "proper" English as he put it. "But I don't know if I really want to talk like that," he went on. "Why not?" I asked. "Because then I wouldn't be black no more," he replied without a pause.

To overcome his marginal status, the middle-class black had to identify with a degree of victimization that was beyond his actual experience. In college (and well beyond) we used to play a game called "nap matching." It was a game of one-upmanship, in which we sat around outdoing each other with stories of racial victimization, symbolically measured by the naps of our hair. Most of us were middle class and so had few personal stories to relate, but if we could not match naps with our own biographies, we would move on to those legendary tales of victimization that came to us from the public domain.

The single story that sat atop the pinnacle of racial victimization for us was that of Emmett Till, the Northern black teenager who, on a visit to the South in 1955, was killed and grotesquely mutilated for supposedly looking at or whistling at (we were never sure which, though we argued the point endlessly) a white woman. Oh, how we probed his story, finding in his youth and Northern upbringing the quintessential embodiment of black innocence, brought down by a white evil so portentous and apocalyptic, so gnarled and hideous, that it left us with a feeling not far from awe. By telling his story and others like it, we came to *feel* the immutability of our victimization, its utter indigenousness, as a thing on this earth like dirt or sand or water.

Of course, these sessions were a ritual of group identification, a means by which we, as middle-class blacks, could be at one with our race. But why were we, who had only a moderate experience of victimization (and that offset by opportunities our parents never had), so intent on assimilating or appropriating an identity that in so many ways contradicted our own? Because, I think, the sense of innocence that is always entailed in feeling victimized filled us with a corresponding feeling of entitlement, or even license, that helped us endure our vulnerability on a largely white college campus.

In my junior year in college I rode to a debate tournament with three white students and our faculty coach, an elderly English professor. The experience of being the lone black in a group of whites was so familiar to me that I thought nothing of it as our trip began. But then halfway through the trip the professor casually turned to me and, in an isn't-the-world-funny sort of tone, said that he had just refused to rent an apartment in a house he owned to a "very nice" black couple because their color would "offend" the white couple who lived downstairs. His eyebrows lifted helplessly over his hawkish nose, suggesting that he too, like me, was a victim of America's racial farce. His look assumed a kind of comradeship: he and I were above this grimy business of race, though for expediency we had occasionally to concede the world its madness.

My vulnerability in this situation came not so much from the professor's blindness to his own racism as from his assumption that I would participate in it, that I would conspire with him against my own race so that he might remain comfortably blind. Why did he think I would be amenable to this? I can only guess that he assumed my middle-class identity was so complete and all-encompassing that I would see his action as nothing more than a trifling concession to the folkways of our land, that I would in fact applaud his decision not to disturb propriety. Blind to both his own racism and to me — one blindness serving the other — he could not recognize that he was asking me to betray my race in the name of my class.

His blindness made me feel vulnerable because it threatened to expose my own repressed ambivalence. His comment pressured me to choose between my class identification, which had contributed to my being a college student and a member of the debating team, and my desperate desire to be "black." I could have one but not both; I was double-bound.

Because double binds are repressed there is always an element of terror in them: the terror of bringing to the conscious mind the buried duplicity, self-deception, and pretense involved in serving two masters. This terror is the stuff of vulnerability, and since vulnerability is one of the least tolerable of all human feelings, we usually transform it into an emotion that seems to restore the control of which it has robbed us; most often, that emotion is anger. And so, before the professor had even finished his little story, I had become a furnace of rage. The year was 1967, and I had been primed by endless hours of nap-matching to feel, at least consciously, completely at one with the victim-focused black identity. This identity gave me the license, and the impunity, to unleash upon this professor one of those volcanic eruptions of racial indignation familiar to us from the novels of Richard Wright. Like Cross Damon in *Outsider,* who kills in perfectly righteous anger, I tried to annihilate the man. I punished him not according to the measure of his crime but according to the measure of my vulnerability, a measure set by the cumulative tension of years of repressed terror. Soon I saw that terror in *his* face, as he stared hollow-eyed at the road ahead. My white friends in the back seat, knowing no conflict between their own class and race, were astonished that someone they had taken to be so much like themselves could harbor a rage that for all the world looked murderous.

Though my rage was triggered by the professor's comment, it was deepened and sustained by a complex of need, conflict, and repression in myself of which I had been wholly unaware. Out of my racial vulnerability I had developed the strong need of an identity with which to defend myself. The only such identity available was that of me as victim, him as victimizer. Once in the grip of this paradigm, I began to do far more damage to myself than he had done.

Seeing myself as a victim meant that I clung all the harder to my racial identity, which, in turn, meant that I suppressed my class identity. This cut me off from all the resources my class values might have offered me. In those values, for instance, I might have found the means to a more dispassionate response, the response less of a victim attacked by a victimizer than of an individual offended by a foolish old man. As an individual I might have reported this professor to the college dean. Or I might have calmly tried to reveal his blindness to him, and possibly won a convert. (The flagrancy of his remark suggested a hidden guilt and even self-recognition on which I might have capitalized. Doesn't confession usually signal a willingness to face oneself?) Or I might have simply chuckled and then let my silence serve as an answer to his provocation. Would not my composure, in any form it might take, deflect into his own heart the arrow he'd shot at me?

Instead, my anger, itself the hair-trigger expression of a long-repressed double bind, not only cut me off from the best of my own resources, it also distorted the nature of my true racial problem. The righteousness of this anger and the easy catharsis it brought buoyed the delusion of my victimization and left me as blind as the professor himself.

As a middle-class black I have often felt myself *contriving* to be "black." And I have noticed this same contrivance in others — a certain stretching away from the natural flow of one's life to align oneself with a victim-focused black identity. Our particular needs are out of sync with the form of identity available to meet those needs. Middle-class blacks need to identify racially; it is better to think of ourselves as black and victimized than not black at all; so we contrive (more unconsciously than consciously) to fit ourselves into an identity that denies our class and fails to address the true source of our vulnerability.

For me this once meant spending inordinate amounts of time at black faculty meetings, though these meetings had little to do with my real racial anxieties or my professional life. I was new to the university, one of two blacks in an English department of over seventy, and I felt a little isolated and vulnerable, though I did not admit it to myself. But at these meetings we discussed the problems of black faculty and students within a framework of victimization. The real vulnerability we felt was covered over by all the adversarial drama the victim/victimized polarity inspired, and hence went unseen and unassuaged. And this, I think, explains our rather chronic ineffectiveness as a group. Since victimization was not our primary problem — the university had long ago opened its doors to us — we had to contrive to make it so, and there is not much energy in contrivance. What I got at these meetings was ultimately an object lesson in how fruitless struggle can be when it is not grounded in actual need.

At our black faculty meetings, the old equation of blackness with victimization was ever present — to be black was to be a victim; therefore, not to be a victim was not to be black. As we contrived to meet the terms of this formula there was an inevitable distortion of both ourselves and the larger university. Through the prism of victimization the university seemed more impenetrable than it actually was, and we more limited in our powers. We fell prey to the victim's myopia, making the university an institution from which we could seek redress but which we could never fully join. And this mind-set often led us to look more for compensations for our supposed victimization than for opportunities we could pursue as individuals.

The discomfort and vulnerability felt by middle-class blacks in the sixties, it could be argued, was a worthwhile price to pay considering the progress achieved during that time of racial confrontation. But what may have been tolerable then is intolerable now. Though changes in American society have made it an anachronism, the monolithic form of racial identification that came out of the sixties is still very much with us. It may be more loosely held, and its power to punish heretics has probably diminished, but it continues to catch middle-class blacks in a double bind, thus impeding not only their own advancement but even, I would contend, that of blacks as a group.

The victim-focused black identity encourages the individual to feel that his advancement depends almost entirely on that of the group. Thus he loses sight not only of his own possibilities but of the inextricable connection between individual effort and individual advancement. This is a profound encumbrance today, when there is more opportunity for blacks than ever before, for it reimposes limitations that can have the same oppressive effect as those the society has only recently begun to remove.

It was the emphasis on mass action in the sixties that made the victim-focused black identity a necessity. But in the eighties and beyond, when racial advancement will come only through a multitude of individual advancements, this form of identity inadvertently adds itself to the forces that hold us back. Hard work, education, individual initiative, stable family life, property ownership — these have always been the means by which ethnic groups have moved ahead in America. Regardless of past or present victimization, these "laws" of advancement apply absolutely to black Americans also. There is no getting around this. What we need is a form of racial identity that energizes the individual by putting him in touch with both his possibilities and his responsibilities.

It has always annoyed me to hear from the mouths of certain arbiters of blackness that middle-class blacks should "reach back" and pull up those blacks less fortunate than they — as though middle-class status were an unearned and essentially passive condition in which one needed a large measure of noblesse oblige to occupy one's time. My own image is of reaching back from a moving train to lift on board those who have no tickets. A noble enough sentiment — but might it not be wiser to show them the entire structure of principles, efforts, and sacrifice that puts one in a position to buy a ticket any time one likes? This, I think, is something members of the black middle class can realistically offer to other blacks. Their example is not only a testament to possibility but also a lesson in method. But they cannot lead by example until they are released from a black identity that regards that example as suspect, that sees them as "marginally" black, indeed that holds *them* back by catching them in a double bind.

To move beyond the victim-focused black identity we must learn to make a difficult but crucial distinction: between actual victimization, which we must resist with every resource, and identification with the victim's status. Until we do this we will continue to

wrestle more with ourselves than with the new opportunities which
so many paid so dearly to win.

Reflections and Responses

1. Consider the two people Steele introduces us to in his essay —
a black friend (pages 396–397) and a white college professor
(pages 403–405). What does each person represent? Of what importance are they to Steele's own self-identity? How does he establish his differences toward each one? Why are these differences
important to Steele's own identity?

2. What do you think of Steele's contention that poorer and less-
educated African Americans are generally considered more "black"
than those from the middle class? What evidence does Steele offer
to support this idea? On what grounds is black "authenticity" or
"purity" based? Do you think the media — especially film, music,
and television — reinforce certain images of "blackness"?

3. Note that toward the conclusion of his essay Steele uses the
word "we." What is the significance of this shift? What identification is he establishing and with whom?

JOY WILLIAMS

The Killing Game

In today's world, survival is a theme that includes all of nature, not merely human life. When the following angry attack on hunting originally appeared in a popular men's magazine, the editors were deluged with equally angry letters from hundreds of subscribers. As you read the essay, you'll see at once why it enraged hunters and hunting advocates. Williams did not choose to write a calm, composed, and gently persuasive critique of hunting but went all out in a savage and often sarcastic attack on American hunters, a group she considers "overequipped . . . insatiable, malevolent, and vain."

Williams is the author of three novels and two collections of stories, Taking Care *(1982) and* Escapes *(1989), as well as a 1987 history and guide to the Florida Keys. Her nonfiction includes articles on sharks, James Dean, the environment, and the electric chair. In 1993 she received the Strauss Living Award from the American Academy of Arts and Letters. "The Killing Game" originally appeared in* Esquire *(1990) and was selected by Joyce Carol Oates for* The Best American Essays *1991.*

Death and suffering are a big part of hunting. A big part. Not that you'd ever know it by hearing hunters talk. They tend to downplay the killing part. To kill is to put to death, extinguish, nullify, cancel, destroy. But from the hunter's point of view, it's just a tiny part of the experience. *The kill is the least important part of the hunt,* they often say, or, *Killing involves only a split second of the innumerable hours we spend surrounded by and observing nature . . .* For the animal, of course, the killing part is of considerable more importance. José Ortega y Gasset, in *Meditations on Hunting,* wrote, *Death is a sign of reality in hunting. One does not hunt in order to kill; on the contrary, one kills in order to have hunted.* This is the sort of intellectual blather that the "thinking" hunter holds dear. The conservation editor of *Field & Stream*, George Reiger, recently paraphrased this sentiment by saying, *We kill to hunt, and not the other way around,* thereby making it truly fatuous. A hunter in West Virginia, one Mr. Bill Neal, blazed through this philosophical fog by explaining why he blows the toes off tree raccoons so that they will fall down and be torn apart by his dogs. *That's the best part of it. It's not any fun just shooting them.*

Instead of monitoring animals — many animals in managed areas are tagged, tattooed, and wear radio transmitters — wildlife managers should start hanging telemetry gear around hunters' necks to study their attitudes and listen to their conversations. It would be grisly listening, but it would tune out for good the *suffering as sacrament* and *spiritual experience* blather that some hunting apologists employ. *The unease with which the good hunter inflicts death is an unease not merely with his conscience but with affirming his animality in the midst of his struggles toward humanity and clarity,* Holmes Rolston III drones on in his book *Environmental Ethics.*

There is a formula to this in literature — someone the protagonist loves has just died, so he goes out and kills an animal. This makes him feel better. But it's kind of a sad feeling-better. He gets to relate to Death and Nature in this way. Somewhat. But not really. Death is still a mystery. Well, it's hard to explain. It's sort of a semireligious thing . . . Killing and affirming, affirming and killing, it's just the cross the "good" hunter must bear. The bad hunter just has to deal with postkill letdown.

Many are the hunter's specious arguments. Less semireligious but a long-standing favorite with them is the vegetarian approach: you eat meat, don't you? If you say no, they feel they've got you — you're just a vegetarian attempting to impose your weird views on others. If you say yes, they accuse you of being hypocritical, of allowing your genial A&P butcher to stand between you and reality. The fact is, the chief attraction of hunting is the pursuit and murder of animals — the meat-eating aspect of it is trivial. If the hunter chooses to be *ethical* about it, he might cook his kill, but the meat of most animals is discarded. Dead bear can even be dangerous! A bear's heavy hide must be skinned at once to prevent meat spoilage. With effort, a hunter can make okay chili, *something to keep in mind,* a sports rag says, *if you take two skinny spring bears.*

As for subsistence hunting, please . . . Granted that there might be one "good" hunter out there who conducts the kill as spiritual exercise and two others who are atavistic enough to want to supplement their Chicken McNuggets with venison, most hunters hunt for the hell of it.

For hunters, hunting is fun. Recreation is play. Hunting is recreation. Hunters kill for play, for entertainment. They kill for the thrill of it, to make an animal "theirs." (The Gandhian doctrine of nonpossession has never been a big hit with hunters.) The animal becomes the property of the hunter by its death. Alive, the beast belongs only to itself. This is unacceptable to the hunter. *He's yours . . . He's mine . . . I decided to . . . I decided not to . . . I debated shooting it, then I decided to let it live . . .* Hunters like beautiful creatures. A "beautiful" deer, elk, bear, cougar, bighorn sheep. A "beautiful" goose or mallard. Of course, they don't stay "beautiful" for long, particularly the birds. Many birds become rags in the air, shredded, blown to bits. *Keep shooting till they drop!* Hunters get a thrill out of seeing a plummeting bird, out of seeing it crumple and fall. *The big pheasant folded in classic fashion.* They get a kick out of "collecting" new species. *Why not add a unique harlequin duck to your collection?* Swan hunting is satisfying. *I let loose a three-inch Magnum. The large bird only flinched with my first shot and began to gain altitude. I frantically ejected the round, chambered another, and dropped the swan with my second shot. After retrieving the bird I was amazed by its size. The swan's six-foot wingspan, huge body, and long neck made it an impressive trophy.* Hunters like big animals, trophy animals. A "trophy" usually means that the hunter doesn't deign to eat it. Maybe he skins it or mounts it. Maybe he takes a picture. *We took pictures, we took pictures.* Maybe he just looks at it for a while. The disposition of the "experience" is up to the hunter. He's entitled to do whatever he wishes with the damn thing. It's dead.

Hunters like categories they can tailor to their needs. There are the "good" animals — deer, elk, bear, moose — which are allowed to exist for the hunter's pleasure. Then there are the "bad" animals, the vermin, varmints, and "nuisance" animals, the rabbits and raccoons and coyotes and beavers and badgers, which are discouraged to exist. The hunter can have fun killing them, but the pleasure is diminished because the animals aren't "magnificent."

Then there are the predators. These can be killed any time, because, hunters argue, they're predators, for godssakes.

Many people in South Dakota want to exterminate the red fox because it preys upon some of the ducks and pheasant they want to hunt and kill each year. They found that after they killed the wolves and coyotes, they had more foxes than they wanted. The ring-necked pheasant is South Dakota's state bird. No matter that it was imported from Asia specifically to be "harvested" for sport, it's South Dakota's state bird and they're proud of it. A group called Pheasants Unlimited gave some tips on how to hunt foxes. *Place a small amount of larvicide* [a grain fumigant] *on a rag and chuck it down the hole . . . The first pup generally comes out in fifteen minutes . . . Use a .22 to dispatch him . . . Remove each pup shot from the hole. Following gassing, set traps for the old fox who will return later in the evening . . .* Poisoning, shooting, trapping — they make up a sort of sportsman's triathlon.

In the hunting magazines, hunters freely admit the pleasure of killing to one another. *Undeniable pleasure radiated from her smile. The excitement of shooting the bear had Barb talking a mile a minute.* But in public, most hunters are becoming a little wary about raving on as to how much fun it is to kill things. Hunters have a tendency to call large animals by cute names — "bruins" and "muleys," "berry-fed blackies" and "handsome cusses" and "big guys," thereby implying a balanced jolly game of mutual satisfaction between the hunter and the hunted — *Bam, bam, bam, I get to shoot you and you get to be dead.* More often, though, when dealing with the nonhunting public, a drier, businesslike tone is employed. Animals become a "resource" that must be "utilized." Hunting becomes "a legitimate use of the resource." Animals become a product like wool or lumber or a crop like fruit or corn that must be "collected" or "taken" or "harvested." Hunters love to use the word *legitimate*. (Oddly, Tolstoy referred to hunting as "evil legitimized.") *A legitimate use, a legitimate form of recreation, a legitimate escape, a legitimate pursuit.* It's a word they trust will slam the door on discourse. Hunters are increasingly relying upon their spokesmen and supporters, state and federal game managers and wildlife officials, to employ the drone of a solemn bureaucratic language and toss around a lot of questionable statistics to assure the nonhunting public (93 percent!) that there's nothing to worry about. The pogrom is under control. The mass murder and manipulation of wild animals is just another business. Hunters are a tiny minority, and it's crucial to them that the millions of people who don't hunt not be awakened from their long sleep and become antihunting. Nonhunters are okay. Dweeby, probably, but okay. A hunter *can respect the rights* of a nonhunter. It's the "antis" he despises, those *misguided, emotional, not-in-possession-of-the-facts, uninformed zealots who don't understand nature* ... *Those dime-store ecologists cloaked in ignorance and spurred by emotion* ... *Those doggy-woggy types, who under the guise of being environmentalists and conservationists are working to deprive him of his precious right to kill.* (Sometimes it's just a *right*; sometimes it's a *God-given* right.) Antis can be scorned, but nonhunters must be pacified, and this is where the number crunching of wildlife biologists and the scripts of *professional resource managers* come in. Leave it to the professionals. They know what numbers are the good numbers. Utah determined that there were six hundred sandhill cranes in the state, so permits were issued to shoot one hundred of them. Don't want to have too many sandhill cranes. California wildlife officials reported "sufficient numbers" of mountain lions to "justify" renewed hunting, even though it doesn't take a rocket scientist to know the animal is extremely rare. (It's always a dark day for hunters when an animal is adjudged *rare*. How can its numbers be "controlled" through hunting if it scarcely exists?) A recent citizens' referendum prohibits the hunting of the mountain lion in perpetuity — not that the lions aren't killed anyway, in California and all over the West, hundreds of them annually by the government as part of the scandalous Animal Damage Control Program. Oh, to be the lucky hunter who gets to be an official government hunter and can legitimately kill animals his buddies aren't supposed to! Montana officials, led by K. L. Cool, that state's wildlife director, have definite ideas on the number of buffalo they feel can be tolerated. Zero is the number. Yellowstone National Park is the only place in America where bison exist, having been annihilated everywhere else. In the winter of 1988, nearly six hundred buffalo wandered out of the north boundary of the park and into Montana, where they were immediately shot at point-blank range by lottery-winning hunters. It was easy. And it was obvious from a video taken on one of the blow-away-the-bison days that the hunters had a heck of a good time. The buffalo, Cool says, threaten ranchers' livelihoods by doing damage to property — by which he means, I guess, that they eat the grass. Montana wants zero buffalos; it also wants zero wolves.

Large predators — including grizzlies, cougars, and wolves — are often the most "beautiful," the smartest and wildest animals of all. The gray wolf is both a supreme predator and an endangered species, and since the Supreme Court recently affirmed that ranchers have no constitutional right to kill endangered predators — apparently some God-given rights are not constitutional ones — this makes the wolf a more or less lucky dog. But not for long. A small population of gray wolves has recently established itself in northwestern Montana, primarily in Glacier National Park, and there is a plan, long a dream of conservationists, to "reintroduce" the wolf to Yellowstone. But to please ranchers and hunters, part of the plan would involve immediately removing the wolf from the endangered-species list. Beyond the park's boundaries, he could be hunted as a "game animal" or exterminated as a "pest." (Hunters kill to hunt, remember, except when they're hunting to kill.) The area of Yellowstone where the wolf would be restored is the same mountain and high-plateau country that is abandoned in winter by most animals, including the aforementioned luckless bison. Part of the plan, too, is compensation to ranchers if any of their far-ranging livestock is killed by a wolf. It's a real industry out there, apparently, killing and controlling and getting compensated for losing something under the Big Sky.

Wolves gotta eat — a fact that disturbs hunters. Jack Atcheson, an outfitter in Butte, said, *Some wolves are fine if there is control. But there never will be control. The wolf-control plan provided by the Fish and Wildlife Service speaks only of protecting domestic livestock. There is no plan to protect wildlife ... There are no surplus deer or elk in Montana ... Their numbers are carefully managed. With uncontrolled wolf populations, a lot of people will have to give up hunting just to feed wolves. Will you give up your elk permit for a wolf?*

It won't be long before hunters start demanding compensation for animals they aren't able to shoot.

Hunters believe that wild animals exist only to satisfy their wish to kill them. And it's so easy to kill them! The weaponry available is staggering, and the equipment and gear limitless. *The demand for big boomers has never been greater than right now, Outdoor Life crows, and the makers of rifles and cartridges are responding to the craze with a variety of light artillery that is virtually unprecedented in the history of sporting arms* . . . Hunters use grossly overpowered shotguns and rifles and compound bows. They rely on four-wheel-drive vehicles and three-wheel ATVs and airplanes . . . *He was interesting, the only moving, living creature on that limitless white expanse. I slipped a cartridge into the barrel of my rifle and threw the safety off* . . . They use snowmobiles to run down elk, and dogs to run down and tree cougars. It's easy to shoot an animal out of a tree. It's virtually impossible to miss a moose, a conspicuous and placid animal of steady habits . . . *I took a deep breath and pulled the trigger. The bull dropped. I looked at my watch: 8:22. The big guy was early. Mike started whooping and hollering and I joined him. I never realized how big a moose was until this one was on the ground. We took pictures* . . . Hunters shoot animals when they're resting . . . *Mike selected a deer, settled down to a steady rest, and fired. The buck was his when he squeezed the trigger. John decided to take the other buck, which had jumped up to its feet. The deer hadn't seen us and was confused by the shot echoing about in the valley. John took careful aim, fired, and took the buck. The hunt was over* . . . And they shoot them when they're eating . . . *The bruin ambled up the stream, checking gravel bars and backwaters for fish. Finally he plopped down on the bank to eat. Quickly, I tiptoed into range* . . . They use decoys and calls . . . *The six-point gave me a cold-eyed glare from ninety steps away. I hit him with a 130-grain Sierra boat-tail handload. The bull went down hard. Our hunt was over* . . . They use sex lures . . . *The big buck raised its nose to the air, curled back its lips, and tested the scent of the doe's urine. I held my breath, fought back the shivers, and jerked off a shot. The 180-grain spire-point bullet caught the buck high on the back behind the shoulder and put it down. It didn't get up* . . . They use walkie-talkies, binoculars, scopes . . . *With my 308 Browning BLR, I steadied the 9X cross hairs on the front of the bear's massive shoulders and squeezed. The bear cartwheeled backward for fifty yards* . . . *The second Federal Premium 165-grain bullet found its mark. Another shot anchored the bear for good* . . . They bait deer with corn. They spread popcorn on golf courses for Canada geese and they douse meat baits with fry grease and honey for bears . . . *Make the baiting site redolent of inner-city doughnut shops.* They use blinds and tree stands and mobile stands. They go out in groups, in gangs, and employ "pushes" and "drives." So many methods are effective. So few rules apply. It's fun! . . . *We kept on repelling the swarms of birds as they came in looking for shelter from that big ocean wind, emptying our shell belts* . . .

A species can, in the vernacular, be *pressured by hunting* (which means that killing them has decimated them), but that just increases the fun, the *challenge*. There is practically no criticism of conduct within the ranks . . . *It's mostly a matter of opinion and how hunters have been brought up to hunt* . . . Although a recent editorial in *Ducks Unlimited* magazine did venture to primly suggest that one should *not fall victim to greed-induced stress through piggish competition with others.*

But hunters are piggy. They just can't seem to help it. They're overequipped . . . insatiable, malevolent, and vain. They maim and mutilate and despoil. And for the most part, they're inept. Grossly inept.

Camouflaged toilet paper is a must for the modern hunter, along with his Bronco and his beer. Too many hunters taking a dump in the woods with their roll of Charmin beside them were mistaken for white-tailed deer and shot. Hunters get excited. They'll shoot anything — the pallid ass of another sportsman or even themselves. A Long Island man died last year when his shotgun went off as he clubbed a wounded deer with the butt. Hunters get mad. They get restless and want to fire! They want to use those assault rifles and see foamy blood on the ferns. Wounded animals can travel for miles in fear and pain before they collapse. Countless gut-shot deer — *if you hear a sudden, squashy thump, the animal has probably been hit in the abdomen* — are "lost" each year. "Poorly placed shots" are frequent, and injured animals are seldom tracked, because most hunters never learned how to track. The majority of hunters will shoot at anything with four legs during deer season and anything with wings during duck season. Hunters try to nail running animals and distant birds. They become so overeager, so *aroused,* that they misidentify and misjudge, spraying their "game" with shots but failing to bring it down.

The fact is, hunters' lack of skill is a big, big problem. And nowhere is the problem worse than in the new glamour recreation, bow hunting. These guys are elitists. They doll themselves up in camouflage, paint their faces black, and climb up into tree stands from which they attempt the penetration of deer, elk, and turkeys with modern, multiblade, broadhead arrows shot from sophisticated, easy-to-draw compound bows. This "primitive" way of hunting appeals to many, and even the nonhunter may feel that it's a "fairer" method, requiring more strength and skill, but bow hunting is the cruelest, most wanton form of wildlife disposal of all. Studies conducted by state fish and wildlife departments repeatedly show that bow hunters wound and fail to retrieve as many animals as they kill. An animal that flees, wounded by an arrow, will most assuredly die of the wound, but it will be days before he does. Even with a "good" hit, the time elapsed between the strike and death is exceedingly long. *The rule of thumb has long been that we should wait thirty to forty-five minutes on heart and lung hits, an hour or more on a suspected liver hit, eight to twelve hours on paunch hits, and that we should follow immediately on hindquarter and other muscle-only hits, to keep the wound open and bleeding,* is the advice in the magazine *Fins and Feathers*. What the hunter does as he hangs around waiting for his animal to finish with its terrified running and dying hasn't been studied — maybe he puts on more makeup, maybe he has a highball.

Wildlife agencies promote and encourage bow hunting by permitting earlier and longer seasons, even though they are well aware that, in their words, *crippling is a by-product of the sport*, making archers pretty sloppy for elitists. The broadhead arrow is a very inefficient killing tool. Bow hunters are trying to deal with this problem with the suggestion that they use poison pods. These poisoned arrows are illegal in all states except Mississippi *(Ah'm gonna get ma deer even if ah just nick the little bastard)*, but they're widely used anyway. You wouldn't want that deer to suffer, would you?

The mystique of the efficacy and decency of the bow hunter is as much an illusion as the perception that a waterfowler is a refined and thoughtful fellow, a *romantic aesthete*, as Vance Bourjaily put it, equipped with his faithful Labs and a love for solitude and wild places. More sentimental drivel has been written about bird shooting than any other type of hunting. It's a soul-wrenching pursuit, apparently, the execution of birds in flight. Ducks Unlimited — an organization that has managed to put a spin on the word *conservation* for years — works hard to project the idea that duck hunters are blue bloods and that duck stamps with their pretty pictures are responsible for saving all the saved puddles in North America. *Sportsman's conservation* is a contradiction in terms (We protect things now so that we can kill them later) and is broadly interpreted (Don't kill them all, just kill most of them). A hunter is a conservationist in the same way a farmer or a rancher is: he's not.

Like the rancher who kills everything that's not stock on his (and the public's) land, and the farmer who scorns wildlife because "they don't pay their freight," the hunter uses nature by destroying its parts, mastering it by simplifying it through death.

George ("We kill to hunt and not the other way around") Reiger, the conservationist-hunter's spokesman (he's the best they've got, apparently), said that the "dedicated" waterfowler will shoot other game "of course," but *we do so much in the same spirit of the lyrics, that when we're not near the girl we love, we love the girl we're near.* (Duck hunters practice tough love.) The fact is, far from being a "romantic aesthete," the waterfowler is the most avaricious of all hunters . . . *That's when Scott suggested the friendly wager on who would take the most birds* . . . and the most resistant to minimum ecological decency. Millions of birds that managed to elude shotgun blasts were dying each year from ingesting the lead shot that rained down in the wetlands. Year after year, birds perished from feeding on spent lead, but hunters were "reluctant" to switch to steel. They worried that it would impair their shooting, and ammunition manufacturers said a changeover would be "expensive." State and federal officials had to weigh the poisoning against these considerations. It took forever, this weighing, but now steel-shot loads are required almost everywhere, having been judged "more than adequate" to bring down the birds. This is not to say, of course, that most duck hunters use steel shot almost everywhere. They're traditionalists and don't care for all the new, pesky rules. Oh, for the golden age of waterfowling, when a man could measure a good day's shooting by the pickup load. But those days are gone. Fall is a melancholy time, all right.

Spectacular abuses occur wherever geese congregate, Shooting Sportsman notes quietly, something that the more cultivated Ducks Unlimited would hesitate to admit. Waterfowl populations are plummeting and waterfowl hunters are out of control. "Supervised" hunts are hardly distinguished from unsupervised ones. A biologist with the Department of the Interior who observed a hunt at Sand Lake in South Dakota said, *Hunters repeatedly shot over the line at incoming flights where there was no possible chance of retrieving. Time and time again I was shocked at the behavior of hunters. I heard them laugh at the plight of dazed cripples that stumbled about. I saw them striking the heads of retrieved cripples against fence posts.* In the South, wood ducks return to their roosts after sunset when shooting hours are closed. Hunters find this an excellent time to shoot them. Dennis Anderson, an outdoors writer, said, *Roost shooters just fire at the birds as fast as they can, trying to drop as many as they can. Then they grab what birds they can find. The birds they can't find in the dark, they leave behind.*

Carnage and waste are the rules in bird hunting, even during legal seasons and open hours. Thousands of wounded ducks and geese are not retrieved, left to rot in the marshes and fields . . . *When I asked Wanda where hers had fallen, she wasn't sure.* Cripples, and there are many cripples made in this pastime, are still able to run and hide, eluding the hunter even if he's willing to spend time searching for them, which he usually isn't . . . *It's one thing to run down a cripple in a picked bean field or a pasture, and quite another to watch a wing-tipped bird drop into a huge block of switch grass.* Oh nasty, nasty switch grass. A downed bird becomes invisible on the ground and is practically unfindable without a good dog, and few "water-fowlers" have them these days. They're hard to train — usually a professional has to do it — and most hunters can't be bothered. Birds are easy to tumble . . . *Canada geese—blues and snows—can all take a good amount of shot. Brant are easily called and decoyed and come down easily. Ruffed grouse are hard to hit but easy to kill. Sharptails are harder to kill but easier to hit* . . . It's just a nuisance to recover them. But it's fun, fun, fun swatting them down . . . *There's distinct pleasure in watching a flock work to a good friend's gun.*

Teal, the smallest of common ducks, are really easy to kill. Hunters in the South used to *practice* on teal in September, prior to the "scrious" waterfowl season. But the birds were so diminutive and the limit so low (four a day) that many hunters felt it hardly worth going out and getting bit by mosquitoes to kill them. Enough did, however, brave the bugs and manage to "harvest" 165,000 of the little migrating birds in Louisiana in 1987 alone. *Shooting is usually best on opening day. By the second day you can sometimes detect a decline in local teal numbers. Areas may deteriorate to virtually no action by the third day* . . . The area *deteriorates.* When a flock is wiped out, the skies are empty. *No action.*

Teal declined more sharply than any duck species except mallard last year; this baffles hunters. Hunters and their procurers — wildlife agencies — will *never* admit that hunting is responsible for the decimation of a species. John Turner, head of the federal Fish and Wildlife Service, delivers the familiar and litanic line. Hunting is not the problem. *Pollution* is the problem. *Pesticides, urbanization, deforestation, hazardous waste,* and *wetlands destruction* are the problem. And drought! There's been a big drought! Antis should devote their energies to solving these problems if they care about wildlife, and leave the hunters alone. While the Fish and Wildlife Service is busily conducting experiments in cause and effect, like releasing mallard ducklings on a wetland sprayed with the insecticide ethyl parathion (they died — it was known they would, but you can never have enough studies that show guns aren't a duck's only problem), hunters are killing some 200 million birds and animals each year. But these deaths are incidental to the problem, according to Turner. A factor, perhaps, but a *minor* one. Ducks Unlimited says the problem isn't hunting, it's *low recruitment* on the part of the birds. To the hunter, *birth* in the animal kingdom is *recruitment.* They wouldn't want to use an emotional, sentimental word like *birth.* The black duck, a very "popular" duck in the Northeast, so "popular," in fact, that game agencies felt that hunters couldn't be asked to refrain from shooting it, is scarce and getting scarcer. Nevertheless, it's still being hunted. *A number of studies are currently under way in an attempt to discover why black ducks are disappearing, Sports Afield* reports. Black ducks are disappearing because they've been shot out, their elimination being a dreadful example of game management, and managers who are loath to "displease" hunters. The skies — *flyways* — of America have been divided into four administrative regions, and the states, advised by a federal government coordinator, have to agree on policies.

There's always a lot of squabbling that goes on in flyway meetings — lots of complaints about short-stopping, for example. Short-stopping is the deliberate holding of birds in a state, often by feeding them in wildlife refuges, so that their southern migration is slowed or stopped. Hunters in the North get to kill more than hunters in the South. This isn't fair. Hunters demand equity in opportunities to kill.

Wildlife managers hate closing the season on anything. Closing the season on a species would indicate a certain amount of *mis*management and misjudgment at the very least — a certain reliance on overly optimistic winter counts, a certain overappeasement of hunters who would be "upset" if they couldn't kill their favorite thing. And worse, closing a season would be considered victory for the antis. Bird-hunting "rules" are very complicated, but they all encourage killing. There are shortened seasons and split seasons and special seasons for "underutilized" birds. (Teal were very recently considered "underutilized.") The limit on coots is fifteen a day — shooting them, it's easy! They don't fly high — giving the hunter something to do while he waits in the blind. Some species are "protected," but bear in mind that hunters begin blasting away one half hour before sunrise and that most hunters can't identify a bird in the air even in broad daylight. Some of them can't identify birds in hand either, and even if they can (*# % *! I got me a canvasback, that duck's frigging protected ...*), they are likely to bury unpopular or "trash" ducks so that they can continue to hunt the ones they "love."

Game "professionals," in thrall to hunters' "needs," will not stop managing bird populations until they've doled out the final duck *(I didn't get my limit but I bagged the last one, by golly . . .).* The Fish and Wildlife Service services legal hunters as busily as any madam, but it is powerless in tempering the lusts of the illegal ones. Illegal kill is a monumental problem in the not-so-wonderful world of waterfowl. Excesses have always pervaded the "sport," and bird shooters have historically been the slobs and profligates of hunting. *Doing away with hunting would do away with a vital cultural and historical aspect of American life,* John Turner claims. So, do away with it. Do away with those who have already done away with so much. Do away with them before the birds they have pursued so relentlessly and for so long drop into extinction, sink, in the poet Wallace Stevens's words, "downward to darkness on extended wings."

"Quality" hunting is as rare as the Florida panther. What you've got is a bunch of guys driving over the plains, up the mountains, and through the woods with their stupid tag that cost them a couple of bucks and immense coolers full of beer and body parts. There's a price tag on the right to destroy living creatures for play, but it's not much. *A big-game hunting license is the greatest deal going since the Homestead Act,* Ted Kerasote writes in *Sports Afield. In many states residents can hunt big game for more than a month for about $20.* It's cheaper than taking the little woman out to lunch. It's cheap all right, and it's because killing animals is considered *recreation* and is underwritten by state and federal funds. In Florida, state moneys are routinely spent on "youth hunts," in which kids are guided to shoot deer from stands in wildlife-management areas. The organizers of these events say that these staged hunts *help youth to understand man's role in the ecosystem.* (Drop a doe and take your place in the ecological community, son . . .)

Hunters claim (they don't actually believe it but they've learned to say it) that they're doing nonhunters a favor, for if they didn't *use* wild animals, wild animals would be useless. They believe that they're just *helping Mother Nature control populations (you wouldn't want those deer to die of starvation, would you?).* They claim that their tiny fees provide *all* Americans with wild lands and animals. (People who don't hunt get to enjoy animals all year round while hunters get to enjoy them only during hunting season . . .) Ducks Unlimited feels that it, in particular, is a selfless provider and environmental champion. Although members spend most of their money lobbying for hunters and raising ducks in pens to release later over shooting fields, they do save some wetlands, mostly by persuading farmers not to fill them in. *See that little pothole there the ducks like? Well, I'm gonna plant more soybeans there if you don't pay me not to . . .* Hunters claim many nonsensical things, but the most nonsensical of all is that they *pay their own way.* They do not pay their own way. They *do* pay into a perverse wildlife-management system that manipulates "stocks" and "herds" and "flocks" for hunters' killing pleasure, but these fees in no way cover the cost of highly questionable ecological practices. For some spare change . . . *the greatest deal going* . . . hunters can hunt on public land — national parks, state forests — preserves for hunters! — which the nonhunting and antihunting public pay for. (Access to private lands is becoming increasingly difficult for them, as experience has taught people that hunters are obnoxious.) Hunters kill on millions of acres of land all over America that are maintained with general taxpayer revenue, but the most shocking, really twisted subsidization takes place on national wildlife refuges. Nowhere is the arrogance and the insidiousness of this small, aggressive minority more clearly demonstrated. Nowhere is the murder of animals, the manipulation of language, and the distortion of public intent more flagrant. The public perceives national wildlife refuges as safe havens, as sanctuaries for animals. And why wouldn't they? The word *refuge* of course *means* shelter from danger and distress. But the dweeby nonhunting public — they tend to be so literal. The word has been reinterpreted by management over time and now hunters are invited into more than half of the country's more than 440 wildlife "sanctuaries" each year to bang them up and kill more than half a million animals. This is called *wildlife-oriented recreation.* Hunters think of this as being no less than their due, claiming that refuge lands were purchased with duck stamps (... *our duck stamps paid for it* ... *our duck stamps paid for it* ...). Hunters equate those stupid stamps with the mystic, multiplying power of the Lord's loaves and fishes, but of 90 million acres in the Wildlife Refuge System, only 3 million were bought with hunting-stamp revenue. Most wildlife "restoration" programs in the states are translated into clearing land to increase deer habitats (so that too many deer will require hunting ... you wouldn't want them to die of starvation, would you?) and trapping animals for restocking and study (so hunters can shoot more of them). Fish and game agencies hustle hunting — instead of conserving wildlife, they're killing it. It's time for them to get in the business of protecting and preserving wildlife and creating balanced ecological systems instead of pimping for hunters who want their deer/duck/pheasant/turkey — animals stocked to be shot.

Hunters' self-serving arguments and lies are becoming more preposterous as nonhunters awake from their long, albeit troubled, sleep. Sport hunting is immoral; it should be made illegal. Hunters are persecutors of nature who should be prosecuted. They wield a disruptive power out of all proportion to their numbers, and pandering to their interests — the special interests of a group that just wants to kill things — is mad. It's preposterous that every year less than 7 percent of the population turns the skies into shooting galleries and the woods and fields into abattoirs. It's time to stop actively supporting and passively allowing hunting, and time to stigmatize it. It's time to stop being conned and cowed by hunters, time to stop pampering and coddling them, time to get them off the government's duck-and-deer dole, time to stop thinking of wild animals as "resources" and "game," and start thinking of them as sentient beings that deserve our wonder and respect, time to stop allowing hunting to be creditable by calling it "sport" and "recreation." Hunters make wildlife *dead, dead, dead.* It's time to wake up to this indisputable fact. As for the hunters, it's long past check-out time.

Reflections and Responses

---

1. In her sixth paragraph, Williams introduces the following quotes: *"He's yours . . . He's mine . . . I decided to . . . I decided not to . . . I debated shooting it, then I decided to let it live . . ."* Who is supposedly saying these things? What point is Williams making about hunters?

2. Williams criticizes not only the morality of hunting but the "manipulation of language" by "hunting apologists." To what extent does she focus her argument on language? What aspects of the pro-hunting language does she most dislike? What euphemisms does she satirize? Do you think she criticizes this language fairly? Explain.

3. Go through the essay systematically and list the pro-hunting arguments Williams introduces. How many can you identify? How do you think she handles them? For example, do you agree with her refutation of the position that people who eat meat are hypocritical in their criticism of hunters?

Alternative
Arrangements

Rhetorical Modes

Any distinguished essay will demonstrate a wide variety of rhetorical techniques. The essays in this volume are no exception. The following classification is designed for those who want to isolate a rhetorical strategy for observation and analysis. The five essays listed under each category were chosen because they distinctly and conveniently show a particular rhetorical mode in action.

NARRATING EVENTS

Anwar F. Accawi, *The Telephone*
Dagoberto Gilb, *Victoria*
Garrett Hongo, *Kubota*
Scott Russell Sanders, *The Inheritance of Tools*
Jamaica Kincaid, *On Seeing England for the First Time*

DESCRIBING PEOPLE, PLACES, AND THINGS

Annie Dillard, *The Stunt Pilot*
Barry Lopez, *The Stone Horse*
Judith Ortiz Cofer, *Silent Dancing*
Henry Louis Gates, Jr., *In the Kitchen*
Gay Talese, *Ali in Havana*

DESCRIBING A PROCESS

Scott Russell Sanders, *The Inheritance of Tools*
Ann Hodgman, *No Wonder They Call Me a Bitch*
Annie Dillard, *The Stunt Pilot*
Frank Conroy, *Think About It*
Lucy Grealy, *Mirrorings*

ANALYZING CAUSES

CONSTRUCTING ARGUMENTS

Some Literary and Journalistic Techniques

As noted in the Introduction, the contemporary essay can be considered in terms of both literature and journalism. Some of the essays in this volume offer excellent models of the essay as a literary form, while others illustrate the art and craft of reportage. The following arrangement focuses on some of the most important features of both kinds of writing.

CLOSE OBSERVATION AND DETAIL

Ian Frazier, *A Lovely Sort of Lower Purpose*
Scott Russell Sanders, *The Inheritance of Tools*
Barry Lopez, *The Stone Horse*
Gretel Ehrlich, *Spring*
John McPhee, *Silk Parachute*

METAPHOR AND SYMBOL

Annie Dillard, *The Stunt Pilot*
Cynthia Ozick, *The Break*
John Updike, *The Disposable Rocket*
Scott Russell Sanders, *The Inheritance of Tools*
Diana Kappel-Smith, *Salt*

IRONY AND SATIRE

Jamaica Kincaid, *On Seeing England for the First Time*
Vicki Hearne, *What's Wrong with Animal Rights*

Contemporary Issues

The essays in this volume are organized around three dominant types of writing. However, selections across the chapters share topical and thematic relationships as well. The following arrangement provides possibilities for linking these essays by their topics of contemporary interest.

THE MULTICULTURAL EXPERIENCE

Anwar F. Accawi, *The Telephone*
Jamaica Kincaid, *On Seeing England for the First Time*
Amy Tan, *Mother Tongue*
Dagoberto Gilb, *Victoria*
Judith Ortiz Cofer, *Silent Dancing*
Henry Louis Gates, Jr., *In the Kitchen*
Gerald Early, *Understanding Afrocentrism: Why Blacks Dream of a World Without Whites*
Garrett Hongo, *Kubota*
Shelby Steele, *On Being Black and Middle Class*

GENDER AND SEXUAL IDENTITY

Joyce Carol Oates, *They All Just Went Away*
Marcia Aldrich, *Hair*
John Updike, *The Disposable Rocket*
Edward Hoagland, *Heaven and Nature*
Natalie Kusz, *Ring Leader*
Cynthia Ozick, *The Break*

Index of Authors